T0329045

The Moral Economy

The Moral Economy examines the nexus of poverty, credit, and trust in early modern Europe. It starts with an examination of poverty, the need for credit, and the lending practices of different social groups. It then reconstructs the battles between the churches and the state around the ban on usury and analyses the institutions created to eradicate usury and the informal petty financial economy that developed as a result. Laurence Fontaine unpacks the values that structured these lending practices, namely, the two competing cultures of credit that coexisted, fought, and sometimes merged: the vibrant aristocratic culture and the capitalistic merchant culture. More broadly, Fontaine shows how economic trust between individuals was constructed in the early modern world. By creating a dialogue between past and present, and contrasting their definitions of poverty, the role of the market, and the mechanisms of microcredit, Fontaine draws attention to the necessity of recognizing the different values that coexist in diverse political economies.

Laurence Fontaine is Director of Research at the French National Center for Scientific Research in Paris. Formerly a professor in the History and Civilization Department at the European University Institute in Florence, Italy, she has published many books, among them *History of Peddlers in Europe* (1996) and *Alternative Exchanges: Second-Hand Circulations from the Sixteenth Century to the Present* (as an editor, 2008), as well as articles in major European journals.

The Moral Economy

Poverty, Credit, and Trust in Early Modern Europe

LAURENCE FONTAINE

Centre National de la Recherche Scientifique, France

CAMBRIDGE
UNIVERSITY PRESS

Shaftesbury Road, Cambridge CB2 8EA, United Kingdom

One Liberty Plaza, 20th Floor, New York, NY 10006, USA

477 Williamstown Road, Port Melbourne, VIC 3207, Australia

314–321, 3rd Floor, Plot 3, Splendor Forum, Jasola District Centre, New Delhi – 110025, India

103 Penang Road, #05–06/07, Visioncrest Commercial, Singapore 238467

Cambridge University Press is part of Cambridge University Press & Assessment, a department of the University of Cambridge.

We share the University's mission to contribute to society through the pursuit of education, learning and research at the highest international levels of excellence.

www.cambridge.org
Information on this title: www.cambridge.org/9781107603707

First published 2008 in French as L'Économie Morale: Pauvreté, credit et confiance dans l'Europe préindustrielle by Gallimard, Paris
First English edition published 2014 by Cambridge University Press & Assessment

English translation by Transfer (programme Investissements d'avenir
ANR-10-IDEX-0001-02 PSL* et ANR-10-LABX-0099)

A catalogue record for this publication is available from the British Library

Library of Congress Cataloging-in-Publication data
Fontaine, Laurence.
[Économie morale. English]
The moral economy : poverty, credit, and trust in early modern Europe / Laurence Fontaine, Centre national de la recherche scientifique, France.
pages cm
Includes bibliographical references and index.
ISBN 978-1-107-01881-5 (hardback) – ISBN 978-1-107-60370-7 (pbk.)
1. Poverty – Europe – History. 2. Credit – Europe – History. 3. Usury – Europe – History. 4. Loans – Europe – History. I. Title.
HC240.9.P6F66 2014
339.4′6094–dc23 2013040408

ISBN 978-1-107-01881-5 Hardback
ISBN 978-1-107-60370-7 Paperback

Contents

Acknowledgements

I would like to express my sincere thanks to D. Gillian Thompson, who translated a first version of Chapter 5; James Turpin and Nelius Carey, who worked on Chapter 7; my dear friend Alice Doolan who time and again helped me translate difficult passages; and my many other friends, colleagues, and former EUI researchers who contributed their bit. Punam Puri translated the rest of the book, which was by far the largest part; it has always been a pleasure to work with her.

The translation was carried out with the support of the laboratory of excellence Transfer (programme Investissements d'avenir ANR-10-IDEX-0001–02 PSL* et ANR-10-LABX-0099).

Introduction

> The tendency to treat economic events as if they constituted independent causal series has been observed frequently. In reality, economic facts are evidently the resultant of other facts that may originate from every imaginable sector ... I am in favor of recognizing the interdependence of any particular historical series with all the other series such that we may see that each element of such a series results from causes attributable to all the others.
>
>   – George Simmel[1]

It is, as they say, the spirit of the age, an age for economists, sociologists, and historians to introspect. Is there an alternative to this new form of savagery that economic liberalism has become, which sees everything – including life itself – as an exchangeable commodity. We have only the bare outlines of the alternatives that draw from the past to imagine the future.[2] At the forefront of the new themes that excite our imagination, or new fetishes, if you will, are microcredit and its supposed virtues. To measure its impact, its effectiveness, as observed in the emerging or third-world countries, is invoked. But the tiny sum of money lent to a destitute woman who is nevertheless an excellent cook to buy her pots and pans so that she can sell her dishes, in other words, create value added by transforming her raw materials, or then to the skilful needlewoman who with her little machine will make bedcovers and clothes

---

[1] Georg Simmel, *Les problèmes de la philosophie de l'histoire*, Paris, Presses Universitaires de France, 1984 [1907], p. 159 note 3.

[2] My thanks to Eric Vigne, who has followed with enthusiasm, rigor, and elegance, this dialogue between yesterday and today.

for the local market, allows more than the mere primitive accumulation of capital. By helping people cast off their poverty instead of making money grow on the international market of financial speculation, microcredit is today endowed with the virtues of a moral economy, for it creates solidarity.

The anti-globalists find in it the distinctive features of a bygone era, that of the dawn of the capitalist society when the economy, in their view, was "embedded" in the social, to draw from the vocabulary of the anthropologist Karl Polanyi. At the time, the gift prevailed over the market, and the economy was more humane. If one reads between the lines, what emerges is the golden age of social solidarity, a world lost.

This alternative proposal alone merits that we take a closer look at it. Was the "embedded" economy really more moral and protective of the weak? Was it only about morality and solidarity, or did these two notions refer to the discursive forms specific to circumscribed eras whose genealogy, if drawn up in the manner of a Michel Foucault, would reveal the extent to which they were the circumstantial mask of Power?

The issues broaden of their own accord: what lessons, if any, can we draw from the study of the economic practices before the industrial revolution? What can we learn from the survival strategies of these eras when each one had to learn to live or, more often than not, survive without any of the social services that have come to characterize our welfare states? What can we learn, if not that microcredit is not a recent invention and that in spite of its seemingly radical novelty, the *subprime* and home loan crisis takes us back to the mechanisms responsible for the financial panic during the ancien régime when the financial system with its banks and last resort moneylenders was yet to develop. Here in the manner of a Marc Bloch, I move back and forth in time, this being my divining rod to probe both the past reality as it can be reconstituted and the utopian prefiguration of a more humane alternative universe.

I thus go back to the times when economics was not as distinct an activity as it may appear on hindsight so that the economic dimension of a phenomenon was always only one aspect of a human activity in which religion, politics and society were intertwined. Those engaged in the practice of exchange and borrowing in modern Europe entered the market in specific ways, in accordance with a diversity of moral values, which not only coexisted but also interpenetrated each other. From this point of view, the economy was truly embedded in the larger social issues that went beyond it.[3] To restore the relationship of men to the economy, it seemed appropriate to me to take credit and trust as the starting point. Both are fundamental mechanisms: trust makes exchange possible and helps reduce the uncertainties of the future; credit, too, inscribes social relationships in time and deferred realization.[4]

In fact, credit irrigates society as a whole. Historians have shown long ago that credit exists in the most elementary of economic exchanges,[5] found as much in the smallest of trades as in bottomry loans,[6] that it weighs on the peasantry and land, that it has its place in the king's court as in the in the finances of the state.[7] The state budget depends on the advances given by financers, the power of the big businesspeople on the cash entrusted to them by the traditional elites, the fortune of the powerful on the credit extended to them by traders and businesspeople, commercial enterprises on the deferred payments of small trade and their

[3] After George Simmel, there were several analysis of the embedding of the economy, influenced by the works of Gary Becker and of Viviana Zelizer as well as by the economic sociology of Mark Granovetter and Richard Swedberg. Gary Becker, *The Economic Approach to Human Behavior*, Chicago, University of Chicago Press, 1976; Viviana A. Zelizer, *The Social Meaning of Money*, Princeton, NJ, Princeton University Press, 1997; *The Sociology of Economic Life*, Mark Granovetter and Richard Swedberg, eds., Boulder, CO, Westview Press, 2002. See in particular their introduction pp. 1–28 in which they argue in favour of a sociological approach to economics which would place the real interactions of the various social actors at the heart of the study.

[4] Niklas Luhmann, *Trust and Power: Two Works by Niklas Luhmann*; translation of the German original *Vertrauen* [1968] and *Macht* [1975], Chichester, John Wiley, 1979.

[5] See, for example, Yves Castan, *Honnêteté et Relations sociales en Languedoc (1715–1780)*, Paris, Plon, 1974, p. 303 sq.

[6] Peter Mathias has shown clearly that enterprises hold a larger part of their assets in circulating capital rather than fixed capital. Peter Mathias, *The Transformation of England : Essays in the Economic and Social History of England in the Eighteenth Century*, New York, Columbia University Press, 1979.

[7] John Brewer, *The Sinews of Power, War Money and the English State*, Londres, Unwin Hyman, 1989. Daniel Dessert, *Argent, pouvoir et société au Grand Siècle*, Paris, Fayard, 1984. Philippe Hamon, *L'Argent du roi. Les finances sous François 1er*, Comité pour l'histoire économique et financière de la France, Paris, 1994. Françoise Bayard, *Le monde des financiers au XVIIe siècle*, Paris, Flammarion, 1988; Alain Guery, "Le roi dépensier. Le don, la contrainte, et l'origine du système financier de la monarchie française d'Ancien Régime," *Annales ESC*, 39, no. 6, 1984, pp. 1241–69. Herbert Lüthy, *La Banque protestante en France, de la Révocation de l'Edit de Nantes à la Révolution*, 2 vols., Paris, SEVPEN, 1959. Marjolein 't Hart, *The Making of a Bourgeois State. War, Politics and Finance during the Dutch Revolt*, Manchester, Manchester University Press, 1993. David D. Biem, "Les offices, les corps et le crédit d'Etat: l'utilisation des privilèges sous l'Ancien Régime," *Annales ESC*, 43, no. 2, 1988, pp. 379–404. *La dette publique dans l'histoire*, Jean Andreau and, Gérard Béaur et Jean-Yves Grenier, eds., Paris, Comité pour l'histoire économique et financière de la France, 2006.

clients. The poor too figure in this scheme of things: they are as much the plaintiffs (unpaid wages) as the defendants in debt litigation.[8] Even the inmates of old people's homes are bound by links of debt.[9] Far from strengthening the compartmentalization of society, the web of credit cuts through it vertically, links together social groups, institutions and regions in dependencies in which each one finds himself both a lender and a borrower. In this way, a series of networks of obligation are woven whose geographical and social spaces are of varying geometry. The ties that link creditors and debtors, lenders and borrowers are a fundamental social link.

However, the relations built around credit are not just an economic and social exchange, they are also an exchange of values. It is as important to try to understand them as to explain the concrete modalities of these interactions. To discover the multiple dimensions of practices, considered today as essentially economic, I have approached the problem from different perspectives. I began with the experience of poverty, the poverty of men and women in urgent need of credit for their very survival. This initial approach allows us to enter the mechanisms of solidarity and profit: it shows that each social group – men and women in accordance with varying modalities – has specific ways of lending money to those in need of it; it brings to light a moral economy shared more or less by the various actors; it opens the doors to the world of urban microcredit and unveils the role played by women and foreigners, including the Jews, in the circuits of credit; last, it defines the attitude of the state vis-à-vis the omnipresence of usury and shows that although some states have opted in favour of creating charitable credit institutions, state-owned pawnshops, others have let the market have a free run.

This historical inquiry led me to define the moral economy and the cultures that reveal themselves in the act of lending and their ways of doing so. The church and the state, both of which have the power to determine good and evil, considered the condemnation of usury as practiced in the Christian civilization. At the same time, theatre, in particular

---

[8] Neil McKendrick, John Brewer, and J. H. Plumb, *The Birth of Consumer Society*, London, Europa Press, 1982. Castan, *Honnêteté*. Scott Taylor, "Credit, Debt, and Honor in Castille, 1600–1650," *Journal of Early Modern History*, 7, no. 1–2, 2003, pp. 8–27 illustrates the horizontal credit chains (A borrows from B who lends to C) and the indebtedness of entrepreneurs on account of unpaid wages.

[9] Craig Muldrew, "Credit and the Courts: Debt Litigation in a Seventeenth Century Urban Community," *Economic History Review*, 46, 1993, pp. 32–8. Benoit Garnot, "Les fortunes populaires à Chartres au XVIIIe siècle," *L'Information historique*, 1987, 49, no. 5, pp. 173–8 (176).

some extremely incisive dramatic works, presented the diverse economic cultures as revealed by the study of the needs of the poorest. The theatre provides a space for complicity in which "performing communities" are revealed, bringing together authors, actors, and spectators. It translates the shared ways in which author and public think and discuss the world.[10] There can be no better guide than Shakespeare and Molière to understand the ways of thinking and experiencing the economy. They allow us differentiate between the two chief modes of being specific to the economy: the aristocratic mode and the merchant. After presenting them in their "pristine" form like the ingredients of a mixture taken apart, I compared these values as enacted on the stage with one of the most common acts of economic life – buying and selling – looking at how the social actors settle, or agree to, the prices at which they buy. The comparison between the values that animate the characters on the stage, the ideal types if you will, with the actual practices enable us to gauge the social effectiveness of these values.

No matter how you consider credit, what lies behind it is the web, both visible and invisible, of power. Of course, there is the power of the state and the church, but a more diffuse, less codified power also runs through society.[11] As far as modern Europe is concerned, all social relationships are permeated by the aristocratic political economy. Pitted against it, the capitalist market economy seeks to impose other values and displace the traditional relations of power. Although the state and public credit are full-fledged actors in this saga, they have not been analysed in themselves in this book. Public credit, which has already received a great deal of attention from historians, does not form part of our discussion. On the other hand, the state is omnipresent behind the numerous laws, institutions, and regulations created by it to exercise control over daily economic practices.

The manner in which men build trust is the last perspective I have adopted to enter the complex relations that individuals maintain with the economy. Trust, just as indispensable to economic life as credit, is founded on the assurance that social partners will act in a predictable manner. Implicit in the analysis of how trust is built are the specificities of

[10] Stephen Greenblatt, *Shakesperian Negociations. The Circulation of Social Energy in Renaissance England*, Oxford, Oxford University Press, 2000 [1988]; Roger Chartier, "George Dandin, ou le social en représentation," *Annales. Histoire, Sciences Sociales*, 49, no. 2, 1994, pp. 277–309.
[11] Michel Foucault, *Sécurité, Territoire, Population. Cours au Collège de France. 1977–1978*, Paris, Gallimard / Seuil, 2004.

social relations and the forms of power in which they are inscribed. The need for trust is universal, but the shared values that underlie it depend on the context.

On the whole, this book brings out not two supposedly successive economic cultures – feudal and capitalist – but two economic cultures, each one upholding different values, which existed together, came close to and clashed with each other but also influenced and merged in each other, emerging transformed from these encounters. Unfurling the gamut of both possible and ordinary experiences restores, by the same token, the multiple tensions that run through societies: at the collective level, between societies of order and status and the parallel development of economic rationales; at the individual level, between the contradictory demands of the diverse belongings of individuals, their aspirations and the reality of their day to day experience.

By the end, the reader will understand that this book attempts to put forth a new approach to the European economy of the ancien régime in the hope of capturing it in its very essence, as close to the way it was, in order to, among others, for people like us living in the twenty-first century, glean some insights into the questions of the gift economy, nonutilitarian exchange, and the waning sway of finance over all human activity.

My approach plays deliberately on the variations of scales and perspectives to bring out to the extent possible societies with all their complexities and tensions, which a single-pronged approach would be hard-pressed to do. It begins by looking at practices and moves on to considering ideal types instead of ideas so as avoid the risk of passing off ideology for the reality of behaviour and highlight the contradictions and inconsistencies of the actors. Nevertheless, we must point out that the European objective of this inquiry has been achieved in a rather imperfect manner; it seems impossible to me to cover the diversity of all the geographical and social contexts and the changes that have taken place, even if variations of scale are inherent to such a project. Consequently, some aspects, like the informal urban financial economy, which can only be apprehended at a microscopic scale, is dealt with based on a single case study – eighteenth-century Paris – the analysis of which will be enriched with the meagre existing bibliography; other dimensions discussed in the book, such as nobiliary indebtedness or the question of usury can draw upon a substantial historiography with the help of which I propose a comprehensive rereading of this set of themes. Alas, a surfeit of material compels one to makes choices and in doing so one cannot do justice to all the regional and contextual differences of modern Europe. You only have to look at the diversity of European nobilities and the major differences that can be seen within the aristocracy of each country. The example of Italy and the Venetian nobility that has little in common with Genoese nobility and even less with the southern nobility is particularly enlightening. What matters however is not the abundance or paucity of sources. The essential is to reformulate in the present as we live it the questions thrown up by the past, a dialogue necessary to shape our common future.

Prologue

The words that will appear know things of us that we know not of them.
— René Char, *Chants de la Balandrane*

Words bear the trace of the uses to which they have been put. They tell us about the values and ways of life of those who have used them. They are our first guide to understand credit and trust. But before that, let us go briefly to the origins of European practices by looking at, in the footsteps of Emile Benvéniste,[1] how the words *gift, credit, credence, trust,* and *debt* acquired their meaning in Indo-European languages.

Fides, says Benvéniste, which means both faith and trust in Latin, refers to a value even older still and slightly different from that of "trust": it signifies the "inherent quality of a person which inspired confidence in him and is exercised in the form of a protective authority over those who entrust themselves to him." This notion is very close to the Germanic *kred.* It is thus clear why, in Latin, *fides* is the noun corresponding to *credo* or "to believe." This implies that

Thus the Latin notion of *fides* establishes between the partners an inverse relationship to that which we generally understand under the notion of "confidence." In the expression "I have confidence in somebody," the confidence is something belonging to me which I can put into his hands and which he disposes of. In the Latin expression *mihi est fides apud aliquem* it is the other who puts his trust in me and it is at my disposal. The "possessor" of the *fidēs* thus holds a security which he deposits "with" (*apud*) somebody: this shows that *fides* is really the "credit" which one enjoys with one's partner. All the early examples confirm this.

[1] Emile Benvéniste, *Le vocabulaire des institutions indo-européennes*, vol. 2, Paris, Editions de Minuit, 1969.

Consequently, *fides* designates the trust that the one who speaks *inspires* in his interlocutor, whose trust he or she enjoys. It then constitutes a "guarantee" to which he or she can take recourse. The *fides* that mortals have in the gods provides them in return a guarantee: it is this divine guarantee that is invoked when in distress.

Benvéniste goes on to review the different links of *fides* and the circumstances in which the notion is used. These instances show that the partners in trust are not on an equal footing: the one who enjoys the *fides* that a man has placed in him has this man at his mercy. This is why *fides* becomes almost synonymous with *dicio* and *potestas*. In their primitive form, these relations entailed a certain reciprocity: to put *one's fides* in someone procured in exchange his guarantee and support. But this in itself emphasizes the unequal conditions. *Fides* is thus authority that is exerted as well as protection for the one who submits to it, in exchange and proportionate to his submission.

These Latin notions were revived in the sixteenth century by the humanists and their rereading of Cicero's *De officilis*. Erasmus and Melanchthon published an annotated Latin edition in 1520 with a hundred odd editions of it being brought out in Europe in the forty years that followed. This filiation and reappropriation is clearly visible in, for instance, the work of the Englishman Thomas Elyot, *The Book named the Governor*, published in 1531. Elyot wrote,

THAT whiche in latyne is called Fides, is a parte of iustice and may diuersely be interpreted, and yet finally it tendeth to one purpose in effects. Some tyme it may be called faythe, some tyme credence, other whyles truste. ... As beleuynge the preceptes and promyse of god it is called faythe. In contractes betwene man and man it is communely called credence. Betwene persones of equall astate or condition it is named truste. From the subiecte or seruaunt to his souerayne or maister it is proprely named fidelitie ...[2]

In this manner, these different notions have been rethought in the context of the hierarchical society of the ancien régime, with its main protagonists, hierarchies, and various forms of relationships between human and God. They slip into the gradations that appear and the contracts into which men enter: from the giving of one's word sufficient among equals

[2] My thanks to Craig Muldrew, who gave me the figures for the Cicero editions and who drew my attention to this text that he cites in his book *The Economy of Obligation: The Culture of Credit and Social Relations in Early Modern England*, Basingstoke, Macmillan, 1998, pp. 133–4. I also express deep gratitude to Jeremy Popkin, who answered my queries until very end and helped me formulate in French a number of obscure expressions and Old English turns of phrase.

to the various forms of dependencies that bound clients and servants to their master.

Benvéniste also analyses the terms *loan, borrowing,* and *debt* and shows how in all Indo-European languages the correlated technical terms for *debt, loan,* and *borrowing* were constituted through the specification and differentiation of other more general terms that belong to another order of representation, that of the language of power. From the very outset, there has been a double construction. On one hand, "loan" and "borrowing" are part of the same process just as "advance" and "repayment" of a sum without interest. The parallelism between to lend and to borrow can be found in German (*borgen*) and old French in which "emprunter" (to borrow) was used for "prêter" (to lend) and "se faire prêter" (to borrow).

Finally, with his analysis of the uses of *prestare,* Benvéniste shows that three different relations of credit were established. *Prestare* was initially and continued for a long time to be used as an interest free loan, a gracious offering, a token of kindness and a nonfinancial transaction. This loan is different from the borrowing *mutuatio,* in which there is reciprocity and the exact repayment of what one has received, and still further removed from *fenus,* a real loan with interest the initial meaning of which is "fecundity" or "prosperity." All these notions are very visible in Cicero's correspondence: he does not speak of one but many relations of credit differentiated according to the social and legal status of the debtor. With respect to the senators' aristocracy, their behaviour was imbued in addition with the cardinal virtue of *liberalitas,* a burdensome generosity but one which brought *gratia.*[3] But the notion of gratia is dual. On one hand, it implies gratitude and, on the other, credit. This means that the term *gratia* can be understood just as well in the passive sense (the debt of gratitude owed) as in the active sense: the debt of gratitude of which one is the beneficiary. In this manner, in its active sense, *gratia* expresses personal credit, which defines a man of influence.[4]

Gift, exchange and trade are a set of economic notions difficult to define in any other way than by the sum of their distinctive features. Greek vocabulary has several words for gift. Those derived from the root *dô: dos, doron, dorea,* and *dosis* convey the idea of a gift that allows the establishment of profitable relations. *Timé* refers to a gift as a contractual

[3] Marina Ioannatou, "Le code de l'honneur des paiements. Créanciers et débiteurs à la fin de la République romaine," *Annales HSS,* no. 6, November–December 2001, pp. 1201-1.

[4] Jean-Michel David, *Le patronat judiciaire au dernier siècle de la république romaine,* Rome, Ecole Française de Rome, 1992, p. 146.

service, imposed by the obligations of a pact, an alliance, a friendship or hospitality; it is the obligation of the host (*xeînos*), that of the subjects toward the king or a god, or then a service because of an alliance.[5]

Thus, belief, faith, and authority lie semantically at the origin of the words *credit* and *credence*. Although these meanings, which refer to the distribution of power and the form of social relations, have practically disappeared today, they were very present in the languages of modern Europe, as borne out by the definitions given in the dictionaries consulted for the late seventeenth and early eighteenth centuries.

In France, Antoine Furetière's dictionary, published in Rotterdam in 1688 and 1689, ascribes three meanings to the French word *crédit* (credit), and these three meanings refer precisely to the old meanings of *fides* that emphasize first and foremost moral authority and then power. The first sense of the word is "Credibility and respect which one acquires in the eyes of the world as a result of one's virtue, integrity, sincerity and merit." The second "also refers to the power, authority and wealth which one attains because of the reputation which one has acquired." This minister has acquired great "*crédit*" (influence) in the court over the mind of the prince. And the third "more usually refers, in the business world, to the reciprocal loan of money and goods, made on the basis of a merchant's reputation for integrity and solvency ..." Furetière goes on to clarify: "We say, to give credit [*crédit*], to sell and buy on credit [*crédit*], when we mean that no cash is being exchanged for a purchase. Credit [*crédit*] is what the merchants grant to the seigneurial lords who subsequently ruin them and their business." To the entry for *credit*, Furetière adds the meaning of the phrase "à credit" [literally, "on credit"]: "often said meaning 'on a whim, pointlessly, groundlessly ...'"

The first meaning relates to one's reputation and character, the second to political and financial power, and the third to reciprocal loans between merchants. The last two uses of the word *crédit* are both based on the first meaning, in other words, on reputation. When not referring to a reciprocal loan between merchants, the word *crédit* is used in verbal phrases, the only example of which Furetière gives here is that of the merchants' financial ruin when they grant credit to the seigneurial lords. The meanings ascribed to the expression *à crédit* all evoke inanity, uselessness, involuntary wastage or baselessness.

Spanish and Portuguese dictionaries list five meanings of the word *credit* that extend to faith, authority, favour, good reputation, and, finally,

---

[5] Benvéniste, *Le vocabulaire*, chap. 5.

commercial records and loans that appear in the language as particular cases.[6] In the Germanic regions, the definitions are the same with a strong emphasis on the Indo-European meaning of a person "of good reputation," "who is creditworthy," which means we place our trust in this person, and he or she will lose it when his or her credit runs out. In addition to these meanings, there is another entry *credito*, which while taking up these same notions ascribes two meanings to the word. The first is fidelity and faith among men and the second is the act of borrowing. Finally, the dictionary dwells on commercial credit and explains that "to give on credit is inseparable from trade as heat is from fire. ...; but it points out the dangers of credit: "the one who gives too much trust (Vertrauen) is unlikely to see his money again."[7]

Last, of the thirteen meanings of the word *credit* listed in *The Oxford English Dictionary*, only the last five refer to an economic activity. The first few meanings refer to faith, trust, authority, something believed, reputation and the acknowledgement of merit. The new feature among the commercial meanings is to include public credit and mention the vote on the budget by Parliament from which the expression *vote of credit* is derived.[8]

These definitions of credit appear complex and puzzling by today's standards because singularly absent from them are both the rationality of the economic activity of credit and a consideration of profit. However, the distinction the dictionaries make between the various types of credit and merchant credit is striking, as if merchants did not belong to the same society and were entitled to a specific set of rules for their group. This differentiation is an old one, which has its roots in the distinction, which theologians and lawyers made from the end of the Middle Ages between business and charity.[9] All this perfectly illustrates the themes I wish to develop in this book. Rather than begin with the conventional approach of studying credit in itself and consider it from the outset as a market

[6] *Diccionario de Autoridades* de la *Real academia española*, 1726; Raphaël Bluteau, *Vocabulario Portuguez e Latino*, Lisbonne, 1712.

[7] *Zedler Universallexikon*, 1733, http://www.zedler-lexikon.de/.

[8] *Oxford English Dictionary*, Oxford, Oxford University Press, first complete edition, 1928.

[9] See the work done by Rodolfo Savelli, "Between Law and Morals: Interest in the Dispute of Exchanges during the 16th Century," *The Courts and the Development of Commercial Law*, V. Piergiovanni, ed., Berlin, Duncker & Humbolt, 1987, and Rodolfo Savelli, "Modèles juridiques et culture marchande entre 16e et 17e siècles," *Cultures et formations négociantes dans l'Europe moderne*, Franco Angiolini and Daniel Roche, eds., Paris, Editions de l'EHESS, 1995, pp. 403–420 (407–8).

and the varying rates of interest as a reflection of this market, I take as my starting point situations that bring the social actors face to face in all their social diversity in order to rediscover, based on practices, the diverse definitions of credit suggested. Such an approach alone enables one to unmask the other face of credit and make nonsense of what is stated in the dictionaries: credit is based on power and deals transacted on the basis of credit were more in the nature of a gift or an obligation (with the exception of the credit relationship between merchants), than a fair recompense for the time and the risk involved.

But to conclude this prologue, let us put aside dictionaries and see how the observers of the times used the notion of credit. The duke of Saint-Simon with his painstaking description of the life at the court in which he was immersed is placed ideally to introduce us to the various facets of credit in the seventeenth century. He always talked of authority in terms of credit that was exercised in a succession of interpersonal relationships. It was important to know the family members who wielded influence. In his family, it was his uncle, for he had "great influence over my father"[10]; in the family of the duke of Lesdiguière, it was the mother, and behind her, her cousin: "Monsieur de Lesdiguière was a child and his mother a sort of fairy over whom her cousin de Villeroy had complete influence."[11] Nevertheless, the mother was of a strong personality: she was une "she was a sort of fairy staying almost always alone in an enchanted palace, and over whom practically no one had any influence"; besides, she "used her influence as she pleased."[12]

When not stated explicitly, the influence of the duchess referred to the fount of all authority: the king. Along with him, all those close to him and who had his ear were constantly solicited by intermediaries, for access to the king's favours in the society of the court in which Saint-Simon lived was the key to influence. He makes us aware of this all the time. The Duchesse de Lude "the Duchesse de Lude would naturally court ministers and all those who were influential, even valets"[13]; "the comtesse du Plessis had the influence to make him [her husband] the first squire of Madame"[14]; "Mme du Maine [...] deluded the bastard into believing that he was in love [with Melle de Lussan], and with the influence of M. du Maine he would have all he wished for by marrying

[10] Saint-Simon, *Mémoires (1691–1701)*, Paris, Gallimard, vol. 1, 1983, p. 86.
[11] Ibid., p. 142.
[12] Ibid., p. 168.
[13] Ibid., p. 308.
[14] Ibid., p. 267.

her."[15] Bontemps, the first of the first four valets of the king's chamber, "never harmed anyone and always used his influence to oblige."[16]

Besides, Saint-Simon, whose own family was very small, knew at a young age that he would have to marry to widen his network and to acquire influence. He was quite forthright about it:

With a considerable establishment, I felt very isolated in a country where influence and consideration achieved more than all else. Son of a favourite of Louis XIII and a mother who had only lived for him, who he had married when she was no longer young herself, without uncles, aunts, first cousins, close relatives nor useful friends of my father and mother out of everything on account of their age, I felt extremely alone.[17]

But influence is never acquired: it is cultivated and used with caution, for if used injudiciously or excessively, it loses its effect. The cardinal Bonsi experienced this in 1703 when "his influence and authority fell completely" because he had lost favour with the king.[18] Similarly, the quarrel between Chamillart, the king's minister, and Bagnols, the intendant of Flanders, that took place in 1708 led him to write that "Never had such a racket been made for so little, nor an intendant so arrogant with a minister who was his superior. Chamillart prevailed, but only after expending much energy and employing much of his influence."[19] Even influence has its economy, and some use it sparingly such as "M. du maine [...] promised miracles, and, as was his wont, never kept a single promise. He spared his influence for himself alone."[20]

Last, credit and business are also related: in 1702, Saint-Simon recounted that the princess of Ursins was entrusted the task of training the queen of Spain and that she performed her duty admirably: "she was no less successful in inspiring in her a taste for influence and business"[21]; however, business is first and foremost social; it also brings in economic profits that reward the intermediary. Business and intermediation are two other practices that we will encounter throughout this book.

The time has now come to take a look at the credit needs of people and see how the notions of credit and trust, fed as they are by power and social relations, play out.

[15] Ibid., p. 732.
[16] Ibid., p. 808.
[17] Ibid., pp. 114–15.
[18] Ibid., vol. 2, p. 340.
[19] Ibid., vol. 3, pp. 147–8.
[20] Ibid., vol. 1, p. 315.
[21] Ibid., vol. 2, p. 209.

I

Poverty, Credit, and Social Networks

... Lost in the nameless crowd, I had to use to gain a mere Subsistence
more Science and Guile than required in a hundred years to govern all the
Provinces of Spain.
     – Beaumarchais, *The Marriage of Figaro*, Act V, Scene 3

Let us begin with those who need credit the most: the poor. Because of
lack of work, their survival depends on their ability to fend for themselves, as well as on charity and credit. How then was solidarity forged?
Did the various social groups show the same willingness to help? In this
chapter we attempt to determine the role of social relations in the face of
impoverishment: Did the nature and the quality of the relations in which
individuals found themselves have anything to do with the unequal manner in which crisis hit men and women in preindustrial Europe? And
what do these inequalities tell us about the relations of various social
groups with the economy?

Before addressing these questions, however, we need to know what is
meant by the term "poor." How did the words of the times and historiography deal with these issues of the poor? The meanings of "poor" and
the social classes to which the term referred were remarkably consistent
between the fourteenth and eighteenth centuries. In the Middle Ages, in
literary text and chronicles, as well as in administrative texts and sermons,
the term "poor" was ordinarily reserved for men who supported themselves from their labours. The word was not used solely in the economic
sense: a poor man was one who suffered, or one afflicted by misfortune.[1]

---

[1] There is a reference to "povres gens mécaniques et de labeur" (the labouring poor), "povres gens de faim et de pouvreté" (the hungry and destitute poor), and "povres et piteables

At the end of the seventeenth century, *Furetière's Dictionary* defined "poverty" as "the lack of possessions, of wealth."[2] Indeed, all analyses of poverty by the politicians of the time – in particular by Vauban in his famous work "Dîme royale" of 1707 – asserted time and again that a man who had no other means of support but his labour was likely to become a poor man if, for whatever reason, he was no longer able to work. In 1788, Condorcet made the same point when he described the poor man as "he who has neither land nor personal property [and who] is destined to fall on hard times should the slightest mishap befall him."[3] These learned definitions matched those of the poor themselves: the inhabitants of seventeenth-century Rome stated they were poor when all they had to live on was their work.[4] In early modern times, other words are used to describe those who become destitute: paupers or beggars.[5] Poverty is, therefore, a potential process as much as a condition, which means that in order to understand it, one must study not only impoverishment mechanisms but also what individuals can do to minimize risks and to slow down and delay the worsening of their situation at times of crisis.

It is not that historians have made mistakes in this area; rather, curiously, they have rarely taken much interest in those mechanisms that allowed individuals to resist their fate and, in particular, in the ways in which financial mechanisms could be exploited and networks utilized. Hence, I trace briefly the historiography of poverty to establish which questions have been asked, which perspectives have been adopted, and how debt has been analysed. I then examine credit more closely in order to demonstrate how debt was both a factor in impoverishment and a protective element in a network of solidarities: in other words, how debt created ties within society every bit as much as it destroyed them. While doing so, I examine the complexity of family strategies and solidarities as well as the saving strategies of the poor. All in all, did these socially different attitudes have an impact on poverty?

---

personnes" (the pitiful poor). M. Mollat, *Les Pauvres au Moyen Age*, Paris, Hachette, 1978, pp. 311–12.

[2] Antoine Furetière, *Dictionnaire universel*, La Haye-Rotterdam, 1690.

[3] Condorcet, *Sur les assemblées provinciales*, 1788, p. 453, quoted by O. Hufton, *The Poor of Eighteenth-Century France 1750–1789*, Oxford, Oxford University Press, 1974, p. 19.

[4] Renata Ago, *Economia Barocca. Mercato e istituzioni nella Roma del Seicento*, Roma, Donzelli, 1998, pp. 82–9.

[5] Jean-Pierre Gutton, *La Société et les pauvres. L'exemple de la généralité de Lyon (1534–1789)*, Paris, Les Belles Lettres, 1971, pp. 8–10.

Historiographical Questions

Historians defined three categories of poor people beyond those who, in the early modern times, were called "the shameful poor."[6] These were the "structural" poor – predominantly the sick and the old – and the temporary poor: craftsmen, small traders, unskilled workers, and others who were without resources at times of economic crisis.[7] This classification endured throughout the ancien régime: the poor came from the same social groups, from among the workers with the least specialized skills.[8] In Bourgogne in the fourteenth century, a distinction existed between destitute households and mendicant households, both of which were insolvent. Both types of households almost always represented 80 per cent of the total households in the towns and between 75 and 80 per cent in rural areas.[9] In Beauvais at the end of the seventeenth century, the situation was not quite so dire: 1,218 households out of 2,252 (almost half) were taxed less than two livres, which related to the temporary poor. At the end of the eighteenth century, in 1790, of 12,960 inhabitants, 4,300 individuals – a third of the total – were "in need of help." This group was almost entirely composed of textile workers and all unskilled workers; the majority of journeymen from the building and clothing industries, the furniture trade, and other modest urban trades; and the host of widows and unmarried daughters with no clear occupation.[10]

To avoid overly rigid categorization and to better capture the fluidity of the process of impoverishment – because to analyse poverty is to analyse risk – historians[11] have preferred to map out circles of poverty, precisely to highlight this dimension of risk, the probability that populations would experience poverty. At the centre of the circle were the structural poor, who were unable to support themselves because of their age, their illness, or their physical handicaps. They represented between 4 and 8

---

[6] The "shameful poor" belonged to social groups who normally were not in need – the nobility, magistrates, and so forth – and whose birth and education meant that they had no manual skills they could fall back on. Gutton, *La Société*, pp. 23–4.

[7] Gutton, *La Société*, pp. 50–3.

[8] Ibid., p. 21.

[9] Mollat, *Les Pauvres*, p. 283.

[10] Pierre Goubert, *Beauvais et le Beauvaisis de 1600 à 1730: Contribution à l'histoire sociale de la France du XVIIe siècle*, Paris, 1960, pp. 263–4.

[11] Bronislav Geremek, "Il pauperismo nell'età preindustriale (sec. XIV-XVIII)," *Storia d'Italia*, V (I documenti), Turin, 1973, pp. 667–98; Brian Pullan, "Poveri, mendicanti e vagabondi (secoli XIV-XVII)," *Storia d'Italia. Annali I, Dal feudalismo al capitalismo*, Turin, 1978, pp. 988–97; Stuart Woolf, *The Poor in Western Europe in the Eighteenth and Nineteenth Centuries*, London, Methuen, 1986.

per cent of the population of the principal European cities between the fifteenth and eighteenth centuries.[12] A second circle encompassed the temporary poor – those living on a meagre salary from an unstable job and those at the mercy of the first fluctuation in the price of bread.[13] These people represented about 20 per cent of the urban population. A third circle encompassed small craftsmen and the smaller retailers – all those who paid the minimum amount of tax in the cities and whom economic crisis on a wider scale or family difficulties would force under subsistence level. Taking the last group into account, between 50 and 70 per cent of urban households found themselves poverty stricken. A final circle included the victims of severe agricultural crises, plagues, and wars.[14]

The triggers for poverty were also either temporary or structural: economic crisis, war, illness, and natural catastrophe were all temporary; the points in the lives of men and women when one sex was more vulnerable than the other, directions that lives had taken (parents' early or late marriage, the individual's place in the birth order the family, and so forth), communities, and economic sectors were structural factors.[15] The importance of the family economy is crucial: workers, generally speaking, earned enough to support themselves, but could not, on their salary, take on the responsibility for many other people; if the woman could not work, or could no longer work, or if children were born, the balance between resources and mouths to be fed was then destroyed.[16]

---

[12] In Beauvais, from 1653 onward, 6% of the population, and more than one-tenth of workers in the wool trade, turned to the Bureau des Pauvres for help. This was "ordinary" poverty relieved by "ordinary" charity, which, in years when prices were low, usually cared for orphans, children from large families, the old, and the infirm. Parish charities and the hospital cared in particular for the poor when they were sick. Goubert, *Beauvais et le Beauvaisis*, pp. 298–9.

[13] When the price of bread doubled, tripled, or quadrupled, the employers would cut salaries by between 10% and 20% to offset the high cost of wool and the slump in business. The workers would accept this rather than find themselves out of work. Goubert, *Beauvais et le Beauvaisis*, pp. 300–1.

[14] Woolf, *The Poor in Western Europe*, pp. 6–9.

[15] *Poor Women and Children in the European Past*, John Henderson and Richard Wall, eds., London, Routledge, 1994, pp. 4–8. For information on Caen and Bayeux, see Robert M. Schwartz, *Policing the Poor in Eighteenth-Century France*, The University of North Carolina Press, Chapel Hill and London, 1988, p. 101. There were more boys aged between five and fourteen than there were girls, but after the age of twenty, there were significantly more women than men. Those older than sixty were, proportionally, the most represented age group.

[16] Hufton, *The Poor of Eighteenth-Century France*, p. 12, 37. Schwartz, *Policing the Poor*, pp. 105–12.

If we now turn to the major questions tackled by the historiography of poverty, at top of the list are the ways in which society treats its poor. Private charity and charitable institutions are the areas that have, for a long time, received the most attention. More recently, historians have worked in two complementary directions. On one hand, they have considered poverty as a political phenomenon and traced its history as a social issue;[17] on the other, they have approached it from a more dynamic and individual angle, no longer confining themselves to the perspective of the rich man giving alms and establishing charitable institutions but also taking the position of the poor man trying to fight against the mechanisms of impoverishment.

In this latter direction, attention has initially concentrated on studying life cycles and the ways in which the poor exploited institutions.[18] Later the theory of an "economy of makeshifts" as a way of resisting impoverishment was developed, but it has emphasized the deviant strategies – theft, smuggling, prostitution, the abandonment of children, and so forth – which were used as means of escape.[19] Interest is currently developing not only in the criminal strategies for coping, evidence of which can be found in the judicial archives, but also in the more positive strategies, in other words how the poor mobilized networks within society as weapons against the logic of impoverishment.[20] But very few sources discuss the poor and the ways in which they lived their lives.[21]

Although this assessment has demonstrated the remarkable wealth and diversity of the historiography of this area, how little attention has

[17] Giovanna Proccacci, *Gouverner la misère. La question sociale en France (1789–1848)*, Paris, Seuil, 1993; Robert Castel, *Les métamorphoses de la question sociale. Une chronique du salariat*, Paris, Fayard, 1995.

[18] *Poor Women and Children*; Daniela Lombardi, *Povertà maschile, povertà femminile: L'ospedale dei mendicanti nella Firenze dei Medici*, Bologna, Il Mulino, 1988; Woolf, *The Poor in Western Europe*; Robert Jütte, *Poverty and Deviance in Early Modern Europe*, Cambridge, Cambridge University Press, 1994; Montserrat Carbonell i Esteller, *Sobreviure a Barcelona. Dones, pobresa i assistència al segle XVIII*, Barcelone, Eumo Editorial, 1997.

[19] Hufton, *The Poor of Eighteenth-Century France.*

[20] *Household Strategies for Survival, 1600–2000: Fission, Faction and Cooperation*, Laurence Fontaine and Jürgen Schlumbohm, eds., Cambridge, Cambridge University Press, 2000.

[21] Woolf, *The Poor of Western Europe*, p. 20, discusses these informal defence mechanisms, underlining how the lack of documentation makes it very difficult to deepen our knowledge of them. R. Jütte devotes a general chapter to them: Jütte, *Poverty and Deviance*, chap. 4; and Carbonell i Esteller, *Sobreviure a Barcelona*, pp. 161–8, could find the family links of the assisted in the Casa de Misericórdia in Barcelona in the last third of the eighteenth century.

been paid, for the most part, to financial mechanisms and social networks should nonetheless be highlighted. Indeed, in analyzing relationships between rich and poor, studies have gone no further than describing acts of charity, although all note the role of patronage and emphasize to what extent society in earlier times was based on interpersonal relationships and the extent to which it was controlled or, in the words of Robert Castel, "cadastré." In fact, the distinction between the poor man and the vagrant was the touchstone throughout the ancien régime of the prominence of social boundaries. In the Middle Ages, the beggar was tolerated and the vagrant despised. The vagrant was the *sans aveu* – a person with no one to speak up for him or her and with no social ties, because to exist socially, people needed someone to answer for them. For these people, having no one who recognized them, no one with whom they could claim ties, pointed inexorably to isolation and marginalization.[22]

Several explanations can be put forward for the lack of interest evinced by historians in the social networks that protected men from the fate of the *sans aveu*. I mention two. The first relates to the strand of historiography that is a product of postwar prosperity and the welfare state: historians have principally set out to understand the genealogy of state-provided social welfare and have placed work at the centre of their inquiries. When such systems started to break down, historians (Anglo-Saxon, in particular, who were the first to deal with the issue in the 1990s) began to show an interest in self-help and the ways in which the poor fend for themselves outside of the welfare system.[23] The second explanation can be found in the importance historians have lent to the economy within historical thought. The majority of analyses of poverty were written in the 1960s and 1970s and, like most historical research of the period, they adhered

---

[22] Mollat, *Les Pauvres*, p. 299. According to Jean-Pierre Gutton and Robert Castel, the concept of the vagrant was established later. The term *vagrant* progressively defined itself between the sixteenth and eighteenth centuries: from meaning one who travelled with no fixed abode, in 1666, it came to mean one who was not only poor (having neither trade nor property to support oneself) but moreover had no one to vouch for him or her; Gutton, *La Société*, pp. 9–13. See also Castel *Les métamorphoses*, pp. 90–7. Gutton cites a letter addressed to a fellow countrywoman, a laundress living and working in Lyon, from a woman servant who had left Lyon and was then in Grenoble, where she could not take up the position she had been promised because there was no one in Grenoble who could vouch for her. She asks her friend the laundress to locate her previous mistress and entreat her to give her a "certificate of service and loyalty"; Gutton, *La Société*, p. 82.

[23] *The Locus of Care: Families, Communities and Institutions and the Provision of Welfare Since Antiquity*, Peregrine Horden and Richard Smith, eds., London, Routledge, 1998; Steve Hindle, *On the Parish?: The Micro-Politics of Poor Relief in Rural England, c.1550–1750*, Oxford, Oxford University Press, 2004.

to a uniquely economic view of causality, in which political, social, and cultural systems did not figure. Admittedly, these works described society as client based, but this in no way had an impact on their explanations of poverty. In these analyses, the social and political considerations were only reintroduced in order to explain how the rich selected particular groups of poor people through patronage, protection, and mediation, thus highlighting their social and political status as benefactor. The social and the political were also reintroduced to show how charitable institutions attempted to inculcate the values of submissive deference, which the elite classes expected from the less-well-off groups in society.[24] This distinction has prevented work from examining the social and cultural processes involved in social marginalization.

In the same way, studies examining the beginnings of the social question curiously leave aside finance. Although work and unemployment are at the heart of Robert Castel's book on the mechanisms of social disaffiliation, capital and credit are absent from it. There is no mention of debt in his analysis of how groups become vulnerable, or of the efforts made by individuals and by the state to remedy excessive debt, or of how societies assumed responsibility for these groups. Yet, then as now, the first instinct of anyone who is unable to make ends meet is to ask for credit and for more time in which to pay off debts. In earlier times, the weakness of the financial infrastructure in Europe meant that, more so than today, credit was at the heart of social relationships.

Admittedly, debt was always mentioned as one of the mechanisms of impoverishment, but – and this is another characteristic of the historiography – credit was seen as a global economic mechanism, the results of which were measured by historians over the longer term. These analyses traced the rise of the bourgeois classes who took advantage of the debt burdening both the aristocratic and peasant classes. In these works, the study of the poor might be carried out on a microscopic level, documenting the cases of individuals, but the economy remained a macroscopic phenomenon, a factor outside the control of individuals. The emphasis on long-term development and the belief that the economy was a completely separate arena governed by its own logic obscured the extent to which economic relationships were also social and cultural relationships. Hence the lack of individual analyses that would have enabled us to trace the effects of credit ties between different social groups and to question whether all creditors – noble, bourgeois, or peasant – operated in the

---

[24] Woolf, *The Poor in Western Europe*, p. 27.

same way. In short, historians have chosen to conduct macro analyses rather than look at this question, noting structural changes in society but not paying attention to the effects these changes had on the individual, thus preventing themselves from understanding the diversity of vocabulary and practices. Although overindebtedness is one of the first manifestations of poverty, historiography has paid scant attention to it, focusing instead on assistance and charity. In doing so, it has considered the question from the viewpoint of the state and the elite. Only very recently have the poor been put at the centre of inquiries on poverty and their ways of thinking, anticipating, and managing the various crises by which they were threatened taken into account.

The Mechanisms of Impoverishment

The invariable element in all these studies of the populations of early Europe is the indebtedness of country and city dwellers alike. Goubert writes that, with fewer than ten hectares of land, a peasant from the Beauvais area would be unable to harvest enough to feed his family, no matter how plentiful the harvest. Yet, he adds, all those peasants who, in theory, could not live off their land did in fact survive: "Miserably, no doubt, with famine and epidemics taking a heavy toll; helped through it by having a cow; their availability to work, their second jobs, and a little fraud and poaching here and there. But they survived by getting into debt." Manual workers, farmworkers, and everyone in between features in European source documents "with a trail of debt which speaks for itself," to quote Pierre Goubert once again.[25] I have cited Goubert, but I could have cited any work on the towns and cities of Europe in order to emphasize the importance of debt. One significant example is that of wealthy Amsterdam in the second half of the eighteenth century, where inventories following the death of the city's craftsmen and day labourers show that almost three-quarters of these workers died leaving more debts than assets.[26]

However, it must be stressed that if historians are able to undertake research into this excessive peasant debt and analyse inventories drawn up after a death, it is only because these men, despite their debts, died

[25] Goubert, *Beauvais et le Beauvaisis*, pp. 182, 160–2.
[26] Anne McCants, "Goods at Pawn: The Overlapping World of Material Possessions and Family Finance in Early Modern Amsterdam," *Social Science History*, 31, no. 2, 2007, pp. 213–38.

in their villages and were not wandering the roads after being stripped of their possessions. Their creditors would have waited for them to die before seizing their livestock and crops, and then it was up to their children, deprived of their inheritance, to negotiate their place within society. As shown in village archives, the creditors' patience, which saved more than one peasant from social exclusion, has enabled historians to study the poor.

In short, there were four or five different types of requests for loans made by peasants: short-term loans for seeds and for food to bridge the gap between harvests, which, for as long as they were granted, protected the peasants from famine in the short term; cash loans to pay taxes; loans made for key family events such as weddings or setting up a home; and the sale of animals, goods, or property to those better-off or between the better-off.[27] In addition, some peasants had rent or farm rent to pay, or, in circumstances in which only one heir occupied a house, he had to pay a certain number of livres to his brothers as their share of the revenue from the property.[28]

In the towns, food trade and rent were the major sources of credit. Bakers were the most exposed, and the rare, preserved account books show the extent of consumer loans: the information provided on forty-one bakers from Lyon in the inventories after death in the seventeenth century allows us to measure the volume of credit they gave to their clients; two-thirds of the bakers, after their death, left tallies worth less than 250 livres, but one out of five was a creditor of more than 1,000 livres with respect to his clients.[29] Inventories drawn up after a death indicate also debts owed to those who sold food (bakers and sometimes even butchers), doctors, and nurses, who turned up to claim their dues.[30] Bakers' inventories made frequent mention of tallies[31] declared to be "of

---

[27] Laurence Fontaine, *Pouvoir, identités et migrations dans les hautes vallées des Alpes occidentales (XVIIe-XVIIIe siècle)*, Grenoble, Presses universitaires de Grenoble, 2003, chap. 3.

[28] Goubert, *Beauvais et le Beauvaisis*, p. 160. In the Beauvais area, one-quarter of manual workers rented their houses, with rent rarely more than ten livres a year.

[29] Anne Montenach, *Espaces et pratiques du commerce alimentaire à Lyon au XVIIe siècle*, Grenoble, Presses universitaires de Grenoble, 2009, p. 343.

[30] Those who turned up to claim their dues did not necessarily represent all the creditors: they were only those who were officially claiming the repayment of loans.

[31] The *Shorter Oxford English Dictionary on Historical Principles*, 6th ed., vol. 2, 2007, Oxford, Oxford University Press, p. 3172, defines tally as "a squared wooden stick or rod scored across with notches representing the amount of a debt or payment and then split lengthways across the notches into two halves (one retained by each party) the correspondence of which constituted legal proof of debt etc."

no value" because the people who owed them were insolvent or had "left for the army"; another baker left seventy tally sticks "all moth-eathen and former parishioners that the said widow ... declared to be of poor silk workers who had died insolvent or had left for the army." The record kept by a baker from Lyon regarding what the wife of a drink vendor (*fontainier*) owed him tells us much about such microcredit: she owed him two round loaves of bread (or two livres), as well as "the baking of two loaves of bread, two pounds of flour, straw and the sum of sixteen sols."[32] Some bakers facilitated the repayment of their clients' debts by spreading them over small monthly instalments. Some of these arrangements took the shape of a convention or promise of payment. Thus, Antoinette Morand came to the following agreement with her baker: she would "pay him 20 sols per month as payment for the sum of seven livres for the sale of bread"; a hotelier promised to pay back 6 livres per month to wipe out a debt of 126 livres. A hatter obtained a period of one year to pay back his debt of 107 livres, and a master glover managed to get three years to pay off 191 livres.[33]

But the main cause of debt was rent arrears. Rent arrears combined with the seizure of property, or even the threat of seizure, forced individuals and families onto the road. Detailed studies of Lyon,[34] Rennes,[35] and Beauvais, which have taught us much about urban debt, all provide ample evidence of the critical role played by rent arrears in the slide into poverty. Measuring the average period by which the rent was late is also to measure urban poverty and its fluctuations. An analysis of this type

[32] Montenach, *Espaces et pratiques*, p. 342.
[33] Ibid., p. 346.
[34] Jean-Pierre Gutton gives numerous instances of this in Lyon; for example, the silk worker who left Lyon because he was being pursued by his creditors – his furniture, which was sold at auction, fetched 459 livres and 12 sols; his debts amounted to 356 livres 5 sols and 9 deniers. A master carpenter, "pressed by his creditors" "went away," leaving behind his wife and six children. Five months later, the landlord initiated seizure of his possessions because of the late payment of the rent, and two days later, the carpenter's wife also disappeared, taking with her the two oldest children. In August 1686, when his tenant died, Pierre David had someone represent him when the inventory was drawn up in order to safeguard his rights – more than two years' rent arrears, at 54 livres a year. Unfortunately, the deceased had left only 56 livres. Gutton, *La Société*, pp. 132–5.
[35] Christine Chapalain-Nougaret has noted the inventories drawn up after death in Rennes for certain poor people, riddled with debt and in arrears with their rent, whose possessions were estimated as being worth 10 livres – less than the annual rent on their tiny one-room dwelling. C. Chapalain-Nougaret, *Misère et assistance dans le pays de Rennes au XVIIIe siècle*, Rennes, Cid éditions, 1989, pp. 122–3.

reveals significant urban poverty in seventeenth-century Beauvais and mid-eighteenth-century Rennes. In Beauvais rent arrears rose in the second half of the seventeenth century: in 1646, 56 tenants had rent arrears of one or two rent periods; in 1688, the 21 tenants of the *paroisse* of Saint-Etienne had between them 116 unpaid rent periods; of the 18 tenants in Saint-Laurent, five were six years in arrears, one had paid his rent on time, and the remaining twelve had on average arrears of six rent periods. As for the seventeen tenants of the other *paroisses*, they were, on average, 2.5 years behind with their rent.[36] In the middle of the eighteenth century, Breton hospices were owed rent for periods easily spanning one to ten years.[37] Hence, rent arrears were not only a cause of poverty but also one of the reasons for itinerancy; in Lyon, in years when the silk industry was in crisis, notices were posted forbidding landlords from demanding rent due on silk workers' apartments until such time as there was work again.[38]

In other words, whatever the reasons, the majority of men and women survived only by borrowing money and signing IOUs from which they would never be free. Therefore, what is surprising is not the number of vagrants and beggars, but rather the number of men and women who, in spite of owing more than they owned, were not expelled from their villages. What is more is that these people did not live in an economy in which risks could be anticipated and calculated; rather, they lived in an unpredictable economy: How could they anticipate high prices or economic crises, protect themselves against unemployment, or insure against illness?

If indebtedness is a gauge of poverty, it is also a sign of being part of social communities, and the poorest people in seventeenth-century Amsterdam were also those with the fewest debts.[39] These observations tell us that economic realities were moderated by social relationships that often served to help and protect those in need. Historians of the modern period are only just beginning to take an interest in these social relationships, which acted as a filter mechanism and which (all other things being equal) point us toward those individuals who were best equipped in times of economic crisis.

---

[36] Goubert, *Beauvais et le Beauvaisis,* pp. 533–4
[37] Hufton, *The Poor of Eighteenth-Century France.* p. 55.
[38] Gutton, *La Société,* p. 78.
[39] Ann McCants, "After-Death Inventories as a Source for the Study of Material Culture, Economic Well-Being, and Household Formation among the Poor of 18th c. Amsterdam," *Historical Methods,* 39, no. 1, 2006, pp. 10–23.

Social Networks and Credit

The various social networks on which people relied point to either horizontal or vertical ties. The former included relations, neighbours, friends, and workmates; the latter covered the elite classes to which the city dweller and the peasant alike were bound by ties of work or power. In certain parts of Europe, in addition to the aforementioned ties, strong religious loyalties existed. In the Netherlands, for example, each religion (or group within a faith community) had its own scheme for aiding the poor: the Protestants had eight such schemes; the Catholics and the Jews, one apiece.[40]

Whether the social relationships were vertical or horizontal, all were crisscrossed by debt. However, an analysis of indebtedness demonstrates that credit relationships varied depending on the people involved and the locus: the social environment determined the type of credit relationship, and this environment depended on geographical relationships. In effect, the creditor-debtor relationship progressed through a certain number of circles, which are discussed in greater detail in the next chapter. The person in need turned first to his or her family. If a person had no family, or the family was unable to help, he or she turned next to friends who belonged to the same social group. In working-class circles, friends were rarely able to provide sufficient help, in which case the person in need would approach those who gave him or her work. For peasants, depending on where they lived, this would be the aristocracy, religious institutions, or the village elite; in proto-industrial urban or rural areas, it would be the merchants. Next to be approached would be the regional elite and, finally, the foreigners, who, depending on the region, would be Jews, Italians, or Savoyards. Evidently, people asked for credit from the person from whom they bought their food. These successive circles can be seen as a spectrum in which the credit relationship was initially situated within the various interpersonal relationships that centred on the individual; gradually it moved outward, ending as a relationship that was more obviously economic and impersonal.

Family solidarity is a controversial issue. In some countries, family solidarity was required by law. In England, the English Poor Relief Act of 1601 stipulated that "the children of every poor, old, blind, lame

---

[40] G. P. M. Pot, "Arm Leiden. Levensstandaard, bedeling en bedeelden, 1750–1854," PHD dissertation, 1994, Hilversum, Leyden. My thanks go to Paul Klep who gave me access to all the Dutch references cited. See also Erika Kuijpers, *Migrantenstad. Immigratie en sociale verhoudingen in zeventiende-eeuws Amsterdam*, Hilversum, Leyden, 2005.

and impotent person shall at their own charges relieve and maintain every such poor person." In Germanic countries and the Netherlands, it was not a legal obligation, but charitable institutions demanded that children should help their parents when they were capable of doing so.[41] Nonetheless, one might well ask whether the aim of these laws was not to impose a practice that, if it had been common, would not have required legislation for it to be implemented. The historians who have laid the most stress on the importance of social networks emphasize the parameters of reciprocity and geographic proximity, stressing that mutual help and reciprocity occurred on an almost daily basis when people lived near one another, but that help was more limited and sporadic when distance came between them. Reciprocity between parents and children was long term and with no conscious thought of return or of the uneven density of social networks being the result of hazard, because they were dictated by the fertility of preceding generations and, subsequently, by personal temperament and the ability of individuals to migrate in order to rejoin their networks if events had conspired to distance them.[42]

Against this optimistic vision, the forums in which family relationships were brought to the fore, such as meetings of family members, neighbours, and friends, showed that family solidarity was anything but natural. In France, for instance, the state sought to protect the property of widows and minors by imposing solidarity on their relatives and friends. Thus, when the head of the household died, a meeting of relatives, neighbours, and friends had to be called to settle the future of the children and to find guardians for them. In addition, the widow and the children had the option of refusing their inheritance or of accepting it on the basis that they would assume the debts of the head of the household, only up to the limit of the value of the estate. This procedure was used to allow orphans to keep property inherited from their mother and legacies they might have received from elsewhere, and to allow the widow to keep what was hers alone. Finally, the state also intervened whenever a situation arose in which the land inherited by the children was to be

---

[41] Jütte, *Poverty and Deviance*, p. 88; C. Lis, *Social Change and the Labouring Poor, Antwerp 1770–1860*, New Haven, CT, and London, Yale University Press, 1986; Naomi Tadmor, *Family and Friends in Eighteenth-Century England: Household, Kinship and Patronage*, Cambridge, Cambridge University Press, 2001; Hindle, *On the Parish?*, chaps. 1, 3, and 5.

[42] Jütte, *Poverty and Deviance*, pp. 84–6.

disposed: guardians were responsible for the day-to-day management of
the estate but could not sell land without meeting and consulting relatives, neighbours, and friends and without the approval of the judge. A
study of these procedures reveals that only the rich had the means to
resort to them.[43]

In addition, English demographers have stressed the importance of
nuclear families in the urban regions of northern Europe, and resulting
from this, the absence of ties to the wider family network,[44] neighbours,
and friends therefore assumed more importance.[45] Indeed, in the eighteenth century, in town, single women living in Denmark rarely had family likely to support them.[46] This model can be extended beyond northern
Europe on the basis that the families of workers with neither capital nor
property – and taking into account how often people in the towns and
cities moved around – had very few means of keeping in touch with family members across large distances.

The composition of the family and the frequency with which people
moved around would thus account for the reduced level of family support. Although these factors are undoubtedly important, they minimize
the role of social background: only the rich had the means to maintain
family ties. Moreover, those examples of solidarity we do have all concern families from wealthy, aristocratic, merchant, or even peasant elite
backgrounds; they are the groups that left behind letters and autobiog-
raphies. Only William Stout (1665–1752), with the help of his family,
could afford to rescue his nephew from debt numerous times. Only Abel
de Servien, magistrate and ambassador, could, in 1678, leave something
in his will to his poor relatives.[47] He requested that 500 livres be distributed to the poor of Claix, the village from which he came, adding that
the money should be given particularly "to our poorest relatives, whom

[43] Laurence Fontaine, "Solidarités familiales et logiques migratoires en pays de montagne à
l'époque modern," *Annales ESC*, 6, 1990, pp. 1433–50.
[44] Peter Laslett, "Family, Kinship and Collectivity as Systems of Support in Pre-Industrial
Europe: A Consideration of the 'Nuclear-Hardship' Hypothesis," *Charity and the Poor in
Medieval and Renaissance Europe*, in *Continuity and Change*, J. Henderson, ed., special
issue, 3, no. 2, 1988, pp. 153–75.
[45] For a discussion of the realities covered by the concepts of household, family and friendship, see Tadmor, *Family and Friends*.
[46] Hans-Christian Johansen, "Never-Married Women in Town and Country in Eighteenth-
Century Denmark," *Poor Women and Children*, pp. 196–206.
[47] Craig Muldrew, *The Economy of Obligation, Culture of Credit and Social Relations
in Early Modern England*, London, Macmillan, 1998, chap. 9. Also see examples in
David Cressy, "Kinship and Kin Interaction in Early Modern England," *Past and Present*,
no. 113, 1986, pp. 38–69 (46–49); and in Tadmor, *Family and Friends*, pp. 29–30.

we must not forget nor treat with contempt."[48] On the other hand, in Languedoc, the ties of family protection for many families were extended to, at most, first cousins,[49] and in his will, Ponç Faig, a Catalan shepherd and moneylender, forewent the 100 florins he had lent his first cousin, the sum of which he had not entered in the record he maintained of his debtors.[50] The fact remains that in every social milieu there are examples showing that, everywhere, whenever there were close relatives, they would help their own.[51] In Barcelona, widows, in their wills, waived the debts of close relatives, and at the end of the eighteenth century, more than half the women who left the *hôpital de la miséricorde* were reclaimed by their relatives.[52]

On the whole, however, studies which reveal the existence of active family networks outside of the nobility and bourgeois merchant classes are few and far between, particularly for the peasant and artisanal classes. In fact, the mechanisms of solidarity established by the state relating to orphans demonstrates that family solidarity was by no means assured: when the inheritance was problematic the family was reluctant to act together in the best interests of the beneficiaries, and no one was willing to take on the role of guardian. Moreover, the number who attended the meetings to settle the child's future was inverse in proportion to the child's need for family unity, and although the notary's report recorded that those who had failed to attend would be pursued in law, repeated meetings were found to be no better attended, despite the protests recorded in the minutes against the relatives who "did not deign to appear."[53] The

[48] Kathryn Norberg, *Rich and Poor in Grenoble, 1600–1814*, Berkeley, University of California Press, 1985, p. 153.

[49] Works by Yves Castan cited by J. -P. Gutton in *La Sociabilité villageoise dans l'ancienne France. Solidarités et voisinages du XVIe au XVIIIe siècle*, Paris, Hachette, 1979, p. 56.

[50] M. Dolors Santandreu i Soler, "El testament i la declaració de deutes i deutors de Ponç Faig, pastor de Sant Martí de Puigbò (segle XV)," *Estudis d'Historia agrària*, no. 14 (2000–1), pp. 91–103 (94).

[51] Cressy, "Kinship and Kin," pp. 38–69. T. Wales, "Poverty, Poor Relief and the Life-Cycle: Some Evidence from Seventeenth-Century Norfolk," *Land, Kinship and Life-Cycle*, R. M. Smith, ed., Cambridge, 1984, pp. 382–4. *The Locus of Care: Families, Communities and Institutions and the Provision of Welfare Since Antiquity*, P. Horden and R. Smith, eds., London, Routledge, 1998; B. A. Holderness, "Widows in Pre-Industrial Society: An Essay upon their Economic Functions," *Land, Kinship and Life-Cycle*, R. M. Smith, ed., Cambridge, Cambridge University Press, 1984, pp. 423–42 (440–1).

[52] Carbonell i Esteller, *Sobreviure a Barcelona*, pp. 186, 194.

[53] An orphan who was physically or mentally deficient encountered even greater difficulties in finding relatives prepared to take him in: "and, should he fall ill, they have agreed that the aforementioned Diaque will look after him for eight days only, and afterwards will take him to the hospital." The guardian of one of Jean Clot's children demanded of

poor were then twice as poor: to the lack of money had to be added the withdrawal of their relatives. Studies carried out on those most in need of family solidarity confirm that whenever need existed, poor families proved themselves incapable of supporting their own.[54] This tends to confirm that family networks were a resource which was unequally distributed between social classes and that deferred reciprocity existed only in families who had sufficient economic stability to allow themselves it.

It is difficult to separate neighbours and friends from family within these networks, because they all fulfilled similar roles and one or the other would be more in evidence depending on where they lived and what the circumstances were. Moreover, family meetings were also attended by neighbours and friends. In the towns, the latter played a more active role in the lives of the poor. Neighbours and friends signed certificates of poverty, lent money, attended funerals, and wrote petitions and requests on behalf of the poor person when necessary. In Cologne at the end of the eighteenth century, more than half of the certificates of poverty (751 of 1,406) bear the signature of citizens who were neither linked to the applicant nor to officials and that 656 (87 per cent) of signatories can be identified as neighbours, the remainder being either friends or relatives. In 1798, for example, Godfried Schaben signed at least seven certificates of poverty for people living in the house next to his.[55] In the Netherlands, some towns, such as Leiden, were divided and run by family networks who took responsibility not just for administrative duties such as maintaining the population register, assisting with funerals, keeping the streets clean, and firefighting, but also for fulfilling more informal social functions, such as taking the necessary steps on behalf of the poor to enable them to get help and supporting them with gifts and food. At the end of the eighteenth-century Leiden had around two hundred of these "gebuurten" family networks. After 1796, in order to counteract their power and fearing riots, the town sought to restrict the activities of these families to the administrative management of their respective districts.[56]

---

the assembled relatives what he should do with the child and his property "given that he could only find people interested in the property without the aforementioned ward." Eventually an uncle took him in, in return for a salary to compensate him for the fact that he couldn't work; if the boy fell ill, the uncle would look after him for eight days and would then take him to the hospital. Departmental archives, Hautes Alpes, 1E 4839, 16 June 1685. Fontaine, *Solidarités*.

[54] See the work done by Lola Valverde, Philip Gavitt, Eugenio Sonnino, and Volker Hunecke on orphans and abandoned children in *Poor Women and Children*, pp. 51–137.

[55] Jütte, *Poverty and Deviance*, p. 97.

[56] Pot, "Arm Leiden."

Saving strategies have hardly been studied, yet poor city dwellers were also in the habit of lending to each other and knew about economies of scale, renting out beds and taking in foreigners in their homes. Censuses in England, for example, reveal foreigners living in the homes of poor families, expressing more complex strategies for coping with the vagaries of life – solutions that were found within the home and were not dependent solely on relatives.[57] In the archives, in France, one can meet women such as Françoise Moreau, previously a maidservant in Lyon who then moved to Grenoble and wrote from Grenoble on 10 March 1743, to a laundress in Lyon asking her (among other things) to recover the 21 sols Moreau had lent to a stocking-darner in the Rue Bellecordière, which she needed back because "she was desperately in need of money." This was a small loan that this woman from the Dauphiné had not recovered when she left Lyon, and only need now forced her to demand its repayment. For the laundress, Marguerite Lambert, in the quai des Célestins, recovering the debt was doubtless an act of loyalty to Françoise Moreau, but it was also a sideline for her – when Lambert died, she left furniture and effects to the value of 153 livres in the room she rented, but she was also owed a total of 2,162 livres. She had made loans to various individuals, once for more than 1,000 livres.[58] This whole activity of small-scale local credit remains poorly documented, and I attempt to deal with it in Chapters 4 and 5.

In the city, small traders supplied on credit; however, many shopkeepers knew they would never be repaid. Some wrote off in their wills the debts of poor insolvent people. Examples of this were found both in England and in Portugal.[59]

These networks of solidarity were all affected by the milieux in which they existed. The urban segregation of the classes destroyed the vertical personal ties that proximity created.

Horizontal solidarities encompassed one final group: the brotherhoods and the guilds. Robert Fossier, moreover, links the development of

---

[57] Jeremy Boulton, "'It Is Extreme Necessity That Makes Me Do This': Some 'Survival Strategies' of Pauper Households in London's West End during the Early Eighteenth Century," *Household Strategies for Survival 1600–2000: Fission, Faction and Cooperation*, L. Fontaine and J. Schlumbohm, eds., Cambridge, Cambridge University Press, 2000, pp. 47–70; and Montserrat Carbonell-Esteller, "Using Microcredit and Restructuring Households: Two Complementary Survival Strategies in Late-Eighteenth-Century Barcelona," *Household Strategies*, pp. 71–92.

[58] Gutton, *La Société*, p. 82, 63.

[59] Muldrew, *The Economy of Obligation*; Maria Manuela Rochas, "Crédito privato num contexto urbano. Lisboa, 1770–1830," PHD thesis, European University Institute, 1996.

brotherhoods in urban milieux to the collapse of the protection provided by the extended family.[60] These solidarities were important to people in the towns, and whenever a craftsman introduced himself, if he was a member of a guild or brotherhood he would always emphasize this, because his membership brought him economic security and a distinctive status within the job market.[61] In fact, in the modern period, the brotherhoods were all willing to help their poorer members. Some of the German guilds kept a stock of wheat that they sold to them at a reduced price. Others, such as the dyers' society in Lübeck, would pay a pension to poor members and a small weekly sum to a master craftsman in straitened circumstances. Help was more likely to be given in the form of a loan with favourable repayment terms rather than as a gift.[62] In addition, employees established tontine funds. In the coastal region of Holland, insurance funds were widely developed from the eighteenth century onward. In return for a weekly contribution they would provide assistance when death or illness struck; very young children were covered, and the sick were generally cared for up to a year.[63] In Portugal, right up to the late nineteenth century, brotherhoods were the principal source of local credit taking care of a fourth of small credit needs.[64] In Germanic countries are numerous examples of members of a brotherhood or guild – such as those belonging to the guild of blacksmiths in Brandenburg – being able to borrow from their collective funds when they were in need. The statutes of the society of joiners and coopers in the town of Lünen, which date from 1736, refer to a special mutual aid fund for its members.[65] On the other side of the Rhine, workers and shopkeepers in Grenoble who left religious donations in their wills would direct them to the brotherhoods rather than to the monasteries, expressing the strength of the ties to professional bodies.[66]

[60] Robert Fossier, *Histoire sociale de l'occident médiéval*, Paris, Armand Colin, 1970, chap. 5.
[61] Schwartz, *Policing the Poor*, p. 112.
[62] Jütte, *Poverty and Deviance*, p. 97.
[63] Pot, "Arm Leiden." See also Erika Kuijpers, "The Metropolis and the Migrant Poor. Paupers in Amsterdam during the Golden Age," unpublished PHD thesis, University of Utrecht (elements of which appear in, Lotte Van de Pol and Erika Kuijpers, "Poor Women's Migration to the City. The Attraction of the Amsterdam Health Care and Social Assistance in Early Modern Times," *Journal of Urban History*, 32, no. 1, 2005, pp. 44–60.
[64] Caroline B. Brettell, "Moral Economy or Political Economy? Property and Credit Markets in 19th Century Rural Portugal," *Journal of Historical Sociology*, 12, 1991, pp. 1–28 (17–18).
[65] Jütte, *Poverty and Deviance*, p. 98.
[66] Norberg, *Rich and Poor in Grenoble*, pp. 248–9.

The way in which people made use of these professional bodies demonstrates the real forward-thinking strategies they employed to protect themselves from the setbacks of circumstance. In seventeenth-century Venice craftspeople even joined more than one guild so that when certain professions faltered, they were left with room to manoeuvre and were able to find work.[67] There were also genuine strategies for savings and financial investments. To avoid spending their old age in hospital the ordinary "poor" people of France would invest what little savings they had in these very same hospitals, attracted by the large income and by the apparent security of these investments. The breakdown of the list of creditors of the hospital in Aix is evidence of this strategy.[68] In 1762, the rector of the hospital described to his intendant in the following terms the creditors of his establishment:

> The largest number of these creditors are working people, artisans, seafaring people, servants, small traders, orphans, old people; they all came to the Hôtel-Dieu as if to a sacred temple to deposit the sweat of their long and hard labour and get a very modest interest out of it, which helps them sustain their family and end their days without having to be supported by pious deeds.[69]

Hospitals served as a savings bank and retirement organization.

A similar analysis of the subscribers to the mounts of piety in Paris at the end of the eighteenth century demonstrates that ordinary folk had no hesitation in investing their savings there.[70] Marseille followed the same pattern with a large number of lenders and small loans, a fact emphasized by the administrators during the French Revolution while speaking of the activity of their predecessors:

> They were careful to borrow only small sums and [from] people who were not rich. This system has always been followed and still is. Thus though at the moment the charity owes more than 460 000 livres, two-thirds of this sum are

---

[67] R. T. Rapp, *Industry and Economic Decline in Seventeenth-Century Venice*, Cambridge, MA, Harvard University Press, 1976, cited by Woolf, *The Poor in Western Europe*, p. 12.

[68] G. Valran, *Misère et Charité en Provence au XVIIIe siècle. Essai d'histoire sociale*, Paris, 1899, Genève, Mégariotis Reprints, 1979, p. 205.

[69] Marcel Courdurié, *La Dette des collectivités publiques de Marseille au XVIIIe siècle. Du débat sur le prêt à intérêt au financement par l'emprunt*, Marseille, Institut historique de Provence, 1974, pp. 188–96.

[70] Robert Bigo, "Aux origines du Mont de Piété parisien," *Annales d'histoire économique et sociale*, V, 1932, pp. 113–26. He gives the example of a woman who invested 3,000 livres for ten years. When she died in October 1778, her heirs were her son, who was an unskilled worker; her daughter, who was married to a poor Parisian; and the three children of her dead brother, who had been a grocer in Saint-Germain (p. 119).

owed in capital from 100 livres to 2000 livres, capital not exceeding 1000 livres being more numerous than that which exceeds this sum.

... we should not think, they wrote, that those who lend to the mount of piety are well-off people and in a condition to work, they are women, pledgees, daily workers who do not know the art of making their money grow. Managing to save a small amount after working their whole life, they take advantage of the service the administration offers them.[71]

Such institutional and financial investments were one of the strategies of the lower classes to guard against an uncertain future.

Varying Social Attitudes to Credit

Attitudes to poverty and credit varied widely between different social groups. They point to the different relationships with the economy that coexisted and were not without bearing on the future of the poor.

The aristocrats were not only the most important source of funds for their peasants, but throughout the ancien régime they showed greatest generosity to the poor under their seigniorial authority. Their attitude retained something of the contracts of an earlier age in which the weak would place themselves under the protection of the mighty.[72] The credit relationship between the nobleman and his poor peasants was characterized in two ways: the relationship was a personal one and the human element took precedence over profitability. To mark the continuity of the relationship, whenever a lord died and was succeeded by the next generation, the wife of the old lord, or his heir, were required personally to distribute to the poor the gifts that the nobility traditionally left them in their wills. In 1681, the Marquis de Virieu left instructions for his heir to distribute several hundred livres to his needy peasants. The Marquis de Valbonnais asked his wife to distribute 500 livres to his poor and deserving peasants.[73] In her work on the aristocracy of the Dauphiné, Kathryn Norberg has calculated that, in the seventeenth

---

[71] Courdurié, *La Dette des collectivités*, pp. 239–40.
[72] From Merovingian times, peasants were driven to seek the patronage of the powerful by debt, insecurity and the scarcity of resources: "As it is common knowledge that I have nothing with which to feed and clothe myself, I have begged you, and you have accepted, to allow me to devote myself to you or place myself under your protection. The terms under which I have done this are as follows: you must help me and support me so that I can both feed and clothe myself, so that I may serve you and be worthy of you. For the rest of my life I shall serve and obey you in such ways as are compatible with my freedom, and I shall not be able during my lifetime to escape your power and protection." Mollat, *Les Pauvres*, p. 44.
[73] Norberg, *Rich and Poor in Grenoble*, p. 152.

century, between 33 per cent and 86 per cent of aristocrats (depending on the year and the size of the sample) left charitable gifts in their wills. If Kathryn Norberg's calculations – often based on samples that are too small – appear random when examined more closely, they nonetheless assume greater pertinence when we compare these figures with the figures for other social groups. Effectively the figures for these latter groups, although they vary just as widely in percentage terms, tended to be much lower.[74]

The aristocracy were the social group who behaved with the most indulgence towards their poor debtors. Jean-Louis de Rodolp, a country gentleman who lived comfortably in Castres with no occupation other than managing his fortune, his tenanted farms, and his seigniorial rights, left at his death a book listing the debts owed to the family. It included the debts he had inherited, those he had granted, and those which his heirs managed after his death. Analysis reveals that, although the debts owed by the peasants were eventually mostly recovered, they were all paid back over extremely long periods. Despite this, the Rodolp family systematically refused to speed up the recovery of these debts by forcing the sale of the peasants' land. Moreover, those rare legal proceedings that did take place demonstrated that accepting the property of smaller property owners as collateral was an illusory guarantee: either they were in debt well in excess of the value of their plots of land, or they had already been forced to dispose of the land to their neighbours, or to city dwellers, who thus increased the size of their own smallholdings. Each new succession in the Rodolp family was an opportunity to revive these rural debts.[75] When the tenants of Gilles de Gouberville fell two months behind in rent, they would go the manor with a woodcock or a chicken, and the matter would be settled.[76] The behaviour of the English aristocracy was similar. In Lancashire during times of economic crisis (in the 1670s, 1680s, and after 1720), landlords were immediately called on to delay collection of the rent or to reduce the accumulated arrears, and in the end, they made very few attempts to take advantage of the situation to evict or replace

[74] Norberg, *Rich and Poor in Grenoble*, p. 123.

[75] G. E. de Falguerolles, "Opérations de crédit en Haut-Languedoc (1728–1748)," *Etudes Rurales*, 9, 1963, pp. 30–46. L. Fontaine, "Relations de crédit et surendettement en France, XVIIe–XVIIIe siècles," *Des personnes aux institutions, Réseaux et cultures du crédit du XVIe au XXe siècle en Europe*, L. Fontaine, G. Postel-Vinay, J. -L. Rosenthal, and P. Servais, eds., Louvain-la-Neuve, Bruylant-Academia s.a., 1997, pp. 206–19.

[76] Cited by N. Z. Davis, *The Gift in Sixteenth-Century France*, Oxford, Oxford University Press, 2000, p. 90.

their defaulting farmers.[77] In the Spanish countryside, monastic communities would commonly grant arrearage and remission of debts in a bad year.[78] The only exceptions were the princes of Hohenloe in southwest Germany, who assumed the lion's share of the debt owed by the small landowners but then proved to be creditors who imposed harsh conditions on their debtors.[79]

The lenient attitude that the majority of the nobility had toward the collection of debts was also reflected in the instructions they left in their wills. Thus, in the middle of the seventeenth century, an aristocrat in the Dauphiné requested that the interest paid by his peasants should be given to relieve the poorest peasants. Others suspended interest payments for a year or instructed their heirs to reduce arrears or to cancel small debts, and one aristocrat cancelled all repayments in grain during a year of famine.[80]

The relationship between the aristocracy and the poor that endured throughout the ancien régime was particular to this social group. Between 1720 and 1789 in the Dauphiné, the number of non-aristocrats who left bequests in their wills to the peasant poor varied between 3 per cent and 6 per cent, depending on the year, whereas for the aristocracy this figure was between 27 per cent and 46 per cent. Other social groups were not interested in reducing the debts of the poor in their home villages. Clauses leaving charitable donations to the poor gradually disappeared from the wills of the urban elite (with the exception of the aristocrats) between the seventeenth and eighteenth centuries: in 1780, a third of lawyers and a quarter of merchants left charitable bequests in their wills, compared to 70 per cent of magistrates. This continued attachment to the old structure of vertical loyalties should not however be allowed to conceal an important shift: although the aristocracy continued to make charitable donations, the average value of such gifts dropped dramatically despite the general increase in wealth of the former.[81]

---

[77] B. A. Holderness, "Credit in a Rural Community 1600–1800," *Midland History*, 3, 1975, pp. 94–115. Keith Wrightson also shows that many peasants died insolvent in seventeenth-century Britain on account of rent arrears owed to their lord, *Earthly Necessities. Economic lifes in Early Modern Britain*, New Haven and Londres, Yale University Press, 2000, p. 281.

[78] Pegerto Saavedra, "Réseaux et culture du crédit en Galice, XVI-XIXe siècle," EUI Working Paper HEC No. 99/3.

[79] Jütte, *Poverty and Deviance*, p. 95.

[80] Norberg, *Rich and Poor in Grenoble*, p. 153. See pp. 254–5 for more detail on the end of the eighteenth century.

[81] Norberg, *Rich and Poor in Grenoble*, pp. 239–57.

Although all the work done in this area indicates that the poor remained in the same conditions throughout the ancien régime, on the contrary, the nobility changed. In effect, the conventions of noble society imposed moral obligations upon them and an extremely costly lifestyle which, during the seventeenth century, cost them their wealth, their possessions and their authority. Their bourgeois creditors settled into the seigniorial estates they acquired and (with a few notable exceptions) set about managing them in the same fashion that had secured their success elsewhere. Thus, in 1789, of fifty-eight gentlemen in the bailiwick of Beauvais, only ten were from the old nobility; the other forty-eight originated from the Beauvais merchant classes or were recently appointed nobles from the capital and neighbouring provinces.[82] The entry of the bourgeois classes into the nobility also explains the changes that took place in this class's relationship to the poor, to credit, and to charity.

Vertical ties based on employment had completely different meanings in the town and in the country. Although one might find a certain number of instructive examples of urban solidarity, it is clear that solidarity between merchants or manufacturers and workers was distinctly limited; the former feeling under no obligation to employ or help the latter unless they had economic need of them. Those contracts of apprenticeship that specified the period during which the apprentice would be cared for by his master before going into hospital were harsh: they allowed between a fortnight and a maximum of two months.[83]

The world of work was similarly a place where authority and dependence were transmitted by debt. In the Beauvais area, an unskilled worker more often than not owed money to his employer: the latter would have ploughed his fields, lent seeds, wood or money, and by working for his creditor, the worker settled his debt.[84] He was in the same position as the seasonal migrants who worked so that they could repay the interest on debts they had contracted at home, or the weavers to whom the merchants had granted an advance on salary, which they then recovered gradually from the weaver's wages. These ties of debt were also contracts of employment, a way for the bosses to keep hold of good workers, or just be sure of having workers during times of labour shortage. With this in mind, some bosses went as far as to lend money against a security – a suit, sheets, a cross – to their workers, despite the fact that numerous

[82] Goubert, *Beauvais et Beauvaisis*, pp. 220–1.
[83] Fontaine, *Solidarités*.
[84] Goubert, *Beauvais et Beauvaisis*, pp. 220–1.

rulings forbade this practice; a report on the sale of wheat in Norfolk, written in 1631 in response to the famines of previous years, refers to "labourers that buy it at an under price of them with whom they work."[85] The need for personnel brought with it both debt and a guarantee against poverty. If the same logic appears less in evidence in Holland, with its system of "diaconies" (an insurance scheme designed to help the poor when they fell sick, financed by rich families of independent means, farmers, and the middle classes), it was nonetheless visible when the biggest landlords, large farmers, and proto-industrial bosses offered credit over the winter to those families with significant personnel, which was to be repaid in labour hours over the rest of the year.[86]

Client relationships and relations of power within the village were also expressed through debt. Once again, debt could work against the debtor, but the nature of such relationships meant that debt primarily represented security: a guarantee that the peasant would have food and a roof over his head for the rest of his life. In exchange, throughout the various struggles between the families, the peasant would give his or her patron support and would be available to work when required. As with all other personal relationships of the time, matters between them would normally only be settled on the death of patron or client as we shall see in the next chapter.

The spiritual ties preferred by the elite classes were meant to reinforce the ties of dependence and protection. During the sixteenth and eighteenth centuries, these ties also crumbled, particularly in England, where, for example, in a village near York in the sixteenth century, in a quarter of all baptisms one of the three named godparents was a member of the gentry – generally a woman – whereas at the beginning of the eighteenth century, in a Catholic community in Lancashire, the practice had almost disappeared and concerned only 2.7 per cent of children who, moreover, were the sons and daughters of previous or present servants. In Germanic countries, on the other hand, the practice remained well established and in Oppenheim, for example, between 1568 and 1798, unskilled workers

---

[85] Cited in John Walter, "The Social Economy of Death in Early Modern England," *Famine, Disease and the Social Order in Early Modern Society*, John Walter and Roger Schofield, eds., Cambridge, Cambridge University Press, 1989, p. 101, quoted in Jütte, *Poverty and Deviance*, p. 94.

[86] Lis, *Social Changes*, and unpublished works by Paul Klep. Hilde Van Wijngaarden shows that at the end of the seventeenth century, a "workhouse" was set up at Zwolle granted frequent advances on salary both to help the poor and to secure the labour of children. Van Wijngaarden, "Credit as a way to make ends meet. The use of credit by poor woman in Zwolle 1650–1700," paper presented at the International Congress of Economic History, Madrid, 29 August 1998.

chose farmers (6 per cent of cases), craftspeople (27 per cent), and officials (32 per cent) as godparents for their children.[87]

Some country notables, such as the tax collectors in France and the
attorneys in England, left behind them when they died numerous inventories, a breakdown of which reveals how active they were as lenders.[88]
Several of these characters who – through ploughing fields, providing
cartage, and lending seeds, wood, hay, and money for taxes or court
cases – had more than half of the families of their village in debt to them
and a number of others from neighbouring villages. Through these loans,
these notables secured their power and made sure of a submissive workforce.[89] The same credit relationships and client culture are found in the
Alps: they formed the basis of village unity. Debt continued from generation to generation; interest payments were reduced when one patron died
and was succeeded by another; credit was never secured on a specific plot
of land: practices such as these convey the preeminence of the social function of debt over its economic function – it was the best guarantee against
economic crisis. Moreover. the village elites recorded separately the credit
they granted to the poorest peasants. For example, in managing the debts
owed to him, Jean Bernard – a rich peddler from the Upper Dauphiné at
the end of the seventeenth century – made a distinction between the loans
he granted to reputedly creditworthy farmers and to those who were not
creditworthy: he recorded in a special book the sums lent to the poorest,
to the "less well-off." These loans totalled 82 livres, compared with 3,665
livres to inhabitants of the village who were not peddlers. The loans to
the poorest peasants were not secured on any land and would never be
paid back. Neither were they easily convertible to labour: in most cases,
they merely added to the network of those who had obligations to him.
His widow sold as a job lot the debts owed to him by the non creditworthy, which she could neither exploit nor recover.[90]

Numerous irrecoverable debts granted to the poor also appear in the
inventories left by English merchants. They represented between 5 per cent
and 7 per cent of the total wealth of the London elite. Craig Muldrew inter-
prets these loans made to the poor as voluntary acts of charity: the merchants

[87] P. Zschuncke, *Konfession und Alltag in Oppenheim*, Wiesbaden, Franz Steiner Verlag,
1984, p. 160, table 18, cited by Jütte, *Poverty and Deviance*, p. 91.

[88] B. L. Anderson, "The Attorney and the Early Capital Market in Lancashire," *Liverpool
and Merseyside, Essays in the economic and Social History of the Port and Hinterland*,
J. R. Harris, ed., Londres, Routledge, 1968. Goubert, *Beauvais et Beauvaisis*, pp. 175–6.

[89] This aspect of the social network is rarely included in explanations of the reasons why people migrated long distances; cf. Castel, *Les métamorphoses de la question sociale*, p. 147.

[90] Departmental archives, Isère, 3E 846, 9 June 1684. Fontaine, "Le marché constraint."

manifested their charitable impulses by not reclaiming debts, rather than by giving to the poor. In fact, in the middle of the seventeenth century, fewer than a third of the London elite left charitable bequests in their wills, and among those who did, almost half left fewer than 10 pounds; however, these merchants each had in their portfolio an average of 378 pounds of irrecoverable debts.[91] This was not necessarily solely charity, and one should doubtless also take into account the vagaries of the economy.

More generally, the merchant bourgeois classes and the entrepreneurs were pivotal in developing credit as a purely economic tool. From the sixteenth century, "the businessman had a very different outlook from that of the feudal landlord," notes Christopher Hill. "He grudged every penny spent over and above the minimum necessary to induce men to work for him. And since they chose 'voluntarily' to work for him, he felt no responsibility for them in hard times. If they did not like what he offered, they might go elsewhere."[92] All studies of the urban bourgeois class emphasize the furious energy it put into acquiring land and seigniorial estates. Goubert goes so far as to describe the collectors of the seigniorial tax as the usurers of the village, and he demonstrates how they exploited debt to increase their possessions.[93]

The fact remains that, taken as a whole, these social ties forced people – particularly ordinary peasants and unskilled workers – into excessive debt. Because several value systems coexisted in seventeenth- and eighteenth-century Europe, credit could act as a protective or destructive force in people's lives. If creditors did not respect the culture surrounding debt, wherein the social relationship was protected, then credit became a powerful force for impoverishment. However, we must look at how debts were repaid on an individual basis and consider the time over which they ran. What is needed is research not into the results of debt, but into individual mechanisms and temporalities that led to these results, for any work done on the poor in Europe in the early modern period requires detailed contextualization because behaviours differed greatly: sometimes ensuring the inclusion of the poorest in a protective whole made up of varied communities, and sometimes pushing the abstract responsibility of providing welfare on to religious institutions and the state, thus releasing individuals from a clear obligation to help.

[91] Muldrew, *The Economy of Obligation*, chap. IX.
[92] C. Hill, *Puritanism and Revolution*, London, 1968, p. 217, cited by Castel, *Les métamorphoses de la question sociale*, p. 122.
[93] Goubert, *Beauvais et le Beauvaisis*.

2

Peasants and Debt Logic

And he did lend his goods
To those who were desirous of them.

O the fine saying! Now let our microcosm be fancied conform to this model
in all its members; lending, borrowing, and owing, that is to say, according
to its own nature. For nature hath not to any other end created man, but
to owe, borrow, and lend.

           – Rabelais, *The Third Book*, chap. 3

In Rabelais's *The Third Book*, Panurge praises loans and debts that,
if they were to become widespread, would enable the world to live in
peace and harmony because both creditors and debtors would need each
other as the sun, the moon, and the stars, or as the various parts of the
body need each other, for debtors need creditors to obtain what they
lack, and creditors need debtors to recover their money. With such a system, Panurge adds, there would be no more wars, usury, or quarrels.
But Pantagruel refuses to hear a discourse that would enter him into
debt. He then undertakes describing the reality of credit with its feared
moneylenders, where debts and lies go hand in hand, and concludes that
money should be lent occasionally, but in very small quantities, and only
to those who in spite of being in work have not managed to earn anything or have lost everything they owned through a stroke of fate.[1] When

---

[1] Rabelais, *Le Tiers Livre*, (*The Third Book*), Paris, Michel Fezandat, Paris, 1552, available
at http://un2sg4.unige.ch/athena/rabelais/rab_tier.html, chap. 3, Where Panurge praises
creditors and debtors and chap. 5, Where Pantagruel hates creditors and debtors. Loans
are, of course, interest free. See N. Z. Davis, *The Gift in Sixteenth-Century France*, 2000,
pp. 187–9, for an analysis of this section in terms of gifts.

Pantagruel proposes to repay all of Panurge's debts, the latter is dejected. He thanks Pantagruel for his undeserved liberalities, using the rhetoric of gift, but refuses to be released from his debts so as not to be forsaken, without anyone wishing for his company, and adds that his aspiration would be to live with creditors and a female companion.[2] This dialogue aptly summarizes the dual logic of credit and the moral commitments it conveys. Panurge's praise also says that credit and gifts are inextricably mingled: both generate social links. As indicated in the previous chapter, debt brings with it obligations: the real poor are those to whom no one has granted a loan. Pantagruel, however, speaks for the other logic he has observed: that of the emerging desire for gain, profit, and individualism.

To start from individuals and interactions, as we did in the previous chapter, and examine "the spontaneous order," to take up Hayek's expression, is not just to reveal categories of creditors that refer to the place of one or the other category in the production process, or to the traditional division of urban creditors versus country borrowers, but also to bring to light circles of creditors to whom individuals have turned successively. Debt portfolios, inventories after death, and accounts of the time show that in every social group, individuals turned successively to different circles of creditors; that the guarantees asked for varied according to the different circles; that these guarantees were often illusory; and that short-term debts was transformed on a massive scale into long-term debts.

Using social actors as the starting point, the next two chapters attempt, by varying scales and angles of observation, to unravel some of the rationales concealed in credit, to enter the circles of creditors, and to show how excessive debt, being one of the structural features of the ancien régime, became widespread. The present chapter focuses on peasants and Chapter 3 on elites.

Circles of Creditors

These circles were first reconstituted in the study that I carried out on the villages of the Upper Dauphiné.[3] A reading of works on other rural regions allows us to widen its scope; however, each region had its own specificities. The credit requirements of peasants were of four types, excluding the credit granted by various traders and itinerant merchants:

---

[2] Rabelais, *Le Tiers Livre*, chap. 9.
[3] Laurence Fontaine, *Pouvoir, identités et migrations dans les hautes vallées des Alpes occidentales (XVIIe-XVIIIe siècles)*, Grenoble, Presses Uuniversitaires de Grenoble, 2003, chap. 2 and 3.

1. Short-term loans for seed and to make ends meet between harvests. These loans were granted for small amounts and usually paid in grain, as and when the need arose. They were linked to crop rotation, to household cycles and to the whims of the weather. They constituted a multiplicity of small-scale written and oral agreements, recorded in cash terms at the prevailing price of grain at the time of the loan. In granting credit in this way, the creditor thus benefited from the seasonal changes in the price of grain, because he or she lent when the market value was highest and was repaid in grain after the harvest when prices were at their lowest. If the borrower was unable to discharge the debt at this point, or, at least, if he was unable to pay the interest, the creditor absorbed the latter into the capital and had the debtor sign a new promissory note. In theory then the interest rates were respected, but in practice, because of the way in which the price of grain was calculated, the real interest rates were much higher; the practice of compound interest was also a way of commanding much higher rates.[4] In some villages in Alsace, the rule of thumb for repaying these grain loans for seeds and the period between harvests appeared to be seven bushels for one bag containing six bushels lent, which meant an interest of more than 15 per cent.[5]

2. Money loans to pay taxes. The repayment deadline for these loans was fixed as a year from the date of the loan after which time, because with the loans of foodstuffs or seed, the creditor introduced compound interest.

3. Loans for family rites of passage (weddings, setting up in business, etc.). These loans were drawn up for medium-term periods. Forms of village mutual aid can be seen in this kind of loan, as well as in loans intended to smooth out, during the different stages of the family cycle, the gap between the number of mouths to feed

---

[4] Examples for Catalonia in Enric Tello Aragay, "El papel del crédito rural en la agricultura del Antiguo régimen: desarrollo y crisis de la modalidades crediticias (1600–1850)," *Noticiario de Historia Agraria*, no. 7, 1994, pp. 9–37 (24). For Galicea, see Pegerto Saavedra, "Réseaux et culture du crédit en Galice, XVI-XIXe siècle," European University Institute – Florence working paper, HEC no. 99/3, 1999. For Venetia, see Gigi Corazzol, *Fitti e livelli a Grano. Un aspetto del credito rurale nel Veneto del '500*, Milan, Franco Angeli, 1979, pp. 24–32.

[5] Jean-Michel Boehler, *Une société rurale en milieu rhénan: La paysannerie de la Plaine d'Alsace (1648–1789)*, vol. 2, Strasbourg, Presses universitaires de Strasbourg, 1994, p. 1185. These are the villages of Hurtigheim and Quatzenheim.

and the number of family members who could contribute to this through their workforce participation.[6]

4. Sales of livestock, goods, and property to or among the wealthiest members of society. Repayment deadlines varied between one year and ten. These were also the only transactions in which cash payments were recorded.

Generally, no notary was used; these multitudes of small loans were recorded primarily in the account books or private promissory notes. The under-registration of peasant credit has been observed in all the studies.[7]

To meet their needs, individuals turned successively to different circles of creditors. Except in certain, specific relations of credit, especially those resulting from the workplace, peasants, like any other social group, first approached the family circle. If the person had no family or the family was completely unable to meet the demand, then peasants turned to those who provided them with work; depending on the region, this might be the aristocracy, religious institutions, or the village elite. In regions where a home industry had begun to develop, people turned increasingly toward merchants for credit. Next they approached neighbours, especially village women and widows, who thus had an opportunity to make their assets grow. Then the regional elite, who often acted as merchant bankers, were approached. Finally, people turned to foreigners who, depending on the region, might be Jewish, Italian, Scottish, from Auvergne or Savoy.

Those seeking credit addressed these circles successively. Families and the immediate elite classes could not refuse providing credit: in a society based on interpersonal relationships, one could not refuse a member of one's family money, even if one knew that he or she would be unable to repay it, any more than the nobility, the religious institutions, and the village elites could refuse their "clients" (politically speaking) because their status obliged them to help.

Although ascertaining family ties was by no means easy because these were not necessarily mentioned in the deeds, one turned first to family. In England during the sixteenth and seventeenth centuries, the kinship

---

[6] Ulrich Pfister, "Rural Land and Credit Markets, the Life Cycle Hypothesis, and Proto Industry: Evidence from Early Modern Zurich," *Continuity and Change*, 22, no. 3, 2007, pp. 489–518.

[7] For Frioul, see Gigi Corazzol, "Prestatori e contadini nella campagna feltrina intorno alla prima metà del '500," *Quaderni Storici*, 9, 1974, pp. 445–500 (464, 489). For Spain see, Saavedra, "Réseaux et culture."

of debtors was a dominant factor for creditors,[8] and in some regions of England, about 40 per cent of the lenders were related to those who, at certain key moments in their life, asked for credit.[9] In a sample of forty-two inventories after death in Lincolnshire in the mid-seventeenth century, for example, 40 per cent of debtors were family members, and it appears that 10 to 20 per cent of them did not live in the immediate neighbourhood of the deceased.[10] The family behaved like a "clan" that provided its members with a large part of the funds they needed. Family credit accounted for the lion's share in the Toulouse countryside of the eighteenth century,[11] and in Germany at Neckarhausen, there was constant lending and borrowing of money in many families without any bond ever being signed; periodically everyone would get together to do the accounts. Sometimes, each one maintained a book containing, among others, expenditures at an inn, wages for work, and loans for the dowry of a sister. Only when there was a dispute was the extent of this mutual microcredit revealed.[12]

Although villagers did have credit associations, it is extremely difficult to bring them to light as until now; no records of these private institutions have been found. We have to rely instead on the observations of travellers touring through the countryside to divine their existence. Thus, Catherine Hutton (1756–1846), in a letter written in September 1797 to her brother, recounted the marriages she had witnessed in Wales: public marriages in the mountains to which the whole village was invited. People, she wrote, ate at a table for forty guests, and at times, her father had seen about 150 guests go by. She goes on to give the following description of the marriage of a sailor to a cobbler's daughter:

The newly-married couple kept their wedding at a public house near our lodgings, where all who came (and the more the better) dined, drank tea, and danced

---

[8] David Cressy, "Kinship and Kin Interaction in Early Modern England," *Past and Present*, 113, 1986, pp. 38–69; Peter Spufford, "Les liens du crédit au village dans l'Angleterre du XVIIe siècle," *Annales Histoire-Sciences sociales*, no. 6, 1994, pp. 1359–73. J. Habakkuk, *Marriage, Debt and the Estates System. English Landownership, 1650–1950*, Oxford, Oxford University Press, 1994, pp. 1–14.

[9] Spufford, "Les liens."

[10] B. A. Holderness, "Widows in Pre-Industrial Society: An Essay upon Their Economic Functions," *in* Smith, Richard M. (dir.), *Land, Kinship and Life-Cycle*, Cambridge, Cambridge University Press, 1984, pp. 423–442 (441).

[11] Jack Thomas, "Crédit et numéraire dans les campagnes toulousaines au milieu du XVIIIe siècle," *Endettement Paysan et Crédit Rural dans l'Europe médiévale et moderne*, Actes des XVIIes Journées Internationales d'Histoire de l'Abbaye de Flaran, September 1995, M. Berthe, ed., Toulouse, Presses Universitaires du Mirail, 1998, pp. 317–33.

[12] David W. Sabean, *Property, Production, and Family in Neacharhausen, 1700–1870*, Cambridge, Cambridge University Press, 1990, pp. 285–8.

if they chose to do so, though some came only to dinner, and others only for the evening. Two female friends sat making tea from three o'clock to seven at night; and at seven o'clock in the morning I saw many persons of the party mounting their horses to return to their homes.

You will think these marriage feasts must be ruinously expensive to poor people – just the reverse. Every guest pays a shilling, at least, for dinner, and sixpence for tea, and many give more, even to half-crowns. A considerable sum is thus collected for the benefit of a young couple setting out in the world; and each, receiving in his turn, is only laying up a fund for his own marriage, or paying a debt contracted at it. If the father of the bride can afford it, he defrays the expense of the entertainment, and the profit is her portion; if he cannot, the people of the public house provide it, and she repays them, keeping only the residue.[13]

At the beginning of the seventeenth century, another observer described the same practice, specifying that it was customary to place a basket in the church at the time of a marriage in which the guests put their gifts that would help establish the new family in the community.[14] Such rare examples have thus been brought to light, and they are invaluable for they suggest the existence of peasant tontines in eighteenth-century Europe.

The weight of religious communities among creditors was preponderant in the whole of Europe during the modern period, for they had to make the income of their domains and the dowries of their members grow.[15] In Spain, this is how female convents turned to good account the nuns' dowries.[16] In Francony and the Middle Rhine Valley, for example, the church held not just temporal power but also financial power:

[13] *Reminiscences of a Gentlewoman of the Last Century: Letters of Catherine Hutton*, edited by her cousin, Mrs. Catherine Hutton Beale, Birmingham, 1891, pp. 125–6. See Bridget Hill, "Catherine Hutton (1756–1846): A Forgotten Letter-Writer," *Women's Writing*, 1, no. 1, 1994, pp. 35–50, to get acquainted with her family origins. I thank Caroline Fontaine for acquainting me with Catherine Hutton.

[14] Karen Newman, "Portia's Ring: Unruly Women and Structures of Exchange in The Merchant of Venice," *Shakespeare Quarterly*, 38, no. 1, 1987, pp. 19–33 (24).

[15] Robert Fossier, "Mort-gage et autres prêts en Picardie au XIIe siècle," *Endettement Paysan et Crédit Rural dans l'Europe médiévale et moderne*, Toulouse, Presses Universitaires du Mirail, 1998, pp. 23–33; Claude Denjean, "Le crédit juif dans les campagnes cerdanes au XIIIe et XIVe siècle," *Endettement Paysan et Crédit Rural*, pp. 185–97; and Serge Brunet, "Fondations de messes, crédit rural et marché de la terre dans les Pyrénées centrales (XVe–XVIIIe siècle): les communautés de prêtres du Val d'Aran," *Endettement Paysan et Crédit Rural*, pp. 217–37. Gilbert Larguier, "Un cahier de doléances du clergé du Roussillon inédit. Saint-Mathieu et les communautés de prêtres du diocèse d'Elne à la fin du XVIIIe siècle," *Société agricole, scientifique et littéraire des Pyrénées-orientales*, vol. 108, Perpignan, 2001, pp. 194–226 (209–10).

[16] Saavedra, "Réseaux et culture."

it owned one-fifth of the agricultural lands in the electorate of Treves; of the twenty-one largest owners, twenty were religious institutions.[17] In Bavaria, the study of Unterfinning village, the lord of which was the church and the convents, shows the financial predominance of the church in the region.[18] This is only one of the many such examples, for wherever they were present, ecclesiastical institutions were the largest creditor in Europe. Congregations or simple village priests, all offered credit to live themselves and to support their pious foundations. In Spain, all studies bring out the major role they played as creditors to all strata of society. In Castile, work based on the mid-eighteenth-century Enseñada land registers attests to the extreme indebtedness of villages and the predominance of the church that collected 90.9 per cent of all rents.[19] The same held true for Catalonia, where the church dominated peasant credit until the middle of the eighteenth century.[20]

As for merchants, in certain areas with weak aristocratic presence, such as areas the mountains or areas very close to the cities, merchants were the principal creditors of the villagers. In the Alps as well as in the Pyrenees, they benefited from the debt of the village labour force or from the pastures. In the regions close to the cities, merchants appropriated the harvests. The example of Naples, where merchants controlled grain production through credit, has been well studied. Indeed, different types of *contratto alla voce*[21] allowed them to appropriate the peasants' harvest during the entire modern period. The loans in kind or the cash given by them to the farmers and sharecroppers at the time of sowing or between harvests were repaid at harvest time. These loans were in fact the anticipated sale of agricultural produce and the contracts were the first link in a chain of intermediaries that ended in the grain supply of Naples, enabling the city to meet its requirements. There were various kinds of contracts, but all played on the seasonal variation in prices. The most common type of contract took advantage of the difference between the high prices of the November sowing or of the period between two harvests in spring

---

[17] Christophe Duhamelle, "La noblesse d'église. Famille et pouvoir dans la chevalerie immédiate rhénane XVIIe-XVIIIe siècle," Paris, Presses de l'EHESS, 1998, p. 107.

[18] Rainer Beck, *Unterfinning. Ländliche Welt vor Anbruch der Moderne*, Munich, Beck, 1993, pp. 460–8.

[19] Conceptión Camarero Bullón, "Endeutament i detraccions a la Castella de l'antic règim (anàlisi de quaranta-nou viles burgaleses)," *Recerques*, no. 18, 1986, pp. 73–106 (82–83).

[20] Enric Tello Aragay, "La utilizació del censal a la Segarra del set-cents: crèdit rural i explotació usurària," *Recerques*, no. 18, 1986, pp. 47–71.

[21] *Voce* is the price paid after the harvests.

and the low prices of the August and September harvests. Another type of contract calculated the value of the loan in the month of May, independently of when the loan when given, in other words, at the highest point in the annual price cycle, and a third type, hardly different from the second, used the month of June.[22]

Married women as well as widows were also major creditors: first, because the husbands managed their dowry and, second, because they made their inheritance profitable. Widows lent according to a dual modality, as illustrated by the examples of the communities of the Agen election: on one hand, they lent small sums to needy inhabitants, and on the other, they accumulated greater debts though the investment of dowries and legacies.[23] The same structure could be found in Spain, as attested by the inventory of Doña Mariana de Lara d'Ojacastro drawn up during her remarriage in 1572 in the mountains south of Logroño. It listed several small, secured claims as well as bonds for higher amounts. Both point to her varied role as a supplier of money to the village.[24] In Portugal, the significant presence of women continued even in the nineteenth century.[25] In England, from the end of the thirteenth century, they appeared regularly as plaintiffs in the English courts,[26] and until the last decades of the eighteenth century, the widows of Lancashire preferred to invest their money, whether or not they were owners, in local loans rather than in state credit.[27] Of course, the presence of a few women in the distribution of village credit must not make us forget that in the society of the ancien régime, widowhood more often than not was a prelude to a lowering of social status.

---

[22] Paolo Macry, "Ceto mercantile e azienda agricola nel regno di Napoli: il contratto alla voce nel XVIII secolo," *Quaderni Storici*, 7, no. 3, 1972, pp. 851–909.

[23] Christophe Blanquie, "La vérification colbertienne des dettes des communautés agenaises," *Endettement Paysan et Crédit Rural*, pp. 299–315. Giuseppe Moricola, "Alla ricerca di un mercato: l'intermediazione creditizia nella città di Avellino nella prima metà dell'ottocento," *Società e Storia*, 9, no. 41, 1988, pp. 559–93 (583). Gilbert Larguier, "Le crédit en Catalogne au XVIIe siècle: les foires de change de Perpignan (1630–1651)," *Annales du Midi*, 117, no. 251, 2005, p. 347–61 (359).

[24] Francis Brumont, "Le crédit rural en Espagne du nord-ouest à l'époque moderne," *Endettement Paysan et Crédit Rural*, pp. 239–81.

[25] Caroline B. Brettell, "Moral Economy or Political Economy? Property and Credit Markets in 19th Century Rural Portugal," *Journal of Historical Sociology*, 12, 1991, pp. 1–28 (16–18).

[26] Philipp Schofield, "L'endettement et le crédit dans la campagne anglaise au Moyen Age," *Endettement Paysan et Crédit Rural*, pp. 69–97.

[27] B. A. Holderness, "Credit in a Rural Community 1600–1800," *Midland History*, 3, 1975–6, p. 100–1.

The last circle called on was foreigners. For a long time, the collective imagination associated Jews with usury, but they were not the only foreigners to live from money lending and, according to the country, Italians, Savoyards, Auvergnats, or Scots, to name the most well known, fulfilled the same role. These foreigners were not stigmatized in the same manner in the countries where they settled, temporarily or permanently, and each country tried to regulate their activity, at least with respect to the Jews. In Spain, Castile fixed the minimum rates since the thirteenth century, and in 1268, it prohibited Christians from lending, restricting this activity to the Jews and Muslims and fixing the annual rate they could charge at 33 per cent.[28] But everywhere, the activity of the foreigners was at the mercy of the manipulation of governments, which were quick to erase whole or part of debts due to them when the economic situation became bad; in troubled times, foreigners were even driven out and their goods confiscated, as was the experience of the Jews everywhere.

Hierarchy of Creditors and Modalities of Credit

If, in these societies based on interpersonal ties, it was difficult to refuse to help one's family financially even if one knew that he or she would not be able to repay, this obligation also extended to the nobility, the religious institutions, and the village elites. The social exchange, which was thus placed in the centre of credit relationships, can be seen not only in the hierarchy of the creditors but also in the modalities of credit and in the guarantees required in exchange for what was lent. The great importance of the personal contract shows the power of personal ties in credit relationships. Each time, it was possible to rely on inventories after death in order to measure this power; the personal contract undoubtedly prevailed, whereas the contract of the notary, which allowed appeal to the law, offered long-term legal guarantees.

The terms of credit extended from six months to ten years in Upper-Dauphiné. But only a small fraction was repaid within the time frame (for the Gourand family in Clavans in the Oisans whom I studied, between the seventeenth and eighteenth centuries, it was to the order of 10 per cent of the amount due). However, each time, these repayments were made by other merchants, that is, men belonging to the same social group. At the beginning, the majority of the credit granted to the villager was

---

[28] M.-A. Ladero Quesada, "Crédito y comercio de dinero en la Castilla Medieval," *Acta historica y aechaeologica mediaevalia*, no. 11-12, 1990–1991, pp. 145–59.

oral. These transactions normally appeared on private promissory notes. Two types of occasions led the contracting parties to the notary to sign an agreement: at the time of economic or family crises like the illness of one of the contracting parties or when the interest had not been paid regularly. At these moments, one realizes that the creditor not only never claimed the repayment of the capital – only the regular payment of the interest mattered to him – but that he granted to his debtor new credits even if he had not begun to repay the previous ones. However, the interest arrears were included in the capital whenever an agreement was signed. Last, if one of the contracting parties died, the debt was renegotiated: either the creditor seized this moment to strip the family of its debtor, even if it meant taking one of the descendants as a farmer on his old family estate, or a new agreement marked the continuation of the bond of credit between the families and thus carried over from generation to generation. The change of partners, more than the contractual stipulations, involved renegotiations of the debt.

On the whole, credits were based on the present and future assets of the debtor without giving details; the spiral of debt developed generally well beyond the value of the inheritance, and everyone was aware of that. However, a more precise analysis of the study such as the one I carried out in the villages of Upper Dauphiné shows differentiated behaviour according to the social groups represented. According to whether the lender was from the family, the community, a notable from the mountains (not from the village), or a foreigner, the guarantees required would differ. The more one moved away from the obligated debt–relation circle, the more specific the required guarantees became.

Between relatives, there were interest-free loans, provisions determining the number of harvests given to the donor to extinguish the debt (in which case the latter would take over weather-related risks), and almost no compound interest rates. Furthermore, securities were usually family based. In villages to the north west of Barcelona, three-fourths of the guarantors, during the medieval period, were family members or neighbours.[29] In sixteenth-century England, loans among relatives were frequent, and the remission of debts was often bequeathed at the time of death.[30]

Between the villagers and their natural social elites, the security for loans was not so much land as harvests and family labour, although

[29] Jordi Fernandez Cuadrench, "Crédit juif et solidarité villageoise dans les campagnes barcelonaises au XIIIe siècle," *Endettement Paysan et Crédit Rural*, pp. 169–83.
[30] Cressy, "Kinship," pp. 51, 52.

this was left unsaid.[31] However, loans granted by outsiders to the community were certified by a notary and were secured on duly described individualized assets. Capital repayment times were spelled out as were automatic transfers of property resulting from nonpayment in due time.[32] Land sale with a repurchase clause was the equivalent of a loan against security and the lender took the produce of the land as interest. Urban creditors, traders, burghers, and especially minor officials imposed very harsh conditions on country people who resorted to them. They often demanded repayment in the form of foodstuff with a 20 to 50 per cent interest rate, and even higher ones in the seventeenth century.[33]

To measure the time gone by before the application of the clause of repurchase tells of the more or less great leniency of the creditor. In fact, many examples show that the guarantees were often symbolic; that no mechanism really put an end to peasant indebtedness because these, being so much more than the registration systems, were very diverse; that the respective creditors of each person who owed him money had trouble knowing who the other committed lenders were; and that peasants, to meet their needs, played the card of secrecy and multiplicity of creditors; all practices which added technical reasons to cultural expectations and which easily let them fall into overindebtedness.

Structural Overindebtedness

Overindebtedness and long-term credits were found everywhere. Both were manifest in the Alps, where periodically, between the fifteenth and nineteenth centuries, all inhabitants were involved in debt well above

---

[31] In the Toulouse region, cash loans for dowries, grain for food and sowing were given frequently by the aristocrats to their sharecroppers. Robert Forster shows how quickly debts swelled and how sharecroppers were constantly in their debt. Although he suspects the aristocrats benefitted from these debts to round off their lands, he acknowledges that there was rarely any mention of this in the deeds. Robert Forster, *The Nobility of Toulouse in the Eighteenth Century: A Social and Economic Study*, New York, Octagon Books, 1971, pp. 51–2.

[32] Laurence Fontaine, "Le marché contraint, la terre et la Révocation dans une vallée alpine," *Revue d'Histoire moderne et contemporaine*, 38, 1991, pp. 275–94; and Laurence Fontaine, "Espaces, usages et dynamiques de la dette dans les hautes vallées dauphinoises (XVIIe-XVIIIe siècles)," *Annales sciences sociales*, no. 6, December 1994, pp. 1375–91.

[33] Gilbert Larguier, *Le drap et le grain en Languedoc. Narbonne et Narbonnais 1300–1789*, Perpignan, Presses universitaires de Perpignan, 1996, pp. 942–50

the top value of their assets.[34] Both were also very present in the seventeenth century in Beauvaisis, where in the Villiers-Saint-Martin parish,
high indebtedness traversed the whole hierarchy of peasant fortunes,
emphasizing the role of creditor of the city's bourgeoisie. Workmen
formed the biggest group of villagers; even if they owned a house or
a plot of land, they had to find work to ensure their subsistence and
that of their family.[35] Rohard, a labourer whose total assets were estimated at 180 livres, had to pay a farm rent of 28 livres to a modest
bourgeois from Beauvais. He owed him 175 livres in arrears. Decaux, a
day labourer (*haricotier*) had assets worth 510 livres, and he owed 253
livres, of which 163 livres were owed to a merchant and a procurator
from Beauvais. Lenglet, a small ploughman, had debts that exceeded his
assets by 212 livres. Two ploughmen of means, Carpentier and Antoine
Rohard, had debts of more than 1,000 livres and assets worth 2,000
livres. They had borrowed from the most prominent bourgeois of the
city. Martin Lorfèvre from Laversines had almost four hectares as well
as a cow with her calf that he had not paid for. He owed large sums to
three moneylenders, a ploughman, and two townspeople from Beauvais.
But, in spite of his debts, like many others involved in debt, he died in
his village with his fields and his cow unpaid for. Even then, only at their
death would their harvests and cattle would be seized, driving their children to give up their inheritance.[36]

   In Alsace, between 1670 and 1699, the balance of outstanding debts
to passive debts in the postmortem inventories was, according to the
epoch, positive in proportions varying between one to three inventories of ten and, consequently, negative in seven to nine inventories of
ten presented. Analysis of the authenticated registers shows that the
loans were first concluded in the short term and were renegotiated periodically but, here also, without preventing the granting of new loans,
hence the importance of delayed payments and accumulated debts.[37]
Of 259 obligations collected in 1751, of which only some pertain to
rural indebtedness, 154 indicate the effective dates of repayment: 29.2
per cent were repaid within five years, 23.4 per cent within ten years,
29.2 per cent between ten and twenty years, and 18.2 per cent between
twenty and thirty years, and there are, moreover, 105 non-receipted

---

[34] Laurence Fontaine, "Espaces, usages et dynamiques de la dette."
[35] Pierre Goubert, *Beauvais et le Beauvaisis de 1600 à 1730. Contribution à l'histoire
sociale de la France du XVIIe siècle*, Paris, SEVPEN, 1960, p. 158.
[36] Ibid., pp. 160–2.
[37] Boehler, *Une société rurale en milieu rhénan*, pp. 1180–1.

debts; that is to say that more than 40 per cent of the total were probably never repaid.[38]

Even in the eighteenth century, the same overindebtedness could be seen among the small owners of Champagne, the average amount of which exceeded the value of the lands they owned by 18 per cent. Debt servicing defined three groups of debtors: those who used less than two-thirds of their income from land to meet their debt obligations, those who paid more than two-thirds, and those who had to pay more than their income from land. A large number of families fell in the first category, with the two other categories accounting for the remaining families who were in great difficulty. The average age of each group being almost identical, fifty-eight and fifty-nine years, this example belies the model that viewed peasant debt as an investment strategy evolving over the life cycle in which the young contracted debt to establish themselves and, on attaining a certain age, changed into lenders. On the contrary, if the young people in debt managed to write off a part of their debts in their old age, they could do so only by selling a part of their land, for generally they ended up owning less land.[39]

However, the enrichment or impoverishment of the peasants can be read in the preponderance of this or that circle of creditor. The general enrichment of the peasants during the eighteenth century is seen in Alsace in the fact that between the seventeenth and eighteenth centuries, the peasants contracted less and less outside debts – urban and in other villages – and found their resources mostly from within their own family and from religious and hospital institutions (urban or rural) to which they were attached as tenants of their land and at the village factory. The relative withdrawal of the Jews and villagers attests to this general enrichment of the Alsatian countryside, which allowed families and the nearby elites more easily to fulfil their obligation to lend.[40]

These examples, taken from very different areas of France, show the recurrence of overindebtedness. But France is not exceptional, and overindebtedness and long-term credits can be found everywhere in early modern Europe, with the lengthening of the loan duration keeping up with changes of financial instruments and official loan legislation.

[38] Bernard Vogler, "Les placements de capitaux à Strasbourg en 1751," *Lyon et l'Europe. Hommes et sociétés. Mélanges d'histoire offerts à R. Gascon*, vol. 1, Lyon, Presses Universitaires de Lyon, 1980, pp. 331–48 (338).

[39] Thomas Brennan, "Peasants and Debts in Eighteenth-Century Champagne," *Journal of Interdisciplinary History*, 37, no. 2, 2006, pp. 175–200.

[40] Boehler, *Une société rurale en milieu rhénan*, p. 1199.

Between 1650 and 1720 in England, 40 per cent of those who listed their assets died with debts.[41] In Spain, the land register of Enseñada drawn up between 1748 and 1752 makes understanding the indebtedness of the villagers possible. The study of forty-nine Castilian villages shows the diversity of situations according to resources and activities and makes it possible to classify them in three main groups: those where a maximum of 25 per cent of the population was in debt, those where a quarter to half of the inhabitants were in debt, and finally the villages where more than half and up to three-quarters of the population was in debt, such as Gumiel de Hizán, in the province of Burgos, where 71 per cent of the inhabitants were in debt and whose debt represented, in 1752, three times the value of the agricultural production for that year. Moreover, the majority of these debts were inherited. The difference in debt refers to the activity of the villagers: those engaged in the tertiary sectors and who had direct access to the market were much less indebted than those who had to go through merchants to sell their produce, such as the wine growers, or those who lived off the traditional agro-pastoral system.[42] The land registers for the year 1744–1745 studied in the case of Catalonia show the same high rates of indebtedness: more than half the capital owed as mortgage represented more than the entire value of all the property recorded in the land registers. In Cervera, half the debtors owed 70 per cent or more than the value of their property.[43] Moreover, these figures were greatly underestimated, as they left aside the multiple forms of private credit[44]: the figures were calculated basis on constituted rents, which accounted for 79 per cent of the capital owed.[45]

[41] B. L. Anderson, "Credit in English Rural Society before the Nineteenth Century with Special Reference to the Period 1650–1720," *The Agricultural History Review*, no. 24, 1976, p. 97–109.

[42] Bullón, "Endeutament i detraccions," p. 73–106 (105).

[43] Aragay, "El papel del crédito rural en la agricultura del Antiguo régimen," pp. 9–37; Aragay, "La utilització," pp. 47–71.

[44] Enric Tello Aragay, "Propietat agrària i percepció de rendes. El paper de l'endeutament en la distribució social de les terres (Cervera 1744–45)," *Estudio d'Historia Agraria*, no. 6, 1986, pp. 57–99 (87).

[45] Concepción Camarero Bullón, "Las detracciones sobre la economia agraria y el endeudamiento del pequeño campesino en el siglo XVIII: aplicación a un concejo castellano," *Agricultura y Sociedad*, no. 33, 1984, pp. 197–252 (231); and Bullón, "Endeutament i detraccions." Pierre Vilar, "Estructures de la societat espanyola cap al 1750. Algunes lliçons del cadastre d'Ensenada," *Recerques, Historia, Economia Cultura*, La Formacio de la catalunya moderna, no. 1, 1970, pp. 9–32.

The credit term was normally extended. The analysis of Catalonia's indebtedness from the fourteenth to the sixteenth centuries illustrates the periodic transformation of the multiple unpaid fixed-term small debts incurred by the peasants into constituted rents.[46] Later, the bonds were converted into rent, and then, when peasants were unable to pay, they were transformed into *carta de gracia* sales, that is, with the possibility to repurchase[47]; in the Bages region during the eighteenth century, it was observed that the *carta de gracia* sales, the term of which was in general fixed at five years, was usually extended more or less indefinitely.[48]

During the extended eighteenth century, which spanned 1648 through 1848, for the peasants in Wurtemberg, the story was one of an always-increasing debt that did not dissolve, until the nineteenth century with the enormous increase in land value, an aspect that then exceeded all the other economic indicators such as wages or the price of grain. In these villages, before the price of land made it possible to erase the debts, the overindebtedness in the countryside was such that an order given to the municipal authorities to draw up the list of all the villagers whose debts exceeded their assets led to violent local revolts. Nevertheless, the *Presser* was sent to all those with tax arrears to seize their property and the town councillors were asked to compel the villagers to clear their municipal and tax debts or then face bankruptcy. Several such legal proceedings were instituted just after the Napoleonic wars.[49] The *Voigt* too could order the *Schultheiss* to make an inventory of the inhabitants' property to verify the extent of their indebtedness. When the *Voigt* asked for the inventory of a large number of peasants believed to be insolvent, a revolt broke out.[50]

---

[46] Mercè Aventín i Puig, "El crèdit a pagès als segles XIV-XVI sobre la logica economica del mercat de rendes," *Pedralbes*, 13-II, 1993, pp. 55–64 (59)

[47] Aragay, "El papel del crédito rural en la agricultura del Antiguo régimen," pp. 9–37 (16–17); Aragay, "La utilització," pp. 47–71. Ll. Ferrer, "Censals, vendes a carta de gràcia i endeutament pagés al Bages (s.XVIII)," *Estudis d'Història Agrària*, 4, 1983, pp. 101–28.

[48] Llorenç Ferrer i Alòs, "Ventas a carta de Gracia y endeudmiento en la comarca de Bages en el siglo XVIII," *Actas del II Coloquio de Metodología Histórica Aplicada. La Documentación Notarial y la Historia.* Universida de Santiago de Compostela, s.d., pp. 409–25.

[49] Sabean, *Property, Production, and Family in Neckarhausen*, pp. 193–4.

[50] Ibid.

In the sixteenth century, in the Frioul countryside of Italy, as in Piedmont, testimonies recall the chronic debt of the peasants.[51] Analysis of the dealings of the Marquis de Groppoli between the sixteenth and eighteenth centuries is a good example of the role of important aristocrats. It shows that they were the first creditors of the villages and the villagers of their domain. Terms of payment and abandonment of debts or interest for the poorest were common practices in difficult years, and analyses of the seventeenth century show that the aristocrats were continuously solicited and never refused lending to the communities. Consequently, the indebtedness that had been contained right up to the 1620s literally exploded during the subsistence crises of 1619–1622, 1629–1632, and 1648–1649. Certainly, the indebtedness ended in the 1650s with the acquisition of community property, but these transfers came into effect after being postponed for several decades and after the amount of the debt had been reduced. It was the same scenario during the crisis at the end of seventeenth century. The resultant enlargement of the domain should not make us forget that the marquis was always there to meet the needs of his communities and that he did not try and extract the maximum benefit from the assistance he rendered.[52] The example of the Marquis de Groppoli in the case of the Genoese lands also shows that in the sale of lands with a repurchase option, it was common for the lords to let the stipulated period overrun, often by five to ten years after the date of repurchase, fixed usually at five years after the sale.[53] In the mid-sixteenth century, the nobility also supported the Friulian peasants in their struggle to obtain more equitable loan contracts whereas the town councils protected the interests of the lenders.[54] Consequently, the practice of selling land with a buyback clause was very common, with only a little over one-fourth of properties being repurchased, unlike Chieri in Piedmont, where such a contract was much less frequent.[55]

As shown by the analysis of the poor and the credit circles, these features emphasize that debt logics vary according to the social actors

[51] Corazzol, *Fitti e livelli a Grano*, p. 53. Luciano Allegra, *La città verticale. Usurai, mercanti e tessitori nella Chieri del Cinquecento*, Milan, Franco Angeli, 1987.

[52] Maria Stella Rollandi, A Groppoli di Lunigiana. Potere e ricchezza di un feudatario genovese (secc.XVI-XVIII), Genova, Società ligure di storia patria, 1996.

[53] Ibid., p. 108.

[54] Corazzol, *Fitti e livelli a Grano*, p. 61, 72.

[55] Luciano Allegra, *La città verticale*, p. 50. Corazzol, "Prestatori e contadini," pp. 445–500.

engaged in the relationship: the nobles show greater leniency as compared to the urban elite. As the terms of the contract and those of the guarantees and their application became increasingly harsh, the successive circles of credit to which the peasants turned may be seen as a barometer of the strength of the social ties and the moral obligations they entailed.

Although the nobility played a protective role almost everywhere, it must be pointed out at the same time that political transformations in conjunction with bad economic conditions could lead to a change in roles, as can be seen in Castile during the eighteenth century when the nobility failed to play its traditional role: more often than not, the court nobility abandoned the villages, and the small nobility was too poor to intervene in any meaningful way; the nobility figured in only 5.6 per cent of the loans to the peasantry, barely more present than the notables (3.5 per cent), leaving the church to be the dominant creditor.[56]

On the other hand, the capitalist economy continued to spread, and its presence in every strata of society was visible in eighteenth-century Northern Europe where the use of credit as a purely economic instrument became perceptible. Even in seventeenth-century England, the multiplication of agencies specializing in intermediation allowed workers and widows the possibility of selling their farms to live off the income from the capital. All the same, as we have already stressed, right up to the last decades of the eighteenth century, most widows from Lancashire preferred investing their money in proximity loans rather that in state credit.[57] From the mid-eighteenth century in Belgium, peasants in Ban de Herve utilized constituted rent on a massive scale, for it gave them a great deal of liberty with respect to their creditors and allowed them to play with the lowering of rates in their debt management.[58] On the other hand, in France during the mid-eighteenth century, the notables alone used rent as monetary income, not just to seize lands. They knew how to threaten the annuitant with repayment to obtain a reduction in rent and

---

[56] Bullón, "Endeutament i detraccions," pp. 73–106 (84).

[57] Holderness, "Credit in a Rural Community 1600–1800," pp. 100–1.

[58] Paul Servais, "De la rente au crédit hypothécaire en période de transition industrielle. Stratégies familiales en région liégeoise au XVIIIᵉ siècle," *in* Fontaine, Laurence, Postel-Vinay, Gilles, Rosenthal, Jean-Laurent et Servais, Paul (dir.), *Des personnes aux institutions, Réseaux et cultures du crédit du XVIᵉ au XXᵉ siècle en Europe*, Louvain-la-Neuve, Bruylant-Academia, 1997, pp. 1393–1409.

such reductions were plentiful from 1720 onward. In many inventories of 1722 and 1723, records exist of "reduced" rents to all deniers that had recourse at the time to Système de Law: 30, 33, 36, 40, even 50; for larger loans to religious establishments, friends and in particular to the most established families, interest bearing loans could fall by 10 to 20 per cent below the maximum legal rate.[59] In Spain, from the mid-eighteenth century onward with the lowering of interest on rent from 5 to 3 per cent, the church disengaged itself from loans to individuals to invest in public debt.[60]

The Logics of Debt

Looking at debt from the point of view of its effects shows that it is a mechanism with several triggers. It makes it possible to grab land, to control other markets, like that of labour and harvest, and especially to consolidate power over men. But this power was akin to the protective authority of *fides* and *credit* that gave authority and imposed duties at the same time.

Access to Other Markets

Thus, according to the place and country, the consequences of debt are not the same. From the end of the fourteenth century, in Tuscany, one saw a concentration of land in the hands of townspeople and a transformation of the modes of production with the spread of the Mezzadria,[61] whereas in Rhenish, country large estates were formed. In the eighteenth century, in many places, it made it possible to own communal goods.[62] In Spain and elsewhere, creditors seized raw materials such as corn and wool.[63] Thanks to the debt, when cottage industry was set up – as in the countries of migration – the elites proceeded to control the labour market. The study of the farmers in the Low Countries shows that the elites

---

[59] Goubert, *Beauvais et Beauvaisis*, pp. 540–1.
[60] Llorenç Ferrer i Alòs, "L'Església com a institució de crèdit: les quotidianes distribucions de la Seu de Manresa els segles XVIIIi XIX," *Recerques*, no. 18, 1986, pp. 7–46.
[61] Jean-Louis Gaulin and François Menant, "Crédit rural et endettement paysan dans l'Italie communale," *Endettement Paysan et Crédit Rural*, pp. 35–67.
[62] Elisa Badosa Coll, "Endeutament col·lectiu i desaparició de bens comunals a Catalunya a la secona meitat del segle XVIII," *Pedralbes*, 10, 1990, pp. 51–66. Maria Stella Rollandi, *A Groppoli di Lunigiana*.
[63] For le Frioul, see the analysis of one these village usurers in Corazzol, "Prestatori e contadini," pp. 445–500.

regularly advanced commodities, raw materials, and carts that would be repaid in labour.[64]

But debt did not only benefit the landowners. Certain peasants used it to transfer their farm to the person of their choice, as observed in Germany, in the estate of von Arnim. The estate comprised eleven villages of *Bauernwirtschaften* peasants and thirteen of *Gutswirtschaften* peasants. The former were free peasants who leased a von Arnim farm for three years. In most cases, they brought their own cattle and work tools. These peasants had to pay for the lease, *Pacht*, the price of their freedom, which differentiated them from the *Gutswirtschaft* peasants who had no right to any form of ownership: neither land, nor animals, nor tools.[65] The von Arnim extended credit to the free peasants when they needed it to establish themselves in *Bauernwirtschaften* to tide them through hard times such as illness and accidents or pay for seeds and buy animals. Normally, such loans remained unpaid for scores of years without their being asked to pay any interest, the peasants repaying some part of their debt in labour by cultivating a part of *Gutswirtschaft* or transporting the produce to the market, and some part in cash.

To provide for their old age on the farm, peasants sought to pass on their farm to their son, a close relative, or even their farmhand. For this purpose, they used debt as a weapon, handing it down to the next generation in the hope of persuading the nobility to keep the inheritors they had chosen on their lands. Several cases illustrate the success of this strategy: the case, for instance, of the old peasant Reinicke who was called before the patrimonial court in 1769 and who was asked to leave the farm on account of his indebtedness and his inability to pay the lease. Reinicke appealed against the decision, stating he had been a farmer for thirty-six years and that his difficulties arose from an unwarranted accident. Von Arnim agreed eventually to help him out, consenting to the transfer of the childless old peasant Pritzkow's farm to his farmhand Michael Bade, who had worked for him for many years without receiving his wages for several years. By doing this, old peasants secured a place for their old age while saving the wages of their servant – who could be their son – and the

---

[64] Thijs Lambrecht, "Reciprocal Exchange, Credit and Cash: Agricultural Labour Markets and Local Economies in the Southern Low Countries during the Eighteenth Century," *Continuity and Change*, 18, no. 2, 2003, pp. 237–261 (245).

[65] Hartmut Harnish, "Bäuerliche Okonomie und Mentalität unter den Bedingungen der ostelbischen Gutsherrschaft in den letzten Jahrzehnten vor Beginn der Agrarreformen," *Jahrbuch für Wirtschaftsgeschichte*, 3, 1989, pp. 87–108 (87–90). My thanks to Christophe Duhamelle for giving me access to this article.

servant bought his independence at the price of the farmer's debts. As for the nobleman, he kept grateful peasants who knew the farm well.[66]

The system of utilizing debt to hand down the farm was also used, with the consent of von Arnim, by the farmers' widows who were able to remarry to transfer their farm to their future husband, provided he was rich enough to take on the liabilities of the first husband; marriage with an indebted farmer's widow ensured entrance into the free peasantry.[67]

In the Villages, Community Belonging Was Based on Debt

The practices showing that the bond of debt could span generations, that interest could be moderate with each succession, and that the debt could be assigned to no particular land; these also indicate, in this relation to time, the preeminence of the social determinant over the economic determinant of the debt. In Upper Dauphiné, it brought about a whole set of rights and duties that cemented membership in the community because the system of compound interest, in particular, never left the debtor the possibility of repaying the start-up capital, and that nonpayment did not mean refusing access to other loans. In its practices, the interpersonal relationship thus created produced a cultural knowledge that transformed the economic relationship into a moral relationship: in exchange for this constant reaffirmation of the bonds of dependence, the creditor undertook to ensure the survival of the debtor and his family. He or she provided them with work, animals for which to care, and even new loans to ensure their subsistence and to pay tax. In the same way, it guaranteed them a roof: one did not find creditors forcing a debtor to sell his house; only exchanges of houses were found. The downgrading of the families was understood in this circulation in which the most beautiful residences were exchanged for others that were more basic. These essential guarantees transformed a material debt into a moral debt: the debtor regarded his or her creditor as a benefactor whom he or she had to defend against his rivals, help in case of lawsuits, and protect from the central authority.[68] In seventeenth-century Clavans, the inhabitants justified their refusal to change the tax collector while arguing that this change could cause the ruin of the poorest who survived thanks to the animals the current

---

[66] Ibid., pp. 93–94, 99.
[67] Ibid., pp. 102–3.
[68] Thus, at the time of the revocation of the Edict of Nanes, the royal administration prohibited Protestants from levying royal charges and their debtors both Catholic and Protestant came to defence of their creditors, arguing that without their help, it would be impossible for them to live in the village anymore.

collector gave them in winter and whose income enabled them to pay fees and charges more easily.[69]

Solidarity and sociability are elements put forward by some authors in their analysis of credit. Thus, in the farms of the Low Countries, the farm owners and the peasants who worked for them were engaged in a constant exchange of reciprocal services. Very little money circulated, but everything was recorded in the books, and once or twice a year, the farmer and his day labourers would do the accounts together with the wages being adjusted against goods provided and services rendered. This was the opportunity for the farmer to pay a call on his workers and to strengthen, over a drink, the personal ties that bound them. But such practices were not widespread, and the farmers of Wallonia, who were paid in foodstuff, cattle, and cash, settled these exchanges every week or fortnight. Over time, the absence of reciprocity would give rise to tougher relations between the farmers and their staff, the former being accused of treating their peasants in a tyrannical fashion.[70] On the other hand, in Flemish farms, such as in Wesphalia,[71] the relationship between the farmer and his servants and day labourers was reinforced by the custom, practiced even in the eighteenth century, of the latter choosing him or his wife as the godfather or godmother of their children. These relationships of credit and reciprocal exchange compelled solidarity between the farmers and their workers.[72]

Debt, a Sign of Power over Men

Regarding creditors, credit was also a political investment because in the Alpine villages, if only the economic game was played, the majority of the lenders were losers. The creditor would give up part of the money owed to him or her in support of the principle that the interest could exceed the capital. In any case, considering the weakness of the credits, they seldom found it profitable to prosecute. So debts that could not be repaid in the stipulated period would be renewed at the end of a certain number of years with the amount being reduced.

Although its economic profitability can be questioned, debt proved to be, on the other hand, a weapon used readily in the struggles among

[69] Archives Départementales de l'Isère, 4E 26 GG9, 13 March 1668.

[70] Lambrecht, "Reciprocal Exchange, Credit and Cash," pp. 237–261 (244–248).

[71] Jürgen Schlumbohm, "Quelques problèmes de micro-histoire d'une société locale. Construction de liens sociaux dans la paroisse de Belm (17ᵉ-19ᵉ siècle)," *Annales, Histoire Sciences Sociales*, no. 50, 1995, pp. XX (790–793).

[72] Lambrecht, "Reciprocal Exchange, Credit and Cash," p. 250 and 254.

the elite. When Jean Jeune was removed as the tallage collector of one
of the villages under his charge (Auris), he obtained the revocation of
this decision, stating that he had not claimed the money due to him on
account of the former roles "to give the contributors the means to cut
their wheat, take it to the market and sell it at their convenience" whereas
he could have "taken these grains cheaply."[73] In individual battles, the
language was the same: to bring a recalcitrant or unfaithful inhabitant
to his senses, his creditor or creditors demanded the immediate repayment of debts, which for many meant being expelled from the village.
Debt was also a pretext for weakening a rival family by starting legal
proceedings the only purpose of which was to cause the ruination of the
adversary forced to incur exorbitant legal expenses, as borne out by the
case between two rival families of a village in Dauphiné, the Bernards and
the Buisson d'Entraigues, that went on for several generations throughout the seventeenth century, the starting point of which was always a
ridiculous amount obtained through the repurchase of the goods of one
their debtors. Such "chicanery" was moreover castigated as the deliberate
desire to extract large sums from the families dragged to the courts and
impoverished into the bargain.[74]

Vis-à-vis this political role of the debt, the only weapon of the villagers
was to dilute their dependence and to borrow from the greatest number
of rival notables and the latter entered this game, not only to weaken
their adversaries but also to capture the markets which went with the
overindebtedness of the families: that of men and of mountain pastures
that allowed true economic profits.

Even in eighteenth-century England, debt remained an instrument of
power and, rediscovering the lessons of Rabelais, Samuel Johnson advocated lending small sums to one's neighbours at a modest rate of interest,
or even without interest, and keeping the acknowledgments of debt for
"securing influence." He supported prison for debt as an instrument of
power and social control; for this reason, many stories and pamphlets
attested to the fact that the laws on debts were a means of exerting
pressure to keep the workers and markets in check and secure personal
favours.[75]

---

[73] Archives Départementales de l'Isère, 4E24 1G69, 3 and 20 November 1675.

[74] Keith P. Luria, *Territories of Grace. Cultural Change in the Seventeenth-Century Diocese
of Grenoble*, Berkeley, University of California Press, 1991, pp. 181–3.

[75] Paul H. Haagen, "Eighteenth-Century English Society and the Debt Law" in *Social
Control and the State, Historical and Comparative Essays*, Stanley Cohen and Andrew
Seull, eds., London, Basil Blackwell, 1983, pp. 222–247 (233–234)

Fragility and Dynamics of Debt Ties

Following the credit ties as we have just done puts the accent on the stability of interpersonal relationships that bind creditor and debtor and on the reciprocal advantages of these negotiated and controlled ties. Noticing how the economic game and the personal will act on these ties partly destroys this image of stability and emphasizes a competing logic: the intense circulation of active debts in the village and, with it, the intermixing of clients. This circulation is due to two sets of factors. The first is purely economic and refers to the lack of cash: debts circulate like paper money. The second factor is related to the social game: the debtors may find it beneficial to multiply their creditors to dilute their dependence while the creditors, on the contrary, try to control this scattering of credit. At the core of the game, access to information is crucial. Moreover, these movements of credits are activated, in Upper Dauphiné, where I studied them, by the presence of merchants and peddlers in extended places of migration: only other migrants, familiar with the plains, were capable of recovering the credits granted outside the valley.

The tangle of various functions of credit thus creates a multiplicity of competing dynamics that makes the systems of credit based on interpersonal relationships evolve. Seeking to transform imposed solidarity and reciprocal dependences, debtors create the dynamics that reflect the credit as a social tie and as a market element. For example, in these patriarchal societies, the exclusion of women from commercial and political affairs obliged the widows to sell "en bloc" the credits of their late husband: the vicissitudes of life then created a market of credits that weakened horizontal ties and eroded the patient constructions built by the elites to control the village families. Besides, peddlers played on the rivalries between the dominant families to reduce dependence and win spaces of freedom.

In the villages existed a veritable active debt market that sprang into action generally after the death of the head of family. It was sustained by widows who sold the debts of insolvent debtors that they could neither use nor recover. The widow of Jean Bernard, the merchant from Besse whom we met in the previous chapter, did precisely that. Indeed, the loans granted to farmers known to be insolvent were noted in a special book. These loans to the poorest were not secured against any land and would never be repaid. As in most cases, they were not really convertible to labour force; they added to the network of debtors. In such a male-dominated society, a widow had no option but to resell them.[76]

---

[76] Archives Départementales de l'Isère, 3E 846, 9 June 1684.

It was not just the debts of the poor that were auctioned: some inheritors sold all of the active debts of their father's inheritance. This practice reveals the fragile nature of the village elite's fortunes. Indeed, the inventories after death of merchants show that for the main part, legacies consisted of active debts in which were mixed private and notarial agreements, notifications, conventions, and legal proceedings. To account for this subterranean part of wealth, one had to find one's bearings in a multiplicity of personal ties and long-standing deals. More than a simple transfer of material goods, inheritance was essentially about the capacity to utilize this subterranean part of wealth. The drawing up of inventories was often a tedious and expensive process (the inventory of Nicolas Giraud, Captain-châtelain of Bourg d'Oisans, cost more than 400 livres; that of Jean Jeune, his brother-in-law, at least 361 livres – the average value of an inheritance being 400 to 500 livres), for the experts who drew them up were alone capable of transferring this knowledge or "immaterial heredity" that constituted the essential part of the wealth of the village elites when a father did not have time to initiate his son into his business. Without direct knowledge of the state, the size, and the reliability of the networks woven by the deceased, the inheritors could not make use of the property inherited. Besides, these moments of a break in family continuity were what the debtors or rival families capitalized on to rid themselves of the obligations tying them to the deceased.

Consequently, when the family structure was such that the father's property could not be managed because the inheritors were too young or were only female, or when relatives were unable to take over, or when the family suspected that the affairs of the deceased were not overly flourishing, the widow or the family assembly would decide against the expensive business of drawing up an inventory that the inheritors would be unable to manage on account of the extent to which the father's affairs were embroiled geographically or socially or the lack of any foreseeable income. In such cases, the debts of the deceased were sold to a relative or were auctioned. These auctions were very popular with the notables who would even join together if the bidding was likely to be high: some cost three times the average price of a succession.[77] They would also acquire

---

[77] On 8 February 1677, Crépin Giraud, the father of Nicolas, Misters Pierre Pelorce, and Pierre Argentier concluded a private convention "to bid in partnership with shared expenses for the active debts of the inheritance of Jean Agentier." To this document was attached the *proof of travel* of 5 May that Nicolas Giraud had undertaken as his father's procurator as well as the amount (1,300 livres) of the bid for the said debts. Archives Départementales de l'Isère, B 627, no. 607. A few years later, Crépin Giraud

the rights that their debtors had on other families. In this market, it was a question not only of recovering money and building a clientele but also of establishing one's power over male labour. The very structure of village power was at stake with these transfers. Once again, indebtedness was the means to hold power over men and villages.

How Then Is Usury to be Dealt with Given These Practices and Their Diversity?

There is no unequivocal answer to this question given that the same word covers a wide range of credit rooted in different realities: circles of creditors, various modalities of lending, not to mention the difficulty in separating interest from capital as it is not to reconstitute the history of each debt. Many deeds included interest with capital, either in pledges, as in England and the Alps, or as in France, in the obligations turned into bonds at the time creditors and debtors got together to do the accounts, adding interest arrears to capital. It has been observed that in certain places and with certain actors, the loan contracts were one-sided whereas as in others, the actual practices and reciprocal advantages protected the debtors.

Accordingly, for some lenders, especially foreigners and a few notables, the aim was, as in the case of credit today, to make money with time and money. For others, it was question of taking possession of something else or entering another market profitably: the labour, the land, or the harvest market. For others still, credit, which entered into a set of social relations marked by political inequality and the submission of the debtor, was first and foremost a sign of authority. But authority also means protection.

What do interest rates tell us about these practices? Although they are certainly not the only indicators of usurious practices, they nevertheless point to the greater or lesser degree of social proximity of the contracting parties. In spite of the general prohibition of usury, which in those times signified the refusal of any interest, the practices were very diverse, and everywhere creditors knew how to hide or disguise the interest received, as we will see in Chapter 7. This large diversity, observable at the microlevel,

joined together with the Protestant Jean Bérard de Mizoen to acquire the active debts of the inheritance of Simon Girard. Archives Départementales de l'Isère, B 627, no. 678, 18 February 1686. Jean Bérard was part of the large network of protestant merchants and he joined his brother, who ran a flourishing shop in Lyon. Crépin was not only interested in acquiring the active debts of his peers but also in bidding for modest sums such as the bid that allowed him to acquire the active debts of Marie Didier and Jean Thomas for the sum of 39 livres 10 sols.

was part of a persistent and widespread macro trend of official rates falling throughout the modern period. This fall was linked to the political
system of the state and was dependent on the citizens' control over public
debt: the more real the control, the more the rates fell.

Thus, initially, legal rates, which fluctuated according to the dictates of the state, were imposed all over, except in the United Provinces
where, from 1658, interest rates were fixed freely: in the seventeenth
and eighteenth centuries, Amsterdam's monetary market had the lowest
rates (they fell to 3 per cent)[78]; now Amsterdam was a merchant republic. In England, Parliament had the right to inspect royal finances and
the maximum rate during the seventeenth century fluctuated between
5 and 8 per cent.[79] On the other hand, in Catholic and absolutist mon-
archies, the king fixed the credit rates as he was God's representative
and he alone had the right to borrow above the rate he had fixed; moreover, that was what kings did when borrowing from financers to find
the money needed for their policies. Nevertheless, in France, the king's
denier decreased during the sixteenth and seventeenth centuries from
10 to 5 per cent[80] in spite of the fluctuations: the rates wavered between
4 and 5 per cent, respecting the legal rate fixed successively at denier
20 in 1665 and denier 30 in 1724, reduced to denier 20 in 1725, lowered to denier 25 in 1766 and stabilized at denier 20 in 1770. Spain
also followed the general declining trend in Europe, as acknowledged in
the Pragmatic Sanction of 9 July 1750 of the Crown of Catalonia and
Aragon,[81] although, here too, the permissible rate for rent fluctuated
between the fourteenth and eighteenth centuries: it began at 7.14 per
cent in the fourteenth century, fell to 5 per cent in the fifteenth century,
rose again to 6.66 per cent in the sixteenth century, fell to 5 per cent in
the seventeenth century, and fell further still to 3 per cent in the eighteenth century.[82]

[78] Peter Spufford, "Access to Credit and Capital in the Commercial Centres of Europe,"
A Miracle Mirrored. The Dutch Republic in European Perspective, Karel Davids and Jan
Lucassen, eds., Cambridge, Cambridge University Press, 1995, pp. 303–37.
[79] Norman L. Jones, *God and the Moneylenders. Usury and Law in Early Modern England*,
Oxford, Basil Blackwell, 1989. Lawrence Stone, *The Crisis of the Aristocracy 1558–
1641*, Oxford, Clarendon Press, 1965, p. 240.
[80] Bernard Schnapper, *Les Rentes au XVIe siècle. Histoire d'un instrument de crédit*, Paris,
SEVPEN, 1957; Goubert, *Beauvais et le Beauvaisis*, pp. 538–40.
[81] M. Peset i and V. Graullera, "Els censals i la propietat de la terra al segle XVIII Valencià,"
Recerques, no. 18, 1986, pp. 107–37 (119).
[82] Llorenç Ferrer i Alòs, "Censals, vendes a carta de gràcia i endeutament pagès al Bages
(s.XVIII)," *Estudis d'Historia agraria*, no. 4, s.d., pp. 101–28 (105).

Some Italian states regulated the rates. In the Venetian republic, they fell from the second half of the sixteenth century to reach, depending on the region, between 6 per cent and 10 per cent.[83] In the Empire as well, the official rates continued to fall from the sixteenth century onward.[84]

However, the analysis of practices reveals the difference between the official rates and the actual rates, which worked both ways. In some places, behaviour induced lower rates whereas in others, the edicts fixing the interest rates were difficult to implement. Thus, we see in Beauvaisis, the denier fall in contracts before the legislation: by holding out the threat of repayment to the annuitant, the party paying the annuity obtained a "reduction" in rent.[85] On the other hand, in the village of Cierp in the Haut Comminges, the denier 16 (6.25 per cent) was dominant around 1675, and the denier 18 or 20 rare between 1692 and 1695.[86] But in Bas-Languedoc, the denier 20, and even the denier 25, dominated from 1660–1670 onward.[87] The edict of December 1665, which established the denier 20 in the kingdom, was not applied and one had to wait till 15 November 1679, when in the jurisdiction of the Parliament of Toulouse interest was moderated to denier 18.[88]

The mechanisms of overindebtedness of some peasantries due to speculation on grain prices and the charging of compound interest, which made for truly usurious rates, were reinforced by social practices that attenuated the apparently stiff rates by granting more time and reduction of debts. This excessive debt, which everyone experienced, showed that the play of economic forces alone was not enough for creditors to emerge winners, even less so as the risks of capital were great. The inventories after death contained many a long list of bad debts,[89] and this even in the very efficient and carefully monitored networks such as those of migrant merchants.[90]

---

[83] Corazzol, *Fitti e livelli a Grano*, chap. 5.

[84] Christophe Duhamelle, L'héritage collectif. *La noblesse d'Église rhénane xviie–xviiie siècle*, Paris, Éditions de l'École des hautes études en sciences sociales, 1998, p. 462.

[85] Pierre Goubert, *Beauvais et le Beauvaisis*, p. 539.

[86] Philippe Patanchon, "La dette paysanne en haut-Comminges au temps de Louis XIV (1675–1695)," *Annales du Midi*, 97, no. 172, 1985, pp. 375–380 (380).

[87] Emmanuel Le Roy Ladurie, *Les paysans de Languedoc*, Paris SEVPEN, 1966, t. 2, vol. 1024–1025.

[88] Bernard Du Puy, *Eclaicissement nouveau sur le prêt et les intérêts*, Toulouse, chez Pierre Calac, 1687.

[89] For Lisbon, see the examples in Rochas, "Crédito private." For the bakers of Paris, see Steven L. Kaplan, *Les ventres de Paris. Pouvoir et approvisionnement dans la France d'Ancien Régime*, Paris, Fayard, 1988, pp. 315–27.

[90] See next chapter.

The question of usury should thus be placed in the framework of these relations of power sought or imposed. Understanding the significance of rates is a difficult enterprise, given that the repayment of loans was not always and necessarily in monetary terms: credit was still not an autonomous market. The complex web of credit needs to be analysed, taking into account the risks capital incurred (there were a large number of defaulters everywhere: about 30 to 40 per cent), the social distance, the repayment, and the economic, demographic, and political situation indicative of the state of competition and which conferred value on repayment (in particular, the changing value of land and labour). Nevertheless, let us recall two contradictory practices that, in some ways, limited the space for development. On one hand, the general practice of compound interest, which made the legal rates illusory, and, on the other hand, the notarial deeds indicative of a village morality intent on ensuring that the interest due did not exceed the principal and that each time such a case occurred, the creditor had to refer explicitly to this rule to "moderate" the sums due and grant a discount. If, at the end of such an analysis, we can conclude that interest rates did not have much meaning for a large majority of the population, we need, on the other hand, to refine our research to see where, when and for whom they became a factor capable of influencing economic behaviour.

One last element needs to be added to complete the picture: the service that credit rendered to those who were in need of it was of such utility that they preferred paying dearly for it rather than foregoing it. Petitions by peasants or poor city dwellers in defence of their usurers were not uncommon. As long as there was no institutional mechanism to regulate credit to the poorest, people defended their private lenders in spite of the high rates they charged. In the Catalonian country, people feared the confiscation of Jewish wealth, for it led to a growing scarcity of money that raised prices,[91] and at the end of the ancien régime, Turgot relates that the biggest defenders of an accused in a criminal case in the Tournelle for an act of usury were the very people who had suffered the most.[92]

In this social and cultural context, accusing someone of usury was undoubtedly indicative of the very low degree of personalization of the credit relationship. As such, only foreigners – who were also

[91] Ubaldo de Casanova Todolí, "Confiscación de bienes a judaizantes en Mallorca. ¿Motivaciones económicas o sociales?," *Peralbes: Rivista d'història moderna*, no. 14, 1994, pp. 187–98 (197).
[92] Turgot, *Mémoire sur les prêts d'argent*, Schelle, 1770, p. 139. See also Chapter 7.

competitors – or rivals were accused. The accusation was a weapon. Although foreigners did in effect charge higher official rates and expect greater adhesion to time periods and guarantees more easily convertible into cash, they were, to a large extent, forced to do so on account of the political and economic conditions with which they were faced: the state, the aristocracies, and the cities used taxation and forced loans to exert the maximum pressure on those who were the most visible, and in particular, the Jews suffered.[93] In this way, the accusation of usury was also a symbolic act of aggression, because the traditional elite lent at hidden rates no less usurious and plundered the very people they accused of usury. However, it was also the reflection of an ideal type of social relationship, based on a morality opposed to profit, as well as the existence of a repressive apparatus that could deal with the matter.

[93] See, for example, Volker Dotterweich and Beate Reißner, "Finanznot und Domizilrecht. Zur Aufnahme jüdischer Wechselhäuser in Augsburg 1803," *Judengemeinden in Schwaben im Kontext des Alten Reiches*, Rolf Kießling, ed., Berlin, Akademie Verlag, 1995, pp. 282–305.

3

The Elite and Debt Logic

A *crédit* [literally, "on credit"]: often said meaning "on a whim, pointlessly, groundlessly [...]." That man ruined himself à *crédit*, on a whim, without having anything to show for it. He threw himself body and soul into this work to no avail [à *crédit*]; no-one attaches any importance to it. Everything this lawyer alleges is baseless [à *crédit*]; he has no proof of it.
  – *Furetière, Dictionnaire universel*

Polonius.... Neither a borrower nor a lender be:
For loan oft loses both itself and friend
And borrowing dulls the edge of husbandry.
  – William Shakespeare, *Hamlet*, Act 1, Scene 3, 75–8

The elite was thus at the heart of the rural financial system. Solicited from all quarters, they often played a significant role in helping peasants tide over times of crisis. Now we will see how the elite managed their own needs and will examine the latitude they had to choose who they would give credit to and who they could not turn down. This is one way of understanding, from the creditor's point of view, the coercive force of circles underlying the demand for rural credit and the intricacies involved in obligatory solidarity and economic calculations. I show that, in spite of the diversity among the nobilities of the European countries and within each country, indebtedness was a component of the wealth of all nobles and this indebtedness was itself dependent on circles of creditors; however, the manner in which it was managed varied according to the country and the proximity of the nobles to royal power. Next, I attempt to examine in greater depth the credit commitments of the elite and to determine through the example of an aristocrat and a local merchant during a successful period the share of credit imposed by their status and social roles and that of the credit they chose to give. In addition to their social obligations, many had to contend with the demands of the aristocratic political economy. A few examples taken from the Italian and Jewish merchants will help us illustrate the weight these demands could have in the finances of any venture. Finally, I follow the social advancement of Samuel Pepys as recorded by him in his diary. His account shows how carefully he followed Polonius's advice, preferring not to give credit rather than suffer its unforeseen consequences from which only the highly placed were really in position to protect themselves.

Indebtedness of the Nobility and Circles of Creditors

The growing indebtedness of European aristocrats in the seventeenth and eighteenth centuries is a well-established fact: nobles borrowed to serve the King, to endow their daughters and younger sons and to pay for the consumption their status imposed on them. It is well known today that even so such indebtedness did not lead them to bankruptcy or being wiped out. *Strict settlement* in England, *fideicommis* in Italy and France, and *majorazgo* in Spain protected the property of the nobles from being seized by their creditors.[1] In her discussion of the archetypal decline of the nobility in the seventeenth century, Arlette Jouanna shows that the examples of Beauvaisis, Burgundy, and Franche-Comté cannot be generalized and that the economic situation of the French noblemen was more prosperous than one would have thought. From her analysis of literature, it emerges that the gentry adapted rather well to the economic conditions of the times and that highly placed families displayed a remarkable capacity to recover. The worse affected were the intermediate ranks of the large seigneuries.[2] Until the beginning of the seventeenth century, the border between nobility and commoners was porous, and the problem of the impoverished nobility needs to be relativized.[3]

---

[1] John Habakkuk, "Debt," *Marriage, Debt and the Estates System. English Landownership, 1650–1950*, Oxford, 1994; Bartolomé Yun Casalilla, "La situación económica de la aristocracia castellana durante los reinados de Felipe III y Felipe IV," *La España del Conde-Duque de Olivares*, J. H. Elliott and A. Garcia, eds., Valladolid, Universidad de Valladolid, 1990, pp. 518–51.

[2] Arlette Jouanna, *Le Devoir de révolte. La noblesse française et la gestation de l'Etat moderne (1559–1661)*, Paris, Fayard, 1989, pp. 95–8.

[3] Michel Nassiet, *Noblesse et pauvreté. La petite noblesse en Bretagne XVe–XVIIIe siècle*, Archives Historiques de Bretagne 5, Bannalec, Presses Universitaires de Rennes, 1993.

A careful examination of the way in which the wealthy managed to avoid bankruptcy testifies to the crucial role of ties with the crown which, while conferring its benefactions, provided regular income and, when required, injected the sums needed to avert bankruptcy.[4] In fact, the wealth of the nobles was very vulnerable. The owners of this wealth spent a great deal of time at the court where, to maintain their rank, they were obliged to maintain an extravagant lifestyle while remaining at the mercy of royal requirements which the king reimbursed at his convenience through gifts, pensions, or tax assignations. In this way, kings depended on the wealth of the nobles and the nobles on the largesse of kings.[5] Debt was thus a normal and inevitable component of any large nobiliary fortune and when it led a family to bankruptcy, the king stepped in to cover the deficit. Every study on the nobility has reported this mechanism. Thus, in Alsace during the eighteenth century, indebtedness reached a proportion even higher than that of the period following the Thirty Years' War[6]; the Nevers spent, without counting the cost, to maintain their position and finance the needs of the monarchy. Louis de Gonzague purchased annuities worth more than 380,000 livres on the Town Hall in 1570 and 900,000 from 1576 to 1578, and to satisfy the royal exigencies, the Nevers mobilized their own client networks, which depended in turn on princely credit. In exchange, the Nevers' debts were a matter of state that Catherine de Médici dealt with personally. Paradoxically, although he lived on royal finances, the duke of Nevers spent the major part of his resources financing the state and his own position in the state.[7] Studies carried out on Spain were in line with the French findings: they point to the obligation of

---

Jean Meyer, "Un problème mal posé: La noblesse pauvre. L'exemple breton au XVIIe siècle," *RHMC*, 18, 1971, pp. 161–88.

[4] Norbert Elias, *La société de Cour*, Pierre Kamnitzer, trans., Paris, Calmann-Levy, 1974 [1969], whose works have been legitimized by historiography.

[5] Arlette Jouanna, *Le Devoir de révolte*. p. 36. Denis Crouzet, "Recherches sur la crise de l'aristocratie en France au XVIe siècle: les dettes de la maison de Nevers," *Histoire, Economie et Société*, 1, no. 1, 1982, pp. 7–50.

[6] Erich Pelzer, *Der elsässische Adel im Späffeudalismus. Tradition und Wandel einer regionalen Elite zwischen dem Westfälischen Frieden und der Revolution (1648–1790)*, Munich, R. Oldenbourg Verlag, 1990, pp. 156–75. My thanks to Christpohe Duhamelle.

[7] Robert Descimon, "Les ducs de Nevers au temps de Blaise de Vigenère ou la puissance de faire des hommes puissant," Blaise de Vigenère, poet and mythographer in the time of e Henri III, *Cahiers V. L. Saulnier* no. 11, Paris, Presses de l'Ecole normale supérieure, 1994, pp. 13–37 (20–22).

munificence of kings and the extravagance of their generosity that was the norm.[8]

A reading of Saint-Simon's memoires bears out this analysis: on almost every page of his voluminous writings, the king paid debts and gave pensions. The pyramidal structure of the aristocracy was so pronounced that everything centred on the king, his family, those close to him, and his ministers. Some offices, which allowed for regular contact with the king, were essential for families to maintain their wealth and power, for when a family lost them, it collapsed. Thus, in 1703, Saint-Simon noted that "the family of the Archbishop of Reims has quite completely fallen out of credit and consideration ever since the ministry was taken from it."[9] When describing Madame de Montchevreuil, he emphasized the power of those close to the royal family, specifying that she was "[a]ll the ladies of the Court were under her surveillance: they depended upon her for their distinctions, and often for their fortunes."[10] In 1709, Saint-Simon fell into disgrace and considered leaving the court. He spelled out the reasons for his failure arising from the conjunction "of the envious and enemies" and "weak and weakened friends." But on the advice of his wife, he gave up the idea of leaving Versailles: "Mme de Saint-Simon, more wise than I, showed me the continual and unexpected changes of courts, the change that came with age, how dependant we were not only for fortune, but for inheritance [*sic*] itself and several other reasons."[11] Montesquieu summed up perfectly the grand seigneur, defining him as "a man who sees the king, speaks to his ministers and who possesses ancestors, debts and pensions."[12]

But when a family did not sufficient credit to lean on the king, the only strategy available to it was leaving the court for some months to come out of the circle of expenses to which it was constrained by the court. Saint-Simon also described the alternative strategies used by the court nobility. Thus, the Comtesse de Fürstenberg, who "was prodigious in all kinds of expenditure," ended up "dismissing most of her household, to go and save for six or seven months at the Bourdaisière, near Tours, which

[8] Antonio Manuel Hespanha, "Cálculo financiero y cultura contable en el antiguo regimen," *Del Ius Mercatorum al derecho mercantil. III Seminario de Historia del Derecho Privato Sitges, 28–30 de mayo de 1992*, Carlos Petit, ed., Madrid, Marchal Pons Editiones juridicas y sociales, 1997, pp. 91–107 (104).

[9] Saint-Simon, *Mémoires (1691–1701)*, Paris, Gallimard, vol. 2, 1983, p. 288.

[10] Ibid., vol. 1, p. 48.

[11] Ibid., vol. 3, p. 515.

[12] Charles de Secondat and baron de La Brède et de Montesquieu, *Lettres Persannes* (Paris, 1875), Paris, Librairie générale française, 1972, p. 170, letter 88.

she first borrowed from Dangeau, and bought later for life. She lived in such distress to have the wherewithal to amuse herself in Paris for the rest of the year,"[13] and the cardinal withdrew to his county of Vadémont "on his way back from Italy to pay his debts."[14] Finally, as a last resort to set right its finances, a family groaning under debt but far too removed from the king to count on his favours would contract an alliance with a rich bourgeois. The story of the Comte de Grignan as recounted by Saint-Simon in 1704 is exemplary in its lucidity: "the Count of Grignan, a knight of the order in 1688, was ruined commanding in Provence, where he was the sole lieutenant general." Accordingly, the family married their son to the daughter of very wealthy farmer, for as the mother said, "From time to time even the best soil needs fodder."[15] The marriage in 1708 of Monsieur and Madame Pompadour's daughter at Courcillon into a rich family but from the small nobility was, according to Saint-Simon, part of the same logic. They sold (that is the term he used) their 13-year-old daughter to extricate themselves from their difficult situation:

They were rich, but heavily burdened, and had nothing to give their daughter; they had no credit and were in obscurity. Far from being able to handle their affairs, they were people who, both with wit, had all the time let everything slip out of their hands, even the property of the fortune, their alliances, their birth, without ever ceasing to be glorious.[16]

Whenever it is possible to discover who the creditors of the aristocratic families were, we find the same circles of lenders: first the family, then the nobility, the church, the bourgeois, and finally foreigners. Studies on the Alsace nobility show that in the eighteenth century such families borrowed little from bankers and turned instead to religious institutions and other noble families. The noble families in the south of Alsace looked first to the bishopric of Basel before approaching the Jews, for the bishopric refused to give large loans. In the Kempf d'Angreth family as well, credit was first sought from relatives before asking the other circles, and the Jews were approached only when the family no longer wanted to or was not in a position to bear the impecuniousness of one of its members.

Yet as long as they lasted, the privileges of the nobility allowed them to easily tide over their financial troubles. Only income from fiefs could

---

[13] Saint-Simon, *Mémoires*, vol. 1, pp. 711–12.
[14] Ibid., vol. 2, pp. 946–1707.
[15] Ibid., p. 523.
[16] Ibid., vol. 3, p. 151.

be attributed to creditors and in Alsace, it was not rare to see as a precautionary measure allodiums being transformed into fiefs; royal intervention alone could save the indebted families, the others being obliged to sell their personal property and then, depending on the composition of the family, transfer their property to their creditors in return for a life pension or live meagrely, increasing the number of their creditors till their successors were compelled to sell.[17]

The situation of the Spanish nobility was not very different. Historiography underlines that the causes of indebtedness were similar: requirements of the monarchy, dowries and payment of legitimate taxes, extravagant expenditure, and administrative expenses.[18] The heterogeneity of nobiliary wealth is reflected in the provinces and the wealth of men in high places follows the same laws: they are both more dependent on the crown and better supported by it.[19] The crisis of the aristocracy in the sixteenth century was also problematic, for the nobility had been indebted right from the end of the fifteenth century, in other words even before the fall in income during the years between 1630 and 1640, because between one- to two-thirds of the income of the grandees was spent on paying the interest on their debts. However, the wealthy nobles showed a great capacity to recover.[20] In point of fact, from 1530 onward, the nobles borrowed in the service of the crown and to put together dowries for their children. In exchange for the money they brought, the monarchy offered them sinecures, favours, and positions that conferred significant benefits. However, these advantages were not used to pay back debts but to continue living in grand style. In fact, in the eighteenth century, many

---

[17] Pelzer, *Der elsässische Adel im Späffeudalismus*, pp. 161–75.

[18] Ignacio Atienza Hernández, *Aristocracia, Poder y riqueza en la Espanña moderna. La casa de Osuna siglo XV-XIX*, Madrid, Siglo XXI di España, 1987, pp. 327–38.

[19] Irving A. A. Thompson, "The Nobility in Spain, 1600–1800," *The European Nobilities in the Seventeenth and Eighteenth Centuries*, H. M. Scott, ed., London, Longman, 1995, pp. 174–236 (174–194). Bartolomé Yun Casalilla, "Carlos V y la aristocracia. Poder, credito y economia en Castilla," *Hacienda Pública Española*, no. 108–9, Homenaje a Don Ramón Carande, 1987, pp. 81–100, 93. Charles Jago, "The Influence of Debt on the Relations between Crown and Aristocracy in Seventeenth-Century Castille," *Economic History Review*, 2nd series, 26, 1973, pp. 218–36.

[20] Irving A. A. Thompson, "The Nobility in Spain," pp. 210–24; Bartolome Yun Casalilla, "Consideraciones para el estudio de la renta y las economias señoriales en el reino de Castilla (s.XV-XVIII)," *Señorio y feudalismo en la Peninsula Iberica (siglos XII-XIX)*, Zaragoza, Institución Fernando el Católico, 1993, pp. 1–35; and Bartolome Yun Casalilla, "La 'crisis' de la Aristocracia en Espana e Inglaterra. Una visión comparative," in *La crisis en la historia*, Chris Wickham et al., eds., Salamanca, Ediciones Universidad de Salamanca, 1995, pp. 77–99 (86).

Castillans, protected by the *mayorazgo*, an institution that prevented the sale or mortgage of the noble properties involved, continued to spend without bothering to reduce the debts with which their states were burdened.[21] When the indebtedness became too high, the nobles could either withdraw and entrust to an intermediary the task of supervising the collection of all or a part of their annuities, or they could declare partial bankruptcy to be settled in court. But such extreme measures were rarely used for the king intervened in most cases, ordering a lowering of the interest rate. Between 1610 and 1635, the king granted this favours to 138 titled nobles and 235 nobles of a lesser rank, going to the extent of reducing the interest to 3.3 per cent. By suspending temporarily the judges' powers to put an embargo on the income from the property of the nobles for the repayment of debts and by providing them, evidently, with all manner of other sources of income, the kings saved them from being wiped out.[22] Needless to say, all these favours increased the dependence of the nobles on the crown. The study on the Catalan nobility also shows the extreme indebtedness of families.[23]

We lack studies on debt portfolios that would allow us to follow the history of debts along through their actors, instruments, and periods. We have some understanding of the instruments with annuity being the preferred contract for aristocratic borrowing till the nineteenth century when bonds were developed. The analysis of the Sentmenat family's creditors confirms the importance of the church and the nobility because 42 per cent of the family's debts were owed to the church, 40 per cent were to the nobility, and only 18 per cent were to individuals whom it is not possible to describe, although one can distinguish a few capellà, notaries, a bourgeois, and even a peasant.[24] This parallel seems to suggest similar strategies in Spain and France.[25]

[21] Jago, "The Influence of Debt," p. 220. Bartolome Yun Casalilla, "Seigneurial Economies in Sixteenth and Seventeenth Century Spain. Economic Rationality or Political and Social Management?" *Entrepreneurship and the Transformation of the Economy (10th-20th Centuries). Essays in Honour of Herman Van der Wee*. Paul Klep and Eddy Van Cauwenberghe, eds., Leuven, Leuven University Press, 1993, pp. 173–182 (178).

[22] Jago, "The Influence of Debt," pp. 229–30.

[23] Eva Serra i Puig, "Evolució d'un patrimoni nobiliari català durant els segles XVII i XVIII. El patrimoni nobiliari dels sentmenat," *Recerques*, no. 5, 1975, pp. 33–71 (47–49).

[24] Ibid., p. 57.

[25] Emiliano Fernández de Pinedo, "Del censo a la obligación: modificaciones en el credito rural antes de la primera guerra Carlista en el País Vasco," *Historia agraria de la España Contemporánea*, Angel García Sanz, ed., Barcelona, Critica, 1985, pp. 297–305.

In England, the indebtedness of the nobles was due the same reasons, namely, dowries, an extravagant life style and the compulsion to take part in political life. This was not linked to the impoverishment of the nobility. On the contrary, some historians have shown it to be a sign of the financial solidity of such families.[26] Richard Tawney uses nobiliary correspondence to give numerous examples of nobles looking desperately to borrow from fellow nobles.[27] The nobility saw to the institutional protection of their property with the establishment of the *Strict Settlement*, displaying at the same time a remarkable ability to recover. Nevertheless, three types of families were at risk: ambitious families miscalculating in their bid to contract matrimonial alliances above their rank by offering lavish dowries or excessively large jointures; families affecting a social rank above their means and whose concern for social standing gave short shrift to financial prudence while fixing dowries; and finally exceedingly prolific families unable to protect their property institutionally from their own proliferation; such families were the most affected. What weakened aristocracies were fixed charges, for they found it difficult to adapt to bad circumstances, meet the expenses of a prodigal son, risky speculation or a costly election. However, rules to regulate credit activity were put into place fairly early, thus obliging the English aristocracy to better manage their affairs. Everywhere, the steep rise in indebtedness led to a better management of seigneuries to increase their income.[28]

However, on the whole, the aristocrats were able to survive their heavy debts. A careful perusal shows that while families which sold their property were indeed heavily indebted, almost all lacked a male heir. Furthermore, the owner had often released himself from the *strict settlement* that obliged one to preserve family assets despite the absence of a male heir or the aristocrat's desire to get rid of them. The sale of property often displayed three characteristics: high degree of indebtedness, absence of male heir, and the absence of the protection afforded by the strict settlement. It remains that if an aristocrat really wanted to preserve

[26] Hugh R. Trevor Roper, "The Gentry 1540–1640," *Economic History Review*, X, supplement no. 1, 1953, pp. 1–55; Lawrence Stone, *The Crisis of the Aristocracy, 1588–1641*, Oxford, Clarendon Press, 1965.

[27] Richard H. Tawney, *Introduction to Thomas Wilson: A Discourse upon Usury*, R. H. Tawney, ed., New York, Augustus M. Kelly, 1963 [1925], p. 33.

[28] Habakkuk, *Marriage, Debt, and the Estates System*, pp. 243–54, 261–8, 314–315, 385–8.

his family lands, no matter how large his debts were, he had a very good chance of succeeding: "Motive was all!"[29]

The Germanic nobilities did not escape this increased indebtedness observed elsewhere in Europe. In the Hesse nobility at the end of the eighteenth century, few seigneuries were free of debt, and most were indebted up to half or more of their estates' value. The second half of the eighteenth century was a period of financial crisis for the German nobility, in Prussia as in southwest Germany. The Seven Years' War meant more expenditure in addition to money spent on dowries, the education and equipment of sons, luxury, and gambling. What is more is that many families inherited heavily indebted seigneuries from extinct branches.[30] Once again, all the accounts show the same circles of creditors: the family, the nobility, the ecclesiastical institutions – often noble institutions[31] – and, finally, the recourse to foreigners, especially Jews.

The analysis of the ninety-two debts owed to Count Prince Friedrich Karl of Stolberg Gedern, which amounted to 750,000 florins in the 1770s, followed this pattern: the family and its allies from other princely families owned 38 per cent of the total debt; the advisors of the count, 9 per cent; and those of other princes, 12 per cent. Of the debt, 16 per cent was held by undefined persons who nevertheless bore an aristocratic surname in 92 per cent of the cases. Of the debt, 20 per cent was held by the clergy, that is, the 140,000 florins owed to the Teutonic Order, an order that also came from the nobiliary and princely group because all its members had to be part of the old nobility. All in all, the princely milieu as well as those closely dependent on it or those acting as a front for it accounted for at least 80 per cent of the debt. The Jews owned 4 per cent, and suppliers and traders, 1.5 per cent.[32]

[29] Ibid.

[30] Gregory W. Pedlow, *The Survival of the Hessian Nobility 1770–1870*, Princeton, NJ, Princeton University Press, 1988, pp. 75–7.

[31] In some cities, the clergy was omnipresent, such as in Trèves or Mayence, which did not have a bourgeoisie powerful enough to eclipse the financial power of an omnipresent clergy. A 1653 statistic shows that in Trèves, 47 per cent of the capital lent in the city came from ecclesiastical institutions. See Christophe Duhamelle, "La noblesse d'église. Famille et pouvoir dans la chevalerie immédiate rhénane XVIIe–XVIIIe siècle," PhD thesis, University of Paris I, p. 107, subsequently published under the title: *L'héritage collectif. La noblesse d'Eglise rhénane, 17ᵉ-18ᵉ siècles*, Paris, Editions de l'Ecole des Hautes Etudes en Sciences Sociales, 1998.

[32] Christophe Duhamelle, "La noblesse du Saint-Empire et le crédit: autour du Von den Reichsständischen Schuldenwesen de Johann Jacob Moser (1774)," European University Institute-Florence Working papers, HEC No. 98/2, 1998, pp. 1–15 (12–13).

The same distribution can be seen in most of the cases we were able to discover. Accordingly, the list of debts obtained from the archives of the bankruptcies of Hessian noble families confirms these circles of creditors. Three examples of Hessian aristocratic families show the variations that can be seen depending on how prominent the family was. In 1773, Wilhelm von Buttlar-Elberberg, a high-ranking officer at the court, owed more than 145,000 talers to fifty-two creditors. He owned 3,400 talers to ten merchants and artisans for unpaid bills and 7,000 talers to the treasury. Four bonds worth 15,800 talers were owed to members of his family, and nineteen loans given by ten nobles amounted to 39,620 talers. Then there remained 96,700 talers in principal and 21,200 talers by way of back interest owed to thirty-seven different creditors including eight administrators who had lent him 17,090 talers spread over twelve loans and six bourgeois employed at the court who had given him sixteen loans totalling 12,124 talers and another bourgeois who had advanced him 1,000 talers. Finally, five Jews had lent him in thirteen instalments 11,149 talers, and thrice, he had turned to charitable institutions for 875 talers.

Another family, the Malsburg family, the four lineages of which owned property worth 61,000 talers and debts worth 103,000 talers, displayed, in the 1771 bankruptcy of the Malsburg-Escheberg branch, the same distribution of debts with out of a total of 49,100 talers without taking into account the back interest from six noble creditors who had lent them 21,500 talers. The remainder came from charitable institutions (6,570 talers from the Haina hospital), and 5,261 talers had been lent by five Jews. Other than a few unpaid bills, the family owed hardly any money to merchants.

Finally, the Löwenstein bankruptcy, which amounted to 14,200 talers plus 2,400 talers in unpaid salaries and bills, reveals a different structure of creditors, for only three creditors came from the nobility: Sophie von Griesheim, owed 3,500 talers, and two others, owed fewer than 300 talers. The family's major creditors were Jews: one Jew had lent the family 2,270 talers, and fourteen others, a total of 4,530 talers. The low proportion of nobles and the high number of Jews among the creditors was a telling commentary on the low social status of the family. In fact, from the 1780s onward, the Hessian nobility could turn easily for its financial needs to Landgrave Frederick II, who had accumulated large surpluses by loaning out his army to the English to fight in America.[33] The setting

[33] Gregory W. Pedlow, *Hessian Nobility*, pp. 82–4.

up of credit institutions reserved for the nobility (Kreditanstalten), which guaranteed the payment of interest and the debts of which had priority, made this easier but increased speculation until the crisis of 1807.[34]

In 1774 and 1775, the German jurist Johann Jacob Moser devoted an entire volume of his monumental work to the indebtedness of the states. With the help of concrete examples, he analysed how princes and counts proceeded when they were no longer in a position to pay their creditors on the due date. The analysis of this collection shows that the indebtedness of the nobility both revealed and mobilized specific social and institutional links. In fact, when faced with excessive debt, princes and creditors appealed to the imperial courts which alone were competent to authorize the sale of a part of the prince's territories. The procedure of the imperial commission amounted to being put under supervision. The imperial court would appoint an imperial commissioner to conduct the enquiry and later, with the approval of the commission, settle the problem of the prince's debts. The indebted prince would then lose all control over the management of his income and be allocated a *Competenz* or income depending on his rank and the number of his dependents. Moser's work provides us information about procedures against a total of fifty-seven imperial states including eighteen princes and thirty-nine counts. However, none of the most prominent princes figured in this list. But we need to include the imperial towns and knights of whom Moser does not speak and whose chronic indebtedness was also a matter of concern for the imperial institutions.

Moser shows that the commission's classification of debts took into account their moral legitimacy. He wrote, "In the case of artisans, suppliers and wages, a great distinction must be made between those who worked or contributed to common good, and those whose debts arose due to expenditure on pleasure, pomp, wasteful spending, extravagances, alchemy, etc." If the debts were incurred on account of pleasure, the prince would be absolved for all intents and purposes, and the fault would lie with the creditors who had little chance of being reimbursed.[35] As a result of these procedures in which the interests of the debtors were placed above those of the creditors, debt moratorium was hardly ever spread

---

[34] Bernd Ristau, "Adlige Interessenpolitik in Konjunktur und Krise. Ein Beitrag zur Geschichte der landschaftlichen Kreditkasse Ostpreußens 1788 bis 1835," *Denkhorizonte und Handlungsspielräume, Historische Studien für Rudolf Vierhaus zum 70, Geburtstag,* Wallstein Verlag, Göttingen, 1992, pp. 197–234 (198–203). I thank Christophe Duhamelle for giving me access to this text.

[35] Christophe Duhamelle, "La noblesse du Saint-Empire et le credit," pp. 10–11.

over periods of fewer than ten years, for repayment was based on the income of the property. Repayment periods of thirty years were frequent, and almost a third of the moratoriums Moser discussed were spread over more than thirty years. The order in which the creditors were paid was determined by the circles of indebtedness: absolute primacy was given to the family, then to the princes who had provided credit and religious institutions; the last to be repaid were Jews and suppliers. It was in accordance with this logic that the ninety-two debts of Count Prince Friedrich Karl of Stolberg-Bedern were classified: the wife had priority. Next came the princes, advisers, members of the clergy, and nobles. The Jews and suppliers were at the bottom of the list. The federal institutions thus worked in the interest of the princes, safeguarding nobiliary groups.[36]

There are hardly any studies on debt portfolios in Italy. The indebtedness of Colonna di Paliano between the sixteenth and seventeenth centuries can be explained by the same set of causes, namely, armed service, dowries, and consumption expenditure, and involved the same creditors favouring family and peers. Thus, in the case of the twenty loans in which the social status of the creditors was known, at least fifteen were nobles. These loans, given in the form of annuities, were handed down from generation to generation.[37] In the entire peninsula, religious establishments were a major source of capital for the aristocrats. Practically all the leading families of Brescia borrowed from convents and monasteries, which offered them favourable terms with relatively low rates of interest and long repayment periods. Such preferential treatment can be explained by the fact that was precisely to these families that the chiefs of the town's religious orders belonged.[38] Looking behind the categories of clergy and aristocracy, an analysis in terms of social relationships never fails to bring out the full importance of the family.[39] The need to give dowries to daughters gave rise to a host of tontines. The first Monte delle Doti was set up in Florence in 1425. By depositing a small amount when

[36] Ibid., pp. 12–13.

[37] Sergio Raimondi, "La rete creditizia dei Colonna di Paliano tra XVI e XVIIe secolo," *La Nobiltà romana in età moderna. Profili istituzionali e pratiche sociali*, Maria Antonietta Visceglia, ed., Carocci, Roma, 2001, pp. 225–53. I thank Renata Ago for bringing this work to my attention.

[38] Joanne M. Ferraro, *Family and Public Life in Brescia, 1580–1650. The Foundations of Power in the Venetian State*, Cambridge, Cambridge University Press, 1993, p. 110. See also Georgio Borelli, "Aspetti e forme della ricchezza negli enti ecclesiastici e monastici di Verona tra secoli XVI e XVIII," *Chiese e monasteri a Verona*, G. Borelli, ed., Verona, Banca Popolare di Verona, 1980, pp. 130–7.

[39] Renata Ago, *Carriere e clientele nella Roma barocca*, Roma-Bari, Laterza, 1990.

their daughters were still young, fathers could, in ten to twelve years, put together a dowry for them.[40] In the Kingdom of Naples, the Monti di Martaggio founded by lineage associations and guilds in the second half of the sixteenth century was organized along the same lines.[41] Along with private initiatives, charitable institutions came up, in particular in Italy, to provide dowries for the daughters of the nobility.[42]

Obligatory Credit

Jean-Louis De Rodolp, a Country Gentleman

The analysis of debt portfolios is the ideal instrument for reconstituting the circles of creditors and revealing the share of credit given freely and that which was obligatory. These mechanisms can only be apprehended through microstudies which, alas, are still too few. I analyse the debt mechanism of a country gentleman whom we have already met in the first chapter. Jean-Louis de Rodolp's life was far removed from the court nobility; he was mainly concerned with managing his fortune, his small-holdings and his seigneurial dues.[43] He managed the debt portfolio he had inherited and had enhanced. The family archives contain a list of the "active debts" owed to the family. It includes the debts he had inherited, the loans he had granted, and those that his inheritors managed after his death. An analysis of these debts enables us to make several assertions concerning the social profile of their debtors, the repayment deadlines, and the number of unpaid debts.

In 1728, Rodolp transcribed sixty-two debts (which remained unpaid) from the portfolio he had inherited from his uncle, who died in 1721. They represented 6,995 livres. It would take him twenty years to recover twenty-five of these debts, the most long-standing of which dated from 1683, and the most recent from 1720; his heirs recovered a further twenty-four. Thirteen debts that were unrecoverable represented a fifth of the total entries and were worth a quarter of the total nominal capital.

[40] Antony Molho, *Marriage Alliance in Late Medieval Florence*, Cambridge, MA, Harvard University Press, 1994.

[41] Gérard Delille, "Un esempio di assistenza privata: i Monti di Maritaggio nel regno di Napoli (sec. XVI)," *Timore e Carità. I poveri nell'Italia moderna*, G. Politi, M. Rosa, and F. della Peruta, eds., Cremona, Annali della Biblioteca Statale e Libreria Civica di Cremona, 1982, pp. 275–82.

[42] Isabelle Chabot and Massimo Fornasari, *L'Economia della carità. le doti del Monte di Pietà di Bologna (secoli XVI-XX)*, Bologna, Il Mulino, 1997.

[43] G. E. de Falguerolles, "Opérations de crédit en Haut-Languedoc (1728–1748)," *Etudes Rurales*, 9, 1963, pp. 30–46.

The sixty-two debts were divided between thirty-five farmers, eighteen rural craftsmen, two professionals (a surgeon and a prosecutor), two consuls representing their community, and five merchants. The thirteen unrecovered debts concerned four farmers, four rural craftsmen, one professional (the surgeon), both the consuls and three merchants. All debts had been drawn up as bonds by a notary and were repayable after a year, sometimes two. Repayments were guaranteed by at least one security, and all debtors pledged both their present and future goods, and sometimes a particular plot of land.

The debts owed by the peasants turned out to be well recovered, as we have seen in the first chapter, but in all cases the time before payment was extremely long: four were repaid within ten years, two took between eleven and nineteen years to repay, five between twenty-two and thirty-two years, eight between forty-one and forty-nine years, and sixteen between fifty-two and seventy-eight years.[44] During his lifetime, Rodolp increased the number of loans made to merchants from the surrounding towns (worth 57,760 livres in total) with sums greater than 2,000 livres in each case. The merchants got into debt because they bought farm produce from Rodolp's farms, paying for only a small proportion of it in cash. Effectively, Rodolp primarily availed himself of their services in those years when prices were too low. Among these loans, the bonds were more significant than the promissory notes: there were fifty-one bonds for 32,200 livres against forty-three promissory notes for 25,560 livres. Rodolp recovered only a fifth of the total: 11,260 livres from the promissory notes and 2,000 livres from a single bond. It seems that that none of these debts was abandoned, but Rodolp relinquished a large proportion of them to his daughters as part of their dowries (10,000 livres to Louise and 26,650 livres to Esther in several instalments); the remaining 10,250 livres were not repaid until 1759. The repayment deadlines granted for the bonds varied between two and six years, renewable by mutual notice of six months. Yet, the actual time scales were again considerably longer, because only ten of the bonds were repaid within ten years, fourteen took between ten and twenty years, seventeen between twenty and thirty years, seven between thirty and forty years, and three between forty-six and sixty-one years. On the other hand, the promissory notes

[44] B. A. Holderness shows for Lancashire that in the periods of crisis (the years 1670 1680 and after 1720), the owners were immediately called upon to delay the collection of rent or moderate the accumulated arrerars and that finally the latter hardly benefitted from the situation to evict or replace their defaulting farmers. B. A. Holderness, "Credit in a Rural Community 1600–1800," *Midland History*, 3, 1975, pp. 94–115.

were repayable after a year, or a few months, and even if most of them required a longer credit period, they were repaid more promptly than the bonds: ten were repaid on the due date, seventeen within three years, eight between five and seven years, six between eleven and eighteen years, and two took between thirty-three and forty-five years to be acquitted. Each time that Rodolp had recourse to the law to speed up repayments, the subsequent proceedings revealed the imbalance between the merchants' debts and their assets, although they bought smallholdings as security for their borrowing and to profit from the harvests. In addition, Rodolp paid his own suppliers (grocers, haberdashers, drapers, and butchers) in part by passing on to them the debts owed to him – with the exception of the bakers, whom he paid in wheat.

Craftsmen got into debt when they bought the raw materials of their trade: bricks for the tilemakers, the cost of wood felling for the carpenters, and wheat or the rental of a mill for the millers. There were loans to rural craftsmen that remained unpaid despite the security of property put up in support by the "farmers."

Another important plank of Jean-Louis de Rodolp's money-lending activities was constituted by the loans he made to his "friends" and relatives. Like him, his friends were "newly converted" gentlemen, officers, or lawyers. Between 1722 and 1748, Rodolp lent 30,750 livres in the form of twelve promissory notes (14,650 livres) and six bonds (16,100 livres). He recovered close to two-thirds of these debts during his lifetime, whereas he recovered only a fifth of merchant or business loans. He relinquished almost a third of these unpaid debts as dowries for his daughters. Those concerning the largest amounts were the most speedily repaid. These loans were reciprocal, and Rodolp himself borrowed from these same people when he needed money for his daughters' weddings, to support his son in the army or meet a friend's urgent need.

He did not charge interest on loans to the gentlemen of his family circle, repayment periods were often lengthy and certain debts were unrecoverable: he lent 7,100 livres to Sieur de la Matte in four instalments in 1722 and 1735, which were repaid in 1736; a lawyer from Castres owed him 500 livres dating back to 1724, which were repaid in 1757 by the purchaser of one house belonging to the succession; in 1725, he lent 60 livres – not having the 100 livres originally requested – at no interest to one of his relatives so that he could go and see his fiancée[45];

---

[45] This is precisely the same reason why Bassanio asked Antonio for money in *The Merchant of Venice*.

the loan was repaid in 1734. He lent money on numerous occasions to his brother-in-law at no interest: 100 livres in 1725, 102 livres in 1739, and yet other loans which are not recorded, until 1746 when de Ligonier signed a promissory note for 1,000 livres. This promissory note formed part of Esther's dowry, and in 1770, her uncle was still unable to honour it. M. de Bonne from Castres owed 3,000 livres between 1727 and 1743. The widow of a gentleman got into debt to the tune of 1,000 livres in 1736, and the lord of Saint Martin by 2,000 livres in 1737; both these debts were passed on to Louise in her dowry in 1737. Pellissier, a former captain of the Auvergne regiment, regularly borrowed sums between 300 and 3,000 livres, taking between nine months and eight years to repay each loan; during the same period, Rodolp borrowed 3,000 livres from him more than thirteen months to put toward a total of 9,000 livres, which he intended to lend to the baron of Sénègas, who was using the money to buy back part of his seigneury. There were others still to whom he lent both small and large sums (ranging from 200 livres at no interest, to sums of 5,000 livres which were repaid over periods between three and eighteen years). Only one debt was the object of legal proceedings: it related to a loan of 90 livres agreed in 1723 with a Dragon's lieutenant, which had become 110 livres by 1732, and was repaid only after the intendant had ordered deductions from the officer's salary.

Rodolp's extensive money-lending activities were in stark contrast to his apparent frequent lack of money. When he died, he left 62,800 livres worth of debts owed to him. A close examination of his debtors reveals the extent to which his money-lending activities were financially risky: the largest loans he made were to "friends" and "relatives," they carried little or no interest, and many of the smaller loans he agreed turned out to be irrecoverable. Moreover, the social status of Rodolp's debtors demonstrates how important was the relationship that linked them to him; in his capacity as feudal lord, he lent to his labourers and tenant farmers, whose repayments were unreliable and late; he lent to the craftspeople, who relied on him as their means of acquiring the raw material for their trade and whose repayments were just as unreliable. (In the case of the latter two groups, Rodolp had improvements made to his house to make use of their labour, because he had no other means of offsetting these debts.) Similarly, the merchants with whom he did business were equally bad debtors – and, when he could, he paid them by passing on debts owed to him that were just as doubtful as their own or, at the very least, likely to take a long time to recover. Finally, he also lent money to members of his family, to whom it was difficult to refuse a loan but who, fortunately, seldom requested one which could not be repaid, and to his friends who, luckily for Rodolp, belonged to noble circles and whose finances, were on the whole, flourishing.

An analysis of the social background of Rodolp's debtors might lead one to think that he had little choice in the question of who to lend money to but that circumstances were not unfavourable for him and those closest to him: in short, that his social circle was enjoying a period of wealth accumulation, although they all extended their credit deadlines. However, assertions such as these raise the question of the role of credit in building fortunes and family estates, just as they cast doubts on the profitability and the availability of dowries bestowed in unrecovered debts. The principal conclusion to be drawn from an analysis of this portfolio of family debts from a landowning elite in the south of France, I would suggest, is that credit fulfilled a fundamentally social function in the lives of wealthy noblemen and, consequently, that the proportion of freely granted loans, which were likely to require rational calculation and for which an inquiry about the trustworthiness of the debtor would be relevant, was extremely small.

The composition of the wealth of the Toulouse nobility reinforces the analysis of Rodolp's portfolio. It shows the importance of loans among aristocrats. These were frequent; advanced in the form of *rentes constituees* (perpetual annuities), they expressed the mutual help families extended to each another when they required money for life cycle events. The interest rates of such loans were between 2 and 5 per cent; the loans rarely exceeded 10,000 livres, and there were many creditors. Riquet de Bonrepos had twenty-two creditors in 1772 half of whom were nobles who had advanced him sums between 5,000 and 10,000 livres.[46] On the other hand, expenditure on consumption required one to turn to other circles and, as in the case of gambling, sent the nobles to moneylenders.[47]

The difficulties of Di Negro, a Genoan noble, bring out clearly the risk of lending to friends when circumstances were unfavourable or turned against them. In his case, his solidarity cost him far more than the bankruptcy of the Spanish crown of which he had been one of the financers. An analysis of his financial affairs shows that he emerged relatively unscathed from the Spanish bankruptcies of 1557–1560, although he had

---

[46] Robert Forster, *The Nobility of Toulouse in the Eighteenth Century: A Social and Economic Study*, New York, Octagon Books, 1971, pp. 117–19.
[47] Ibid., pp. 161–2.

invested heavily in the Crown of Aragon whereas he suffered greatly on account of what happened in Genoa in 1575. He said he had suffered very heavy losses due to the loans he had granted to his friends during the period of civil discord.[48]

Pressure on Merchant Wealth

Merchants were not exempt from the constraints of aristocratic power or their relationship obligations. To carry on with their business in a feudal world, entrepreneurs never refused credit to well-placed aristocrats. Social relations maintained through patronage, gifts, and loans went a long way in reducing bureaucratic and political interference in their business. To illustrate our point, I discuss the case of a merchant whose business was doing well and who, more importantly, was integrated in a network of merchants from the same region, a factor that normally helped in putting a business on a sound footing.

Jean Giraud, Protestant Merchant

Jean Giraud from La Grave in the Haut Dauphiné, summarized after the Revocation of the Edict of Nantes and before his flight to Switzerland, the status of debts owed to him.[49] Giraud was a Protestant merchant who had opened a shop in Lyon and whose business affairs were healthy. His portfolio of debts reveals debts owed by merchants, by villagers, and by his family.

The debts owed to Jean Giraud by merchants reveal an extremely high proportion of bad debts. These totalled 11,188 livres and concerned thirty-eight individuals, plus a certain number of other debtors grouped under the heading "Debtors who are worthless and where no hope exists, whether as a result of error or otherwise." Sixteen other merchants were recorded in Giraud's account book, as well as debts owed from the Beaucaire fair, but Giraud did not record for them the sums owed, merely indicating "business," "on account," or "allocation of funds" next to their names (which is why it is difficult to calculate the total amount owed). Of the 11,188 livres, 4,542 were owed by eight merchants who were classified as bankrupt. The bulk of the debtors bore names from the

---

[48] Giorgio Doria, "Mezzo secolo di attività finanziaeie di un doge di Genova," *Nobiltà e investimenti a Genova in Età moderna*, Genoa, Istituto di Storia Economica, 1995, pp. 175–88 (187).

[49] Departmental archives of the Isère-France, 1J 1102.

Haut Dauphiné and comprised forty-five merchants from the Alps who had shops on the trade route between Italy and Spain.

In one particular book, he recorded the debts he granted in his home village. The details he gives of them reveal that forty-two individuals were in debt to him for a total of 9,145 livres when he left La Grave in 1687.

Credit granted to members of his family was of significant proportions. It stemmed from unpaid dowries, unsettled successions and various cash loans. The capital bestowed on him on his marriage (1,000 livres) and his sister's dowry, both dating from 1665 (their father died in 1672); the dowry of his second wife, Madeleine Chicot (1,200 livres); and the legacies from their parents were not always settled. 1,345 livres remained unpaid from his first wife's inheritance, in addition to the 2,132 livres owed to him by her mother and brother. His second wife owed him 1,518 livres, and his sister Anne owed him 557 livres for the goods she ordered from him. Credit worked both ways, because in 1675, he was managing more than 8,668 livres entrusted to him by his uncle, Paul Giraud, in addition to 2,000 livres from his father. He managed the money of his widowed sister and her children, to whom he was guardian. Last, he lent his brother-in-law, Jean Monnet, the 1,000 livres, which he invested in their merchant firm.[50] Jean Giraud kept accurate accounts of the money he managed for different members of the family (dowry, pension, survivorship inheritance, and funds held in trust as guardian of a minor), and as far as it's possible to ascertain, interest was paid at 5 per cent.

There is a remarkable absence of debts owed by the state or by towns in Giraud's business affairs. This is explained by the merchant's Protestant faith that, at the time of the revocation of the Edict of Nantes, excluded his family from state business. A study of debts owed to other merchants would reveal different divisions. But the three pillars of credit – to the family, to other merchants, and to those in the surrounding areas were universal – and all merchants were dependent on the good or bad fortune of the members of their family. Credit granted to the family thus appears as an extremely important element in the success, or failure, of businesses in the eighteenth century: financial overcommitment by a family, just as much as conflict within it, was one of the causes of business failure that was most difficult for those involved to control, because both were

---

[50] The loan was granted on 13 November 1670, with no interest for three years. Jean Monnet retired from the firm in 1674 and was re-employed in 1677 as Jean Giraud's clerk, this time on a salary of 300 livres a year.

guaranteed to affect the capacity to fund business ventures.[51] Analysis of about sixty business failures in Lyon between 1763 and 1771 demonstrate the imbalance between the merchants' debts and their assets, and confirms the destabilizing role (as Furetière notes) of credit granted to the official or administrative aristocracy.[52]

Thus, even the merchants' portfolios of debt did not escape the complexity of their social roles and the contradictions these forced on them: on one hand, they had to meet their obligations as members of immediate and wider family groups, of networks of "friends" and as providers of work, and on the other, they had to invest in the various centres of power to realize their strategies for upward mobility and market conquest. The important thing was to know with how many people a successful entrepreneur would have to share his profits. Saul Bellow says that in "the old system,"[53] the number could be high in the Jewish families from Eastern Europe; in Asia, modern economists contrasted merchant networks that successfully restricted their membership to those whose with more loosely defined social structures that suffered on account that, although only one of the numerous groups to which the individuals belonged was the mainstay of a business, members of other groups could legitimately demand a share of the profits, the multiplicity of potential claims introducing a strong element of uncertainty.[54]

If we look at it from the perspective of the foreign merchants trading in money, we realize the complexity of their activity. For many, lending to princes and nobles was a means to buy the right to exist as a trader. In the Germanic countries, Jews and Italians were not allowed to settle and open

---

[51] The Lacombe family of Bordeaux and the Delorme publishing house in Avignon, among others, are good examples of business failures of this type. J. Cornette, *Benoit Lacombe, Un révolutionnaire ordinaire*, Paris, Aubier Montaigne, 1986; M. Moulinas, "Une famille d'imprimeurs-libraires avignonnais du XVIIIe siècle: les Delorme," *Revue française d'histoire du livre*, no. 3, 1972, pp. 45–78.

[52] Maurice Garden, "Aires du commerce lyonnais au XVIIIe siècle," *Aires et structures du commerce français au XVIIIe siècle*, P. Léon, ed., Lyon, Centre d'histoire économique et sociale de la région lyonnaise, 1973, pp. 265–99 (270-2). For more on the debt commitments of these groups, see D. Biem, "Les offices, les corps et le crédit d'Etat: l'utilisation des privilèges sous l'Ancien Régime," *Annales ESC*, no. 2, 1988, pp. 379–404.

[53] In *Mosby's Memoirs and Other Stories*, Harmondsworth, 1971, pp. 45–81.

[54] Mark Granovetter, "Les institutions économiques comme constructions sociales: un cadre d'analyse," *Analyse économique des conventions*, André Orléan, ed., Paris, Presses universitaires de France, 1994, pp. 79–94. Clifford Geertz, *Peddlers and Princes*, Chicago, University of Chicago Press, 1963, p. 123. Avner Offer, "Between the Gift and the Market: The Economy of Regard," *Discussion Paper in Economic and Social History*, 42, no. 3, January 1996, pp. 12–13.

shop in towns. It was only by lending to the elite that they were able to do so. The Brentano, like other Italian merchant peddlers, thus managed to enter the city.[55] In Alsace, ruined nobles sold to the Jews the right to settle down in the neighbourhood of their chateaux.[56] After being expelled from the major cities of the empire at the turn of the sixteenth century, the Jews inched their way back into the city on the basis of the exceptions granted to a few of them as a token of gratitude for the loans given to various princes.[57] The imperial cities, unlike the traditional cities, are good examples of "aristocratic power" because they were governed by closed patriciates recognized as forming part of the empire's nobility and maintaining an aristocratic way of life. The moneys lent were in the ultimate analysis just a right to enter other remunerative markets. Admittedly, these rights were precarious and could be revoked at any time to placate local merchants who complained of competition from foreigners. On the other hand, the city councils favoured the entry of the main Jewish merchants in order that they pay the charges, as in any case they always found a way to trade and the orders they placed provided a livelihood to local artisans.[58] As the Jews struggled to enter Augsburg in the early nineteenth century, the council agreed in principle to take them in provided they financed on favourable terms a loan the city desperately required. The local merchants tried to fight back with the same weapon but they could not furnish the money needed: the imperial city of Augsburg owed in particular and without any further extension whatsoever 87,000 florins to the Jewish bank Kaulla and Obermayer. Finally, a convention was signed with the three Jewish exchange houses; on 12 November 1803, they were authorized to take up domicile in Augsburg without any time limit, provided they confined themselves to big business, currency, and jewellery trade and, among others, kept their accounts in German.[59] The city placed such stringent requirements that after less than a year, two Jewish families went bankrupt and the third succeeded in getting the second loan promised reduced

[55] Laurence Fontaine, *Histoire du colportage en Europe XVe-XIXe siècle*, Paris, Albin Michel, 1993, chap. 1.
[56] Erich Pelzer, *Der elsässische Adel im Späffeudalismus*, p. 160.
[57] Volker Dotterweich and Beate Reißner, "Finanznot und Domizilrecht. Zur Aufnahme jüdischer Wechselhäuser in Augsburg 1803," *Judengemeinden in Schwaben im Kontext des Alten Reiches*. Herausgegeben von Rolf Kießling und Sabine Ullmann, eds., Berlin, Akademie Verlag, 1995, pp. 282–305. I thank Christophe Duhamelle. Hanna Sonkajärvi, *Qu'est-ce qu'un étranger. Frontières et identifications à Strasbourg (1681–1789)*, Strasbourg, Presses universitaires de Strasbourg, 2008.
[58] Dotterweich and Reißner, "Finanznot und Domizilrecht," pp. 286–8.
[59] Ibid., pp. 289–91.

from 300,000 to 125,000 florins. All in all, the Jews brought credit worth 325,000 florins.[60]

A New Type of *Homo Creditus*

Samuel Pepys, an Employee of the State

We can see to what extent the businesses of merchants were undermined by the debt obligations imposed by the power of the aristocracy. As it was impossible to say no, many were tempted to follow the advice of Polonius who swore Laerte, Ophelia's brother getting ready to leave the kingdom, to neither lender nor borrower be. Samuel Pepys is one of the few people who almost succeeded in following Polonius's advice. Thanks to his voluminous and precious diary, we can follow the manner in which he attempted to plan his social success while managing his daily life.

He came from modest origins in the Cambridge region, although some of his cousins had done well in life, one becoming recorder of Cambridge and another, Lord Chief Justice of Ireland. His father migrated to London at the end of the sixteenth century where he learned to be a tailor, married a laundress, and set up shop on his own without being admitted into the tailors' guild. His family connections allowed young Samuel to study at Cambridge; after graduating, he was employed in a clerical position by his second cousin Edward Montague, the earl of Sandwich, as a Treasury agent for the commonwealth. Thanks to his cousin's patronage, Pepys was able to secure a post in the nascent bureaucracy of the English state and went on to be appointed clerk of the acts to the navy. His wife was the portionless daughter of a Huguenot refugee.

Pepys is the perfect example of social and financial success based entirely on the prudent management of his income as a civil servant. His salary was estimated at 50 pounds per annum. When he started his diary in 1659, he was concerned about his low salary, noting that he did not have enough money to heat his house. This was due in part to the difficulty he had in collecting his bonuses, but mainly to his lifestyle: he preferred the pleasures of London, its taverns, and its theatres to work. Yet he was ambitious and quickly decided to do his accounts regularly and discipline his life sufficiently – but not excessively! – to increase his wealth steadily. Pepys became a rich man. When he ended his diary in 1669, he had saved 10,000 pounds, and ten years later, in 1679, the government

---

[60] Ingrid Batori, *Die Reichsstadt Augsburg im 18.Jahrhundert. Verfassung, Finanzen und Reformversuche*, Göttingen, V&R, 1969, pp. 124–8.

owed him 28,007 pounds for his services. Needless to say, this debt was never repaid.[61]

The remarkable thing about Pepys's life is that he was a man who built his fortune entirely from his income as a state employee; however, we should not discount the fact that family patronage went a long way in furthering his career. His account is of great value to the extent that he made clear his intention to get rich and rationalized the means to do so. To achieve his ends, he adhered to three rules of conduct: he did his accounts regularly; he disciplined his life and work, that is to say that he thought of his work as a profession and not merely as a source of income; and, finally, he refused as far as possible to lend money to friends and family. Now, he and his father were visited frequently by distant relatives, many of whom he met for the first time during their trip to London. In fact, Pepys named in his diary more than eighty members of his family most of whom were distantly related and whose exact relationship was often difficult to understand. The figure was all the more impressive as he had no relatives on his wife's side, she being the daughter of a French émigré.[62] Nevertheless, his bonuses and the income he got from the tax he collected gave him access to ready cash. He chose to hoard in the literal sense of the term the money he managed to accumulate rather than lend it, even though it could have fetched him a high rate of interest.[63] Although noting in the 1660s that money was scarce, he added that he had no desire to incur the risk of lending money and this theme recurred frequently in his diary. He observed in particular the loss of credibility of the Naval Office, because it lacked the money to repay its debts,[64] and how this fact caused a merchant to lose credit as the office had not paid him back the money it owed him.[65]

Such were his misgivings that he was not prepared to trust even the bankers with whom he dealt when he borrowed for the Naval Office, for he knew how fragile their wealth was, being as it was at the mercy of bad debts.[66] Pepys was thus perfectly aware of the dangers of structural over indebtedness; he had also taken the measure of the limitations and

[61] Craig Muldrew, *The Economy of Obligation: The Culture of Credit and Social Relations in Early Modern England*, Basingstoke, Macmillan, 1998, pp. 250–6.

[62] Naomi Tadmor, *Family and Friends in Eighteenth-Century England Household, Kinship, and Patronage*, Cambridge, Cambridge University Press, 2001, p. 115.

[63] Samuel Pepys, *The Diary*, New and complete transcription, London, Bell, 1970–83, vol. 3, pp. 292, 296.

[64] Ibid., vol. 2, p. 119.

[65] Ibid., vol. 3, p. 136

[66] Ibid., vol. 5, p. 269.

singularity of his social position. In fact, as his fortune was based not on the goods he owned but wholly and solely on his salary as a civil servant, he avoided the social compromises that merchants were compelled to make, thus managing to escape from the obligation of giving risky loans to earn profit and win markets. The only time he broke the rule he had imposed on himself was when he gave a loan of 1,000 pounds to his cousin Lord Sandwich, the man who had offered him his first position. He explained in his diary that he given this loan because he wanted to strengthen his *interest* and his ties with the earl, although he knew perfectly well that the aristocracy had a bad reputation when it came to repaying their debts.[67] After giving the loan, so great was his concern about that nobleman's dissolute behaviour at court that he went personally to tell him on several occasions how his reputation was suffering on account of it.[68]

Indeed, if Pepys had a choice between thieves and bad debtors, he would have opted for the former. So he hid his money in the secret recesses of his house. When the Dutch ventured onto the English Channel, he asked his father and his wife to remove his bags of money from London and bury them, taking care that no one saw them doing so. He hid in his cellar 6,000 pounds that accrued to him from the navy. He alternated his hiding places from the cellar to the lying-in room.[69] He believed in being sparing with his money, but generous with his hospitality, for hospitality created and strengthened ties. It was a gift that called for a gift in return and encouraged the exchange of services. Pepys extended his hospitality to all his relatives, even those he did not know, but he could not be induced to part with his money![70]

Thus, through a shrewd appraisal of England's social functioning in the seventeenth century and the regulation of his life just to the extent needed to live well and yet be protected against the unforeseen, Pepys lived a joyous life while advancing his career. Because he had no descendants, he did not bother to found a lineage or buy a house or land.[71] A man of humble origins, he was adept at using the credit of his noble protectors but loath to part with his own, taking good care to keep his money separate from the bonds of love that lie at the

---

[67] Ibid., vol. 5, p. 199.
[68] Ibid., vol. 5, pp. 132, 175, 186, 192, 206–8, and vol. 6, p. 33.
[69] Vincent Brome, *The Other Pepys*, London, 1992, pp. 126–8 and 132–3 that quotes from I 247, 255, 305, II 76, III 100, 148, and V 9–10, 201.
[70] Samuel Pepys, *The Diary*, vol. 1, p. 32; vol. 3, pp. 186, 190–11; and vol. 6, p. 1.
[71] Craig Muldrew, *The Economy of Obligation*, pp. 255–6.

heart of aristocratic credit; on the other hand, he did not skimp on his hospitality!

These examples, taken from the nobility and the merchant bourgeoisie, show that credit, because it was embedded in an aristocratic political economy based on interpersonal relationships and a gift culture, was an activity not easy to regulate; it is not for nothing that there are so many sayings warning us against the danger of credit, that Polonius advised Laerte to neither borrower not lender be, and that Pepys built his fortune by literally burying his money rather than making it grow.

4

Urban Financial Microcircuits

Cléante. Five and a half per cent? By Jove, that's honest!

La Flèche. That's true.
But as the said lender has not in hand the sum required, and as, in order to oblige the borrower, he is himself obliged to borrow from another at the rate of twenty per cent., it is but right that the said first borrower shall pay this interest, without detriment to the rest; since it is only to oblige him that the said lender is himself forced to borrow.

Cléante. The deuce! What a Jew! what a Turk we have here! That is more than twenty-five per cent....
Is there anything else?

La Flèche. Only a small item.
Of the fifteen thousand francs which are demanded, the lender will only be able to count down twelve thousand in hard cash; instead of the remaining three thousand, the borrower will have to take the chattels, clothing, and jewels, contained in the following catalogue, and which the said lender has put in all good faith at the lowest possible figure.

– Molière, *The Miser*, Act 2, Scene 1

How does the city, the marketplace par excellence, work? How is credit regulated daily in these laboratories of modernity and change? Very little is known about urban financial microcircuits, yet in the city, most social groups have a structural need for credit, for the simple reason that money does not come at regular intervals but expenditure does.[1] In Paris of the

---

[1] Michael Sonencher, "Journeymen, the Courts and the French trades," *Past and Present*, no. 114, 1987, pp. 92–9.

early eighteenth century, 65 per cent of day labourers and 60 per cent of servants were indebted at the time of their death; this proportion went up over time to 83 per cent and 80 per cent, respectively, in 1790.[2] In Lisbon as well, indebtedness was widespread.[3] Even eighteenth-century Amsterdam, always held out as the model of a modern economy before the others, could not escape indebtedness. Although during the last quarter of the century three-fourths of the artisans and day labourers in the city had more assets than liabilities, only one-third did not have debts more than a year old, whereas one-fourth had at least between one- and two-year-old debts; another one-fourth had two- to five-year-old debts; and 18 per cent had more than five-year-old debts.[4] It must not be forgotten that before the seventeenth century in Amsterdam, the eighteenth in London, and the nineteenth century elsewhere, there was no real banking system, no specific institution to finance small enterprise or help those temporarily in need.

Following the urban daily economy circuits is difficult, for lack of the sources to identify the multiple means employed by city dwellers each day to make ends meet. This is undoubtedly one of the reasons that explain why works on the city take us to space, architecture, construction, social groups, professional activities, living spaces, and lifestyles, and yet remain silent on the circulation of money.[5]

In modern Europe, markets to fulfil the needs of daily life were atomized, because both needs and sales were always miniscule. Goods were bought and sold in tiny quantities. Loans for such transactions were therefore also small and frequent: these were high risk–low volume loans that brought no income to those who gave them. Because there was no real financial interest, these small requests for loans had to do with neighbourhood credit or social forms of credit described in the previous

---

[2] Daniel Roche, *Le Peuple de Paris*, Paris, Aubier, 1981, p. 84. He prefers talking about wage earners rather than about day labourers.

[3] Maria Manuela Rochas, "Crédito privato num contexto urbano. Lisboa, 1770–1830," PhD thesis, European University Institute, 1996.

[4] Anne McCants, "Goods at Pawn. The Overlapping Worlds of Material Possessions and Family Finance in Early Modern Amsterdam," *Social Science History*, 31, no. 2, 2007, pp. 213–38.

[5] Some elements, however, are in Roche, *Le Peuple de Paris*. The role of a few notaries was studied in Philippe T. Hoffman, Gilles Postel-Vinay, and Jean-Laurent Rosenthal, "Deposits, Bankruptcy, and Notarial Credit in Late Eighteenth-Century Paris," *Des personnes aux institutions, Réseaux et cultures du crédit du XVIe au XXe siècle en Europe*, L. Fontaine, G. Postel-Vinay, J. -L. Rosenthal, and P. Servais, eds., Bruylant-Academia s.a., Louvain-la-Neuve, 1997, pp. 245–67.

chapters, or then pawnbroking, the only form of credit capable of over-coming the weaknesses of high risk and low volume.

Relatives, friends, providers of labour, and credit specialists – merchants, all manner of individuals, and institutions to be ferreted out – constituted the circles of creditors to which the urban lower classes turned.[6] Like elsewhere, women invested their gains, their dowries, and their inheritances in neighbourhood loans. This was an informal activity often difficult to trace but clearly visible in Lisbon between 1770 and 1830 when widows played a major role in the supply of credit, a role they shared with the large merchants.[7] However, the sources available to us have not so far revealed whether townswomen in ancient Europe had established solidarity-based and rotating savings of the kind found today in Africa and Asia.

Compensation and Credit for Small Trade

In the city, an infinite number of transactions took place on the basis of verbal promises: goods were exchanged for work, small loans of money, foodstuff, or objects against other loans or days of work, and each one kept a mental record of all that had been given and received. There is hardly any record of disagreement; the Narbonne police registers provide some accounts, but these above all deal with goods taken from shops, labour supplied, or small loans. Some of these records traced a long history of mutual exchange until such point as a misunderstanding about the value of the services occurred. When debts accumulated, a security was demanded in the form of clothes, furniture, or utensils. There was frequent mention of securities in the inventories of butchers, apothecaries,[8] and, above all, innkeepers, so much so that the city of Lyon forbade the latter to accept payment on credit or security.[9] Most important, guarantors were asked to stand surety and promise to "take responsibility"

[6] For the end of the Middle Ages, see the analysis in Julie Mayade-Claustre, "Le petit peuple en difficulté: la prison pour dettes à Paris à la fin du Moyen âge," *Le petit peuple dans la société de l'Occident médiéval*, B. Boglioni, C. Gouvard, and R. Delort, eds., Paris, Publications de la Sorbonne, 2002, pp. 453–66.
[7] Rochas, "Crédito private."
[8] Maurice Garden, "Le contrat de mariage lyonnais: une source de l'histoire sociale du XVIIIème siècle," *89th Congrès des Sociétés savantes*, book 2, vol. 1, Lyon, 1964, Paris, Imprimerie nationale, 1965, pp. 51–75.
[9] Anne Montenach, "Une économie de l'infime. Espaces et pratiques du commerce alimentaire à Lyon au XVIIe siècle," PhD thesis, European University Institute, October 2003, p. 73.

should a borrower default. At the police station, complainants would cite their guarantors, who never shirked their obligations.[10] The paucity of records of such multiple exchanges should not make us forget their pervasiveness.

In the food trade, credit was all pervasive. It underpinned the transactions of suppliers who advanced goods and were paid only after the goods had been sold and those of clients who purchased on credit.[11] Traders also extended credit to each other and periodically settled the purchases they made from each other. In England,[12] as well in some towns of the Netherlands, such settlements took place once a year.[13] The rare account books that have survived show that besides consumer credit, shopkeepers lent small sums of money to their clients. In Versailles, the grocer was generally paid every year, and the butcher, every six months.[14] In the seventeenth century, of the forty-one bakers from Lyon for whom information is available in the after-death inventories, enabling the measurement of the volume of credit given to clients, two-thirds of the bakers left at the time of their demise tallies worth fewer than 250 livres, but one out of every five had given credit of more than 1,000 livres to his clients. A baker even totted up 158 tallies for a little more than 3,045 livres. Some butchers had tallies, which went up to several thousand livres.[15] A tally is a squared wooden stick or rod scored across with notches representing the amount of a debt or payment and split lengthways across the notches into two halves, one-half being retained by the merchant and the other by the client, recording in this way the new credit granted. Among butchers, tallies were only granted to worthy clients whose solvency was

[10] Gilbert Larguier, *Le drap et le grain en Languedoc. Narbonne et Narbonnais 1300–1789*, Perpignan, Presses universitaires de Perpignan, 1996, pp. 936–40.

[11] See Montenach, "Une économie de l'infime," chap. 9; Maurice Garden, "Bouchers et boucheries de Lyon au XVIIIe siècle," *Histoire moderne*, vol. 2, 92è Congrès national des sociétés savantes, Strasbourg, 1967, Paris, Bibliothèque nationale, 1970, pp. 47–80 (59–60); for Lisbon during the eighteenth and nineteenth centuries, see Rochas, "Crédito private"; for Paris in the eighteenth century, see Steven L. Kaplan, *Les ventres de Paris. Pouvoir et approvisionnement dans la France d'Ancien Régime*, Paris, Fayard, 1988, pp. 120–8; and for Amsterdam in the eighteenth century, see McCants, "Goods at Pawn," pp. 213–38.

[12] Craig Muldrew, *The Economy of Obligation: The Culture of Credit and Social Relations in Early Modern England*, Basingstoke, Macmillan, 1998, p. 173.

[13] I thank Herman Van der Wee for this information.

[14] Jacques Levron, "La vie commerciale à Versailles à la fin du XVIIIe siècle d'après quelques livres de comptes," *Revue d'histoire de Versailles et de Seine-et-Oise*, 1957-8, pp. 75–92.

[15] Montenach, "Une économie de l'infime," p. 393.

well established; sales were recorded daily[16] through regular entries in notebooks; at times, even hoteliers acted as bankers. In the account books of one hotelier, there are five mentions of "money lent" for sums between 1 livre 10 sols and 5 livres.[17]

In the case of consumer loans given by small traders, the books did not mention interest except when a trader registered a complaint. Interest was only mentioned in court orders: it was charged from the day of the complaint to that of the execution of the order. Thus, on 14 August 1700, a certain Petit, a *guimpier* (craftsman who made silver and gold threads), was sentenced by default to pay the sum of 54 livres due to the butcher Pierre Jacquin for meat on the strength of the tallies he had presented. To this sum was added interest from the day the complaint was lodged.[18]

Workers Associations

Another source of credit in the towns came from workers associations that functioned like banks for their members. The funds collected by the companies were used for mutual aid, public utility works, and small loans for its members. Thus, the company of masons of Cevio lent money more or less willingly to its members; that of the Palermo chimney sweeps acted sometimes as a small establishment for rural credit: in 1792, it lent in all to six individuals 4,389 liras. The credit and pawn bank activities of these brotherhoods have been documented in the account books of "la scuola di Palermo e de l'università degli artigiani di cervio."[19] In Bologna, such mutual benefit activities were very widespread among workers excluded from guilds; they would meet at the numerous religious congregations such as the one of San Vitale where the employees of cobblers, whether local or foreign, would gather. Money was put into the

---

[16] Garden, "Bouchers et boucheries," p. 59.
[17] Montenach, "Une économie de l'infime," p. 391.
[18] Ibid., chap. 9.
[19] Raffaello Ceschi, "Artigiani migranti della Svizzera italiana (secoli XVI-XVIII)," *Itinera*, fasc 14, 1993, pp. 21–31 (26–7). See alsoi Rinaldo Boldini, "Piccole banche in Calanca, ovvero: della funzione sociale delle confraternité," *Quaderni grigioni italiani*, 34, no. 3, 1965, pp. 210–22, which examines the registers of the brotherhood of the very holy sacrament Santissimo Sacramento de Cauco from the end of the seventeenth century to the nineteenth century and of Cesare Santi, "Le Confraternite," "La voce delle Valli," 18 November 1982, which refers to the loans granted by the brotherhood of Santissimo Rosario at Lostallo.

fund through monthly instalments and solidarity was intended for the ill and the aged.[20]

The World of Pawnbroking

An Instrument of Poor Economies

Private pawnbroking was exceedingly common in ancient Europe. In the working-class urban milieux, people pawned objects all the time when there was no work. In the records of requests made to charitable institutions, there is regular mention of loans granted to buy or get back tools left as security.[21] Numerous examples of this can be found for eighteenth-century Lyon. Claude Gariot and his wife "were destroyed by the cessation of work. Their loom and their entire household were up for hire"; they only managed to keep a bed and a spinning wheel. But "with neither sol nor maille to tide them over, they pawned their spinning wheel with a certain Fillon … for 6 livres"; on 20 December 1738, the Office of the Council of Charity granted 66 livres to a widow so that she could get back her ribbon frame. She was to pay 3 livres a month starting 1 January 1740, until the final payment. On 7 March 1739, 16 livres were granted similarly so that the wife of Jean Martin could get back her spinning wheel kept with Mr Jarsoy Esquire.[22] Taking care of the poor in their quarters, a widespread practice at the end of the seventeenth century and during the eighteenth century under the influence of Catholic philanthropists with a view to maintain the household's independence, testifies to the prevalence of pawnbroking. The offices of charity of Tours, Besançon, and Troyes,[23] and the Charitable Council of Lyon, a private charity set up in the seventeenth century to provide legal aid and loans to the poor, were all engaged in the large scale repurchase of pawned tools.

Indeed, pawnbroking was a sale, not a loan: it was a buy-back contract. An individual in need of money sold his or her good for a sum lower than its value and was given time to buy it back, having to pay both principal and interest at the time of repurchase. The duration of the transaction

[20] Mario Fanti, "Istituzioni di mutuo soccorso in Bologna fra Cinquecento e Settecento: la Compagnia dei lavoranti calzolari," *Povertà e innovazioni istituzionali in Italia del Medioevo ad oggi*, Vera Zamagni, ed., Bologna, Il Mulino, 2000, pp. 225–45.

[21] Jean-Pierre Gutton, *La Société et les pauvres en Europe XVI–XVIIIe siècle*, Paris, Presses Universitaires de France, 1974, pp. 62–9.

[22] Ibid., pp. 68–9.

[23] Olwen Hufton, *The Poor of Eighteenth-Century France 1750–1789*, Oxford, Oxford University Press, 1974, p. 57; Stuart Woolf, *The Poor in Western Europe in the Eighteenth and Nineteenth Centuries*, London, Methuen, 1986, pp. 32–3.

was calculated according to the value of the security. But in general, the duration was short: one to six months, and this suited perfectly the agents of poor economies. Such loans, it goes without saying, did not involve expensive legal procedures (registration, notary, mortgages, etc.).

Pawnbroking gave rise to an informal economy in which linen, clothes and small items of jewellery were sold and resold. The secondhand clothes market was undoubtedly one of the largest markets of the times.[24] It was controlled by Jews in the main Italian towns,[25] the Alpines in the Rhine area, and the natives of Auvergne in France and Spain. Various guilds attempted to maintain or secure the monopoly of this market and the guild of the secondhand clothes dealers always counted among the richest. In addition to these more organized groups a whole host of small merchants and intermediaries, men and women, dressmakers, linen maids, and dealers were active in this market whose importance can be seen in the numeric division between occupations in the clothing industry: those involved in the production of new clothes around 1725 totalled 3,500 tailors and dressmakers compared with 700 secondhand clothes dealers, as many linen sellers, and between 6,000 and 7,000 female resellers.[26]

The All-Pervasive Intermediary

It is difficult to bring to light and study these circuits, for lack of the documentation to do so: here we are often dealing with the informal economy that, unless it turned to crime, almost never entered into any record. Writers, pamphleteers, and criminal records are the only sources we have to shed light on the underground world of financial circulations. Louis Sébastien Mercier is a good guide to help us penetrate this urban economy. His pen may be readily moralizing, determined to castigate licentiousness and the decline in morals, or lecturing when an opportunity for praising family values arose, but his eye is extremely sharp. His ability to apprehend, whenever they existed, economic micro circuits, the social and cultural practices attached to them, and the menial jobs they created is always corroborated by other sources.

With its graphic description of the numerous kinds of intermediaries who made their living by bringing together those in urgent need of money,

[24] *Alternative Exchanges: Second-Hand Circulations from the Sixteenth Century to the Present*, L. Fontaine, ed., Oxford and New York, Longman, 2008.

[25] Patricia A. Allerston, "The Market in Second-Hand Clothes and Furnishings in Venice, c. 1500–1650," PHD thesis, European University Institute, 1996.

[26] Daniel Roche, *La culture des apparences. Une histoire du vêtement XVIIe-XVIIIe siècle*, Paris, Fayard, 1989, pp. 328, 344.

be they rich or poor, and those who had money to give, *Le Tableau de Paris* demonstrates how the city was the kingdom of small money lending. Go-betweens, brokers, resellers, secondhand goods dealers, both men and women, are recurring figures in Mercier's writings.

Go-betweens gained from the needs of the nobility:

The nets are cast far and wide; and the tastes of the one whose opulence is coveted are so carefully studied beforehand that were he lacking in ingeniousness, his vanity would serve to deceive him. The talk is all about the control of his property, the value of his debts, and free reign is given to his every desire such that after of four years, he sees himself reduced to one-sixth of his annual income.

The despoiler, a veritable Proteus, affects a perfidious compassion; and consummating his hypocrisy, he finds himself, by joining interest and capital, the owner of the finest part of the property of the one he called his pupil.

The moment of awakening is marked by dread, surprise, despair, every feature burning with the most righteous indignation: but it is vain, for all is in order; the law can do no more than confirm the unworthy possession of the traitor; the courts would be in his favour, should the injured party reclaim his property. The ruination of a young man can only enlighten another about this fascination that leads so many victims to the brink. The new owner, riding in his carriage, splashes the wretched man, who scampers past houses.

It is not uncommon to see such and such rich businessman endowed with the finest lands of his client, the prosecutor own four of his houses, the intendant reside in the mansion his master occupied. And how did they acquire the property of the man dispossessed? By lending him his own money.

These unofficial brokers appear rarely; they have frontmen. They create moments of distress and profit from them.[27]

The preceding description underscores the existence of real specialists who turned to account the diversity of economic cultures. Mercier brings to light another type of intermediary, *the city collector*. They would collect annuities on behalf of others whose ethic or status kept them away from the pernickety business of dealing with the courts. They were called "grippe-sols," their commission being 1 sol per livre. Their commission had been reduced to 6 deniers but their main profit came from the money they advanced so that debtors could pay the interest on the annuities:

Sollicitors of process, those who buy them, those involved in the Treasury, city collectors, called grippe-sols, tax-collectors who rent some private income of kings and princes are all also called by this name, which they mask most often behind the title of advocate in parliament, that they buy in Reims against payment of five hundred livres.

---

[27] Louis Sébastien Mercier, *Tableau de Paris*, edition prepared under the supervision of Jean-Claude Bonnet, vol. 2, Mercure de France, Paris, 1994 [1781–1789], pp. 302–4.

This title proves that the individual can read and write: most importantly, he learns how to calculate. Today we mock at this science; we are wrong; it was not so common four hundred years ago, far from it; one can save one's neck, as soon as one can read from a book. There is but a small fraction of the human race in the world that can read, and one can perhaps reduce my estimate even further.[28]

In the words of Regnaud de Saint-Jean d'Angély, "very decent folk" in the eyes of their peers were not embarrassed to lend – through an intermediary – at rates from 20 to 30 per cent. "Pursued earnestly by the police, only a few miserable individuals bereft of a protector were punished with much hue and cry by parliaments, for pawnbroking was tacitly accepted, silently protected and secretly practiced." Even the nobility was suspected of making their income grow through small money lending, hiding behind dummies.[29]

In the very Catholic Spain, right from the Middle Ages, everywhere in the towns prosecutors were in charge of recovering debts from recalcitrant debtors,[30] and in the Languedoc, peasants made numerous complaints against these townsmen who recovered on behalf of their natural creditors the debts they were unable to honour. The city authorities attempted at times to fight against these intermediaries like the Toulouse parliament, for example, in 1785, when it created a committee to contend with the abuses committed by lawyers who were able to make large profits for themselves from all these debts, which were difficult to recover and were handled on to them, without worrying about the human consequences.[31]

In England, *brokers* brought people together, drew up deeds, and charged for their services. They tried to ensure that the loans were renewed every six months to draw up further deeds. Brokers served as

---

[28] Mercier, *Tableau de Paris*, vol. 1, p. 366, "Gens d'affaires."

[29] *Moniteur*, 28 January 1804, quoted by Robert Bigo, "Aux origines du Mont de Piété parisien," in *Annales d'histoire économique et sociale*, 1932, pp. 113–126 (p. 115).

[30] Antoní Furio, "Endettement paysan et crédit dans la péninsule ibérique au Bas Moyen Age, Actes des XVIIe Journées Internationales d'Histoire de l'Abbaye de Flaran, *Endettement paysan et Crédit rural dans l'Europe médiévale et moderne*, M. Berthe, ed., Toulouse, Presses universitaires du Mirail, 1998, pp. 139–68.

[31] The notary and clerk of the court of Planchamp in the diocese of Mende was accused by 94 witnesses of "exceeding his legal power, use of false documents, breach of trust and other abuses which led to the ruin both of debtors and those who were imprisoned," since one of his favourite strategies for accumulating wealth was to buy a share in the recovered debts. The notary was also criticized for profiting from peasant debt to increase the number of seizures. Nicole Castan, "Révoltes populaires en Languedoc au XVIIIe siècle," in *Actes du Congrès des Sociétés savantes, Toulouse, 1971*. Section d'histoire moderne et contemporaine, Paris, 1976, t. II, p. 223–236. Jean-Pierre Gutton, *La Sociabilité villageoise dans l'ancienne France. Solidarités et voisinages du XVIe au XVIIIe siècle*, Paris, Hachette, 1979, pp. 63–64.

intermediaries mainly in London and were very expensive because, in
addition, the cost of their travel, stay, and sometimes their assistance in
finding guarantors had to be paid for to the extent that some said borrowing in London was 30 per cent more expensive than in the countryside. At the beginning of the seventeenth century, *scriveners* dominated
brokerage. During this period, some *money scriveners* and jewellers
accepted money deposits and paid interest on them. Very often they
had to act as guarantors and thus bear the risk the transactions they
had organized. In 1614, their commission was limited to 2 pence per
pound.[32]

The Role of Women and Brokers

The absence of financial institutions combined with the poor circulation
of money and the numerous occasions on which people needed cash created openings for intermediaries, positions that required discretion and
the ability to enter into every type of home. Moreover the aristocracy
could not openly engage in business. Some of these professions, such
as *revendeuse à la toilette* were the province of women; others, such as
courtiers (brokers), were exercised by both sexes.

> The *revendeuse à la toilette* [fine clothes reseller] is welcome anywhere. She brings
> you fabrics, lace and jewelery that belonged to someone who needs cash to pay
> gambling debts. She is in the confidence of the finest ladies, who ask for her opin-
> ion and arrange several matters on the basis of her advice. They have strange
> secrets and ordinarily keep them quite faithfully.
>
> It has been said that a *revendeuse à la toilette* must prattle endlessly but none-
> theless maintain unfailing discretion, must possess boundless agility, a memory
> for objects, unflagging patience and a strong constitution.
>
> Women such as this exist only in Paris. They make their fortune in a very short
> time ...[33]

Trevoux's dictionary also mentions their existence: "In Paris those women
who go to private houses with old clothes or jewels which others wish to
be rid of are called *revendeuses à la toilette*."[34] Savary also insists on the
uniquely Parisian aspect of the profession whilst further underlining their
role in the diffusion of contraband goods:

[32] Norman L. Jones, *God and the Moneylenders. Usury and Law in Early Modern England*,
Oxford, Basil Blackwell, 1989, pp. 80–90.
[33] Mercier, *Tableau de Paris*, vol. 1, p. 392, "Revendeuses à la toilette."
[34] Ibid., p. 392 n1.

In Paris those women who go to people's houses to sell second-hand clothes and jewellery that others wish to get rid of are called *revendeuses à la toilette*. They are also often involved in the clandestine sale of smuggled or illegally imported goods, such as fabrics from the Indies, painted canvases, Flanders lace, and so forth ..., either on their own account or acting on behalf of someone else ..."[35]

Molière has often put on stage these lower-class women who, as Saint-Simon has shown, had their counterpart in the aristocracy. In *The Miser*, Frosine is a "business broker" (entremetteuse d'affaires) who charges for her services. Here she is trying to arrange a marriage:

La Flèche. Ah! ah! it is you, Frosine; and what have you come to do here?
Frosine. What I do everywhere else, busy myself about other people's affairs, make myself useful to the community in general, and profit as much as I possibly can by the small talent I possess. Must we not live by our wits in this world? and what other resources have people like me but intrigue and cunning?.
La Flèche. Have you, then, any business with the master of this house?
Frosine. Yes. I am transacting for him a certain small matter for which he is pretty sure to give me a reward.[36]

In Monsieur de Pourceaugnac, Sbrigani and Nerine are intriguers who know each other well and in this dialogue where they are complimenting each other on their prowess, Sbrigani praises Nerine's work:

Sbrigani. I am ashamed to hear the praises with which you honour me, and I could most justly extol the marvellous things you did in your life; I could particularly speak of the glory you acquired when you cheated at play that young nobleman we brought to your house, and won twelve thousand crowns from him; when you handsomely made that false contract which ruined a whole family; when with such greatness of soul you denied all knowledge of the deposit which had been entrusted to you, and so generously gave evidence which hung two innocent people.[37]

These actions remind us of characters encountered in the Archives of the Bastille such as the woman Leonard, *courtière* (broker) and *revendeuse à la toilette*, who owed five creditors, including two haberdashers, nearly 30,000 livres for "merchandise entrusted to her" and who dealt in all kinds of goods: Persian rugs, fabrics from the Indies, satins, dresses, jewellry, and watches. Marie-Anne Riffant was another *revendeuse à la toilette* who specialized in cloth and muslins, competing illegally with the

[35] Jacques Savary des Bruslons, *Dictionnaire universel de commerce, d'histoire naturelle et des Arts et Métiers*, vol. 5, Copenhague, 1759, art revendeur, revendeuse.
[36] Molière, *The Miser*, Act II Scene 5. The translation comes from the Gutenberg project.
[37] Molière, *M. de Pourceaugnac*, Charles Heron Wall, trans., e-book DP Project, URL http://onlinebooks.library.upenn.edu/webbin/gutbook/lookup?num=6923, Act 1 Scene 4.

women who sold household linen. She also lent money to other (female) usurers.[38]

These examples of *revendeuses à la toilette* show the range of their activities and the diversity of their clientele. They found themselves at the Bastille for usurious loans, resale of securities, or handling stolen goods. Resale was tempting in as much as these *prêts sur gage* (secured loans) were made with a very great disproportion between the value of the security and the money lent. So I came across one woman from Grassy, a *revendeuse à la toilette* who was arrested on the complaint of a priest who had entrusted to her a necklace to sell, which she had passed on to her husband, a prisoner at the Petit Châtelet;[39] Marie Ursule Mazerine, a widow, *revendeuse à la toilette*, and *prêteuse sur gage* (pawnbroker), who refused to return two watches to a watch-dealer who had given them to her, together with a satin gown lined with flamed taffeta belonging to the wife of a Parisian bourgeois who had left them against a loan of 25 livres for a month with interest paid in advance, although the dress was worth 150 livres[40]; Marie Suzanne Peret alias Germain alias Richard, who kept the securities of a master enameler,[41] and Jeanne Françoise Lefèvre, *revendeuse à la toilette* and shopkeeper's wife, accused of being "an untrustworthy pawnbroker who kept an item entrusted to her.[42]

The more lenders dealt with a poor clientele, the more difficult it is to trace their activity, because it escaped the notice of the state and its various accounting systems; in any case, the stakes involved were not worth the effort of denouncing such activities. But the sense one gets is that women were very present at this micro level need for credit. Some account books of pawnbrokers in England illustrate their role, a few inventories after death hint at this, such as that of Johannna van Lint, who died in Amsterdam in April 1744, leaving behind 26,000 florins in debt and more than 10,000 florins in credit although there was no sign of a workshop or shop to justify these financial investments.[43] Stories, when read alongside the inventories after death, help us enter into the world of moneylenders; for example, the story of "Claudine," a servant working

---

[38] Roche, *La culture des apparences*, pp. 336–7.

[39] Archives de la Bastille, dossier 10884, year 1725, 12 March 1725.

[40] Ibid., dossier 11580, year 1745, 3 October 1745.

[41] Ibid., dossier 11898, year 1755, 31 August 1755.

[42] Ibid., dossier 11911, year 1755, 31 March 1755.

[43] Anne McCants, "Petty Debts and Family Networks: the Credit Markets of Widows and Wives in Eighteenth-Century Amsterdam," *Women and Credit: Researching the Past, Refiguring the Future*, Beverly Lemire et al., eds., Oxford, Berg Publishers, 2002, pp. 33–50.

for a former master *guimpier* and "bourgeois of Lyon," speaks of a ring with seven stones set in gold offered to her by her master that he would borrow from her each time he went out and that, four months before his death, he asked her to pawn, but on seeing the paltry amount the money-lender was prepared to offer for it, he changed his mind.[44]

Only the legal archives, in which particular women and the excesses of the trade were from time to time severely criticized, allow us to guess at the most ordinary practices. The Bastille archives contain details of a number of these working-class women in eighteenth-century Paris, arrested because their demands exceeded the amount they lent out, because they charged exorbitant rates of interest, or because they sold articles pawned or used them to yield further profit by renting them out. Some examples of such women show us different aspects of this small-scale female financial delinquency: excess usury by a woman named Lestrade who lent 36 livres on two silk robes and three petticoats worth 150 livres, earning her more than 3 livres 12 sols per month in interest[45]; sale of secured items by Marie Magdeleine Le Fort, the wife of a pit sawyer, who had sold a baker's coat and smock that she had accepted as security from him for a loan of 22 livres[46]; or a woman named Roger and her daughter who had not given back the outfit of gray cloth braided with gold with which a gentleman had secured a loan of 120 livres.[47]

These women worked in collaboration with other lenders. They took on responsibility for a loan and made it pay, such as la Demoiselle Benoist, who charged 2 sols per livre in interest and served as *courtière* (broker) to pawnbrokers, although she could not resist reselling the securities when she herself did business.[48] To stand surety, however, was not without its risks. Thus, the widow La Tour found herself threatened with prison when the grocer's son she had invited to the house of the Demoiselle Prunier stole from her. Prunier then claimed against the intermediary.[49]

The file on Dame Bertrand, a pawnbroker arrested in 1735, contains all of these elements. She worked for herself, in association with Dame Noret, and M. (*Sieur*) Lafosse, who acted as a lender. Through these

---

44 Maurice Garden, "Les inventaires après décès: source globale de l'histoire sociale lyonnaise, ou juxtaposition de monographies familiales?," *Cahiers d'Histoire*, 12, no. 1–2, 1967, pp. 153–73 (168).
45 Archives de la Bastille, dossier 11573, 7 June 1745.
46 Ibid., dossier 10697, 1720.
47 Ibid., dossier 10899, 26 July 1725.
48 Ibid., dossier 11885, 21 December 1755.
49 Ibid., dossier 11891, 1755.

women's intermediary, *Sieur* Malbay pawned an outfit with Lafosse, against 3 louis and 12 livres interest for four months. When he retrieved the item, he found "in the pockets love letters and a note for 444 livres in favour of a certain Dasarsis." Malbay went to see Dasarsis, who confirmed that he had rented the outfit from the women Bertrand and Noret. Once arrested, the complaints came flooding in: Bouin, a laundry worker, said that the Dame Bertrand charged her 12 livres interest for a dress and petticoat that she had bought for 68 livres with her savings and pawned to help her parents secure a loan of 21 livres given by M. Desmaret through the intermediary of Dame Bertrand. Others complained of her propensity for keeping the securities entrusted to her: a certain Régnier, captain in the Nanterre regiment, described all the clothes and objects that he had had the imprudence of pawning to borrow 84 livres and that the usuress refused to give back to him: an outfit with a silver fabric waistcoat worth 550 livres, a damask chamber robe worth 100 livres, two embroidered shirts worth 60 livres, a pair of silvered candlesticks worth 24 livres, and two tortoiseshell snuffboxes worth 30 livres. Luckily for her, Dame Bertrand had a sister who had caught the eye of an aristocrat, who therefore rapidly signed her release papers.[50]

Finally, the world of prostitution was also very much tied to pawnbroking, both because prostitutes had to invest in their appearance and because they also received in payment from their clients gifts of clothing. The archives of the Bastille reveal borrowers such as La Dubuisson, a *fille du monde*, who borrowed 40 livres, with 4 livres interest for the first month, on a blue silk waistcoat embroidered in silver from La Leloup. She gave it to La Sagest to find a lender, but the two go-betweens doubtless sold the item.[51] Lenders such as Marie Anne de Lostaing, the widow of a footman, who had been banished to Dijon, his hometown, for public debauchery: Elisabeth Le Tellier, employed by a female linen merchant, feared getting nothing back of the 350 livres of cloth and lace that she had entrusted to de Lostaing.[52] Friendships were formed: Marie Catherine Bellemont, a sixty-year-old prostitute and lender on security, had fallen into the company of a guardsman's wife and his sister, a prostitute, a madam, and a brothel keeper. All three caused quite a stir in the street.[53]

All of these women, whatever the scope of their business, also worked together. They represented one of the links in the business of finance

50 Ibid., dossier 11273, 24 January 1735.
51 Ibid., dossier 11904, 19 August 1755.
52 Ibid., dossier 10706, 1720.
53 Ibid., dossier 10868, 1725.

and of resale, which was a driving force in the urban economy, whereby money, goods, clothes, and other objects changed hands in a long chain of intermediaries. These women knew whom to approach to borrow money or to sell secondhand goods, and shopkeepers came to them when one of their female customers needed money. It was not unusual for three or four intermediaries to be involved in a transaction. Thus, Madeleine le Dagre used a dealer, Hérissier, to dispose of two pieces of cloth for 355 livres. Hérissier gave them, with other items, to Delaunay, the widow of a ship's lieutenant, associated with a man "without wealth or profession," who paid only half of the value of the pieces of cloth and owed him 1,500 livres for other items.[54] The female broker (*courtière*), Deshayes, who remitted the engraved gold watch of the assistant to a major of the battalion of the Mantes militia to a second broker, who placed it with a third, who disappeared with it.[55] A tailor approached Javotte Gouillon to lend 10 *écus* to one of his clients against a dress that the *revendeuse à la toilette* sold three months later.[56] Catherine Villers, wife of a cork maker's assistant (*garçon bouchonnier*), gave two outfits placed by Lerson as security for a loan of 60 livres to a lackey of the Bishop of Autun, and the poor borrower could not recover his clothes.[57]

It was easy for the women and petty merchants who used the services of the lenders living in the vicinity of les Halles[58] to act as intermediaries. More generally, in this scheme of micro credit, they would provide information about possible lenders and borrowers, act as intermediaries, and sometimes even stand surety. Mercier does not seem to be overly critical of "this crowd of mercenaries who lend on a weekly basis." He even compares them favourably to those who knew how to make money from the inexperience of young people: "I am not speaking here of this crowd of mercenaries who lend on a weekly basis; they are often less greedy, less barbaric; besides, they are poor. But I'm talking about these rich … these moneylenders do not lend against pawns …"[59] The broker is another figure who did the rounds of the city and attracted Mercier's attention:

The man who offers you money looks gaunt and half-starved; he wears old clothes. He is always tired; he sits down when he comes in, for in a day he covers

[54] Ibid., dossier 11282, 26 November 1735.
[55] Ibid., dossier 11916, 22 June 1755.
[56] Ibid., dossier 11899, 16 November 1755.
[57] Ibid., dossier 11915, 30 November 1755.
[58] Mercier, *Tableau de Paris*, vol. 1, p. 548, "Prêteurs à la petite semaine."
[59] Ibid., vol. 2, pp. 300–3, "Usuriers."

all parts of the city in order to match sales and purchases and to link the frequent exchanges of various goods.

First you place in his hands your bills of exchange. He leaves: within the hour they will have been scrutinized by the entire clique of *courtiers*. Then he comes back to offer you cheap stockings, hats, braid, cloth, raw silk, books – he will even offer you horses. It is up to you to turn these objects into money. Suddenly you are a hatter, a hosier, a bookseller or a horse dealer.

Your bill of exchange has been paid in merchandise; sometimes you will get a quarter of it as cash. And the same *courtier*, whom you are obliged to turn to again, is also the man to take this merchandise off your hands: a new piece of sharp practice which soon reduces your bill of exchange to a third of its original value.[60]

The lack of cash, then, was both cause and pretext for a parallel exchange of goods.

In *The Miser*, Molière puts on stage this world of intermediaries which draws Cléante, short of money, towards his father Harpagon. The terms of the loan are spelled out in three episodes. First, the courtier explains to him that he will have to sign a bond with the notary bearing an interest of 5.5 per cent. Next, he says the borrower must himself borrow at 20 per cent, and finally, some part of the amount will be delivered to him in goods:

Cléante. Five and a half per cent? By Jove, that's honest! There is no cause for complaint.

La Flèche. That's true.

But as the said lender has not in hand the sum required, and as, in order to oblige the borrower, he is himself obliged to borrow from another at the rate of twenty per cent, it is but right that the said first borrower shall pay this interest, without detriment to the rest; since it is only to oblige him that the said lender is himself forced to borrow.

Cléante. The deuce! What a Jew! What a Turk we have here! That is more than twenty-five per cent. ...

Is there anything else?

La Flèche. Only a small item.

Of the fifteen thousand francs which are demanded, the lender will only be able to count down twelve thousand in hard cash; instead of the remaining three thousand, the borrower will have to take the chattels, clothing, and jewels, contained in the following catalogue, and which the said lender has put in all good faith at the lowest possible figure.

Cléante. What is the meaning of all that?

La Flèche. I'll go through the catalogue.

[60] Ibid., vol. 1, pp. 57–60, "Courtiers."

The lengthy and detailed catalogue, complete with colour, usage and material, resembles a notary's inventory or then a poem by Prévert:

A fourpost bedstead, with hangings of Hungary lace very elegantly trimmed with olive-coloured cloth, and six chairs and a counterpane to match; the whole in very good condition, and lined with soft red and blue shot-silk.... the tester of good pale pink Aumale serge, with the small and the large fringes of silk. Tapestry hangings representing the loves of Gombaud and Macée ... A large walnut table with twelve columns or turned legs, ... Three large matchlocks inlaid with mother-of-pearl, with rests to correspond.... A brick furnace with two retorts and three receivers, ... A Bologna lute with all its strings, ... A pigeon-hole table and a draught-board, and a game of mother goose ... A lizard's skin ... The whole of the above-mentioned articles are really worth more than four thousand five hundred francs, and are reduced to the value of a thousand crowns through the considerateness of the lender.[61]

Molière was having fun with his lampooning, but loans through a succession of intermediaries with hidden interest rates and a mixture of goods and money were common currency. So much so that on his return from Russia, Diderot invested with a notary the money Catherine II had handed over to him and had it written in the contract that it would be returned to him in cash and not in goods.[62]

An Activity Practiced by Rich Individuals

"Secondhand trade" and "business" were the terms used by Mercier to stigmatize these parallel markets in which objects were sold frequently among rich individuals. These practices were deeply entrenched: in seventeenth-century France, a fair number of curio collectors personally resold all or part of their paintings and curios, so much so that the time of their death, the duke of Richelieu and the knight of Lorraine were without a cabinet.[63] Apart from second hand goods dealers who hid behind collectors, fashion resale was an important activity among individuals. It was simply referred to as "business" (*affaires*):

This is the generic term to describe any form of trading in second-hand goods. Rings, cases, jewellery and watches circulate in place of money. If someone needs

[61] Molière, *The Miser*, Act II Scene 1.
[62] I thank Dominique Poulot who told me of this contract.
[63] Antoine Schnapper, *Curieux du grand siècle. Collections et collectionneurs dans la France du XVIIe siècle*, vol. 2, Œuvre d'art, Paris, Flammarion, 1994, p. 426.

money, he starts out with the contents of a shop. He will lose, it is true, more than half his investment when he wants to turn it into cash; but this is what is called *affaires* (business).

Young people are often involved in this type of business. Dresses, skirts, negligees, cloth, lace, hats, silk stockings are all traded. They know that they will be tricked, yet need pushes them onwards and they take on all sorts of merchandise. A mass of men are engaged in this destructive industry, and the upper classes are among the most skilful of them.[64]

The count of Forges condemned the ruinous circulation of objects that went under the guise of "business": "There are far too many noble men who know to their misfortune this way of finding money. They buy for 20,000 livres goods that are worth only 12 and give them for 8 and this is what they call *doing business*."[65]

Further on, Mercier returns to this activity: "There is an enormous trade in jewellery: among rich men items of jewellery are constantly being resold. Certain individuals have in their homes stocks of jewellery to rival the shops of the jewellers themselves: they're jealous and proud of this honourable reputation."[66]

Mercier sees the origins of this circulation of luxury goods between individuals lying in the rapid tempo of changing fashions and in the need to possess several versions of certain objects such as snuffboxes and items of jewellry.[67] In this he agrees with Georg Simmel's analyses, which have recently been supported by Carlo Poni's work on the strategies employed by silk merchants in Lyon.[68] This circulation is generated both

[64] Mercier, *Tableau de Paris*, vol. 1, pp. 365–6, "Affaires."
[65] Conte de Forges, *Des véritables intérêts de la Patrie*, Rotterdam, 1764. I thank Daniel Roche for acquainting me with this work and for giving me the quotation.
[66] Mercier, *Tableau de Paris*, vol. 1, p. 415, "Les bijoux."
[67] "Thus different snuffboxes for summer and winter: light in one case and heavy in the other and which must be changed every day." "It is this characteristic that distinguishes a man of taste. One can dispense with a library, a natural history cabinet and paintings when one has three hundred boxes and as many rings." Ibid.
[68] Georg Simmel, "Fashion," first published in *International Quarterly*, 10, 1904, republished in Georg Simmel, *On Individuality and Social Forms. Selected Writings*, with an introduction by D. N. Levine, ed., Chicago, The University of Chicago Press, 1971, pp. 294–323; C. F. Sabel and J. Zeitlin, "Historical Alternatives to Mass Production: Politics, Markets and Technology in Nineteenth-Century Industrialisation," *Past and Present*, no. 108, August 1985, pp. 133–176; Carlo Poni shows how merchants used this intrinsic trend of fashion; see Poni, "Fashion as Flexible Production: The Strategies of the Lyon Silk Merchants in the Eighteenth Century" *Worlds of Production: Flexibility and Mass Production in Western Indistrialisation*, C. F. Sabel and J. Zeitlin, eds., Cambridge, Cambridge University Press, 1997, pp. 37–74. See also Carolyn Sargentson, *Merchants and Luxury Marfets. The Marchants Merciers of Eighteenth-Century Paris*, London, Victoria and Albert Museum Studies in the History of Art and Design, 1996, p. 97 sq.

by fashion's need to renew itself and by a basic need for money, whether to help acquire the latest stylish objects or for other reasons altogether. In London, this activity was institutionalized, and in the nineteenth century, some families such as the Attenboroughs specialized in pawnbroking for the aristocracy, setting up a chain of shops which only accepted fashionable goods that did not take up much space: jewellry, watches, and silver cutlery as well as law books and a few pieces of furniture; unrecovered goods recovered were dispatched to "Messrs Debenham," who resold them.[69]

Whenever one wished to borrow in early modern times, one ran the risk of having to negotiate goods. Thus, what Louis Sébastien Mercier and Diderot have to say for Paris also holds good for the small Piedmontese town of Chieri.[70]

As Mercier wrote, goods were circulated among aristocratic families partially on account of gambling debts. In order to understand the role of luxury goods in financial circuits, the specificity nature of gambling debts in the culture of the nobility and the way they affected debt practices deserve to be emphasized. In the eighteenth century, credit was for the most part interpersonal, as shown in the earlier chapters, and its modalities were specific depending on who borrowed and who lent: everything hinged on the time granted or denied, and not everyone had the same access to time. This depended on one's social status: the higher the status, the more time worked in favour of the debtor and against the creditor.[71]

However, one type of debt fell outside of the equation linking time and social status: gambling debts that had to be paid without delay. Indeed, gambling debts fall outside the ordinary culture of credit because, by its very nature, to gamble is to consume money. The motivations for gambling were complex but, in the given social context, it is worthwhile highlighting two elements which constituted the self presentation of the gambler: he displayed his wealth and his magnificence by accepting to lose large sums, and he proved his relationship of equality with chance, his potential power to control it, and, in this way, his proximity to God who was the master of chance – two features that distinguished a man from the run of the mill. It is therefore out of the question, because it risks distorting the very act of gambling, to include these debts within

---

[69] Beverly Lemire, *The Business of Everyday Life: Gender, Practice and Social Politics in England, c. 1600–1900*, Manchester, Manchester University Press, 2005, chap. 4.

[70] Luciano Allegra, *La città verticale. Usurai, mercanti e tessitori nella Chieri del Cinquecento*, Milan, Franco Angeli, 1987, p. 39.

[71] This aspect is developed further in Chapters 8 and 9.

an economy of credit that was oriented towards the future when they were really part of a consumer economy rooted in the present. Gambling was extremely common both at the court and in the town.[72] The fact remains that jewellry and fashion items circulated as though they were paper money, except that their drop in value was significant and rapid. Those working in the clothing industry were all caught up in this financial circulation, which was essentially usurious, given the huge drop in value once an item had been sold on once.

Trade, Crafts, and Pawnbroking

This corpus of literary and legal information testifies to the proliferation of pawnbrokers, although it is hard to identify them in the records: like secondhand clothes dealers, pawnbrokers, often linked to the former, were infinitely more diverse than the traditional Jew, the memory of whom remains engraved in the imaginary. Like Harpagon, many hid behind intermediaries. When Cléante finally confronts his father, he tells him his conduct is disgraceful: "Cléante. Are you not ashamed of dishonouring your station by such dealings, of sacrificing honour and reputation to the insatiable desire of heaping crown upon crown, and of outdoing the most infamous devices that have ever been invented by the most notorious usurers?"[73]

Mercier also condemns "the hidden usurer who every year can earn one-third of his capital without industry or risk."[74]

The diversity of those who practiced the trade of lending was great, ranging from the small clandestine transaction behind the shop to the activity carried out in the open by those well established in the trade. In both cases, neither the clients nor the goods accepted were the same.[75] The count of Forges demanded that there be a pawnshop in each town to fight against the proliferation of usurers: "there is no quarter in Paris where there isn't the ubiquitous usurer and what is worse, they live peacefully, and the secrecy of their residence and profession is worthy of the theatre." He reproached them for charging exorbitant interest and not even giving a quarter of the value of the objects entrusted them which

---

[72] Francis Freundlich, *Le monde du jeu à Paris 1715–1800*, Paris, Albin Michel, 1995.

[73] Molière, *The Miser*, Act II Scene 3.

[74] Mercier, *Tableau de Paris*, vol. 2, pp. 300–3, "Usuriers."

[75] Melanie Tebbutt, *Making Ends Meet. Pawnbroking and Working Class Credit*, London, Methuen, 1984, p. 20.

they sold or lost, not to mention the fact that they often changed their residence, disappeared or went bankrupt.[76] The Bastille archives tell us about some of these usurers in Paris who did not stay long in their shops. Their favourite haunts were located around the Rue Quicampoix and between the Odéon and the Seine.

In documents relating to bankruptcy, certain jewellers with wide business connections turned out to be no more than large-scale usurers. Aubourg is one of them. The account books he left behind give us a clear picture of his business and fully justify Mercier's stigmatism of courtiers and aristocrats acting as intermediaries as well his criticism of the count of Forges for demanding pawnshops to fight against the usurers; his own his large business was unable to survive the setting up of a Parisian pawnshop; he went bankrupt a year after its establishment. Let us look at his business for a moment[77]: His shop was on the Rue Mazarine. He would not lend money on pledges but, worse still, he bought jewellry, watches, and other luxury items at very low prices from individuals who needed money and from the brokers who were the original contacts between those in need of money and the jeweller himself. His purchase book describes "lusterless ring, poor quality chain, yellowed diamonds, cheap ring, agate ring and broken gold box, poor quality walking sticks and watches, old key, old clock, old silverware etc." He also bought at auctions. Most of this jewellery ended up in the hands of other middlemen to be resold. This resale business was entered in his jewellry account books as "given with the *option to return*" or "*on trust.*"

Aubourg was in the middle of a double network: he bought, either directly or through brokers, from those who were in financial difficulty and had to resell their belongings, and he resold directly or through brokers or from other jewellers to those people who wanted to invest their money or acquire jewellery. The official brokers took 49 per cent of the *objets donnés à conditions* (with the option to return them) and 66.5 per cent of the sales and made up more than 50 per cent of his sales turnover. Two noblemen made up 21 per cent of the *objets pris à condition*, 15.5 per cent of the sales and a little less than a quarter of his sales figures; this means almost as much as four jewellers with a total of 80,342 livres, whereas the two aristocrats together sold for 90,667 livres;

[76] Forges, *Des véritables intérêts de la Patrie*, pp. 142–5.
[77] Natacha Coquery used this case raising questions about the consumptions. I examine it from the point of view of informal finance. See Natacha Coquery, "La boutique à Paris au XVIIIe siècle," dossier d'habilitation à diriger des recherches, Université de Paris I, June 2006 from which I draw my data.

the following three clients came in for between 1 and 5 per cent of his
various operations. However, the activity of one fashion dealer is worthy of attention: she took 3.5 per cent of the *objets donnés à conditions*,
sold at 0.5 per cent, bringing in business worth 14,124 livres in the total
custom of the six best clients worth 464,354 livres. Aubourg distributed
the merchandise that he gathered among his fellow usurers, or he sold
directly to other brokers who in turn placed it with other individuals,
or indeed he would entrust the merchandise to aristocrats who had no
qualms about selling it on.

The jeweller-usurer was thus at the centre of large number of brokers working for him, allowing him access to all levels of society and to
offload all the merchandise, good or bad, which he had bought: female
brokers dealt with the poor, and aristocrats hid their sales activity behind
a passion for fashion and collecting. The nobleman Dorat is an example
of the activity that Mercier describes as "business" (*affaires*). He is frequently present in the jewellers account books, and Aubourg constantly
entrusted sapphires, rubies, solitaires, rings, earrings, and watches to him
for days at a time, jewellery that had a value of up to 2,000 or 3,000
livres per item, On the other hand, this same Dorat would take three
months to pay for a walking stick with a golden apple handle worth 150
livres. A small-timer who handled a lot of business! Thus, these jewels
circulated in a market rich in intermediaries, each of whom took his or
her commission at every transaction.

Therefore, this economy touched directly, or via intermediaries, every
level of Paris society. All over the city there are indications of occasional
dealers who sold him jewellery or watches, even a glazier who sold silver
cutlery. These occasional vendors, such as a wood and a salt merchant
or a hair dresser, were individuals who needed money and who bought
and sold watches and jewellery depending on their income and financial
needs. For the most part, these people of modest means came only once
to Aubourg; others such as the Marquise Dez de Courtaumont sold a
lot to him over several months: during an eleven-month period between
1774 and 1775, for unknown financial reasons, she divested herself of
more than 23,000 livres of extremely valuable jewellery.

Moreover, snuffboxes, rings and watches were for sale at all prices:
in Aubourg's account books, snuffboxes sold from 3 to 320 livres, rings
from 3 to 5,600 livres, and watches from 12 to 3,300 livres. A female
broker bought the least expensive rings; as to watches, the purchaser
of the one for 12 livres is unknown, but the poor-quality silver watch

for 24 livres – the lowest price for whom the purchaser is known – was also bought by a female broker. Judging from the purchase price and the price for which items were sold, the jeweller made for himself enormous profit: a gold-plated bronze watch bought for 30 livres on 3 June 1774, was resold on 6 June for 72 livres (more than double!). Other examples show at least 30 per cent profit: a plain gold watch from Geneva of poor quality bought for 57 livres was resold for 96 livres; a poor-quality gold watch from Geneva went from 72 to 114 livres; a quite old gold watch from Paris from 98 to 114 livres; and a "gilded double lidded box, gold watch the colour of Paris" allowed the broker to double his price as he bought it for 216 livres and sold it for 432 livres; finally, the most expensive item, a "speckled green enameled gold watch adorned with pink and ruby" brought a profit of 400 livres, going from 1,200 to 1,600 livres. Maybe these articles which he describes as "random, old, poor quality or bad" were perhaps not so!

Aubourg recorded his business in four books: purchases, sales, items given on condition "donnés à condition," and credit because he listed credit separately as he saw his business as a lender as an activity in its own right. The amounts loaned ranged from 6 to 4,800 livres: he lent to his suppliers; he held the accounts of certain clients and received their money on deposit. He handled many different financial instruments: different notes, letters of exchange, bonds, and even, six months after the establishing of the official pawnshop, the tickets of the said shop; he himself was very little involved in the business of pawnbroking, preferring to buy outright at low prices. He was especially involved in short-term lending at a rate of 10 per cent: he would lend for a few days or weeks, whereupon, the wheel seemed to have turned and the debts became non recoverable.

Pawnshops were the only institution capable of fighting against the financial practices of intermediaries such as Aubourg who depended on the need for short-term loans. In fact, one year after the founding of the Paris pawnshop on 7 December 1777, Aubourg's business fell into decline: it took only this much time for the pawnshop to become powerful. The jeweller's bankruptcy testifies, as we shall see later in Chapter 6, to the meteoric success of the lending institution to which the jeweller's clients were quick to turn.

The proliferation of pawnshops can be explained by the fact that to start a trade, the initial investment required was very low. In England, in 1747, the author of a commerce book declared that only 500 pounds were required to set up a pawnshop and, in 1761, another book indicated that the sum of 1,000 pounds was required as start-up capital.[78] In the middle of the eighteenth century, an English apologist for the trade held that 2,000 pounds was adequate to set up a sound business. However, examples of success with half the initial investment were not uncommon. Yet, prosperity was slow to come and those who started in the trade with insufficient capital thinking they would manage somehow often failed.[79]

For Paris, Mercier talks of robbers' dens in which raged "the greedy passion of rapacious usurers."[80] The Bastille archives reveal some private offices, more often than not owned by merchants, which employed middlemen to scout for clients and make them pay. Many did not give any acknowledgment, argued over the date of maturity, and substituted the bills entrusted, and it was against the backdrop of this criminal economy that philanthropists were in favour of making pawnshops official.

To go by the gossip doing the rounds in Paris, the inhabitants of Auvergne and the Jews were the biggest usurers in the capital. Indeed, a gang of pawnbrokers operating in Paris finds mention in the archives of Clermont.[81] The ringleaders, including one J. Cayron, were said to have owed their success to the fact that they lent to the highest in the kingdom. Accusations of this kind were made repeatedly, and one is very pointed: "J. Cayron the elder lives in the street of Mauvaises-Paroles ... he has an insatiable greed for interest and is known to lend money at extortionate rates." He lent to Du Parc without charging interest, a clever ploy to earn his gratitude, and then "got several wealthy inhabitants of Auvergne lend money on interest, given that Monsieur Du Parc and his wife, desirous of adopting the tone of people of quality ... are obliged to borrow."[82]

Among the goods received in exchange for loans in the working-class milieu, there were no pieces of furniture but clothes and linen, and at best a few paintings or watches, snuffboxes, silver cutlery, copper objects, caldrons, and bowls that Besson could easily circulate among his fellow colleagues. The amounts paid were in the vicinity of 10 to 15 livres and

---

[78] P. Earle, *The Making of the English Middle Class: Business, Society and Family Life in London 1660–1730*, London, 1989, p. 107.

[79] Tebbutt, *Making Ends Meet*, p. 103.

[80] Mercier, *Tableau de Paris*, vol. 1, p. 662, "Mont-de-piété."

[81] Françoise Raison-Jourde, *La Colonie auvergnate de Paris au XIXe siècle*, Ville de Paris Commission des travaux historiques XIV, Paris, 1976, pp. 115–6. AD Puy de Dôme, C 3283, packet of letters.

[82] Archives de la Seine, D5 B6 4707, account book of the secondhand dealer Besson whose shop was located in 1771 in the fifth arrondissement, cited by Raison-Jourde, *La Colonie auvergnate*, pp. 114–6.

the clientele came from the sixth and fifth arrondissements. Besson dealt mainly with servants, doorwomen, dressmakers, laundrywomen, and milliners and, among the men, with water carriers, printers and cobblers. The frequent entry "withdrawn" added later in a special column along with the signature of the client show that he was indeed a pawnbroker. Obviously, the sums returned were never indicated, but the objects seem to have been taken back fairly quickly, within less than a year.[83]

Of all the merchants who engaged in pawnbroking, jewellers were the best placed to do so: they were discrete in their dealings and quick to make an estimate. They were less expensive and lent between 50 and 80 per cent of the value of the object pawned to people known to them and whom they trusted. The clothes trade, of course, attracted all these circuits of usury. The link between secondhand clothes dealers and pawnbroking was an organic one all over Europe in the modern era. Secondhand clothes dealers and resellers of both sexes were at the heart of the urban circulation of clothes. The Jews and the Irish were known for their lending houses because they were very involved in the sale of secondhand clothes, and many illicit lenders hid behind secondhand clothes shops so much so that the black wooden doll used in England as the sign for secondhand clothes dealers became the nickname for informal pawnshops called "dolly-shop."[84] Alehouses were also known for their links with lenders: they did not give credit but accepted securities, directing clients to the neighbouring lender who would pay them for services rendered; in England alehouse owners had a long history of lending to their clients.[85] In fact, many lenders did not have any outward sign of their activity; instead, they advertised their business by indicating that they could be found next to such-and-such well-known tavern.[86]

Because these trades were for the most part clandestine, it was only by chance that some houses emerged from the shadows. We are sufficiently

[83] Raison-Jourde, *La Colonie auvergnate*, pp. 114–6.

[84] Tebbut, *Making Ends Meet*, p. 123.

[85] An anonymous bill of 1678 condemned their daily usury: "There is yet another Pack of the charitable Vermin that make it / their Business to lend Money by the Week. This crafty / Extortioner commonly keeps a blind Ale-house, and you must / first, besides a World of Compliments, spend two or three / schillings at several Times, before he be at pleasure, or money / comes in, or that you can persuade him to like your security; at / least you get but eighteen shillings for every twenty shillings; / but must give bond, (and him Twelve-pence for making it), to / repay full twenty shillings at two shillings per week. Quoted by Tebbutt, *Making Ends Meet*, p. 112.

[86] Tebbutt, *Making Ends Meet*, pp. 112–13.

well informed about such informal finance in the case of England.[87] Besides, several lenders' account books have come down to us such as those of John Pope for the years 1666 to 1671. He was an ironmonger in a South London quarter who also sold cloth and accessories and was at the same time a well-known pawnbroker. His books inform us about 440 credit transactions that took place for the most part in 1669. The clients came from two major groups. The first comprised very small operations by craftspeople, broom and string makers, tailors, weavers, and various trades associated with construction and services. The second major group comprised women without a profession whose names were recorded in the books along with the name of their husbands.[88] Pope's books allow us to reconstruct with precision such financial circuits: he indicated the amount, the period, and gave information about partners and guarantees. The payment schedules that he presented show that his clients paid him back with payments of 6 pence to a few shillings per week for durations of ten to twenty weeks. Between men and women, differences in respect to the amount and the construction of the relationship of trust can be found. Thus, more women than men had to furnish guarantees for loans fewer than 2 pounds, and 86 per cent of the women borrowed fewer than 2 pounds compared to 73 per cent of the men.

The initial contact was made through sponsors. The analysis of the loans given by John Pope displays a clear trend towards sponsorship within the professional activity. Men and women were the first link, and once the newcomers became known, they borrowed directly.[89] Kinship, trade, and neighbourhood ties were the links and the main security in such neighbourhood credit.[90] The cost of such loans was not mentioned

[87] Beverly Lemire, "Peddling Fashion: Salesmen, Pawnbrokers, Taylors, Thieves and the Second-Hand Clothes Trade in England, c. 1700–1800," *Textile History*, 22, no. 1, 1991, pp. 67–82; Beverly Lemire, *Dress, Culture and Commerce: The English Clothing Trade before the Factory, 1660–1800*, London, Macmillan, 1997; J. Boulton, *Neighbourhood and Society: A London Suburb in the Seventeenth Century*, Cambridge, 1987, pp. 88–90. Beverly Lemire "Petty Pawns and Informal Lending: Gender and the Transformation of Small-Scale Credit in England, Circa 1600–1800," *From Family Firms to Corporate Capitalism: Essay in Business and Industrial History in Honour of Peter Mathias*, Kristine Bruland and Patrick O'Brien, eds., Oxford, Clarendon Press, 1998, pp. 112–38. Margaret Hunt, "Women, Credit and the Seafaring Community in Early Eighteenth-Century," presented at the session C 59, "Women and the Practices of Credit (17th to 19th Centuries)," M. Berg, L. Fontaine, and C. Muldrew, coordinators, of the 12th International Congress of Economic History, Seville, 1998.

[88] Lemire "Petty Pawns."

[89] Ibid.

[90] R. Tittler, "Money-Lending in the West Midlands: The Activities of Joyce Jefferies, 1638–49," *Historical Research* 47, 1994, pp. 256–260.

in the account books.[91] Undoubtedly, as was often the custom, interest was added to the principal to be repaid or to the price of the goods sold. In the debate on the regulation of pawnbroking, fierce criticism was levelled against the practices of the lenders who "prosper like cancer" and who were of both sexes. The petition criticized them for taking securities worth three or four times the value of the money lent and lending at rates, which amounted to about 60 per cent per annum. They forced the poor borrowers to exceed their time limits in order to make them pay one or even two months of interest for a delay of a few days. Most of the time, they did not lend money but goods that the borrower had to make do with, and obviously, they had a gift for losing securities and working with a whole host of intermediaries among whom the objects pawned circulated and vanished into thin air.[92]

Philip Henslowe was another London lender; 278 loan deeds for his activity over a period of fourteen months from 1594 to 1595 were found.[93] Only a quarter of Henslowe's loans were against securities; the remaining loans fell within a network of social surety, a sign of the strength of the economy of obligation in the sixteenth century, so aptly described by Craig Muldrew. An English petition acquaints with another such lender who came after John Pope: Richard Grainger, a large pawnbroker who, in 1745 on Ladyday, granted 328 loans of an average value of 3 shillings.[94]

The hierarchy of lending houses followed that of the towns with the largest lenders doing business in the capital cities. In England, the richest were established in London where they quickly grouped together into a society to protect the trade. Right from the eighteenth century, they were accused of elitism, of keeping aloof from other trades and of associating only among themselves in clubs. The oldest of these societies was the Bouverie Society, but most of these trade associations go back to the 1810s.[95]

The picture is no different for Italy, and in the sixteenth century, Jewish and Lombard bankers rubbed shoulders with a wide variety of lenders

---

[91] Lemire "Petty Pawns."

[92] British Library, I-816 m. 13 (2 n. 84), Great Mischiefs Daily Arising by the Common Practice of Pawn-Brokers and their Accomplices in and about the City of London ... s.d. (end 17th). I thank Caroline Fontaine for acquainting me with this document.

[93] Boulton, *Neighbourhood and Society,* pp. 88–9.

[94] Lemire "Petty Pawns."

[95] Tebbutt, *Making Ends Meet*, p. 103.

and intermediaries who in general relied on a trading activity.[96] In Siena in the first half of the sixteenth century, the inventories after death have kept a record of such activities. Two modes of operating have come to light: on one hand, artisans and shopkeepers who displayed their ownership of luxury goods disproportionate in respect to their income and status. This disproportion testifies to the circulation of these goods and their role as instruments of saving when the artisans, who received them by way of payment, either kept or bought them. On the other hand, the inventories of artisans and small merchants include, in nearly one out of two cases, mention of the objects that they held as security. Two categories of merchants can be seen depending on the number of objects left as security: most gave the occasional loan. They had only a few rings or small jewels left as payment before being bought back by their owners. But then there were the real professionals who lent against security on a large scale. They were mainly innkeepers and secondhand clothes dealers. Thus, an innkeeper had 156 pawned objects in his house, along with cash kept in a chest, and a secondhand clothes dealer who had only kept 60 such objects, but his house was full of furniture, objects, and fine lace that came undoubtedly from his activities as a lender.[97] During the same period in Piedmont, accusations against usurers spoke of interest between 20 to 50 per cent per annum and complained that the intermediaries, omnipresent in such transactions, were increasing further the cost of credit. These intermediaries were an indispensable front for aristocratic lenders. They also helped find clients or lenders and later recover the money lent.[98]

An Activity Difficult to Regulate

Identifying and regulating this proliferation of pawnbroking agencies was a permanent concern of governments. Usurious rates of interest for the poor and pawning of stolen goods were the main items in the discussions on informal pawnshops.[99] In 1770, a memorandum drawn up on the order of Sartine at the request of Marie-Thérèse admitted: that

---

[96] Allegra, *La città verticale*, p. 14, 31.
[97] Paula Hohti, "Artisans, Pawn-Broking and the Circulation of Metal Goods in Sixteenth-Century Sienna," *Siena nel Rinascimento: l'ultimo secolo della Republica*, Parte I: *Le Arti a Siena nel Rinascimento*, Florence, Edizioni Cadmo, 2006, pp. 1–11.
[98] Allegra, *La città verticale*," pp. 28, 36–8.
[99] Lemire "Petty Pawns."

"given the difficulty of abolishing moneylenders is as great as preventing those in need from going to them, we considered that conditional tolerance was the sole and best course of action possible."[100]

The position of the street lender was in fact ambivalent. He lived off the despair of the small operations by craftspeople, traders, and women who sought to eke out their daily existence. But since he was necessary for the day to day life of the locality, he was, in spite of all this, the recipient of the community's gratitude. But, on other hand, he was the bête noire of philanthropists. Turgot defended them in his Mémoire *sur les prêts d'argent*. Although he shows that the highest rates of interest were charged on small loans, he also adds that clients didn't complain, for thanks to them, they could ply a trade and live off it:

> Do we not know that there are usuries we are obliged to tolerate. There is perhaps none any sharper than the one known in Paris by the name of week loan and at times it went up to 2 sous a week for an ecu of 3 livres: it is on the foot of 173 and one-third for 100. Nonetheless, it is this truly enormous usury that makes run the retail trade of the foodstuff sold in the markets of Paris. The borrowers do not complain about the terms of this loan, without which they would not be able to ply their trade to earn a living, and the lenders do not get much richer because this exorbitant interest is but the compensation for the risk the capital runs. Indeed, the insolvency of a single borrower wipes out all the profit the lender can make on thirty; such that if the risk of unfaithfulness or insolvency of the borrower was one on thirty, the lender would earn no interest on his money, and were the risk greater, he would lose the principal.[101]

Louis Sébastien Mercier shows that to insure themselves against this risk, lenders asked the women from the market a joint guarantee, and Turgot stresses the fact that thanks to these loans, small merchants were able to make a living and were "far from complaining about the lenders" and that for this reason, the "police and the public prosecution left them well alone."

In England, private pawnshops, but recognized officially, sought to contain the proliferation of financial circuits that escaped all regulation and asked Parliament to check them. As opposed to these clandestine practices, they emphasized their morality, and the fact that they had served an apprenticeship before becoming masters and that they were not exercising any other profession concurrently. They underlined their

---

[100] Commissaire Le Maire, "La police de Paris en 1770," Paris, Mémoires Soc. Histoire de Paris, 1879, quoted by Bigo, "Aux origines," pp. 113–126, (114).
[101] Turgot, *Mémoire sur les prêts d'argent*, Schelle, 1770, vol. 3, p. 116.

honesty when compared to the informal sector of certain merchants among whom were many gin and candle sellers.[102] Periodically, some members of Parliament would express concern and demand that those trading in money be registered.[103] In 1745, the parliamentary commission proposed the imposition of a licence for 40 shillings annually and to admit in these trades (pawnbroker, broker, secondhand clothes dealer) only such individuals who had a shop and to exclude those who worked from a room or in carriage entrances, in order to fight against all informal, marginal, and part-time forms of lending. Except for the prohibition of accepting securities against spirits liable to a fine of 40 shillings, hardly any of the recommendations had the force of law. However, the trade was progressively regulated and, in the second half of the eighteenth century, interest could not exceed 10 per cent.[104] Cases filed by women who had been charged a very high rate of interest attest to the progressive regulation of the activity in the eighteenth century.[105]

The question of the ownership of the goods pawned was the leitmotiv of legislations intended to prohibit or regulate the activity. It was about fighting against the highly informal nature of practices that helped conceal stolen objects: hardly any receipts were issued. The links between peddlers and secondhand clothes dealers were also criticized, for clothes were the objects the most frequently pawned and stolen. The first Act Against Brokers of 1603 attempted to curb the malpractices of the trade, targeting hundreds of small traffickers who bought, sold, and took as security basic family objects. The law sought to impose the maintaining of registers, but the idea was highly unpopular as it would compromise the reputation of the elite who were obliged as well to take recourse to brokers in order to put together the dowry of a daughter or overcome temporary difficulties.

The contradiction between protecting the rights of those who needed to pawn their property and regulating the dubious origin of goods made legislation impossible and were hardly ever enforced. Fraud was at the centre of all legislation until 1757 when one of the first Acts also dealt with the question of regulating the relationship between lender and borrower. However, there was no reference to the rate of interest. The lender held responsibility for objects pawned worth more than 10 pounds for

[102] Lemire, "Petty Pawns."
[103] In 1661, a "Register sales and Pawns made to retailing Brokers in London and Westminster and places adjacent" was established.
[104] Tebbutt, *Making Ends Meet*, pp. 70–3, 112.
[105] Hunt, "Women, Credit and the Seafaring Community."

two years. Clients could claim the profits on the sale of their goods once the charges had been paid and could, on payment of a denier, inspect the sales books to regulate the price. Although such registers recorded only goods more than 2 pounds, these legislations were a first step towards protecting the small borrowers.[106]

In 1750, the "Tipping Act" imposed a 40-shilling fine on accepting a pawn in payment for spirits and the loss of the object; however, the offense was always difficult to prove. In 1784, an attempt was made to regulate interest on loans less than 10 pounds. A commission of half a d per month was introduced for sums up to 2 shillings 6 d and on each 2 shilling 6 d up to 10 pounds, amounting to an annual rate of 20 per cent. Making a copy of the transaction became obligatory, and the lender had to account for the sale of objects of more than 10 shillings, the buyback period being reduced to one year. The following year, all pawnbrokers had to get themselves registered on payment of 10 pounds in London and Edinburgh and 5 pounds elsewhere. Other acts were passed, one of which reduced the interest to 15 per cent per annum in 1789, and all these measures were put together in the Pawnbrokers' Act of 1800, which governed the trade during most of the nineteenth century. The act made it obligatory to maintain accurate books and to issue duplicate copies. Pawnbrokers' interest was fixed at 20 per cent per annum for all sums less than 42 shillings and 15 per cent for all loans more than this. For sums greater than 10 pounds, the period and interest were mentioned in a written agreement signed by the lender and the borrower. This was all very well in theory, but in reality, loans were never given for such long periods, and the custom was to charge 0.5 d per 2 shillings 6 d whatever be the duration.[107]

However, being far too complex to implement and ill suited to the practical realities of the trade, the act failed to make the profession more ethical. As such, the fixed interest rate did not correspond to any known unit of measurement and resulted in impracticable fractions whenever it was a question of calculating intermediary amounts. The interest tables that should have been available to everyone were not always so, not to speak of the fact that only a few were capable of reading and understanding them. Similar problems cropped up in the calculation of the period for which the article had been pawned. Although the theoretical annual rate was 20 per cent, a deposit at 6 d claimed the same day

---

[106] Tebbutt, *Making Ends Meet*, pp. 70, 74.
[107] Ibid., pp. 8–13, 74–5, and 112–13.

meant 3,000 per cent! In fact, the smaller the loan, the higher the interest, and it was precisely the poor who borrowed miniscule amounts for very short periods. Asking for the name and address of clients was also not always possible. In any case, because clients were ignorant or incapable of asserting their rights, the new act advocated a strategy of denunciation and rewarded possible informers, giving them half of the fine paid by the lender if accused of any wrongdoing.[108]

The various rules and regulations were intended to control the trade and keep out informal usurers. But to be profitable, small loans had to have a quick turnover and be large in number, for the costs were the same irrespective of the length of the deposit. Consequently, many pawnbrokers, especially in London, declined to give very small loans, and the poorest were left with no choice but to put themselves in the hands of unlicensed lenders to obtain minuscule loans that were only profitable at an illegal rate of interest. Besides, what the poorest had to pawn would not have been accepted by the larger agencies. The illicit sector thus continued to flourish in the shadow of the recognized profession, and in 1798 in London, it was estimated to be as large as the official pawnshops – about 400 houses.[109]

Regardless of the weaknesses presented by the monetary circulation, the world of pawnbroking refers to economic behaviour that betrays a desire not to save in the form of cash. This preference for illiquidity – highlighted by anthropologists in the countries in the south – is the expression of the wish to curb the urge to spend. It also a reveals a strategy for not lending to one's entourage in a cultural system in which such refusal is viewed unfavourably, as we have seen in the previous chapters. The preference for illiquidity may even have been a response to the monetary manipulations and the royal privilege of striking money. But here there is a form of saving that needs to be considered in itself. This was in the shape of metals, precious objects, or marketable goods. These goods that were bought and sold easily and that were pawned if need be also served as currency. In view of all this, it is easy to understand why pawnbroking was the financial instrument favoured by the urban poor; their precarious existence and income insecurity obliged them to live in a random economy that dealt only with the moment.

But these financial micro circuits have always been viewed very poorly. Philanthropists have condemned in their time the usurious loans of this

---

[108] Ibid., pp. 90–2.
[109] Ibid., pp. 13, 121–3.

small, urban economy, and many sociologists followed in their foot-steps.[110] Perhaps we need to nuance this wholesale condemnation by tak-ing into account the services rendered by this economy. On one hand, it helped some avoid the worst by providing them the means to tide them over. On the other, we must not forget that many of these loans were for a very short time, which skewed the calculation of annual interest. This short-term economy allowed for the existence of a large number of tiny entrepreneurs who borrowed in the morning to buy a few goods that they would sell or raw materials, which they would transform and pay back in the evening with the profit they earned. To them, as Turgot emphasizes, what mattered was not that they borrowed at high rates but that, thanks to such loans and despite these rates, they succeeded in making a profit: for them, the only thing that counted was the return on money. Usury on a weekly basis was thus – and still remains – an important element in the survival strategy of the low-income city dwellers.

[110] Clifford Geertz believes it to be static and archaic "The Rotating Credit Association: A 'Middle Rung' in Development," *Economic Development and Cultural Change*, 10, 1962, pp. 69–89.

5

Women's Economic Spheres and Credit

He then goes to an out-of-the-way house, to a room where there is only one bad tapestry, a pallet, three chairs and a crucifix. There he grants an audience to sixty fish sellers, street hawkers and fruit sellers. Then he speaks to them in a solemn voice: "My friends, as you can see, I am not better off than you; here is my furniture, here is the bed I lie on when I come to Paris; I give you my money and rely on your conscience and religion; as from you I have no signature, you know, I can ask nothing of the law. I am useful for your trade; and when I lavish my trust, I must have my surety. So be all of you jointly liable, and swear in front of this crucifix, the image of our divine Saviour, that you shall do me no wrong, and that you shall faithfully return to me that what I shall entrust to you.

– Louis Sébastien Mercier, *Tableau de Paris*, chap. CCXIX,
"Prêteurs à la petite semaine"

To link together the multiple feminine figures encountered in towns and villages, lenders, borrowers and intermediaries, and understand the multiplicity of relationships among women, debt, credit, and financial circuits, we need to examine those economic spheres acknowledged as the preserve of women. Their capacity to make use of time and money, in other words credit, depended thus on a complex set of equations between social institutions and roles, their cultural construction, and the authorities that regulated and defined the place of women and their access to resources, be it land, labour, or capital. In Europe, such equations varied greatly. Before going any further, it must be emphasized that to benefit fully from the interplay of time and money, money was required. Having money meant not only earning or receiving it, but also having the freedom to spend it as one wished or give it away. In other words, it meant managing it freely, and hence being able to enter into legally binding arrangements; it also meant being able to safeguard it. In a period when private and public were largely interdependent and when economic success was dependent on the prince who bestowed economic privileges, trading rights, and monopolies, the ability to play a role in politics was essential for building up, holding onto, and consolidating wealth. To understand the relationships women maintained with credit it is necessary to explore the wide range of legal capacities that defined women's autonomy and finally determined what a woman's word and a woman's honour were.

I would like to stress the relationship between the rights of women in Europe and the economic spheres which they created and to emphasize three distinct cleavages which gave rise to change: the linking of the law to a woman's life cycle, the development of the market, and the migration of men. After this, one can better understand why women were omnipresent as financial intermediaries and merchants and ask questions relating to the existence of specifically female financial practices and economic cultures.

The Law and Women's Economic Activities

The three principal branches of law to be found in Europe were far from being internally consistent. Germanic laws varied: Saxon, Burgundian, Visigoth, and Frankish law; canon law was a juxtaposition of elements, many of them contradictory, because it reflected the history and the ambivalence of the church, always torn between the desire to see both sexes as equal and the determination to subjugate women.[1] Law, despite its "a-historical" appearance and like all social activities, is a product of the play of power and contradictory perceptions that cut across society. For instance, France in the modern era had a tendency to remain rigorously attached to keeping women under close domination, a rationalist current that proclaimed equality of rights and a current driven by the royal legislator who, in day-to-day management, adjusted the law so that the woman's position hinged on the goods of the family and those of the state.[2]

---

[1] René Metz, "Le statut de la femme en droit canonique médiéval," *La Femme. Recueils de la société Jean Bodin*, Bruxelles, Éditions de la librairie encyclopédique, 1962, XII, pp. 59–113 (59).

[2] Jean Portemer, "La femme dans la législation royale aux XVIIe et XVIIIe siècles," *Mélanges Petot*, Paris, Montchrestien, Dalloz, Sirey, 1958, p. 441. The conditions were such that they led to changes in the law. An example from the Paris basin bears this out.

This was to satisfy the royal will to assert itself against the power of feudal clienteles and the church. In other words, law is also something that is practiced, that draws on complex and contradictory bodies of work, and that thus allows a certain latitude to lawyers and judges to interpret it.

In this way, the rights of women progressed, receiving an indirect fillip from other battles being fought, such as the affirmation of the State through the royal judges and the battle of Parliament when women, excluded from the crown by Salic law, became regents thrice in less than a century. The first time was with Catherine de Médici through the application of old principles; the second, in 1610, following an audacious move by the Parliament of Paris that used this fact to assert its prerogatives with respect to the crown; and the third, with Anne of Austria who, on the death of Louis XIII, obtained from the Parliament of Paris the annulment of the king's testament and the regency of the kingdom until such time as Louis XIV was a minor. In the contemporary period, it may be pointed out that the wage increment for women after the Second World War came about through men who sought to protect their own income and who feared the social dumping of badly paid female employment.

Three main tendencies are apparent within this diversity.

Life Cycle

The first followed the life cycle and separated married women from unmarried women and from women who were no longer married. Everything – notarial records, the wording of rulings, memoirs, plays, and novels – proves that this tradition of placing married women in a position of dependency grew stronger in the early modern period, starting in the sixteenth century. Between the sixteenth and eighteenth centuries, women's legal incapacity became progressively more widespread, but, in return, their financial interests came to be more protected everywhere.[3]

In sixteenth-century France, a debate began on personal properties. The debate intensified as more and more dowries were given in money, a trend that necessitated the redefinition of the notion of immovable goods so that the money given in dowry, movable according to earlier definitions, could be included in it. It was for this reason that the debate shifted from movable and immovable property to the more controversial notions of spouse's separate and after-acquired property. This gave rise to two conflicting interpretations, one favouring lineage and the other the couple; the first considered that reuse was tacitly understood; the second, favouring the new household and the husband to the detriment of the wife's lineage interests, considered that the choice should be left to the individuals.

[3] John Gilissen, "Le statut de la femme dans l'ancien droit belge," *La Femme, Recueils de la société Jean Bodin*, pp. 255–321 (255–6).

In northern France, Belgium, the Netherlands, and Germany, a married woman was *"une incapable,"* and both she and her property came under her husband's authority. In France, a married woman could not go to court in any civil or criminal matter except with a prosecutor and the authorization of either her husband or a legal authority; though she could be called upon as a witness, she could not be a witness to any legally binding contract. She was allowed to have her own separate property, but her husband managed it and received income from it as though it were his own. He was not allowed to sell it, use it as collateral, divide it, or initiate any legal action involving it without his wife's consent.[4] From the sixteenth century onwards, married women benefitted from an increased protection of their pecuniary interests, and in the seventeenth century, jurisprudence introduced the *hypothèque légale* or legal claim in favour of the wife, which was a characteristic of regions of written law, and applied it to the husband's real property and to jointly owned property, but the woman could legitimately relinquish her claim. The new provisions prompted persons who had dealings with the husband with respect to a spouse's separate or after-acquired property to take the precaution of asking the wife to relinquish her legal claim on the good in question. As such and despite their incapacity, married women strengthened their control over the disposal of assets by their husband.[5] If, during the marriage, the woman feared her husband's financial ruin, she could ask for the division of property *(séparation des biens,* which came from Roman law). She thus regained the administration and use of her estate, disposed of her movables as she pleased, but she required the permission of her husband or that of the law, to dispose of her immovable property. Conversely, she remained in a less advantageous position in the modern era than at the end of the Middle Ages when she regained the free disposal of her estate.[6] However, until the end of the eighteenth century, certain customs, such as those obtained in Normandy, which favoured lineage, remained extremely restrictive for women kept under strict marital authority and did not allow them to accede to their full estate till after the death of their husband when, as favoured

---

[4] Portemer, "La femme," pp. 465, 460, 454–5. Pierre Petot, "Le statut de la femme dans les pays coutumiers français du XIIIe au XVIIe siècle," *La Femme, Recueils de la société Jean Bodin,* pp. 243–254 (252).

[5] Petot, "Le statut de la femme," p. 251.

[6] Portemer, "La femme," p. 462. Petot, "Le statut de la femme," p. 247.

creditors, they took back their dower, even paternal property, be it to the detriment of their children.[7]

Catalan jurisprudence in the modern era was very similar: it limited the access of women to the transmission of property, and they could not go to court or file a case without the permission and support of their husbands. In fact, both secular and ecclesiastical discourse subordinated women to men, be they their husband, brother, or father.[8]

Germanic women were subjected to *mundium* or permanent guardianship. They were thus incapable, such as minors, to alienate, administer, or go to court without the consent of their father, husband, or curator.[9] The power to ask for the division of property was denied to them by numerous customs of the Germanic sphere.[10]

The various Italian regions were divided between the mixed influences of Roman, canon, and Germanic law. Despite the equality within the family proclaimed in principle by Christianity,[11] the Lombard invasion brought with it – as happens in all military societies – conditions that were even more restrictive for women. As they were not able to bear arms – a fundamental prerequisite for the status of legal subject – Lombard women were placed under the permanent guardianship of their father, relatives, husband, or, failing these, of the king, the ultimate guardian. The system of the personality of laws, which allowed the juxtaposition of various rights on the same territory with different professionals, placed the Lombard women along with the Roman women in a significantly inferior position. When the law was unified in the Middle Ages, whereas

[7] Jean-Claude Perrot, *Genèse d'une ville moderne Caen au XVIIIe siècle*, vol. 2, Paris, Mouton, 1975, p. 245.
[8] Montserrat Carbonell i Esteller, *Sobreviure a Barcelona. Dones, pobresa i assistència al segle XVIII*, Barcelona, Eumo Editorial, 1997, pp. 120–21.
[9] In 1820, this guardianship was abolished in the Rhenish regions. David W. Sabean, *Property, Production, and Family in Neckarhausen, 1700–1870*, Cambridge, Cambridge University Press, 1990, p. 26.
[10] *Frauen in der Geschichte des Rechts. Von der Frühen Neuzeit bis zur Gegenwart*, Ute Gerhard, ed., Munich, Verlag C. H. Beck, 1997.
[11] Christianity imposed on all members of the family certain duties towards one another, recognizing in marriage "a divine and indissoluble institution" and attributing to the father and to the mother reciprocal rights, shared duties, and equal authority over the children. However, increasingly this equality was considered as pertaining to spiritual and moral status rather than on a practical level: Christian asceticism, which glorified celibacy; the tradition that placed women under the guardianship of men; and descriptions of woman that emphasized her physiological and psychological weakness explain why, despite the proclaimed equality, women were only allowed "limited legal responsibility." Cf. Guido Rossi, "Statut juridique de femme dans l'histoire du droit italien. époque médiévale et moderne," *La Femme, Recueils de la société Jean Bodin*, pp. 115–34.

the Lombard women gained in autonomy, the Roman women lost out. As the various elements of Roman, church, and Germanic law converged, overlapped and merged in the Middle Ages, the trend was for these prejudices and restrictions to continue.[12]

In those territories exempt from Germanic law, such as Rome, Venice, and Ravenna, women could engage in any legal action when they attained their majority. Yet here too the trend was to restrict women's autonomy. One of the first changes arose from the need for communes and families to control the circulation of capital. Women's freedom was restricted so as to prevent them taking their wealth elsewhere if they married outsiders. A second development was the strict reinforcement of lineage. A husband's permission was not always enough, and the consent of the relatives in charge of the family group might be required in a case of the alienation of a patrimony. In the same way, a woman's right to be the beneficiary of a will was limited, just as she herself was often obliged to draw up her own will according to the wishes of her protectors. This situation, which was sometimes imposed even when the law allowed otherwise,[13] persisted in several regions of Italy to the end of the ancien régime.[14] But in places where Roman ideas remained strong, it was not unusual, especially in merchant circles, for women to have personal wealth not derived from their dowry, which they could dispose of as they saw fit, even though normally its administration would be their husband's responsibility.

In Italy as in France, although men had the right to administer and invest the dowry, they could not alienate the property and were required to return to their wives the equivalent of the movable assets; for that purpose, they could mortgage their own property with the husband's kin also being also held responsible.[15] But the dowry could be invested in family businesses, either of the family of origin or of the husband with the wife receiving only the income it generated. In any case, the legal

[12] Ibid., p. 117.
[13] In some Italian regions, where in law the woman was free *sui iuris* in accordance with Roman principles, in practice, she could not bind herself without the presence of a man, husband, guardian, prosecutor, or judge. Rossi, "Statut juridique de la femme," pp. 125–6.
[14] Ibid., p. 122.
[15] F. Ercole, "L'instituto dotale nella pratica et nella legislazione statuaria dell'Italia superiore," *Rivista italiana per les Scienze Giuridiche*, 45, 1909, pp. 191–302; 46, 1910, pp. 167–257 both are connected in the volume dated 1908. On the rights of husbands and their limitations, see 46, pp. 167–182, 222–223, 246.

incapacity of women was useful in protecting their separate property from the community creditors.[16]

Only in England was the trend in the opposite direction. Common law was undeniably one of the strictest in Europe, prohibiting the married woman from owning anything (all that she owned, including her moveable goods, was given to her husband who, in exchange, settled her debts), from entering into any contract, and, of course, from making a will. It was not until the sixteenth century and the development of the concept of equity law (which had begun, hesitantly, to make an appearance in the ambit of the chancery in the fourteenth century) that the severity of common law was mitigated. Secular Lords Chancellor, such as Francis Bacon (1561–1621), succeeded in extending women's legal capacities. They introduced the system of trusts, which meant that a woman handed over all that she owned to trustees – in most cases professionals – through whose mediation she had use of her property and could sell, give, bequeath, or otherwise dispose of it as she saw fit. Moreover, the Court of Chancery imposed the famous "settlements" on recalcitrant husbands, whereby a woman was assured of the equivalent of a dowery and income in keeping with her social standing during her lifetime. In the matter of property reserved for her in this way, the married woman had the legal rights of a single woman.[17]

These changes in the rights of married women corresponded to the increasingly categorical assertion that the role of women was in the private sphere. However, although this reinforced the guardianship of husbands, paradoxically it also opened spheres of freedom for women by reshaping their economic roles. In effect, women's primary task was to find a way to match irregular income with the daily need to feed the family. So she could provide for her family, in several regions of customary law as in Belgium, the married woman had the right to make contracts and incur debts for the needs of the household such as food, clothing, and so on, and in the seventeenth century, it seemed that this was never explicitly stated, it was accepted.[18] In the northern Netherlands, married women even had the right to enter into a contract

[16] Renata Ago, "Ruoli familiari e statuto giuridico," *Quaderni Storici*, 88, no. 1, 1995, pp. 111–33.

[17] F. Joüon des Longrais, "Le statut de la femme en Angleterre dans le droit commun médiéval," *La Femme, Recueils de la société Jean Bodin*, pp. 135–241 (145–6).

[18] Gilissen, "Le statut de la femme," p. 299.

and incur debt for household needs, independently of the control of her husband.[19]

A central concern nowadays,[20] but one about which historical documents have very little to say, is to understand the extent of women's bargaining power within the family and the couple and how income was brought in and parcelled out within the family. We know very little about everyday money management in the early modern era, although the law allows us certain glimpses. A few letters from the wives of the nobility of Toulouse reveal the ambiguous attitude of women towards the expenses of their husbands: they took the liberty of advising them but stole their information. Thus, in a letter dated January 1745, Mme de Bonrepos explained to her husband M. de Riquet that she knew of his intention to borrow in town, for she had intercepted the letter he had sent to a certain M. Saget, adding that if he was in need of money, she could get it for him at a cheaper rate from her friends.[21] For the working class, English studies show that the refusal to talk about income and money matters was a predominant feature of the relationship between husbands and wives. Neither did the wives know what their husband's total salary was nor did the husbands know how much their wives earned from their additional activities. However, the wife's money was spent in household expenditure, for she had to manage the family budget and feed the family. Melanie Tebbutt points to the contradiction between the economic dependence of wives on their husbands and their financial responsibility to keep the family alive. For this purpose, they borrowed, often at very unfavourable conditions, which only went to reinforce the prejudices against their sex and their incapacity, whereas they were placed in situations in which they were left with hardly any other choice.[22]

On the other hand, one of the consequences of hypothecation, which became widespread in the seventeenth century as a way of protecting married women's rights despite poor management by husbands, was that those who had dealings with the husband, either over property that she owned or over property that was acquired during marriage, now took

---

[19] Jan Willem Bosch, "Le statut de la femme dans les anciens pays-bas Septentrionaux," *La Femme, Recueils de la société Jean Bodin*, pp. 323–50 (334).

[20] Amartya Sen, *Ethique et économie*, Paris, Presses Universitaires de France, 2002 [first English edition 1987], pp. 229–70.

[21] Quoted by Robert Forster, *The Nobility of Toulouse in the Eighteenth Century: A Social and Economic Study*, New York, Octagon Books, 1971, p. 140.

[22] Melanie Tebbutt, *Making Ends meet. Pawnbroking and Working Class Credit*, London, Methuen, 1984, pp. 37–8, 66–7.

the precaution of asking the wife to waive her legal right to the property in question. In consequence, the married woman, despite her legal incapacity, found her control over how her husband disposed of her property strengthened.[23] The protection of the wife's inheritance met with stiff resistance. Husbands fought to benefit from the dowries of their wives, and creditors exerted a great deal of pressure to ensure that their loans were secured against women's dowries. The outcome was that the inalienability of dowry was frequently contravened, for women did not always have the capacity – or the requisite knowledge – to protect it in its entirety.

For the husbands in Florence in the second half of the sixteenth century, in order to pay the fee to be admitted into the Order of the Knights of San Stefano, some nobles obtained from Cosme the use of the dowry money of their wives in disregard of the contract that obliged them to invest it only in municipal properties or debts. Others obtained the same special dispensation to pay their taxes or debts.[24] Everywhere women signed contracts alienating their property to meet the needs of the family or husbands. I hardly ever found a counter to this spoliation except in Catalonia, where the bishop used his power to undo oaths for cancelling contracts of husbands and parents who profited unduly from the money of minors and married women.[25]

As for the creditors, they constantly attempted to have included legally the property of wives as a guarantee for the debts of men, and at the end of the nineteenth century, they finally met with success. In Germany, notaries, innkeepers, merchants, and lawyers – groups that provided the State the bulk of its servants – were also the principal creditors of the peasantry and were unquestionably behind the alterations made between 1825 and 1828 to the law on guarantees, *Pfandgesetz*. These laws allowed the mobilization of properties belonging to the wives to secure the debts of husbands. Previously, a woman could keep her property separate from her husband's business. She could continue to do so, but in this case, the husband could not become Bürgermeister –because henceforth the charge was levied not only on his property but also on that of his wife – and it would be difficult for him to get credit.[26] In

[23] Pierre Petot, "Le statut de la femme," p. 251.
[24] Bresnahan Menning Carol, "Loans and Favors, Kin and Clients: Cosimo de' Medici and the Monte di Pietà," *Journal of Modern History*, no. 61, 1989, pp. 487–511 (499, 501, and 506–7).
[25] Archives of the cathedral town of Barcelona.
[26] Sabean, *Property, Production, and Family*, pp. 47–8, 430.

England, The Married Women's Property Act of 1870 granted only limited property rights to women and did not make them wholly liable for their debts: the husbands had to take responsibility for those arising out of household needs, which gave rise to much litigation with men citing their wives' appetite for luxury to avoid discharging their debts.[27]

Unmarried women, whether of the age of majority or widowed, in northern France, Belgium, the Netherlands, and Germany, were not, in principle, legally incapacitated; however, constraints gradually appeared in these places too. If classical Roman law had gotten rid of the legal guardianship of women,[28] in numerous regions of Germany the practice of *cura sexus* was very much alive.[29] In several customs of Western Europe, Belgium, the Netherlands,[30] and elsewhere, at the time of dissolution of their marriage, women could always relinquish the communal estate to dodge the burden of debt; furthermore, she could avail of the *benefice d'emolument* (limitation of a spouse's liability for the community debts her share of the community's assets). But in Brussels and almost the whole of eastern Flanders, as well as in the nonurban law of western Flanders until the sixteenth century, widows were prohibited from relinquishing joint property. The effects of this relinquishment varied according to the customs. The woman who relinquished was not no longer bound by debts, except her own (but under the full community property regime, there were no personal debts) and those she had expressly contracted during marriage.[31]

Moves in the opposite direction were evident in certain Germanic regions, in particular in the Rhineland, where widows gradually acquired the right to manage the property coming from their dowry and their dower, on their own, only being required to have recourse to a male intermediary (in most cases a professional) in case of

[27] Erika Rappoport, "'A Husband and His Wife's Dresses' Consumer Credit and the Debtor Family in England, 1864–1914," *The Sex of Things, Gender and Consumption in Historical Perspective*, Victoria de Grazia with Ellen Furlough, eds., Berkeley, University of California Press, 1996, pp. 164–87. Amy Louise Erickson, *Women and Property in Early Modern England*, London, Routledge, 1993.

[28] Jean Portemer, "Le statut de la femme en France depuis la Réformation des coutumes jusqu'à la rédaction du code civil," *La Femme, Recueils de la société Jean Bodin*, pp. 447–497 (453). Scarlett Beauvalet-Boutouyrie, *Etre veuve sous l'Ancien Régime*, Paris, Belin, 2001.

[29] *Frauen in der Geschichte des Rechts.*

[30] Bosch, "Le statut de la femme," p. 336.

[31] Gilissen, "Le statut de la femme," pp. 317–8.

dispute or important agreements.[32] Widows were also involved in providing surety.

Finally, in England, widows benefited from a dower provided by the husband, which had to correspond to their social standing as assessed by the legal authorities.[33]

If, broadly speaking, widowhood bestowed freedom on women everywhere, once again we must be cautious. Young widows with their own property were likely to remarry, even against their wishes, and in any case, many preferred to put themselves back under the protection of a man and to enjoy the material support he could provide, for, in too many cases, widowhood meant poverty.[34] Official terminology makes the predominant attitude clear: it ranks widows among the groups characterized by structural poverty, on the same level as orphans, the infirm, and the elderly.

The Market

The second major area of change was the marketplace, and this meant primarily the town. Since the Middle Ages the development of trading everywhere was accompanied by an expansion of women's legal autonomy. For men, running a business had been a way of escaping paternal authority, and for women it also became a reason for acquiring the capacity to enter freely into legally binding agreements.

The rapid expansion of large towns in Flanders, Brabant and the region of Liège from the eleventh and twelfth centuries onwards had created a town law which was codified in the thirteenth century and remained in force until the end of the *ancien régime* and which was very favourable towards women. Town law abolished male privilege in matters of inheritance, bestowed on widows full guardianship of their children, brought property acquired during the marriage into joint ownership, and prevented the man from disposing of the most significant assets without the agreement of his wife. Finally, when a marriage ended, town law allowed

---

[32] Claudia Opitz, "Contraintes et libertés (1250–1500), *Histoire des femmes en Occident t. 2 Le Moyen Age*, Klapisch-Zuber, ed., Paris, Plon, 1991, pp. 278–335 (325). In 1820, this guardianship was abolished in the Rhenan regions. Cf. Sabean, *Property, Production, and Family*, p. 26.

[33] Longrais, "Le statut de la femme en Angleterre dans le droit commun medieval," p. 184.

[34] Scarlett Beauvalais-Boutouyri, *Etre veuve sous l'Ancien Régime*, pp. 311–12; Olwen Hufton, *The Poor in Eighteenth Century France, 1750–1789*, Oxford, Clarendon Press, 1974, pp. 116–7.

the surviving spouse – male or female – to retain either full ownership of all jointly owned property or the use thereof. In addition, a woman had the right to make a will, to spend the household's money and to defend herself in the criminal courts. Naturally, there were subtle differences between established customary law and practices as they evolved, with coastal Flanders, which was more commercial, having the most liberal law, and with eastern Flanders offering an example of how the law evolved in the other direction.[35]

Moreover the legal category of female trader was created. The female trader was usually a woman who "kept shop." She did not need prior permission to do this; it was enough for her to conduct her business in the plain view and knowledge (*au vu et au su*) of her husband. His tacit permission was sufficient, because he had only to exercise his right of counteraction to bring the situation to an end. Thus, within the legal limits applying to her business, she was responsible for all contractual arrangements and all debts. As a consequence of the permission granted to her by her husband to engage in commerce, her property, their jointly owned property, and his property were at stake in her business. A woman trading publicly could be arrested for debt, whereas a married woman could not. If a woman suspected her husband of squandering her estate, she could request a legal division of property. In many traditions, a woman who had been granted a separation of property had full legal capacity, just as if she had been widowed.[36] Under the customary law of Belgium, the Netherlands,[37] and certain German towns, she had to run her business separately from that of her husband because, if she worked for him, it was he and not she who was legally responsible. (But if she was involved in her husband's business, then she was jointly liable for his bankruptcy.)[38]

The legal female trader enjoyed a favoured legal status for everything related to her trade. In France as in Italy,[39] in almost all medieval customs and till the end of the ancien régime, she could go to court for matters

---

[35] Gilissen, "Le statut de la femme," pp. 256–8, 286.

[36] Ibid., pp. 287–99. In the Netherlands, imprisonment for debt was not applicable to women; Bosch, "Le statut de la femme," p. 346. In France, it was to female public vendors for trader-to-trader commitments and merchandise, but not to septuagenarians, minors, wives, and daughters if it were not matter of trade swindle; Law of 15 Germinal an IV; Portemer, "La femme," p. 493.

[37] Bosch, "Le statut de la femme," pp. 335–6.

[38] Order of 4 October 1540; Gilissen, "Le statut de la femme," p. 297.

[39] Rossi, "Statut juridique de la femme," pp. 126–33. In Italy, trade alone allowed women to administer freely their inheritance.

related to her business,[40] she was free to administer her property, dispose of it, and, in case of bankruptcy, separate her liability from that of her husband.[41] Imprisonment for debt was not applicable to women in the Netherlands.[42] In France, it did apply to legal female traders but only for trader to trader commitments and goods. Septuagenarians, minors, wives, and daughters, except if guilty of trade swindle, were excluded from its purview.[43]

Amongst urban artisans, women's autonomy was less widely accepted. French and Spanish women were excluded from professional organizations, such as the guilds. A widow could take over her husband's business, however. Conversely, there were many women active in small and large businesses in the Netherlands and in certain German towns (such as Lübeck, Bremen, and Cologne), where they had access to existing guilds or were organized in their own guilds.[44] In the Germanic sphere, they were, in the Middle Ages, as numerous in the craft industry as in trade. They did not work merely as "family labour" and instead had a place in guilds and the unregulated sectors as independent artisans and wage earners.

The manufacturers of clothes and luxury goods were the first to open their guilds to women as apprentices, journeymen, or masters. Some trades such as the spinning of gold threads or silk embroidery became the exclusive domain of women who set up their own guilds as in Paris and Cologne. The fur trades were particularly egalitarian: in Bâle, the statutes of the guild drawn up in 1226 gave the same rights to men and women. Later, the furriers guilds in Cologne, Frankfurt am Main, Ratisbon, Lübeck, and Quedlingburg did likewise. Women were also very present in the food trade: bakery, butchery, fish mongering, oil manufacturing, market gardening, and brewing beer. At the same time, many women worked "outside" the guilds, such as the women who spun gold threads in Nuremberg who were registered only from 1526 onwards and who had previously plied their trade outside the purview of the town council's

[40] Petot, "Le statut de la femme," p. 253.
[41] Rossi, "Statut juridique de la femme," pp. 126–33. However, there were few such women. They were particularly active during the fifteenth and sixteenth centuries. Cf. Opitz, "Contraintes et libertés," pp. 308–10.
[42] Bosch, "Le statut de la femme," p. 346.
[43] Law of 15 Germinal 15 germinal an IV; Portemer, "La femme," p. 493.
[44] Bosch, "Le statut de la femme," p. 347. Merry E. Wiesner, *Working Women in Renaissance Germany*, New Brunswick, NJ, Rutgers, 1986, p. 18 sq.

control and regulation. In Strasbourg, women were engaged in a major way in spinning wool outside the guild.[45]

Men benefited from the exclusion of women from public service and from the right to say what is right and lawful in order to exclude or marginalize them from economic activities. The inferior position of women without any political weight or support from trade organizations, being too poor to pay the admittance fee, obliged them to shift their workshops outside the city or to give up the craft industry. In periods of crisis, the battle intensified. The sixteenth century also saw a net decline in the role of women in the craft industry. Journeymen first fought against their right to employ female servants and then against their right to train apprentices. In this way, there were no women left to carry on the trade. In Nuremberg, all new training of women for the trade was prohibited as early as in 1540: only the old hands could continue. Thus, the masters of the trade no longer had to face competition from women. In France, women were excluded from trade organizations and widows who took over their husband's business were restricted in their activity by the numerous rules imposed on them.[46]

In Strasbourg, weavers' guilds stepped up their attacks against women artisans, obliging them to pay the fees due to the guild or give up their trade. After 1500, there was no trace of their activity in the wool industry.[47] The eviction of women from the town's craft industry and trade organizations was almost complete by the end of the sixteenth century so much so that in 1688 the German jurist Adrian Beier could write, "In accordance with the rule, no person of the female sex may enter into business as an artisan, even if she is just as skilled as a person of the male sex."[48] This exclusion did not mean that women no longer worked as artisans but that they were forced into working at home or into subordinate roles.[49]

---

[45] Opitz, "Contraintes et libertés," pp. 314–16.

[46] Ibid., p. 316; Beauvalet-Boutouyrie, *Etre veuve sous l'Ancien Régime*, pp. 276–7.

[47] Opitz, "Contraintes et libertés," p. 316.

[48] Ibid. In 1566, in Strasbourg, the journeymen who worked in a belt workshop cited guild regulations that stated they could not be obliged to work alongside a woman to get rid of the competition from the employer's two daughters; in the face of the master's insistence to make them work, the entire guild stopped working and the case was brought before the college of the cities of the diet of Augburg; the master had to give in and the girls stopped working; Opitz, "Contraintes et libertés," p. 317.

[49] Sara Mendelson and Patricia Crawford, *Women in Early Modern England 155–1720*, Oxford, Clarendon Press, 1998, chap. 5, "The Makeshift Economy of Poor Women."

Business was not exempted either from such restrictive legislation on
women's economic activities with a view to limiting them to retail selling.[50] In keeping with their more confined role in the house, women were
restricted to the small-scale foodstuffs distribution and services sectors.
In sixteenth-century Nuremberg, they had hardly any more access to
trade and the traditional crafts trade than elsewhere in Europe, and widows could only take over their deceased husband's shop for one or two
years.[51] Their right to start up a business was likewise restricted.

In England, retail business was the preserve of freemen of the towns.[52]
However, women in the country who produced poultry and dairy products had the right to sell them at market either in person or through a
servant acting as an intermediary. Nonetheless, it should not be forgotten that here they faced competition from farmers having a garden, gardeners, fruiterers, and the army of peddlers who traded in anything they
could get their hands on – from baskets of fruit to leftover meat – and
that the majority of these traders were also women. A specific analysis
of criminal offenses for the Lyon markets in the seventeenth century, as
well for the Oxford markets in the eighteenth century, shows that women
did not adhere to restrictions and frequently mixed authorized products
and products they were prohibited from selling, playing on space and
clienteles. Thus, in the county of Oxford in 1712, twenty-four regrat-
ers were prosecuted for buying commodities from a market and reselling them in the same or another market within a radius of four miles.
They were prosecuted for reselling vegetables and fruit and three of them
for reselling fish. Now, of the twenty-four persons arrested, twenty-one
were women. Among them were four widows, two single women, and
eleven married women, of whom two were married to ploughmen and
one to a gardener. This case shows that ploughmen's wives were adept
at treading the fine line between legal and illegal activities: they sold the
produce of their gardens quite legally but added to it other produce they
had acquired, something they were not allowed to do.[53]

Other changes were taking place between the seventeenth and nineteenth centuries, brought to light by studies that took into consideration

[50] Opitz, "Contraintes et libertés," pp. 317–19.
[51] Merry Wiesner Wood, "Paltry Peddlers or Essential Merchants? Women in the Distributive
Trades in Early Modern Nuremberg," *The Sixteenth Century Journal*, 12, no. 2, 1981,
pp. 3–13.
[52] Wendy Thwaites, "Women in the Market Place: Oxfordshire c. 1690–1800," *Midland
History*, 1984, pp. 23–42 (32).
[53] Ibid., pp. 30–2; Anne Montenach, *Espaces et pratiques du commerce alimentaire à Lyon
au XVIIe siècle*, Grenoble, Presses Universitaires de Grenoble, 2009.

the material aspect of the installations (the existence of a covered or open-air market), the structure of the shops, changes in the law and attitudes, and the more or less complex form of financial circuits, for each of these factors had a bearing on the woman's place in merchant circuits. Accordingly, the covered market of Oxford consisted of shops and stalls given on rent. In 1790, it counted forty-eight shops, of which forty were run by butchers and eight by gardeners, and forty stalls occupied by sellers of eggs, bacon, cheese, poultry, and so on. Of the forty-one tenants summoned to appear in 1795 for late payment of rent, only two were women, but in 1808, for which a list of all the tenants is available, fifty-three shops and thirty-eight of the forty stalls were run by men. This indicates that women were practically excluded from the official market structures. However, other court cases demonstrate that some women set themselves up as grocers and bakers in town in defiance of the prohibition, "on their own initiative and without paying for any licence and entrance fee," even if that meant paying a 1-shilling fine. The low rate of the fine imposed on those who defied the prohibition was an indication of how representations on behalf of women, and consequently how the law, were evolving: through their attitude, women were in the process of doing away with this discrimination.

With the dismantling of guild structures and market regulations, one would have expected that women enter the food trade in a big way. In point of fact, nothing of the sort happened and the rise of liberalism left them without support. Thus, the wives of small farmers, who had been very active in the sale of farm produce, vanished with the ruin of this social class, a victim of enclosures and the sale of communal property that deprived them of the space required to breed a pig, a cow, or, in the case of the poorest, a few hens. At the same time, transaction volumes went up, especially close to towns where the fresh-food trade was increasingly in the hands of specialized middlemen, edging women out of such markets. In addition, covered markets held an advantage over the open-air markets in which women invested traditionally. These movements, which required ever more capital, more professionalization, and more access to credit to feed the towns, spelled the marginalization of women. These developments explain why, in England, the cheese seller, a woman at the end of the seventeenth century, became a man by the eighteenth century.[54]

---

[54] Thwaites, "Women in the Market Place," pp. 26, 32–4.

On the other hand, some widows achieved notable success in large retail becoming major entrepreneurs such as in Saint-Malo where, between 1680 and 1720, forty women, almost all widows, were merchants.[55]

Thus, although the social and political hegemony of the husband continued, the economic importance of the wife was increased *nolens volens* by the growth of markets. Even if wives did nothing more than help, they gained sufficiently in importance that, at least in the artisan milieu, conflicts grew up within couples, as illustrated in innumerable bawdy and misogynistic farces and *fabliaux* on this theme. These were a product of the development of the marketplace and the transformation of social roles in business and among urban artisans.[56] However as always, this was not the case everywhere: in sixteenth-century Nuremberg, in trade and the craft industry, the role of women as their husbands' associates was fully recognized. There are several pointers to this: clients' debts were often addressed to them, for they managed the shop's financial affairs; they were responsible jointly with their husband for the payment of taxes and for the quality of the products they sold; and, if for instance, a butcher's or baker's wife was imprisoned for some offense, the shop had to shut down until she was released and, in case of any breach, there was stiff fine to pay. The recognition of the role of the wives of artisans was such that the latter were obliged to marry and that the same terms were used for wife and widow, a telling indication of the fact that widowhood did not entail any change in role. The baker's wife was "die Frau Bäckerin" and the tailor's wife "die Frau Schneiderin," appellations that designate clearly their professional roles.[57]

The Departure of Men

The third area of change was women's replacement of men. The departure of the men, whether to go off to war or to go off to earn a living, meant that women gained a de facto autonomy during their absence. Thus, in the families of sailors and peddlers, husbands' long absences and their high mortality rate gave women an essential role, both in the organization of the family and in the decisions made within it. The husband often bestowed power of attorney on the wife so that she could

[55] Beauvalet-Boutouyrie, *Etre veuve sous l'Ancien Régime*, pp. 278–280.
[56] Opitz, "Contraintes et libertés," p. 295.
[57] Wood "Paltry Peddlers or Essential Merchants?," pp. 3–13.

manage their affairs in his absence and have recourse to the law. In the port of London, women collected all or a part of their wages, which they managed, turning themselves into lenders or pawn brokers as soon as they could.[58] Conversely, those who were too poor took advantage of their status as minors to live on credit even after their husband had left them. William Hutton, judge and chronicler at the Court of Requests of Birmingham, tells us how the town was full of such women abandoned by their husbands on account of their debts and that to live, they used "all kinds of subterfuges … to extract the maximum from small traders. They live on little bit of cash and a little bit of credit. Money is temporary, credit is eternal. Their swindling is written in chalk on the door of every shopkeeper in the area"; if one wished to prosecute them for debt, they replied that they could not be prosecuted by law and that the person had to prosecute their husband (but he had left!): the manipulation of credit thus became one of their survival strategies.[59]

War also created trading opportunities around drinking, eating, and men's sociability. Women were omnipresent in the food and spirits trade. In Nuremberg, they served in inns, made beer wine, distilled spirits (half of the ninety-two distillers were women) and ran most of the taverns. During the Thirty Years' War, about one hundred outlets for selling brandy were authorized in Nuremberg. These outlets where clients could only drink standing were almost all run by elderly women.[60] Jobs such as these allowed women to get around the general rule that if a woman wished to borrow more than 5 livres she had to have the consent of her husband. These women were free to lend and borrow money and were absolutely free to conduct their affairs as they saw fit. Their freedom was, in fact, greater than that enjoyed by rich widows. In these spaces of professional freedom backed by the required legal recognition, it is hard not to see the influence of war. *Mother Courage*, popularized by Bertolt

---

[58] Margaret Hunt, "Women, Credit and the Seafaring Community in Early Eighteenth-Century," presented at the session C 59, "Women and Credit Practices (17th and 19th centuries), M. Berg, L. Fontaine, and C. Muldrew, coordinators, of the 12th International Congress of Economic History, Seville, 1998.

[59] Craig Muldrew and Steven King, "Cash, Wages and the Economy of Makeshifts in England, 1650–1800," *Experiencing Wages. Social and Cultural Aspects of Wage forms in Europe since 1500*, Peter Scholliers and Leonard Schwartz, eds., New York and Oxford, Berghahn, 2004, pp. 154–79 (172–3). They cite William Hutton, *Courts of Requests: Their Nature, Utility, and Powers Described*, Birmingham, Printed by Pearson and Rollason, 1787, p. 42, and give an estimate of the hopeless debts which were abandoned.

[60] Wood "Paltry Peddlers or Essential Merchants?"

Brecht, came from this world of women who made their living from the movements of men.

We can draw two conclusions from this brief summary of the relationship between the law and women's economic spheres. First, we cannot talk about women in general, given the wide variations in law from region to region, and the equally wide gap in women's experience, determined by their social milieu and their business activities. Second, it should be emphasized that women's autonomy was doubtless promoted by the fact that Europe was a patchwork that juxtaposed very different legal traditions with territories that were very close to one another. It could be argued that the indecision and contradictions of the law allowed women to take advantage of new freedoms and to widen the horizon of their thinking. This trait is perhaps specific to Europe and could well explain the early development of women's autonomy. Throughout Europe, women lived surrounded by other women who, because they were widows, were in particular religious orders or were involved in running a business, had attained a greater degree of autonomy. Moreover, they were aware that, over the course of their lives, they too might gain access to these areas of relative autonomy, Although women still lacked far too many rights, especially political and legal rights, the juxtaposition of the various statuses of women in a single territory in accordance with their age and their changing avatars, and the favoured status of widows everywhere – very numerous in ancient Europe and found in all strata of society[61] – meant that women were able to hold onto ideas of what was possible. Reservoirs of reflection and encouragement to imitate other women helped them to sustain an imaginary horizon of the mind and to preserve other, freer and more independent ways of doing things, and this, perhaps, also explains why women had such little regard for the law. Finally, to get round the legal proscriptions, married women also built up mutual support networks in town: they acted as one another's guarantors, borrowed money, and pawned goods.[62] But these networks of female solidarity, which were a response to women's legal exclusion, are very difficult to document.

[61] Residents' lists registered widows with a frequency that made them a real social group. Jean-Claude Perrot observes this in eighteenth-century Caen; see Perrot, *Genèse d'une ville moderne Caen au XVIIIe siècle*, p. 245.
[62] Beverly Lemire, "Petty Pawns and Informal Lending," *From Family Firms to Corporate Capitalism: Essay in Business and Industrial History in Honour of Peter Mathias*, Kristine Bruland and Patrick O'Brien, eds., Clarendon Press, Oxford, 1998, pp. 112–38; William Chester Jordan, *Women and Credit in Pre-Industrial and Developing Societies*, University of Pennsylvania Press, Philadelphia, 1993, p. 93.

Women as Financial and Trading Intermediaries

Pawnbroking and Secondhand Markets

Women were faced with a challenge: notwithstanding the fact that they were subject to guardianship and restrictive laws, they were expected to manage family expenditures and constantly juggle the regular need for money with an irregular income, and this with a budget over which they rarely had any control. In fact, their limited political, administrative or legal capacities constrained them to staid and unimaginative administrative functions and kept them in state of dependency, the service sector, as wage earners or domestic help, because they were excluded from entrepreneurial activities because they did not have full control over their capital, nor even the right to bear the risk involved in decisions. To try to square the circle, they entered into the heart of the informal circuits of urban credit, namely, pawnbroking and secondhand markets.

We would do well to recall certain features of the economy of the ancient regime that influenced the economic activities of women, beginning with the lack of cash. First, money did not circulate as freely as today, and a large proportion circulated in the form of goods. Salaries, pensions, and loans were systematically paid at least partly in kind. The circulation of money as goods has been largely obscured in the work done on the economy of the *ancien régime*. Second, the economy of Europe at this time was based on credit. This credit was still largely between individuals, however, and the conventions governing it were very specific, depending on who was borrowing and who was lending. Those outside the social networks who had no property to offer as guarantee only had access to such credit which was, in effect, a deferred sale. In other words, their sole access to credit was the pawnshop, which was, as seen in the previous chapter, the financial tool par excellence of poor economies. These two characteristics explain why the market for second-hand clothes and all other objects produced by society was one of the most important in Europe at this time, and why the used-clothes business was linked to pawnbroking.[63] Women were at the heart of this small economy in which clothes circulated like money and were rented or pawned according to the need. Hence, the social role of women in an incompletely monetarized economy and a legal environment that marginalized them explains

---

[63] *Alternative Exchanges: Second-Hand Circulations from the Sixteenth Century to the Present*, L. Fontaine, (ed.), Berghahn, Oxford and New York, 2008.

why they were, since the Middle Ages, at the helm of the sale and resale circuits of old clothes and active in pawnbroking.

A few studies allow us to penetrate these female specializations. Thus, in Nuremberg in the sixteenth century, women were equally well established in the secondhand clothes trade as in pawnbroking. In 1542, 111 *Keuflinnen* controlled the secondhand market: clothes, shoes, furniture, armours and arms, household utensils, tools, leather, bottles, and containers of all kinds. These women had to prove that they had property to offer as security, and two citizens had to vouch for their honesty. Most of them had designated spots at the marketplace; the others had a special license to sell door to door; however, there was a limit on the number of hours they could sell and on the amount of profit they could earn. They were also pawnbrokers. Such was their expertise that 95 per cent of the appraisers of movable goods listed in inventories after death were women (*Unterkeuflin*). They clashed frequently with other guilds, which accused them of selling prohibited foodstuffs such as bread and meat. In spite of the many problems, the city recognized their role and often decided in their favour. They acted as a very close-knit group, and there were few instances of a *Keuflin* denouncing another whereas to protect their trade, they were relentless in attacking other professions.[64]

In Amsterdam too, women specialized in assessing ordinary inventories: in the seventeenth century, one of five inventories were assessed by women appraisers under oath (*gesworene taxeersters*). These women had to take an oath before a magistrate, after which they were accredited to the municipality. But for the inventories of the elite that comprised collections, the guilds concerned delegated masters to appraise them.[65]

Peddling

Peddling of foodstuffs was also handled mainly by women. In Nuremberg in the seventeenth century, the market was full of women selling food, candles, and even books and pictures. Their small-scale retail operations included the distribution of household production. Generally, these women were allowed to sell only one kind of merchandise. Permitting these small traders to exist was a political strategy employed by the city to give them the means to support themselves and thus avoid their falling back on charitable institutions. Moreover, the strategy of reserving

---

[64] Wood, "Paltry Peddlers or Essential Merchants?"

[65] John M. Montias, *Le Marché de l'art aux Pays-Bas (XVe XVIIe siècles)*, Paris, Flammarion, 1996, p. 67.

segments of small retail (the distribution of official news, for example) for the poor was very common in the cities of Europe. But the women of Nuremberg were also present in the retail distribution of exotic items of long-distance trade such as citrus fruits, dyestuffs, and spices. They shared this market with the networks of Italian peddlers, and as in Paris, they were active in the urban peddling of books, engravings, and news.[66] Most of them borrowed from usurers on a day-to-day basis to buy their merchandise. Louis-Sébastien Mercier recounts that the latter set up their agencies around markets and insisted the women merchants accept collective liability:

The women selling fruit and vegetables which they carry in a basket, retailers of every kind need more often than not a modest advance of an écu of six livres to buy mackerels, peas, currants, peaches and cherries. The lender gives it to them, provided that at end of the week he gets seven livres four sols. Thus, his écu, when it works, brings him nearly sixty livres a year, in other words, ten times its value. This then is the modest rate of lenders who lend by the week.

He [the usurer] then goes to an out-of the-way house, to a room where there is only one bad tapestry, a pallet, three chairs and a crucifix. There he grants an audience to sixty women, – food sellers, street hawkers and fruit sellers. Then he speaks to them in a solemn voice:" My friends, as you can see, I am not better off than you; here is my furniture, here is the bed I lie on when I come to Paris; I give you my money and rely on your conscience and religion; as from you I have no signature, you know, I can ask nothing from the law. I am useful for your trade; and when I lavish my trust, I must have my surety. So be all of you jointly liable, and swear in front of this crucifix, the image of our divine Saviour, that you shall do me no wrong, and that you shall faithfully return to me that what I shall entrust to you."

All the fish sellers and fruit sellers raise their hands, and swear to strangle the one who would not be faithful in payment: dreadful oaths are taken and long signs of the cross made. Then the skilled flatterer takes the names, and distributes to each one an écu of six livres, telling them: "I don't earn what you earn, far from it." The crowd starts to melt away, and the ogre remains alone with two emissaries, settling their accounts and paying them their wages.[67]

Although it was not managed by development-oriented bankers, as is the case today, solidarity microcredit is not a contemporary invention: it has long history of helping multiple small women traders to eke out a living despite the high rates of interest and their institutional marginalization.

---

[66] Wood "Paltry Peddlers or Essential Merchants?" For Paris, see, Beauvalet-Boutouyrie, *Etre veuve sous l'Ancien Régime*, p. 282.

[67] Louis Sébastien Mercier, "Prêteurs à la petite semaine," *Tableau de Paris*, Jean-Claude Bonnet, ed., vol. 1, Mercure de France, Paris, 1994 [1781–1789], p. 548–51.

Maidservants

Maidservants, too, were at the heart of this redistribution, often receiving clothes by way of payment. With the urban population growing rapidly, the city of Nuremberg established a system of employment agents for domestic service. These positions were reserved for women and held by the wives or widows of craftsman or minor officials. It was their job to find domestic servants in the city and the neighbouring countryside, and they were held responsible for the quality of the young girls they placed as well as of the families with which these girls were employed. Entrusting this job to women speaks volumes about their capacity to gather information through informal networks of relatives and gossip.[68]

Specific Economic Practices

Did the economic marginalization of women and the particular nature of their monetary worth, comprised predominantly of letters of credit, cash and moveable goods, give rise to specific economic behaviour? Because they were often obliged to live on small, irregularly paid incomes, did they manage their money differently from men?

To be sure of having an income, widows and single women were accustomed to investing their money in annuities (*rentes*) arranged with individuals as well as with institutions such as hospitals, pious associations, churches, guilds, and so forth. This entry into financial markets took place gradually across Europe as early as the sixteenth century (and doubtless before in Italy), in the seventeenth century in England,[69] and probably not until the eighteenth century in France and Germany. This rough time frame is approximate and was largely dependent on social groups and phases of the life cycle.

Can We Talk about Specifically Female Money Management?

The first variation was social. Aristocratic and bourgeois women did not invest their money in the same places as women from the lower orders. Among the aristocracy, women, like their fathers and husbands, chose to invest in annuities to secure a regular income for themselves.[70] Widows

---

[68] Wood "Paltry Peddlers or Essential Merchants?"

[69] B. A. Holderness, "Widows in Pre-Industrial Society: An Essay upon Their Economic Functions," *Land, Kinship and Life-Cycle*, Richard M. Smith, ed., Cambridge, Cambridge University Press, 1984, pp. 423–42.

[70] Examples for the French nobility in Natacha Coquery, "Les courtisans et le crédit à Paris au XVIIIe siècle," European University Institute, Florence, *Working paper* HEC no. 98/5,

also invested their money in convents in exchange for a life annuity.[71]
For France, if we compare the late eighteenth-century creditors of the
hospitals and the *mont-de-piété* (pawnshop) of Marseille, it is clear that
women invested far more in the pawnshop than in the hospitals. At the
Hôtel-Dieu about 34 per cent of the investors were women, and at the
Hôpital de la Charité, barely 30 per cent, and within the womens' group,
47 per cent were widows in the case of the Hôtel-Dieu and 31.6 per cent
in that of the Hôpital de la Charité.[72] On the other hand, 69.5 per cent of
women invested in le mont-de-piété and strangely enough, few widows
were among them (11 per cent). A social divide is at work here: it was
predominantly the widows of merchants or nobles who invested in the
hospitals, as their husbands had done before them, whereas the pawnshop
received deposits of money from the wives of sailors and day labourers
and from small-scale women traders and workers.[73] When women were
admitted to the Salpêtrière Hospital, if they came with a nest egg of more
than 1,000 livres, the hospital would invest it directly in the pawnshop
to make it grow.[74] In Beauvais at the end of the seventeenth century and
at the beginning of the eighteen, widows and elder daughters from the
bourgeois milieu would invest in commercial ventures as annuitants so
that there was no risk involved. Just like officers and the bourgeois, they
"put" their available funds in the business of a merchant who inspired
confidence in them, satisfied with a fixed interest, often fairly low, without asking for a share in the profits. Thus, the inventory of the merchant
Daugy in 1732 shows that four daughters and two widows had lent him
23,600 livres through the purchase of annuities. The inventory of Bigot
in 1727 attests to the same type of loan of 31,250 livres given by seven
daughters and widows, his brother, a canon, a councillor at the Présidial,
and a notary. In both cases, the sums were lent at denier 20, 25, 30,
and more than half the sums at deniers 40 and 50.[75] Aristocratic families favoured annuities on public institutions to endow their daughters
and invest the money of their wives. In 1759, 55 of the 105 creditors
of the states of Languedoc were nobles of Toulouse, and most of the

1998; and Natacha Coquery, *L'Hôtel aristocratique. Le marché du luxe à Paris au XVIIIe siècle*, Paris, Publications de la Sorbonne, 1998, p. 160.

[71] Beauvalet-Boutouyrie, *Etre veuve sous l'Ancien Régime*, pp. 305–6.

[72] Courdurié Marcel, *La Dette des collectivités publiques de Marseille au XVIIIe siècle. Du débat sur le prêt à intérêt au financement par l'emprunt*, Marseille, Institut historique de Provence, 1974, pp. 188–9.

[73] Ibid., pp. 239, 248.

[74] Beauvalet-Boutouyrie, *Etre veuve*, pp. 330–1.

[75] Pierre Goubert, *Beauvais et le Beauvaisis de 1600 à 1730. Contribution à l'histoire sociale de la France du xviie siècle*, Paris, SEVPEN, 1960.

beneficiaries of these annuities were women, the daughters and wives of the best families of Toulouse, who earned an income of 100 to 400 livres. The same social characteristics can be seen in all the loans issued by the states and municipalities.[76]

Works on England confirms these social distinctions among women making financial investments. After 1680, the number of aristocratic and bourgeois *rentières* who lived comfortably from money invested in government loans increased,[77] however, on the whole, the source of widows' income was not specific.[78] We should not forget that, in order to safeguard women's standard of living, the law required that families employ professionals to manage women's inheritances and that husbands leave them the means to live out their life in a manner consistent with their social status.

Otherwise, in less-well-off milieu, widows and single women very often played a central role in loans within communities – to relatives, neighbours, and other villagers. Between 1660 and 1799 all the widows without occupation who were creditors when they died had placed at least a third of their fortune on account with relatives.[79] Of the 170 inventories after death of deceased widows with debts, 116 among them (68 per cent) left at least 60 per cent of their movable assets in credit, and 18 left more than 90 per cent. It is always difficult to ascertain correctly the social status of the debtors and the bonds that tied them to the creditors, but the wills of the widows reveal that at least a third of their debtors were relatives. Sons and daughters as well as brothers and sisters appeared the most frequently, but that did not preclude more distant relatives. Nevertheless, the scales were tipped in favour of close relatives, for they were generally mentioned, as the widow intended to cancel their debts.[80] In Lancashire, fifty-two inventories of widows, who were not engaged in the business of their husband, show that, on an average, each

---

[76] Forster, *The Nobility of Toulouse in the Eighteenth Century*, pp. 115–16.

[77] Holderness, "Widows in Pre-Industrial Society," Richard M. Smith, ed., pp. 423–42 (438–9).

[78] Ibid., pp. 438–9. Of the 620 widows who lived in Lincolnshire and East Anglia in the seventeenth century, no more than 10–15% of the debt contracts were mortgages. They existed alongside unsecured loans, bills and bonds, promissory notes, stocks and shares, pawns, and sales on credit. Pawns rarely accounted for more than 5%, except when the widow entered into pawnbroking.

[79] B. A. Holderness, "Credit in a Rural Community 1600–1800," *Midland History*, III, 1975, pp. 100–1.

[80] Holderness, "Widows in Pre-Industrial Society," pp. 440–1.

left 76 pounds; about 50 pounds per head were in loans and unpaid debts, and among these widows, several only had a few possessions in a room of the family house. Single people, both male and female, manifested similar behaviour: of the 4,300 pounds owned by forty-five single people between 1660 and 1799, 2,721 pounds were in loans. Credit represented 64 per cent of the wealth of unemployed widows and of single people, and this percentage takes into account the sixteen inventories of ninety poor people. Among the gentry and the clergy this figure was 27 per cent, for the farmers and merchants 13 per cent.[81]

Similarly, in Gdansk in the first half of the seventeenth century, of the 846 small loans 609 (i.e., 72 per cent) were issued by women, who were responsible for a number of small loans within their neighbourhoods. As elsewhere, widows were very active in this sort of enterprise, but the wives of craftsmen working in the clothing trades as tailors or furriers also played a part. This is in keeping with a widespread tradition in Germanic Europe where women were legally associated with their husbands.

In Italy, women invested their savings in *luoghi di monte* or with private companies: the *censi* and the *compagnie d'ufficio*, where returns were fixed from the outset for the duration of the investment. The income varied from 3 to 7.5 per cent except for the "compagnie d'ufficio" the duration of which was 6 months with an income of 12 per cent. These notes could be exchanged or sold. As the income was fixed at the outset for the entire duration of the investment, it was a no-risk investment. In Florence, people favoured investing their wife's dowry in pawn shops. In the second half of the sixteenth century with the decline of the Monte delle Doti and its absorption in Monte Comune, Florentines used it increasingly as a savings bank to put together dowries for their daughters. From 1574 onwards, pawnshops kept two kinds of books: one for ordinary deposits, *depositi libri*, which could be withdrawn at any time, and the other for deposits subject to restrictions, *depositi condizionati*, such as dowry moneys.[82]

In the imperial territories, between the seventeenth and eighteenth centuries, the dower of women in the form of cash annuities went up sharply. Before 1670, they were rare and modest. In the eighteenth century, they were almost always present in the immediate Rhenish chivalry, generally

---

[81] Holderness, "Credit in a Rural Community 1600–1800," pp. 94–115 (101).
[82] Carol, "Loans and Favors," pp. 503–6.

amounting to 600 florins per annum if the widow had an additional income in kind, and 2,000 or 3,000 florins if cash was her sole dowery as was most often the case.[83]

The division between men and women, and the nature of the goods in the inventories after death of the municipal orphanage of Amsterdam – those of parents who died leaving their minor children in the care of the municipality – in the second half of the eighteenth century substantiates the fact that men and women did not share the same monetary circuits and that women depended on the informal sector and faced insecurity. Here we are dealing with the middle and lower classes of the crafts industry and trade. The average value of the assets of women head of families was one-fourth less than that of men (62.9 florins for women against 78.5 florins for men). The average of families headed by a married couple was nearly 10 per cent higher than of families with only a father (83.5 florins) whereas families financially dependent on widows had an average of only 60.5 florins. The most significant difference was between widows and widowers, the latter having 66.7 florins as compared to 48 florins for the former.

An analysis of the composition of this meagre wealth shows that widows possessed more gold, coins, and jewels than other groups.[84] Admittedly, these assets were traditional forms of momentary investment, but they stood in contrast with the changes observed in the eighteenth century when people invested increasingly in financial instruments proposed by large companies and the state.[85] Widows did not follow these changes and preferred, when they could, to have coins. Of the twenty-four women owning such assets, only two had state annuities whereas three of the thirteen married men had various types of annuity bonds as did three out of sixteen widowers. Conversely, married women owned annuities rather than cash, as was the case in a sample of twelve women in which five were married. Credit portfolios indicate the same trend: in nearly 65 per cent of the inventories, the debts were greater than the assets, and excessive

[83] Christophe Duhamelle, "La noblesse d'église. Famille et pouvoir dans la chevalerie immédiate rhénane XVIIe-XVIIIe siècle," PhD thesis, University of Paris I, p. 418, published subsequently under the title *L'héritage collectif. La noblesse d'Eglise rhénane, 17e – 18e siècles*, Paris, Editions de l'Ecole des Hautes Etudes en Sciences Sociales, 1998.

[84] Anne McCants, "Petty Debts and Family Networks: the Credit Markets of Widows and Wives in Eighteenth-Century Amsterdam," *Women and Credit: Researching the Past, Refiguring the Future*, Beverly Lemire et al., eds., Oxford, Berg Publishers, 2002, pp. 33–50.

[85] Thera Wijsenbeek-Olthuis, *Achter de Gevels von Delft*, Hilversum, Verloren, 1987, pp. 306–7, 341.

debt was in a ratio of 2 or even 3 of debts left behind to assets owned. But when seen in the context of the eighteenth-century crisis, the behaviour of women was atypical because many were indebted: they had on an average 70 florins whereas the other groups fell in the bracket between 112 and 178 florins. More than an economically rational behaviour, this low indebtedness is indication of their economic marginalization.[86]

If we study their debts, we find that not only did women not borrow as much as the others from shopkeepers and craftsmen, but that they also made much less use of the more official credit markets. On the other hand, they were used to pawnshops: 17.3 per cent of widows had at least one of their assets pawned at the time of their death. In comparison, 13.5 per cent of widowers had pawned an object, as had 14.3 per cent of married women, but the record was held by married men (23.7 per cent). Besides, widows pawned cheaper objects.

The example of Amsterdam highlights the heterogeneity of the group of widows: although some were rich and used the help of professionals in their financial matters, there were also those who were among the groups the most vulnerable to poverty. Between the two, were widows who owned a few assets, the fruit of their labour or inheritance, and who invested heavily in neighbourhood loans and pawnshops; these were forms of credit of which they had experience when they found themselves in need and for which information was readily available to them.

A Specific Economic Culture?
Did the specific experiences of women produce a specifically feminine economic culture? Of course, in a study such as this, one is confronted all the time with subtle differences in behaviour, depending on the country, the time, the status, and life-cycle phases. Understanding female behaviour is all the more difficult, because we have no way of measuring the degree to which it was influenced by the advice of men. Still, the case studies I have chosen allow us to identify two very different types of behaviour. The behaviour of the women of Nuremberg working on a small-scale in the retail business was perfectly consistent with standard business practices: they put prices up when products were in short supply, entered into contracts with farmers to ensure a constant supply of produce, and were always on the lookout for new supply networks, thus exhibiting a true spirit of enterprise. Was it the legal recognition of their

[86] Anne McCants, "Petty Debts."

economic role and of their status as workers that allowed these women to take part fully in the whys and hows of the marketplace?[87]

At the other end of the spectrum, life on the fringes of the law, and in the informal economy which accommodated numerous ordinary women in other parts of Europe, caused women to develop economic cultures based on subterfuge and secrecy, which served to hide and reinforce their illegal (or quasi-illegal) economic practices, and a culture of solidarity to compensate for the fact that they were legally less protected. These subterfuges had two aspects. The first involved exploiting all the possibilities of the system, such as hiring out clothes that had been pawned, as we have already seen. The culture of solidarity was imposed on women by societies that refused them, on the whole, the right to exist individually, outside the power of men. That is why usurers who lent on a weekly basis compelled them to stand surety for each other and, in doing so, learn how to exist collectively.

The second aspect demonstrates women's ability to twist the image assigned to them by society. This comes out clearly in the criminal economy where they became the main fences and dealers in stolen goods, exploiting not only their sewing skills but also the fact that the law imposed more lenient punishments on them. It was in just such a case, in eighteenth-century Paris, that the famous crook Cartouche was accused of making use of women of the lower orders on a grand scale.

Of course, neither attitude is uniquely feminine, and other groups also learned the economic cultures of marginality and the subterfuges required by anyone who, in order to survive, had to break the rules. Finally, I should point out that women were in the same financial slot as other minorities. Not having full political rights, foreigners found it equally difficult to get into business or to become established as craftsmen; like women, many of them had to turn to ventures in which their legal incapacity was not a hindrance: the world of money lending and the informal economy.

[87] Wood, "Paltry Peddlers or Essential Merchants?," p. 10.

6

Between Bank and Assistance: Setting Up Pawnshops

What I know for sure is that I have seen between 60 and 80 people waiting their turn there, each one come to borrow not more than *six livres*. One was carrying his shirts, another a piece of furniture, another what remained of a wardrobe, and another his shoe buckles, an old picture, some poor clothes, and so forth. They say that there is a new crowd there almost every day, and this gives a very clear idea of the extreme shortage of money from which most of the city is suffering ...

> – Louis Sébastien Mercier, "Mont de piété," *Tableaux de Paris*,
> chap. CCLXII pp. 662–4

We have already seen the extent to which borrowing money by pawning objects was widespread in ancient Europe. The practice extended to almost all strata of society: the poorest left clothes and small items of jewellery to secure petty loans; the more affluent exchanged luxury goods, silverware, and jewellery to satisfy their consumption needs, pay their gambling debts and deal with unforeseen situations; even craftspeople and small traders took recourse to pawning goods to tide over moments of crisis. Yet this economy proved expensive for the poor, and the trade produced unscrupulous moneylenders.

Towards the end of the Middle Ages, some Récollet and Franciscan monks were deeply concerned about usury which had become all pervasive in society. Prompted by the monks, a growing number of initiatives were taken to set up institutions that could free the poor from the clutches of Jewish and Christian moneylenders.[1] These monks initiated a

---

[1] Michel Mollat, *Les Pauvres au Moyen Age*, Paris, Hachette, 1978, pp. 315–16, 335–6. Carol Bresnahan Menning, "Loans and Favors, Kin and Clients: Cosimo de' Medici and the Monte di Pietà," *Journal of Modern History*, no. 61, 1989, pp. 487–511; Michele

trend that advocated instituting honest forms of credit for the poor that were different from gifts. Lending was seen as having two advantages over almsgiving: it was morally more in keeping with human dignity because it helped people to get back on their feet; it was more efficient because it was easier to prevent people from falling than to pick them up and rehabilitate them when they become rootless. They were the first to discern, in the general condemnation of credit, especially by the church, virtuous credit for the poor just as they were the first to try to promote forms of assistance other than charity. I will come back to these points in the next chapter.

The first pawnshops were created in Italy as early as in the fifteenth century. They multiplied in Italy and in Spain in the fifteenth and sixteenth centuries and became widespread from the seventeenth century onwards in other countries, except in England, which had to wait until the nineteenth century as it favoured private initiative.[2] The situation in France was more ambiguous with a contrast between rather early creations of pawnshops in the outer provinces, where the custom was already anchored, and their difficulty in settling elsewhere.

Attempting to grasp the reasons for such large time differences leads us to a web of contradictory interests pitting the economic needs of the people, the will of churches to fight usury, the determination of states to deal with social issues against the capacity of merchants to defend their market share of money and their commercial interests. Beyond the equations of power, the diversity of economic relationships is obvious in the way pawnshop regulations deal with the question of remuneration of initial capital and the rate of interest that was asked of borrowers. The domination of a religious or a merchant culture and the interactions between the two is reflected in the diversity of choice.

Cassandro, *Gli ebrei e il prestito ebraico a Siena nel Cinquecento*, Milan, Giuffre, 1979; Giacomo Todeschini, *Ricchezza francescana. Dalla povertà volontaria alla società di mercato*, Bologna, Il Mulino, 2004.

[2] Between 1471 and 1500, sixteen pawnshops were set up in Emilie Romagne. Those in southern Italy came up around 1550. P. Vittorino Meneghin, *I Monti di Pietà in Italia dal 1462 al 1562*, Vicenza, LIEF Edizioni, 1986, p. 33, quoted in Paola Avallone, "The Credit upon Pledge in the Kingdom of Naples (16th–19th centuries)," presented at the symposium on "The Bank of the Poor. The Credit upon Pledge and the 'Monti di Pietà' in the Mediterranean Countries (15th–19th Centuries)," Naples, 24–25 September 2004, pp. 1–28. Massimo Fornasari, "Tra banchi publici e istituti di credito al consumo: i Monti di pietà nell'area emiliano-romagnola dal Seicento al Settecento," *Povertà e innovazioni istituzionali in Italia del Medioevo ad oggi*, Vera Zamagni, ed., Bologne, Il Mulino, 2000, pp. 383–401; Jose López Yepes, *Historia Urgente de cajas de ahorro y monts de Piedad en España*, Confederacion española de cajas de ahorro, Madrid, 1973, chap. 1.

The pawnshops resulting from Catholic culture were influential mainly in southern Europe. They bear the seal of ambivalence because they acknowledged the necessity to lend to the poor while rejecting the trade of currency needed to find necessary funding. The purpose of charity was also apparent considering the status of the shops, which were linked to charitable institutions.

The Question of Funding: Between Donation and Capital

The limitations of funding through donations and interest free loans were soon obvious. As long as the pawnshop's activity was limited – initial donations and keeping the shop open only two days a week involving minimum cost – they were able to stay afloat. Yet their success made such an option impracticable: keeping the shop open for regular hours and the corresponding increase in staff required to manage the shop's activity soon made expenditure hard to bear. First running costs were taken into account: from 1515, with the *Inter Multiplices* bull, Pope Léon X authorized levying a modest interest to cover such costs.[3] On the other hand, because financing through donations had not proved sustainable, the question of funding through free donations or interest-bearing loans had fuelled much debate during the entire modern period in the Catholic countries, and each institution found solutions, which were more or less efficient to resolve its financial crisis. However, the choices made partially changed the nature of the pawnshops. A few examples from Italy and Spain illustrate the diversity of solutions adopted.

Thus, Sienna, established in 1472, and Lucca, in 1475, were the only two Tuscan pawnshops that accepted returns on capital from the very outset.[4] But, in Florence, the pawnshop founded in 1495, thanks to Savoranole's encouragement, received its funding mainly from donation. Loans could not be extended more than one year and could not exceed more than two-thirds of the value of the pledge: they could not exceed 25 liras for the *cittadini* and ten liras for the *contadini* and were granted with an interest rate of 5 per cent. The profits had to be given to charitable institutions. In the case of the pawnshop in Florence, in 1498, the state deposited the amount from the sales of the goods seized from Pisan

---

[3] G. Barbieri, *Il pensiero economico dall'Antichità al Rinascimento*, Bari, Università di Bari, 1963, pp. 439–40, quoted by Avallone, "The Credit upon Pledge."
[4] Paola Massa, *Lineamenti di organizzazione economica in uno stato preindustriale. La repubblica di Genova*, Genova, ECIG, 1995, p. 410.

rebels.[5] The consequence of the recycling of war treasure into an act of charity was apparent in the fact that the pawnshop was not only used as relief to the poor but also as a bank by the nobility, for both themselves and their clients. For instance, Cosme made use of this to help his relatives – who moreover were, at his behest, taken on in the administration – as well as his political connections. He would have loans granted to them at 5 per cent, sometimes against a security, sometimes with just an assurance of security and sometimes, he himself stood surety for the borrower. Once they were well established in power, the Medici used pawnshops to finance their foreign policy, granting huge loans to foreign personalities. In this way, Philippe II benefitted from a loan of 3,000 scudis in 1583 that he never returned.[6] Such misappropriation, very widespread in sixteenth- and seventeenth-century Italy, greatly reduced or even wiped out the capacity to bring relief to most of the Italian pawnshops intended for the poor.[7] They were criticized for giving loans to friends and taking on increased staff and the same problems were encountered by the food pawnshops even though theoretically they were supposed to be better suited to the needs of country folk.[8]

In the Venetian region, the ruling groups tried opening pawnshops that offered returns on capital. In Brescia, for instance, the governing council approved the foundation of a second pawnshop in May 1553, insisting it was required as the financial lung of the town and referred to other Venetian establishments that offered returns on deposits. The first pawnshop, established in 1489, was already offering returns on deposits.[9] The councillors suggested 5 per cent for capital and 7 per cent for "engagistes." The proposal was not followed up, and when it was reviewed thirteen years later, in 1566, it met with the same fate. Indeed, on one hand, in 1569, Pie V reaffirmed his dislike for usury in the *Reformatio contractuum de annuis censibus* bull, and, on the other, Bishop Charles Borromée was explicit in his condemnation of all forms of return on capital and deposits at the pawnshops. It was only in 1586, after the

[5] Menning, "Loans and Favors," pp. 490–1; and Carol Bresnahan Menning, *Charity and State in Late Renaissance Italy: The Monte di Pietà of Florence*, Ithaca, NY, Cornell University Press, 1993.
[6] Menning, "Loans and Favors," pp. 495–502.
[7] See the several examples of misappropriations Jean-Claude Waquet, *De la corruption. Morale et pouvoir à Florence aux XVIIe et XVIIIe siècles*, Paris, Fayard, 1984.
[8] Alessandro Pastore, "il governo dei Monti di Pietà," in *Storia d'Italia*, annali 9, Giorgio Chittolini e Giovanni Miccoli, eds., Torino, Einaudi, 1986, pp. 151–6.
[9] Massa, *Lineamenti di organizzazione economica*, p. 410.

bishop died, that the initial proposal was adopted. Although aware of the impossibility of furthering the pawnshop's activities if these were limited to giving non remunerative capital, most Italian pawnshops were not able to get a return on deposits; however, there were exceptional cases such as that of Mantua: after the imperial troops sacked the town, it was permitted to offer 5 per cent on money deposits and ask for 7 per cent on loans.[10] However, the additional activities of the pawnshops did not prevent them from maintaining their main vocation, which was to help the poor by offering them small loans against objects pledged. Moreover, all Italian pawnshops added pawnbroking to their multiple charitable functions. That of Bologna, established in 1473, added among other activities the distribution of dowries to poor young girls.[11]

The Madrid pawnshop was established in 1711 with the specific purpose of lending without interest. In order to collect the large amount of capital it required, Don Francisco Piquier called on three main sources. First, he turned to the royalty from whom he obtained donations and rights on a certain number of incomes. In 1710, he won the right to ask for alms for the pawnshop on American soil. Then, in 1716, he succeeded in having agents appointed for the pawnshop in all the provinces and getting a fixed income (4,000 pesos) drawn from the India income. Legates and gifts were another source of capital though they remained modest and irregular. The third source was individual deposits without interest. The curve of such deposits was parallel to the owned assets curve, and between 1738 and 1758, it was even higher in some years.[12]

The pawnshop in Barcelona – el Mont de Pietat de Nostra Senyora de l'Esperança i Salvaciò de les Animes de Barcelona – created in 1751, still retained a funding partly through donation and partly through a resort to the capital market when financial crises were close to attract funding and respond to the demand. Its finances thus vacillated between donations and recourse to the capital market. An analysis of lenders establishes their diversity. Pawnshops were financed in several different ways: lower-class women, aristocratic benefactors, the church, and the administration. Most of the lenders were men. Only a fifth of them

---

[10] Daniele Pawnshopanari, "I Monti di pietà della Lombardia (secoli XV-XVIII). Prime riflessioni," *Annali di Storia Moderna e Contemporanea. Università Cattolica del Sacro Cuore*, 2, 1996, pp. 9–43; and "I Monti di pietà bergamaschi (secoli XVI-XVIII)," *Studi Veneziani*, n.s., 27, 1994, pp. 165–267.

[11] Isabelle Chabot and Massimo Fornasari, *L'Economia della carità. le doti del Monte di Pietà di Bologna (secoli XVI-XX)*, Bologna, Il Mulino, 1997, pp. 151–2.

[12] Yepes, *Historia Urgente de cajas de ahorro*, chap. 4.

were women, and among them, slightly fewer than half were widows. The study of deposits between 1751 and 1808 confirms the ambivalent status of pawnshops: they dealt in alms, donations, quitrent, and all kinds of temporary deposits or those that did not yield any return (dowries, sums given while awaiting the return of a family member who had gone to America, etc.). A debate was initiated on interest on deposits, prohibited in the late 1760s. Thus, pawnshops found themselves in dire straits due to a lack of capital, and although deposits were interest free in theory, interest between 2 and 2.5 per cent was offered until the late 1770s. The year the pawnshop was set up in Barcelona, it registered 808 loans against security, and fifteen years later, in 1776, it gave 9,975 loans in a city of 70,000 inhabitants. Difficulty in finding funding led to a decline in the number of loans, which fell to just 2,910 at the end of the year 1772.

As was the case of practically all pawnshops, the Barcelona pawnshop was associated with charitable institutions into which it ploughed back its profits. As it was governed by the pious congregation Notre Seigneur de l'Espérance, it financed partially a welfare institution, *la Casa del Retir de Barcelona*, which took in penitent prostitutes and women in distress. Its problems were aggravated when it had to face competition from three new banks set up at the same time: in 1776 the banc de Canvis de Barcelona and the banc de Fons Perduts and, in 1785, the Monte Pio General para Viudas, Pupilos e Impedidos.[13]

On the contrary, the pawnshops in Northern Europe resorted to the capital market more easily and were not reluctant to develop links with banks rather than with charities. They were also founded much later; Nuremberg was one of the few cities in the Germanic area to open a pawnshop at the end of the fifteenth century (in 1498),[14] after beseeching the emperor to expel Jewish usurers. The preexistence of charitable organizations that partially fulfilled the same role was a first explanation for such backwardness. In the Netherlands, for instance, the presence of the Tables of the Poor delayed the establishment of pawnshops. The creation of these charities was prompted by the need to support unemployed workers and quell popular unrest in times of crisis. This development is noticeable in Beauvais as early as at the end of the fifteenth century: whenever a crisis occurred, the "Three Bodies" (bishopric, chapter, and

[13] Montserrat Carbonell i Esteller, *Sobreviure a Barcelona. Dones, pobresa i assistència al segle XVIII*, Barcelona, Eumo Editorial, 1997, pp. 63, 173–8; and Lluís Castañeda, "Sector financer i mercat de capitals al primer terç del segle XIX," dans *Història econòmica de la Catalunya Contemporània*, vol. 5, Barcelona, 1991, pp. 338–51.

[14] Mollat, *Les pauvres au Moyen Age*, p. 338.

town), would come together to deal with poverty, unemployment, revolt, and contagion. In the sixteenth century, "an office of the poor was held" and, in 1653, the "Office of the Poor" was founded, with its buildings, its autonomous revenues, and its administration.[15]

In the south of the Netherlands, in the sixteenth century, permissions and interdictions of the Lombard alternated and a first reduction of the rates was imposed. On Wenzel Cobergher's initiative (1560–1634), the idea of replacing the private pawning counters by state pawnshops appeared. Between 1618 and 1634, he succeeded in creating pawnshops in fifteen towns in the Southern Netherlands: Brussels, Antwerp, Mechlin, Ghent, Arras, Tournai, Mons, Valenciennes, Cambrais, Bruges, Lille, Douai, Namur, Courtai, and Bergues. Then, two more institutions opened: in 1665 in Ypres and in 1782 in Louvain.

In the wake of this movement, the northern Netherlands developed credit banks capable of competing with the private activities of the Lombard (in Amsterdam in 1614, in Rotterdam in 1635, in The Hague in 1673, in Leyden in 1675, etc.). A credit bank, the Bank van Lening, was established in Zwolle in 1636 after several years of petitioning.[16] The pawnshops in the capital of Cobergher were not financed by donation but by resorting to private capital funded by perpetual loans (*rentes perpétuelles*). Resorting to the capital market proved to be a huge success: from 1618 to 1650, the population bought more than 8,000 perpetual loans, thus allowing the pawnshops to dispose of several million florins. However, such use of capital overburdened the pawnshops with debt, and the excessive cost of construction and maintenance of the buildings placed them in a complex financial situation. It was not until drastic reforms were undertaken in 1760 that they ultimately became viable.[17] These institutions had specific characteristics: the loan was anonymous, and the interest rate ranged from 6 per cent to 15 per cent. Certain other pawnshops followed the same rule, in particular the one in Paris.

England was the only European country that did not try to create a pawnshop after the Italian model of a charitable organization.

---

[15] Pierre Goubert, *Beauvais et le Beauvaisis de 1600 à 1730: Contribution à l'histoire sociale de la France du XVIIe siècle*, Paris, SEVPEN, 1960, pp. 302–3.

[16] Hilde Van Wijngaarden, "Credit as a Way to Make Ends Meet. The Use of Credit by Poor Women in Zwolle, 1650–1700," presented at session C 59, "Les femmes et les pratiques du credit (XVIIe–XIXe siècles)," L. Fontaine and C. Muldrew, coordinators, of the 12th International Congress on Economic History, Madrid, 1998.

[17] Paul Soetaert, *De Bergen van Barmhartigheid in de Spaanse, de Ootenrijkse en de Franse Nederlanden (1618–1795)*, Brussells, Historiche Uitgaven, reeks in 8°, nr. 67, 1986, pp. 328–9.

Nonetheless, a debate did take place in the seventeenth century to try to limit the excesses of pawnbrokers. Some suggested it be made obligatory to register their activity in special registers and to deposit these in specific offices where they could be checked and consulted; others held the only way out was to set up pawnshops of the kind existing in Southern Europe and Flanders.[18] A lively controversy also arose about the utility of such institutions: some considered them a symbol of authoritarianism; others thought that the creation of an institution likely to compete with private lenders could be defended provided it was viable. The only attempt we know of was The Charitable Corporation. Presented in 1699, it opened in 1707 in London. Willingly characterized as philanthropic and as a way of counteracting the misuse of private loan, this organization proposed an interest rate of 5 per cent to its subscribers. It developed until rumours of embezzlement of funds and of fake pledges aroused suspicions. In 1731, after an investigation was launched, the cashier and the investor fled to the continent. The loss was estimated at a half million pounds, and the institution was closed in 1732.[19] This failure sounded the death knell on attempts to offset private-loan establishments. Projects that flourished before the 1830s also remained unaccomplished.[20]

In the French region, the first establishments were located in the outer reaches of the kingdom, regions that had earlier benefitted from other traditions: Avignon in 1577, Beaucaire in 1583, Carpentras in 1612, Arras in 1615, Nancy in 1630,[21] and Marseilles in 1696.[22] However, most of these institutions could not withstand the merchants' hostility. The latter refused to be dispossessed of the lending deals they had the upper hand on and feared for their business – especially the sale by auction of objects that were deposited and never reclaimed. Their opposition was strong enough to hinder the setting up of pawnshops, although some such as Colbert favoured their establishment.

---

[18] British Library I-816 m. 13. See, for instance, 1 n. 83 to 86. My thanks to Caroline Fontaine who acquainted me with these documents.

[19] J. M. Bulloch, "The Charitable Corporation," notes and queries, 4 April 1931; Melanie Tebbutt, *Making Ends Meet. Pawnbroking and Working Class Credit*, London, Methuen, 1984, p. 109.

[20] Tebbutt, *Making Ends Meet*, pp. 110–11.

[21] Yannick Marek, "Au carrefour de l'économique et du social: l'histoire du mont de piété de Rouen (1778–1923)," *Le Mouvement social*, no. 116, 1981, pp. 67–94 (69).

[22] Marcel Courdurié, *La Dette des collectivités publiques de Marseille au XVIIIe siècle. Du débat sur le prêt à intérêt au financement par l'emprunt*, Marseille, PUBLISHER Institut historique de Provence, 1974, p. 237.

As a matter of fact, for a long time in France, the conception of pawnshops remained a project. Around 1608, Pierre de Fontenu submitted to the King's Council a plan to set up a Banque de France, and envisaged, with the opening of deposit accounts, a system of lending against security at denier 12 (i.e., 8.33 per cent); the difficulty of building a financial corpus doomed the project to failure.[23] In 1611, Hugues Delestre, former member of the League and civil lieutenant at the royal seat of Langres, conceived of a pawnshop that would be

the eyes of the blind, the feet of the lame, the ears of the deaf, the veil of the virgin, the guardian of the widow, the staff of the old man, the father of the orphan, the teacher of the child, the guide of the disciple, the master of the apprentice, the doctor of the sick; in a nutshell, all things for all men.

This plan, presented in 1611 to Marie de Medici, was then submitted to the Etats généraux in 1614 by some gentlemen who suggested a pawnshop

where there shall be deniers to lend at the interest of denier 16 [6¼ per cent] for securities to be given by those who deal with money." Supported by the lower nobility, this bill was opposed by the Tiers-Etat which viewed it as "a means to introduce new usurers in France where there were already too many."[24]

In 1643, letters patent provided for the establishment of a pawnshop in Paris and in fifty-eight other cities. The operation did not yield any result either in the capital or in any other city.[25]

Théophraste Renaudot, a Protestant doctor and journalist, revived the plan in 1637. He suggested associating an Address Bureau (which supplied the names of people requiring help and listed the situations vacant and situations wanted) with a pawn-broking establishment that would lend for two months, with the possibility of renewal, at a rate of interest of 15 per cent per month. These two organizations were to be installed in the premises of *la Gazette* in Paris. Before Cardinal Richelieu, he justified his pawnshop emphasizing the importance of helping people when they were in need:

Monseigneur, experience has taught in the affairs of life, that succor provided in time acquires the import of a treasure. A worker, without an advance, cannot take charge and, pushed to despondency, gives himself up to drink, the mother

---

[23] Robert Bigo, "Aux origines du Mont de Piété parisien," *Annales d'histoire économique et sociale*, 1932, pp. 113–26 (115).

[24] see Yannick Marec, Le *"clou" rouennais des origines à nos jours (1778–1982) du Mont de piété au Crédit municipal. Contribution à l'histoire de la pauvreté en province*, Rouen, Éditions du P'tit normand, 1983, pp. 23–4.

[25] Bigo, "Aux origines," pp. 115–16.

of poverty and ill health; the merchant, the entrepreneur without a nest egg succumbs at the first impediment he experiences or cannot execute a good deal or an order; I could carry on forever, Monseigneur, if I were to enumerate all the circumstances where timely assistance is worth, I repeat, a veritable treasure.

In the face of opposition from the Faculty of Medicine and the Parliament of Paris, which accused him of usury and practices unworthy of a doctor, he was forbidden in March 1644 "to sell or lend in future against security."[26]

Finally, in 1673, an edict ruling pawnbroking allowed the creation of several pawnshops (Apt in 1674, Tarascon in 1676, Brignoles in 1677, Angers and Montpellier in 1684, and Marseilles in 1696).[27] They lent either money or seeds. The Aix pawnshop established by the Brotherhood of Notre-Dame de l'Espérance de St Sauveur d'Aix in 1637 acquired its final organizational shape in the eighteenth century. The charity granted loans against securities to all and gave a third of the value of the objects deposited; it accepted as securities all that was not "subject to worms" (metal, linen, etc.). The loan, which could not exceed 30 livres, was given for a period of only six months; it was renewable for another six months "in the case when the crops were yet to be harvested"; once this maturity period elapsed, a notice was sent one month in advance that the security would be put up for sale.[28] In Brignoles, a pawnshop instituted in 1667 would lend to the poor "with the option of duration and withdrawal for as much and whenever they wished."[29]

The letters patent instituting the Arles pawnshop in 1698 illustrate the difficulty in setting up such establishments: "Several establishments of this kind had gone bankrupt, it was written, on account of poor administration by rectors." In 1703, the Brotherhood of Notre-Dame du Bon Secours, called mont-de-piété or charitable Present, lent its name to the organization in Arles. It was open on Mondays and lent up to 100 livres for a maximum duration of six months.[30]

The Marseille pawnshop had been in existence for a long time. After several unsuccessful attempts to establish a system of free loans, the city like others – Aix being an exception – adopted loans with interest.

[26] Marec, *Le "clou" rouennais*, p. 24.
[27] Ibid., p. 25.
[28] Gaston Valran, *Misère et Charité en Provence au XVIIIe siècle. Essai d'histoire sociale*, Paris, 1899, Geneva, Mégariotis Reprints, 1979, pp. 278–9.
[29] Ibid., p. 281.
[30] Ibid., p. 310.

The pawnshop acquired its final organizational shape in 1696, thanks to the generous donation of Jean de Puget, who bequeathed 69,000 livres to it and the permission granted by Louis XIV through letters patent of July 18. The office, open two days a week, Tuesdays for pawning and Saturdays for releasing pledges, was closed from Easter to the month of June. Loans were free, even if in 1702, it was decided to subject transactions to a fee equal to 2.5 per cent of the sales price of securities. The fee was abolished in 1730, and in 1734, it was decided that an interest of 3.75 per cent would be levied on all pawning, in view of the fact that the number of transactions kept increasing.[31]

The seed advance was even more widespread than money loans. The Arles pawnshop, which offered both kinds of loans, had as its mission to help poor farmers. Besides, it indirectly contributed to reestablishing the reputation of the grains of the region, which in the past had attracted merchants from Toulouse and Marseille:

The threat of an agricultural crisis loomed over Arles at all times. It is the land of grains: share cropping is the system of farming; in the bad years, the farmer can hardly pay for his share of the seed; he is forced to borrow; he suffers serious losses; very expensive and of very poor quality, the seed thus acquired does not produce enough in the following years to free him, and he is constrained to contract fresh debts. He is the victim of speculation: the lender values at the highest price the wheat he delivers for the seed and at the lowest price the wheat he receives as payment. As a result, grain cultivation is suffering in Arles, and trade is slowing down: the markets visited in the past by merchants from Toulouse and Marseille have now been abandoned because of the bad reputation of the grain.[32]

Le Prêt charitable – the name given to the pawnshop – lent free wheat at current prices fixed at Saint-Michel, after conducting an inquiry on the peasant who was also required to furnish a guarantee. The wheat was repayable at the time of harvest on June 24 if the harvest had been sold. After September 1, if the loan was not returned, the debtor was dispossessed. When the pawnshop lacked wheat to distribute to all those who had made a request, lots were drawn to determine the fortunate beneficiaries. Peasants in need were required to identify themselves in August. The pawnshop established in 1699 encountered great difficulty in the early stages on account of the terrible winter of 1709 and the 1720 plague. It only started functioning in the true sense of the term in the

---

[31] Ibid., pp. 303–5.
[32] Quoted by ibid., p. 311.

second half of the eighteenth century. In 1738, the council refused to set up new establishments giving the reason that the funds allocated (10,000 livres) did not seem sufficient. In 1766, the 30,000 livres collected still did not allow them to function. Rectors had to borrow, and to secure their loans they asked for official recognition, which was not granted to them until 1770.[33]

In the big towns, setting up a pawnshop was extremely difficult. After failing the first time in the sixteenth century, the city of Lyon attempted once again to set up a pawnshop in 1678. The main traders of Lyon were opposed to official lenders and invoked the municipal privileges and trade interests of the city.[34] They feared above all being dispossessed of the control of the highly profitable private-lending houses, even though in their discourse they played on the fear that the bankrupt would use the institution to conceal their merchandise and take it away from their creditors. In Rouen, traders and bankers – led by Lecouteulx de Canteleu, one of the founders of the discount bank and future regent of the Bank of France – were responsible for the failure of the attempt in 1778 and undoubtedly of the one made in 1786: they claimed that pawnshops would only encourage fraudulent bankruptcy:

merchants and manufacturers whose businesses did not appear to be doing well would take their merchandise to the pawnshops, receive two-thirds of the price and disappear with the money, that it was only an opportunity for young people to steal the effects from the houses of their fathers and mothers in order to procure money for themselves.[35]

At last, after an unsuccessful attempt in 1637, the Parisian pawnshop was created in 1777, at a time of great impoverishment. The initiative came from a group of bankers and politicians who thought that affordable credit was more efficient than charity to help the poor.[36] In June 1777, M. Framboisier de Beaunay[37] suggested to the lieutenant general of police Lenoir the plan for a pawnshop. The project modelled along the organizational lines of the six institutions in the French Flanders aimed at "ensuring cash assistance on easy terms and using the profit to

---

[33] Ibid., pp. 310–14.
[34] Jean-Pierre Gutton, "Lyon et le crédit populaire sous l'Ancien Régime: les projets de monts-de-piété," *Studi in memoria di Federigo Melis*, vol. 4, Napoli, Giannini Editore, 1978, pp. 147–154.
[35] Yannick Marek, "Au Carrefour de l'économique et du social," p. 71.
[36] Marec, *Le "clou" rouennais*, p. 70.
[37] Honorary prosecutor in the bailliage of Lyon, former subdelegue to the intendant of Lyon, he looked after since 1760, visits to the bourgeois children placed with wet nurses

provide relief to the poor." In the words of Necker, the following social strata were targeted: "The pawnshop was established, he wrote,[38] with a view to provide assistance to subjects so that they could get relief in their domestic affairs; assistance to traders for them to avoid the ignominy and the damage caused by the seizure of their goods"[39]

Despite Necker's support, the conception of pawnshops in France was not a won cause because, although he encouraged the creation of such an organization in Paris, he was not willing to bridle the system of private loans that prevailed in the provinces:

I do not believe however that we should establish such institutions in provincial towns: such precautions must be regarded as a softening of misuses we cannot hinder; but in those places where the police are not overburdened, it is easy to destroy the usurers' profession, or at least to contain the traffic within known bounds. It is only in the commotion of a great capital that moral depravation needs accommodating, and a sort of conciliation needs to be made with vice that cannot practically be wiped out: elsewhere, the antidote would only point at the evil.[40]

In the end, the Parisian pawnshop was created on 9 December 1777, and from 5 January 1778, an internal regulation completed its constitutive charter. Although placed under the control of the lieutenant of police, this institution possessed an autonomous regime, and its own accounts were checked each year by a commission, composed of four councillors of the *Grand Chambre* of the *Parlement* and of a representative of the procurator general. It was granted the monopoly over pawn broking.

The success was immediate and as early as in the first months, more employees were hired. On 12 February 1778, a cashier-controller, an assessor, and a chief clerk (*premier commis*) managed the establishment with seven assistants (*commis*) to whom five extras were very soon added. On 2 March a further three assistants (*commis*) were recruited. From 30 March the flow of business was such that the shops had to be expanded and several divisions created. By the end of the year, the *mont-de-piété* comprised no fewer than twenty-seven employees and twenty-six pawnbrokers.[41]

---

in the Parisian suburbs. He established the Office of Wet Nurses. Bigo, "Aux origines," p. 116.

[38] Oeuvres t. II, p. 454, quoted by Bigo, "Aux origines," p. 117.

[39] Bigo, "Aux origines," pp. 116–17.

[40] Jacques Necker, *De l'administration des finances de la France*, Paris, 1784, book 3, p. 293, quoted by Yannick Marek, "Au carrefour de l'économique et due social," p. 70.

[41] Bigo, "Aux origines," p. 118.

Louis Sébastien Mercier[42] relates what he saw and heard at the time of the opening of this pawnshop:

A *mont-de-piété* has finally just been established, known elsewhere as a *lombard*; and the administration, by this wise, long-desired, establishment, has issued a mortal blow to the barbarous and harsh fury of voracious usurers, always ready to despoil the needy ...

Nothing better demonstrates how much the capital needed this *lombard* than the endless flow of applicants. Such peculiar and incredible tales are told that I dare not set them down here without first having sought more precise information, which will allow me to guarantee their veracity. There is talk of *forty barrels filled with gold watches*, doubtless to express the prodigious quantities that have been deposited. What I know for sure is that I have seen between 60 and 80 people waiting their turn there, each one come to borrow not more than *six livres*. One was carrying his shirts, another a piece of furniture, another what remained of a wardrobe, and another his shoe buckles, an old picture, some poor clothes, and so forth. They say that there is a new crowd there almost every day, and this gives a very clear idea of the extreme shortage of money from which most of the city is suffering ...

Rich people borrow as well as the poor. One woman gets out of her carriage, wrapped up in her coat, and deposits 25,000 francs' worth of diamonds so that she can go gambling in the evening. Another takes off her petticoat and asks for the price of a loaf of bread. ...

We are assured that a third of the effects are not collected: a further proof of the strange shortage of cash. The sales that take place offer many luxury goods at low prices, which may harm the smaller merchants somewhat. But besides this, it is no bad thing that these goods, which were excessively highly priced, should now experience a drop in their exorbitant rates.

It is said that the system is already being abused. The poor are bullied, and the objects offered by the destitute are estimated at too low a price, which means that they are being offered virtually no help. Charity should be the driving force and should be more important than other superficial and vain considerations. It would not be hard to turn this establishment into a *temple of mercy*, generous, active and compassionate. The good work has begun: why should it not be completed in a way that will satisfy the poorest people most?

On opening, the *mont-de-piété* had in its tills a sum of 558,200 livres, thanks to the discounting of notes to the bearer under the guarantee of the Hôpital général. After one month, it had already lent 101,154 livres. At the inaugural meeting on 22 December the director was authorized to borrow at 5 per cent. The funds were drawn in several ways.

---

[42] Louis Sébastien Mercier, *Tableau de Paris*, edition prepared under the supervision of Jean-Claude Bonnet, vol. 2, Mercure de France, Paris, 1994 [1781–1789], vol. 1, p. 662–4, "Mont de piété."

On 14 November 1778, exchange agents were invited to procure funds at six months, averaging a commission of 1/8 per cent, that is, 25 sols per 1,000 livres. The establishment, which sought long-term deposits, offered premiums for two-year deposits. From 3 December 1778, the Hôpital Général, which had already contributed to the constitution of the initial capital, had to guarantee further sums up to four million. At the same time, the number of administrators was increased from four to six. It offered 4.5 per cent for deposits of one year and 3.5 per cent on loans of six months. Funds grew, and, after a year, the accounts were healthy. In February 1789, the pawnshop had received so many deposits that it decided to give only 5 per cent interest on deposits of a year, up to a limit of 6 million. Beyond this sum, interest would be given only at 4.5 per cent. On 31 December 1789, the operating capital reached more than thirteen million livres, of which close to five million were placed at 4.5 per cent, and the rest at 5 per cent.

On 31 December 1778, there were 128,508 objects pawned for 8,309,384 livres and 60,551 objects released for 3,179,523 livres and 67,957 objects in stock for 5,129,861 livres; five years later, there were more than 400,000 articles whose value exceeded 16.5 million livres and in 1787 and more than 470,000 objects worth more than 18 million livres. From 1780 to 1787, the number of employees went up from fifty to eighty-four. In 1789, the brisk business of the two preceding winters kept busy 7 warehousemen, 82 pawnees and 88 assistants who, along with the management staff, added up to 194 agents. This huge success reflects the great need for small, short-term credit of the people of Paris.

With paper money being issued increasingly, the revolution kept away lenders who preferred securing a movable asset and borrowers too became scarce. Shops were empty and the pawnshop dwindled before being closed down on Fructidor, Year IV.[43] It was from the time of the directoire that public authorities encouraged the pawnshop to fight against usury and several laws, under the consulat and the empire, gave them the monopoly over pawnbroking, but they continued to allocate the profits of the pawnshop to hospices, thereby maintaining the link between these credit establishments and charitable institutions in accordance with the old Catholic tradition to the detriment of the banking institutions that were being developed at that time.

In spite of everything, all over Europe, the nineteenth century witnessed the development of pawnshops. In France, many were set up, and

---

[43] Bigo, "Aux origines," pp. 119–23.

if we are to compare the figures for items pawned and renewals in the main establishments between 1833 and 1875, the increase was spectacular: 157.4 per cent in Paris, 204.79 per cent in Lyon, and 158.16 per cent in Bordeaux. These figures notwithstanding, several pawnshops faced serious problems: the association of hospices that received the pawnshop profit prevented the required investment to be made to lighten the operational costs and, on account of this, prohibited the lowering of rates. As a result, pawnshops had a bad reputation. They were accused of lending at very high rates, thereby favouring usurers who could lend at similar, even better rates, as well as merchants who had come to an understanding to acquire extremely cheap the objects put up for auction. Trafficking in acknowledgments of debt was also condemned. The example of Rouen, as well as those of the Irish establishments, illustrates these problems. The pawnshop in Rouen appeared in 1808 after the prohibition of private-lending houses. Ten years later, it went bankrupt under the pressure of creditors suspected of working to protect the private houses. A new establishment was set up in 1826. The rate of interest charged was 12 per cent, and until the end of the nineteenth century, it remained a welfare establishment. The last creations, in Catholic Europe, took place in Ireland: eight pawnshops were built in the 1830s and 1840s in Limerick, Belfast, Newcastle, Cork, Lismore, Dugannon, Tandragee, and Portadown. But they all failed because the interest rates they offered were a lot higher than those of the private houses. The latter had, moreover, planned together to stand against them in fierce competition.[44]

Breaking ties with charitable establishments proved to be a long struggle in Catholic Europe. It only really succeeded in France in the aftermath of the First World War. The opponents refused to see the similarity of operations between pawnshops and savings banks.[45]

Institutions That Won the Immediate Acceptance of the People

These pawnshops, set up during the ancien régime, were made to fulfil multiple functions by the people. In addition to the donations from the elite by way of charity, the lower orders invested their savings, using pawnshops similar to a savings bank. An analysis of monies invested in the Marseille pawnshop is an eloquent testimony: the pawnshop borrowed as and when required from lenders who were for the most part

---

[44] Tebbutt, *Making Ends Meet*, p. 110.
[45] Marec, *Le "clou" rouennais*, pp. 72–5.

people of limited means who demanded they be paid back when they asked. Thus, low return perpetual annuities (generally 4 per cent) represented 76.7 per cent of the total value of borrowings during the eighteenth century.[46]

The clientele was everywhere more diverse than the initial intentions had foreseen. The mission of the pawnshops was always to assist the poor, but they also helped other social classes that were deep in debt.

The rules governing deposits and loans tell us of the will to reach out to the poorest, although the other social strata were accepted everywhere. The loan-to-value ratio varied from one pawnshop to the next. In southern Italy, people borrowed for at least three months and at the most three years, and some objects likely to wear out quickly were excluded such as a ball of wool or iron objects. Only the inhabitants of the town in which the pawnshop was set up could go there and the loans were modest: from 1.5 deniers to 40 deniers.[47] As for the loans, the letters patent of 9 December 1777, fixed for Paris the quota of loans at four-fifths of the value by weight for gold or silver and two-thirds of the estimated value for other objects. The valuers, chosen from among the attendant auctioneers (*huissiers-commissaires priseurs*) of the Châtelet, had a commission rate (*droit de prisée*) of one denier per livre. The rate of loans had an implicit upper limit of 10 per cent to the extent that the administration was authorized to retain only 2 deniers per livre and per month for the administration costs (making 2 sous per livre per year). The loan could not be for less than three livres.[48]

In Marseille, gold and silver obtained three-fourths of their intrinsic value; diamonds and pearls, two-thirds; and furniture and clothes, half. The pawnshop charged on such loans an interest varying between 3.75 and 5 per cent throughout the century. In 1757, loans less than 5 livres were given free, and in 1782, the interest was 4 per cent for loans of more than 5 livres and 5 per cent for deposits of more than 15 livres.[49]

In Barcelona, loans given for six months and a day could not exceed 56 Catalan livres. This ceiling was often crossed in the initial years when the pawnshop had solid reserves but it was once again maintained from

[46] Courdurié, *La Dette des collectivités*, pp. 240–1.
[47] Paola Avallone, "The Credit Upon Pledge," in the Kingdom of Naples (XVIth–XIXth centuries)," communication to the colloquium "The Bank of the Poor. The credit upon pledge and the "Monti di Pietà" in the Mediterranean countries (XVth–XIXth Centuries)" Naples, 24–25 September 2004, pp. 19–20.
[48] Bigo, "Aux origines," p. 121.
[49] Courdurié, *La Dette des collectivités*, p. 238.

the 1770s when pawnshops faced a crisis. The jewels deposited received two-thirds of their value and cloth half. At the time of retrieving their security, debtors would pay alms to respect the spirit of the gift[50] when its practice was not observed. The amount was fixed in 1652 at 8 deniers per livre of the sales price of the security; from 1664, the alms were no longer calculated on the basis of value but on the quantity loaned. This practice was only legalized in 1667. From 1770, on the intervention of the king, such alms lost their obligatory character; 6 deniers per livre were still charged from 1772 (2.5 per cent); however, there is no evidence of the king having ratified the said measure. Such alms were used to finance the functioning of the institution and pay interest on deposits.[51]

Finally, credit institutions were everywhere, in Italy, France, Spain, England, and the Netherlands,[52] providing consumer credit to the poorest, short-term commercial credit, and emergency credit to the middle classes and even the elite. In Amsterdam in the second half of the eighteenth century, an analysis of pawnshop clients according to gender and life-cycle stage shows that credit was widespread, even if the poorest were not as well represented: of 912 families for whom we have inventories, 14 per cent left tickets for possessions they had pawned and not recovered at the time of their death. The poorest, those who left goods for a maximum of fifteen guilders only represented 6 per cent of those who left behind tickets for securities they were unable to claim. Among them, widows belonged to the category, which made the largest amount of small loans and had difficulty in recovering their securities. A season-wise analysis of loan distribution reveals a significant concentration of loans during the winter months (November to February) and a notable decline in summer (July and August). This calendar holds good especially for married couples, because widows escaped the traditional work market with its slack periods, being part of a more informal economy.[53]

In Marseille, account books, preserved only for the years 1791 to 1793, indicate 23,000 loans in a common year for an average amount of 19 livres 5 sols. For the year 1734, based on the volume of loans

[50] Bartolome Clavero, *Antidora, Antropología católica de la economía moderna*, Milan, Giuffrè Editore, 1991. The French translation has been used here: *La grâce du don. Anthropologie catholique de l'économie moderne*, Paris, Albin Michel, 1996.
[51] Carbonell i Esteller, *Sobreviure*, pp. 174–5.
[52] Soetaert, *De Bergen van Barmhartigheid*, pp. 112 et seq.
[53] Anne McCants, "Goods at Pawn: The Overlapping World of Material Possessions and Family Finance in Early Modern Amsterdam," *Social Science History*, vol. 31, no. 2, 2007, pp. 213–38.

given, it is estimated that about 5 per cent of the population had pawned a good.[54]

The Parisian pawnshop played the role of a real bank for the Parisian artisans, as the quality of the objects and the lowness of the loans testified. Of 600,000 annual loans, 550,000 loans for between 3 and 24 livres were given at a loss. Four divisions of the establishment, each receiving close to 80,000 articles for a value of about 1 million livres in 1789, were reserved for clothes, linen, sheets, and remnants of fabrics. In two other divisions, the most precious objects were pawned. In the first were deposited diamonds, jewels, lace, and new goods. In 1789, the sum of the 52,221 pawned items of this order reached 7,630,667 livres. Such figures corroborate Mercier's assertions: "The opulent borrow as much as the poor. One woman gets out of her carriage, wrapped up in her coat, and deposits 25,000 francs worth of diamonds so that she can go gambling in the evening." The second division took silver, watches, bronzes, buckles, swords, and pictures, and was well supplied: records show 89,461 articles to a value of 5,420,145 livres. On a single day – 26 August 1783 – 139 gold watches were deposited. Already at the time, the number of goods pawned daily reached 1,800 to 2,000 items for an amount of 60,000 livres. Of this sum, 43,000 livres, that is, more than two-thirds, were paid to five to six hundred clients of both the rich divisions, whereas one-third (17, 000 livres) was paid to thrice that number of clients (approximately fifteen hundred), of the five ordinary divisions. Of the 1,500,000 livres that came from the sale of securities in 1788, 600,000 came from the sale of rags belonging to the needy, 300,000 livres from silverware, 200,000 livres from watches, 200,000 livres from jewels, and only 200,000 livres from merchandise.

An inspection of the registers on a daily basis clearly shows the diversity of the clientele. Here is an example of an ordinary morning in 1788. That morning, the appreciators have estimated the 84-pound gold watches of two midwives, a wine merchant, and a tailor. Then a cobbler showed up with 32-pound silver rings; a jeweller with a clock estimated to cost 252 pounds; a burgess living on rue d'Argenteuil deposited 150 pounds' worth of silverware; a joiner brings Voltaire's works in seven volumes; a dancer at the Comic-Diversion pawned his theatrical belongings; a private individual deposited four paintings estimated to cost 260 pounds, and so forth.[55]

[54] Courdurié, *La Dette des collectivités*, p. 238.
[55] Bigo, "Aux origines," pp. 121–5.

The help given by the pawnshop to artisans and small merchants was constantly criticized. In January 1789, Desbois de Rochefort, in his short essay on the winter calamities of 1788–1789, held that unemployment in watch- and clock making was due partially to pawnshop sales. In the register of grievances, the community of merchants in the feather fashion also complained of such unfair competition. Now, according to a pawnshop inspector, those who pawned were often the merchants themselves. This statement seems to be borne out by attendant auctioneers who, in their *Observations sur le mont de piété* published in 1790, noted that goldsmiths and watchmakers bought silverware and watches from pawnshops, even though prices were on the whole higher than on the market.[56]

In Avignon, the increase in the number of visits to pawnshops was almost continuous. The threshold of 5,000 deposits was reached in 1694, 1695, and once again in 1699. A record maximum of 6,386 tickets were issued in 1713, and then the number of clients fell and only regained the 1710s' level in the 1740s. Thereafter in the following years, the success of the pawnshop continued to grow: 8,504 loans in 1751, which in theory represents one loan per adult, and the activity kept increasing. Silk workers were the main users of pawnshops; in fact, they were mainly women workers, because since 1674, the share of women never fell below 83 per cent, whereas men in an average year accounted for only 10 to 15 per cent. Its success, which was not directly linked to the industrial environment of the time, did not indicate an increase in the number of the poor but the fact of its becoming a credit establishment used regularly by the people.[57]

An analysis of the English clientele in the middle of the nineteenth century reveals the importance of very small traders and artisans:

First the poorest, such hawkers who cry fish, fruit and other wares, all those belonging to the poorest class without personal credit were obliged to go to pawnbrokers and, thanks to the money they borrowed from them, were able to buy the various goods they would resell to live and support their families.

Another group of users were the middleclass merchants who engaged many day labourers and borrowed from pawnbrokers the wages they had to pay them.

And lastly, workers and craftspeople who bought with the money borrowed from pawnbrokers the material required for their business; very few of them could do otherwise for lack of personal credit.[58]

[56] Ibid., pp. 122–3.
[57] Madeleine Ferrières, *Le bien des pauvres. La consommation populaire en Avignon (1600–1800)*, Paris, Éditions Champ Vallon, 2004, pp. 64–75.
[58] Peter Earle, *The Making of the English Middle Class: Business, Society and Family Life in London 1660–1730*, Berkeley, University of California Press, 1989, p. 118.

In Glasgow, a bankruptcy that occurred in 1836 showed that of the six thousand deposits, three-fourths were of clothing, of which 58 per cent were women's and the others belonging to one or the other sex. Bed linen accounted for 14.5 per cent; watches, rings and medals for 7.4 per cent and bibles for 1.6 per cent. The most modest craftspeople and street sellers were regular clients of such lenders. Several small fruit and fish sellers in Glasgow would borrow the few shillings required for their trade by pawning their blankets; shoemakers pawned part of their stock to pawnshops to renew or purchase material, and the small carpenter did likewise with his saw to buy nails and glue that would allow him to finish his work. Hawkers too were habitual clients of pawnshops whenever they experienced financial difficulties. Yet none of them had access to official establishments, and many had to be content with backyard lenders who asked for much higher rates of interest. However, thanks to these small loans, the world of small independent workers found the means to eke out a living.[59]

Pawning items was such a common practice that Charles Dickens was surprised at these "strange afterthoughts" highly visible among costermongers and fishmongers: "the former often wearing great squab brooches as convenient pledges, and the latter massive silver rings." Indeed, seasonal trade workers were in the habit of buying objects of value (furniture, household utensils, and ornamental clothing) which they pledge in winter as and when there was a financial need.[60]

An analysis of the loans granted by the pawnshop in Barcelona in January 1764 shows that 80 per cent of the loans around 2 Barcelonian pounds were given to a similar clientele. The fabrics and clothes that constituted the high majority of the deposits (sheets, shorts, raw wool fabrics, and, seldom, cotton canvas and printed calico) testified to the strong presence of the weavers. Then came the peasants, the carpenters, the ironworkers, and the sailors. Those who managed to reclaim their deposits, generally the most modest, were textile and construction workers and farmers, and almost half the traders – those who worked in the foodstuffs sector – could not reclaim their loan.[61] In times of crisis, the most ordinary and profitable uses of pawnshops tended to get hidden.

Very soon, pawnshops became part of the popular culture, and all over Europe, people were able to turn them to their advantage and make

[59] Tebbutt, *Making Ends Meet*, pp. 33–34, 22.
[60] Ibid., p. 19 and citations on p. 17.
[61] Carbonell i Esteller, *Sobreviure*, pp. 180–4.

them reenter the informal urban economy. They were quick to learn how
to use every possible resource to earn a little money. Popular expressions
such as *ma tante* or *le clou* were a reflection of these familiar and shared
appropriations of the pawnshop, some of which deserve to be highlighted.
When the season changed, they were used on a large scale as storage units
by individuals and tradespeople such as this tailor, who in the summer
of 1845 deposited the winter clothing that cluttered his shop to reclaim
them with the coming of the winter months thanks to the money he had
been loaned.[62] Some people would pledge an item every morning only
to reclaim it every evening: thus, more than one individual removed the
blanket from his bed to reclaim it before nightfall in exchange for a coat
or a jacket; others would pledge every Monday their Sunday suit; still
others deposited their winter clothes that cluttered their cupboards and
shops to reclaim them as soon as winter set in.

People also considered pawnshops sufficiently safe to protect their
valuables from theft and fire and more than one woman deposited her
jewels there to keep them safe from thieves.

Pawnshops allowed some small craftspeople as well to make their
money grow by pawning goods hired, purchased, or handed over before
or after having worked them. Thus, no sooner had tailors bought cloth
pieces with the advance they had received that they pledged them and
took them back as and when required. Apprentices, servants, and daily
workers in the jewellry business brought the precious metals with which
they worked. In 1744, the author of an apology of pawnbroking acknowledged that it was a common habit in many professions.[63] Laundry women
were also known to adopt such practices: they would tell their clients' to
come back after a week to collect their linen and used the time to deposit
the washed linen at the pawnshop. With the money they got, they would
buy various small items to sell and with the money earned through their
resale, the cycle was completed and the linen reclaimed in time for the
client to collect it.[64]

The records of a pawnbroker from the mining district of Salford inform
us of popular practices in English towns in the early nineteenth century: 5
per cent of the goods were reclaimed on the very day they were pawned,

[62] Marec, *Le "clou" rouennais*, p. 81.
[63] T. S. Ashton, *Economic History of England in the Eighteenth Century*, London,
    Routledge and the Taylor & Francis Group, 2006, p. 210, as cited in Tebbutt, *Making
    Ends Meet*, p. 72.
[64] Tebbutt, *Making Ends Meet*, p. 73.

8 per cent on the next day, and 20 per cent within three days. It was not uncommon for deposits of blankets or clothes to be exchanged twice in the same day and pawnshops in England too were used as safe deposits and protection against fire.[65] A late-seventeenth-century text thus relates the back and forth of a certain Mrs Joan's finery; it would leave the pawnshop every Saturday evening only to come back on Monday morning. So great was the extent of the phenomenon that some establishments had to refuse blankets and coats deposited there in the summer months.[66]

The trafficking of IOUs flourished in many towns, showing the extent to which the informal economy had managed to appropriate an institution intended to prevent its spread. In Paris, for instance, if the average number of transactions was taken – objects pledged, reclaimed, renewed, and sold – in a common year, from 1785 to 1789, then one would observe that out of the 490,000 articles deposited (i.e., about 14 million), hardly 25,000 were sold (i.e., 1,200,000 livres),[67] which seems to reveal that the large majority of clients were solvent, but those who withdrew the objects were not necessarily those who deposited them.

Loan tickets soon became a part of the popular economy. If one compares the business of Avignon's pawnshop with that of Salon, we see that in Avignon only 4 to 12 per cent of the items were withdrawn and 5 to 11 per cent in the eighteenth century, whereas in Salon, nearly 50 per cent of the items were not withdrawn. The reason is that since the seventeenth century, people resold pawn notes. From the 1620s onwards, the name of the person depositing the items was not always the same as that of the person withdrawing them. In this way, tickets circulated like paper money: they were sold and resold. In Avignon, a priest was called on to settle a dispute between three women over the circulation of pawn tickets. The widow Petitjean had withdrawn four tickets, which she resold to the widow Tardieu, who, before paying for them, gave them immediately to Madeleine Bressy. Another case shows that the same pawn was used in several loans: Marguerite Bourge, another widow, acknowledged before the notary that she owed 34 livres to the merchant Antoine Peyrol, "who as security declares being in possession of a ticket from the pawnshop containing a stripped bourrette petticoat and Indian apron that the said

---

[65] Ibid., pp. 13, 19.
[66] "Four for a Penny: Or Poor Robin's Character of an Unconscionable Pawnbroker, and Ear-mark of an Oppressing Tallyman: With a Friendly Description of a Bum Bailey and his Merciless Setting Cur or Follower With Allowance," 1678, Harlein Ms., vol. IV, quoted by Tebbutt, *Making Ends Meet*, p. 21, 31.
[67] Bigo, "Aux origines," p. 125.

Bourge handed over to him, and he promises to return it to her when the said Bourge pays the 34 livres on 22 July of the following year."[68]

An analysis of the deposits of Barcelona's pawnshop shows that in the first year in 1751, a little less than 16,500 items were withdrawn against more than 92,000 items deposited. But from the very next year, the number of withdrawals increased significantly, proof of the fact that the resale of tickets spread rapidly.[69] We need to know a little more about the micro profits of this secondary circulation of loan tickets. The fact remains that women were at the heart of this circulation as they were of every scheme of the small urban economy.

Traditional usurers too knew how to use the pawnshop and once again, they relied on women to act as their intermediaries. The example of Avignon shows that the pawnshop was both a storage place and a supply store: the women acting as their intermediaries went there regularly to deposit and withdraw clothes, as is emphasized in a memorandum of 1756 that notes that "the shops are full of pawns deposited by usurers through intermediaries" and that, in his shop, the usurer had as many tickets as clothes. Women frequently seen at the pawnshop were usually brokers. Their business flourished in particular at the end of the seventeenth and early eighteenth centuries and accounted for as much as one-fourth of the total interventions. In 1771, their business was made official by fixing a rate; it was displayed in the city as well as at the entrance of the pawnshop; they could charge 1 sol for 3 livres, 2 sous for 6 livres, and 3 sous for 12 livres.[70]

The functioning of pawnshops raises the issue of the common people's infatuation for the consumption of luxury objects, such as gold watches and jewels, which are mentioned so often in after-death inventories[71]: apart

---

[68] Ferrières, *Le bien des pauvres*, p. 69.
[69] Yepes, *Historia Urgente de cajas de ahorro*, p. 107.
[70] Ferrières, *Le bien des pauvres*, pp. 71–2, 84.
[71] Towards 1700 in Paris, 13% of domestics and 5% of wage earners had a watch. Watches became increasingly common during the eighteenth century, as indicated by 70% of the inventories of domestics and 30% of those of wage earners in the decade of the 1780s; Daniel Roche, *Le peuple de Paris*, p. 226. Initially, cheap watches were acquired (27.1% in 1725 and 17.2% in 1785), but the main trend was phenomenal increase in gold watches (7.1% in 1725 compared to 54.7% in 1785). Jewellry followed the same trend, and the number of times they were listed in inventories rose from 49.2% in 1725 to 78.1% in 1785; C. Fairchild, "The Production and Marketing of Populuxe Goods in Eighteenth-Century Paris," *Consumption and the World of Goods*, John Brewer and Roy Porter, eds., London, Routledge, 1993, pp. 228–48 (230). The fall in the number of cheap watches has to be taken with a pinch of salt: it could simply mean that many did not think they were worthy enough to be included in an inventory.

from their mere usefulness and from the will to imitate the aristocrats,[72] watches could easily be converted into money. The purchase of luxury items might testify to the fact that town dwellers in early modern Europe already favoured "illiquidity." By investing money beyond the sheer pleasure of consumption, they tied up capitals, which were thus freed from the relations' enticement and which, in case of need, could be used to borrow ready money.

Just like merchandise, clothes, and objects were pawned and resold among individuals. Clothes and objects are as much a part of wealth as anything else, a fact we seem to have forgotten with the trivialization of material goods in today's consumer society. When a widow from Barcelona said in her will that she would bequeath her shirts to such a one as would help her until her last breath, it was money she gave, and no one thought otherwise.[73] In Rome, women loaned their luxury goods so that others could pawn them and get back some money.[74] The increase in popular consumption is also to be read as an accumulation of savings.

The functioning of pawnshops, such as that of many pawn agencies, shows the extent to which it is important to reposition the purchase and sale of goods, not only in a symbolic economy but also in the way things actually worked and in everyday logic. This implies that we cease to think of luxury trade in the context of the developed economies of Europe of the twentieth century, in which the market and the financial sectors each have their own institutions and autonomy, and to go back to the ancien régime, in which money was scarce, work and life precarious, and financial institutions had just started to take shape. Besides, the history of the institutionalization of pawnbroking tells us at the same time about the extent to which the subterranean financial economy drove the cities.

In spite of the impossibility of pawnshops investing their profits to modernize and reduce their costs and despite the stiff opposition of merchants to their establishment, their immediate and obvious success testifies to the need for such institutions. Delinking pawnshops from welfare and placing them in the banking system was a long battle won only in the twentieth century after the First World War. This victory was marked by a change in the name of such establishments, thereafter called Municipal

---

[72] Fairchild, "Production and Marketing."
[73] Carbonell i Esteller, *Sobreviure*, p. 186.
[74] Renata Ago, "Credit, Consumption and Women's Work: Rome in the XVIIth Century," presented at the session C 59, "Les femmes et les pratiques du crédit (XVIIe–XIXe siècles)," L. Fontaine and C. Muldrew, coordinators, of the 12th International Congress of Economic History, Madrid, 1998.

Credit. Now, the linking with welfare cost pawnshops dearly. It hampered considerably return on capital and gave to charitable institutions the profits they made thereby stopping them from reinvesting to modernize and lower their running costs. These drawbacks contributed to the bad reputation of pawnshops, accused of lending at excessively high rates. Yet in spite of these difficulties, they won immediate acceptance from the people who were able to use them to their own advantage and earn unexpected profits.

The history of the institutionalization of pawnbroking reveals the strength of ideologies and their impact on economic practices: pawnshops paid dearly because of their inability to choose whether to be a bank or to provide welfare, to be profitable or charitable. This fact has hardly ever been emphasized, yet it is the central reason for the failure of pawnshops in Southern Europe, required as they were to maintain high rates to meet their operational costs. They were soon to become more expensive than private lenders.

7

The Battle of Prohibitions against Usury

Here enter not base pinching usurers,
Pelf-lickers, everlasting gatherers,
Gold-graspers, coin-gripers, gulpers of mists,
Niggish deformed sots, who, though your chests
Vast sums of money should to you afford,
Would ne'ertheless add more unto that hoard,
And yet not be content, – you clunchfist dastards,
Insatiable fiends, and Pluto's bastards,
Greedy devourers, chichy sneakbill rogues,
Hell-mastiffs gnaw your bones, you ravenous dogs
Part of the inscription set upon the great gate of Theleme.
            – François Rabelais, *Gargantua*, chap. 54

Although credit and debt were omnipresent in the lives of individuals in early modern Europe, church and state, which universally condemned their usage, developed an intense intellectual and legislative response to these questions. Understanding how this contradiction unfolded thus forms the backdrop to all thinking on the experiences of men and women arising out of the practice of lending, need and the price of time. What moral values were in conflict, how did they evolve and how did practice reconcile itself with these diverse doctrines? In this chapter, the multifaceted debate concerning credit and usury is not analysed (a volume would not be sufficient). Our aim is simply to highlight the major patterns in the confrontation over the censure of credit and see how the discourses, institutions, and practices relating to credit and usury became intertwined over time. In an attempt to capture the essence of this European diversity, this chapter is organized around the intersection of three specific realities which are rarely studied together in the context of usury, namely, the currents of the ideological tensions that have influenced representations of usury; the institutional concretization of such representations because they reveal the political play of forces working behind these debates (i.e., whoever holds judicial power decides who is competent to define right and to ensure it is respected); finally, the manner in which social agents establish financial instruments and practices to sidestep and overcome the rules.

The chosen approach, which mingles these controversies with their social concretization, allows in return for the approach concerning the discourses to be more complex by showing to what extent the social efficacy of such discourses is variable depending on the power of those who elaborate them, and, on the power of resistance of those who receive them. This approach should also make it possible, to avoid the simplifications of a long-term history of "mentalities"[1] in order to emphasize the conflicts concerning concepts crucial to the same epoch, their struggles, their negotiations, and their transformation.

The First Tensions Concerning Time, Work, and Charity

Urbanization and the development of commerce in the Middle Ages are the first evolutions that shifted the framework of ethical reference that had, up to then, been exclusively religious. Certainly, the relationship between "morality" and "religion," as far as usury was concerned, just as for sexuality and temporal power, had never been exempt from tensions.[2] The concepts that these social developments set in motion are, in the first instance, those of time (with God's time and that of the merchant),[3] work, gift, and charity. But, with them, other concepts are redefined like those of nature, property, and contract. The evolution, noticeable everywhere, has always had, depending on the country, its own rhythms. The Italy of the Middle Ages had the first ethical, religious, and moral conflict with the merchant.[4] Holland and England partook in debates, practices, and

---

[1] Bartolome Clavero, *Antidora, Antropología católica de la economía moderna*, Milan, 1991. The French translation has been used here: *La Grâce du don. Anthropologie catholique de l'économie moderne*, Paris, Albin Michel, 1996, p. 57.

[2] Michel de Certeau, "La formalité des pratiques. Du système religieux à l'éthique des Lumières (XVIIe–XVIIIe)," *L'écriture de l'histoire*, Paris, Gallimard, 1975, p. 153.

[3] J. Le Goff, *La bourse et la vie, Economie et religion au Moyen Age*, Paris, Hachette, 1986.

[4] *The Courts and the Development of Commercial Law*, V. Piergiovanni, ed., Berlin, Duncker & Humbolt, 1987, see his introduction; R. Savelli, "Modèles juridiques et culture marchande entre 16e et 17e siècles," *Cultures et formations négociantes dans l'Europe moderne*,

institutions of finance ahead of France and Spain. One could say that if usury is a subject that has given rise to a substantial body of scholarship and that has given rise to numerous controversies, these same debates, often with the same conceptual reference points – but with different chronologies and institutional effects – recur throughout Europe.

The first tensions were born of the financial needs of the merchants and of the necessity to fight against the poverty that urbanization was exacerbating. In fact, the end of the Middle Ages was concerned not only with how to base the duty of alms giving but also with credit and poverty alongside making gifts.[5] These debates form part of a tradition founded in the Old Testament and certain precepts of the New Testament. Usury is there defined as any interest demanded beyond the capital sum. The sense is thus very different from that of today where only excessive interest is seen as usury. According to the original definition, all forms of credit were usurious.

The Old Testament forbids making interest bearing loans to one's kin, but authorizes loans to strangers. The laws of Moses state, "Non foenerabis fratri tuo ad usuram pecuniam, ne fruges, ne quamlibet aliam rem, sed alieno" (Do not loan to your brother with interest, not money, nor fruits, nor any other thing but to the stranger). Ezekiel praises the just one who never engages in usury and concludes that whoever deals in usury should not live. When King David asks who shall live in the tabernacle of the Lord, Psalm 15:5 replies that the just will help his neighbours and will not make loans with interest.[6] The Christian tradition rests on these teachings and on St. Luke's injunction: *Date mutuum, nihil inde sperantes*.[7]

The needs of commerce were the first to cause a shift in this body of religious precepts by introducing the element of the time of transactions to notions of risk, or the nascent damage *damnum emergens* and loss of profit *lucrum cessans*. In the *damnum emergens*, a loan offered without interest could be offset if a loss occurred during the loan period, that is to say that if the lender on account of lending lost opportunities to use his money. The case of *lucrum cessans* could only be invoked

---

F. Angiolini and D. Roche, eds., Paris, Éditions de l'EHESS, 1995, pp. 403–20. See also in the same work the article by Gorgio Doria.

[5] Le Goff, *La bourse et la vie*.

[6] Exodus 22:25: "If thou lend money to any of my people that is poor by thee, thou shalt not be to him as an usurer, neither shalt thou lay upon him usury"; Deuteronomy 23:20–1 and Leviticus 25:35–6: do not lend to one's kin only to one's enemies; Ezekiel 18:7–8 and 18–13.

[7] Luke 6:35: "Lend hoping for nothing in return."

when three criteria were met: the compensation demanded had to be reasonable and never superior to the loss, proof of the loss had to be provided, and the loan had to have been granted initially without interest or other charges.

John Noonan dates the redefinition to the fifteenth century with the transformations of the economy,[8] but Jacques Le Goff has shown it to be earlier.[9] In fact, from the beginning of the fifteenth century, the legitimacy of insurance is admitted, and some therefore think that the risk can be sold.[10] That A lends to B with C as guarantor is an accepted practice. The position of the church at the time was, and had been for several centuries, firmly represented by St. Thomas Aquinas (1225–1274) who retained from Roman law the concept of the *mutuum* – a loan contract with interest, sometimes called a *foenum* to distinguish it from a contract of hire. This distinction is combined with that of movable property, which is worn with use, and immovable property, which cannot be destroyed, to allow for the conclusion that one cannot rent a movable object. Thomas Aquinas continues by defining money as a movable object. It is the equivalent of food and, if one lends food, one must concede the right to eat it or else the loan is of no use. Pursuing this logic, Thomas Aquinas decides that one can no more demand rent for money than for food.[11]

To the argument of the fungible nature of money, Thomas Aquinas adds another element borrowed from Aristotle: money was invented as a means of exchange; its proper use is to be consumed in exchange. Because it has no use outside of exchange, money cannot be bought for money and to do so means using it for an aim which is against its own nature. Aristotle's argument on the nature of money forms part of the general framework of assumptions shared by Thomas Aquinas: all things have two uses, one natural and the other corrupt. Nonnatural use is improper

---

[8] John T. Noonan, *The Scholastic Analysis of Usury*, Cambridge, MA, Harvard University Press, 1957, pp. 199–201.

[9] Le Goff, *La bourse et la vie*. On the role played by Pierre de Jean Olivi, see Giacomo Todeschini, *Un trattaro di economia politica francescana: il "De emtionibus et venditionibus, de usuris, de restitutionibus" di Pietro dil Giovanni Olivi*, Rome, Istituto Storico Italiano Per II Medio Evo, 1980, pp. 51–112; and Alain Bourreau and Sylvain Piron, ed., *Pierre de Jean de Olivi, Pensée sclolastique, dissidence spirituelle et société*, Paris, Vrin, 1999.

[10] Giovanni Ceccarelli, "Risky Business: Theological and Canonical Thought on Insurance from the Thirteenth to the Seventeenth Century," *The Journal of Medieval and Early Modern Studies*, 31, no. 3, 2001, pp. 607–58, which moreover fits into the chronology of Jacque le Goff.

[11] Noonan, *Scholastic Analysis*, pp. 53 et seq.

and, Thomas Aquinas would add, is a sin because God created nature and the divine law to which human laws must conform. Consequently, to betray the nature of money by lending it with interest is condemned both by natural law and by the word of God and must be condemned by human law.

But money is a form of property, which, if given for a time, deprives its owner of its use. Moreover, to outlaw the use of capital in commerce is impossible, and Thomas Aquinas, who is conscious of these problems, retains the distinctions made from the thirteenth century concerning the use of money in commercial affairs. In question 78 of his *Summa Theologica*, he admits the legitimacy of making money on a loan if the lender shares the risk with the borrower. The lender must therefore be associated with the borrower and the loan must be an investment. Only two circumstances justify asking for more than the principal: the cases of *damnum emergens* and *lucrum cessans*. Underlying these redefinitions of time, redefinitions of the concept of money, of nature with its human and divine components are also developing and this carries with it tensions over the notion of contract.

The other great conceptual tension concerns the relationship between work and charity. In the debates at the end of the Middle Ages, Antonino of Florence (1389–1459) and Bernardino of Siena (1380–1444), to cite only the two most celebrated contributors to these debates, did not compromise on either the fraud committed against the poor by usury or the obligation to give alms; the latter could not excuse the former. They were at the heart of a current of opinion that advocated the institution of honest forms of credit for the poor that were distinct from donations.[12] The loan is seen as endowed with a double advantage over alms: it is morally more in conformity with the dignity of humans, for it helps them to be the master of their own circumstances; it is more effective, for its is easier to prevent a person from falling than to lift him or her up and to reintegrate the person once he or she is undone. Behind the questioning of alms as the sole form of social exchange lies a questioning of the aristocratic economic culture and, with it, aristocratic power. Once it appeared, this current of thinking never died out – more or less a minority view but always present. Indeed, this same aim animated the founders of the *monts-de-piété* in medieval Italy and in Marseilles at the end of the seventeenth century: "The *Mont-de-Piété*, wrote the administrators, has not so much as its objective the comforting of the poor as to prevent citizens

---

[12] Michel Mollat, *Les Pauvres au Moyen Âge*, Paris, Hachette, 1978, pp. 315–16.

from falling into poverty."[13] Thomas Aquinas and his school established the legal categories: the loan bearing interest is forbidden and the exceptions clearly defined, even if disputes remain surrounding themes such as that of lending with interest to support charitable activities, which was authorized by the Lateran Council in 1515.

The church, which defines what is good, also has the institutional power to ensure its respect. Ecclesiastical tribunals were thus concerned with cases of usury. They fell under both Episcopal jurisdiction and that of the Inquisition in the following manner: the bishop was charged with enforcing morals whilst the inquisitor concerned himself with thoughts. Under the reign of the Inquisition, faith became the only important concern, with morality reduced to a decidedly secondary role. It is not the act but the mental state that determined the gravity of the offence. Thus, a misdeed consciously perpetrated is treated with more leniency and came under different tribunals than cases of ignorant good faith. To trample on the Eucharist, knowing it to be the body of Christ, is less serious than to do it without believing in the divine presence; in one case, there is no heresy whereas in the other, there are grounds for an accusation of heresy. Similarly, to lend usuriously knowing that one is acting wrongly saves the creditor from the charge of heresy that would have been justified if, in lending with interest, he or she believed him- or herself to be acting correctly. Thus, the usurer was only answerable before the tribunal of the Inquisition when he or she affirms, or his or her actions demonstrate, that usurer did not consider usury to be a crime; if he or she recognized its criminal character, the person was amenable to the jurisdiction of the bishop.[14]

An examination of part of the immense literature on the Inquisition confirms this analysis and allows us to draw some conclusions on the relations between the church, the state, the inquisitor, and the creditor. Ordinarily, the Inquisition did not hear cases of usury, preferring

---

[13] Report sent to the Controller General of Finance Mémoire on 29 August 1760, quoted by M. Courdurié, *La Dette des collectivités publiques de Marseille au XVIIIe siècle. Du débat sur le prêt à intérêt au financement par l'emprunt*, Marseille, Institut historique de Provence, 1974, p. 238.

[14] Henri-Ch. Lea, *Histoire de l'inquisition au moyen âge*, 1st American ed., New York, Harpers and Brothers, 1887, 1st French ed., Paris, Société nouvelle de librairie et d'édition, 1901. The edition of Jerôme Millon, (Grenoble, Jerôme Millon, 1990), vol 3, has been consulted, vol. 3, p. 800 and vol. 1, pp. 358 and 452. Jaime Contreras, *El santo oficio de la Inquisición de Galicia (poder, sociedad y cultura)*, Madrid, Akal Editor, 1982, p. 580, emphasizes the dual function of the holy office: to extirpate heresy and moral irregularities. Concerning usury, Lea's distinctions seem pertinent.

to sentence the Jews for heresy. The index of offenses shows no cases either in Corte, Murcia, Grenada, Barcelona,[15] Valencia,[16] Galicia,[17] or Portugal.[18] Nor were the bishops very active. There are some trials for usury in the first decades of the fourteenth century in the Episcopal archives of Barcelona and, during that period, at the end of pastoral visits, some usurers were invariably pursued. Many of these offenses were punished by excommunication, loss of civil rights, and financial and spiritual penalties such as a forced pilgrimage to Montserrat or by being placed at the church door with a placard around the neck indicating the crime and the promise never again to offend. Women accused of usury had to go about with their heads uncovered. But from the fifteenth century, the Episcopal archives indicate that such trials became increasingly exceptional.[19] This leniency also shows that the church was in reality at the core of the loans system.

In medieval England, the church pursued moneylenders in a less frequent, although more consistent, manner.[20] The Netherlands and the Germanic sphere presented a diverse picture; whereas in north and east Germany civil law books made no mention of usury, in the south, they came to follow canon law. Until the middle of the fourteenth century when there was a court case against a city, the city preferred appearing

---

[15] J. -M. Blázquez, "Catálogo de procesos inquisitoriales del Tribunal de Corte," *Rivista de la Inquisición*, no. 3, 1994, pp. 205–57; "Catálogo de procesos inquisitoriales del Tribunal del Santo oficio de Murcia," *Murgetana*, 74, 1987, pp. 7–109; J. -M. Blázquez, "Algunas precisiones sobre estatistica inquisitorial: el ejemplo de la actividad antijudia del Tribunal de Granada en el siglo XVII," *Hispanica sacra*, 40, 1988, pp. 133–64; J. -M. Blázquez, "Catálogo de los procesos inquisitoriales del Santo oficio de Barcelona," *Espacio, Tiempo y Forma*, Serie IV, 3, 1990, pp. 11–158; and J.-M. Blázquez, *El tribunal del Santo oficio de Barcelona 1487–1820*, Toledo, 1990, pp. 291 et seq., for a list of offenses.

[16] S. Haliazar, *Inquisition and Society in the Kingdom of Valencia 1478–1834*, Berkeley, University of California Press, 1990. The trials concerned faith, sexuality, and blasphemy but never usury.

[17] Contreras, *El santo oficio de la Inquisición*, p. 587. Offenses concerning heresy (Judaism, the moriscos, Lutheranism), blasphemies, superstitions, disturbances of the holy office, and sexuality.

[18] J. Romero Magalhaes, "La Inquisición portuguese: intento de periodización." *Rivista de la Inquisición*, no. 2, 1992, pp. 71–93.

[19] Processos de l'Arxiu diocesà de Barcelona, J. M. Martí i Bonet, L. Niqui i Puigvert, and F. Miquel i Mascort, *Els processos dels segles XIV i XV*, vol. 2, introducció a cura de Josep M. Martí i Bonet, Barcelona, Departament de cultura de la Generalitat de Catalunya, 1984.

[20] R. H. Helmholtz, "Usury and the Medieval English Church Courts," *Speculum*, 61, no. 2, 1986, pp. 368–9. Norman L. Jones, *God and the Moneylenders. Usury and Law in Early Modern England*, Oxford, Basil Blackwell, 1989, p. 108.

before the communal judge, and it was only from the mid-fourteenth century onwards that the situation changed in favour of canon law, first in
Bruge and then in Cologne.[21]

To all these observations should be added some nuances resulting
from local circumstances and the whims of judges. Thus, for example,
for want of heresy in the city of Florence in the middle of the fourteenth
century, the inquisitor invoked the crimes of usury and voluntary blasphemy and amassed a considerable fortune. But these crimes, which the
Florentine bishops committed regularly by lending church funds with
interest, never put the bishops in fear of the inquisitors.[22] Trials against
Jews were always under cover of heresy, never for their financial activities, even if their goods were confiscated and usually ended up in the
coffers of the inquisitor.

The lay authorities were also concerned with the act of usury. In
Flanders and Hainault, repression by the lay authorities came particularly
early on, with Baudoin IX, during an economic crisis in 1199, forbidding
usurious lending. Certain cities legislated on these matters, and for example, a municipal proclamation in Douai in 1236 prohibited interest loans
on pain of a fine of 50 pounds.[23] The adoption of canon law from the
fourteenth century onwards made conditions far more stringent.[24]

In Italy, in spite of canonical legislation, lending was openly practiced
in numerous cities in the thirteenth century with very high rates of interest. Sometimes the city imposed a rarely respected ceiling of 20 per cent.

Spain only forbade the loan with interest tardily and the measures
taken were applied to Christians before Jews and Muslims. In fact, it was
more a question of regulation than prohibition.[25]

In France, in the thirteenth century, royal legislation regulated secured
loans and fixed the maximum rates to consumption loans (two *deniers* per
pound and per week), but it had no penal sanctions, leaving this to the
church. One must wait until 1312 for royal power to arm itself with penal
sanctions. In periods of crisis, the king was content to eliminate debts by

<hr>

[21] Gerhard Rösch, "Wucher in Deutschland 1200–1350. Überlegungen zur Normdidaxe
und Normrezeption," *Historische Zeitschrift*, 259, 1994, pp. 593–636 (628–35).
[22] Lea, *Histoire de l'Inquisition*, vol. 1, p. 543.
[23] Bernard Schnapper, "La repression de l'usure et l'évolution économique (XIIIe–XVIe
siècles)," *Tijdschrift voor Rechtsgeschiedenis*, 37, 1969, pp. 47–75 (50–51).
[24] Rösch, "Wucher in Deutschland 1200–1350," p. 636.
[25] Antoni Furió, "Endettement paysan et crédit dans la péninsule ibérique au Bas Moyen
âge," Actes des XVIIe Journées Internationales d'Histoire de l'Abbaye de Flaran,
Endettement paysan et Crédit rural dans l'Europe médiévale et moderne, M. Berthe, ed.,
Toulouse, Presses Universitaires du Mirail, 1998, pp. 139–167.

invoking usury.[26] However, prison for debt became a reality in Paris at the end of the Middle Ages, when one-third of the people imprisoned in 1488–1489 were debtors (629 cases for 2,513 prisoners), although their brief stay in prison, not more than a few days, was intended to make the creditor wait and to incite the debtor to pay while giving a legal debt guarantee.[27]

In the fourteenth century, these loans, which were regulated and for which loan tables were kept in general by the "Lombards," conferred with a license issued by the princes or the cities, multiplied in the Low Countries as in France. The legislation had a fiscal as much as a regulatory dimension, but it gave a legal basis for the intervention of the king's judges to the detriment of the ecclesiastical courts. Examination of the cases shows that royal judges were particularly inactive in the thirteenth and fourteenth centuries. But from the fifteenth century, and especially in the sixteenth century, the law became once again much more restrictive in Italy, Spain, and France. As of 1560 in France, there is increasing evidence of a lay campaign against usury.[28] In the decade before, the Venetian Senate had endorsed the measures taken by some twenty towns and villages to regulate the interest paid by the peasants of various Venetian localities, especially Frioul.[29] The thirteenth and fourteenth centuries, which are the moments of strongest pressure on usurers, reflect more the complexity of the relations between state, church, and usurers than a progressive and continuous disengagement vis-à-vis Christian morality.

Ecclesiastical and lay prohibitions resulted in increasingly sophisticated drafting of loan contracts in order to preclude the possibility of prosecution. The chosen formulations have two goals: to avoid falling under the law of usury and to indemnify against loss if the debtor does not pay. One can group together the principal devices according to five categories, which consist of

- masking, quite simply, the interest by including it in the capital sum until the loan expires.
- introducing an element of risk in the transaction to show that the interest is not guaranteed. In general, linking the rate of interest to the

---

[26] Schnapper, "La répression de l'usure," pp. 52–3; and Bernard Schnapper, *Les rentes au XVIe siècle: histoire d'un instrument de crédit*, Paris, 1957, pp. 202–3.

[27] Julie Mayade-Claustre, "Le petit peuple en difficulté: la prison pour dettes à Paris à la fin du Moyen âge," *Le petit peuple dans la société de l'Occident médiéval*, B. Boglioni, C. Gouvard, and R. Delort, eds., Paris, Publications de la Sorbonne, 2002, pp. 453–66.

[28] Schnapper, "La répression de l'usure," pp. 61–2, 72–3.

[29] Gigi Corazzol, *Fitti e livelli a Grano. Un aspetto del credito rurale nel Veneto del '500*, Milan, Franco Angeli, 1979.

longevity of the parties to the contract by deciding that the loan will be free for X years and thereafter an interest would accrue.

- playing on the drafting of contracts such as, for example, in the triple contract that comprises (1) a contract between the lender and the borrower for sharing the profits and losses in the borrower's business, (2) an insurance contract by which the borrower guarantees the restitution of the capital, and (3) another insurance contract by which the borrower guarantees the lender against all losses if the latter renounces sharing the profits against a fixed but reduced return on the investment. Although the triple contract had been condemned by Sixtus V (1585–1590), the Casuists continued to debate its merits throughout the seventeenth century.[30] This type of contract in which A guarantees B against a loss by giving him or her a weaker but guaranteed rate on the loan is allowed from about 1480. But this practice does not cease to be a problem because the lender no longer assumes the risk as he or she has a guaranteed rate of return.

- using every formula that hides the credit behind a sale. Thus, exchange may allow for the interest to be concealed. The bills are payable in another place and in another currency and the interest is set out in the letter of exchange. The exchange is thus not considered as a loan but as a sale (*cambium non est mutuum*) just like the purchase of foreign currency is taken to be a sale and not loan.[31] The *cens* is not considered as a loan but as a sale of rights: the right to pay. This idea is supported in Italian and Spanish circles.[32]

- not setting any time limit; this explains why annuities were the most common instrument of credit in France, Italy and Spain, because the capital did not have to be returned within a period fixed beforehand. The *annuity*, because it does not require the return of the capital, is legal whereas the loan, because it requires the reimbursement of the capital, is not.[33] The history of annuities reveal their use as an

[30] Raymond de Roover, "Scholastic Economics in Business, Banking, and Economic Thought in Late Medieval and Early Modern Europe," *Selected Studies of Raymond de Roover*, Julius Krishner, ed., Chicago, University of Chicago Press, 1974, p. 318.
[31] Raymond de Roover, "Scholastic Economics in Business."
[32] Clavero, *Antidora*, p. 115–17.
[33] For Catalonia, see the examples in Enric Tello, "La utilizació del censal a la Segarra del set-cents: crèdit rural i explotació usurària," *Recerques*, no. 18, 1986, pp. 47–71. In France, at the end of the fifteenth century, annuities were generally redeemable, with the exception being life annuities on houses in the city of Paris and its outskirts. Schnapper, *Les Rentes au XVIe siècle*, p. 62.

instrument of credit as also the will of the pope in the two papal bulls "Regimini" of 1425 and 1455 to regulate its usage.[34]

Interest can also be disguised in the sale, and depending on the partners and the reasons for the loan, it might relate to a money loan with reimbursement in cereals at a higher prices, a sale of merchandise to the borrower with its resale to the lender at a lower price (the interest is hidden between the two transactions), a more expensive sale of merchandise in order again to cover the interest, signing the papers with a certain sum and then reselling them more cheaply, and, finally, making acts for the sale of land with the possibility of buying back:

- Saving the good faith intention by setting a penalty if the capital is not paid within the term. Thus, short time periods are always provided for in the deeds: right from the Middle Ages, a few months to a year are the normal periods, because this allows one to break the commitment given under oath, the best way of covering oneself.[35] This subterfuge explains, it is submitted, why so many contracts throughout the modern period are drawn up with a very short term and are never paid within the period without the creditors being inordinately troubled. To avoid allowing an intention to charge interest in the establishment of the contract to be observed, some add the interest in the initial contract; others have it paid in cash; and some draw up two documents, one for the interest and one for the principal; others again rent out a piece of land for the duration of the loan, the revenues of which serve to pay the interest.

The subterfuge by lenders and merchants that allow them to give credit with complete impunity had, in turn, a double influence. On one hand, they served to draw theologians, engaged in the controversies surrounding usury, into the subtleties of the contractual relations between the actors. Exchange thus permanently defined the moralists' debates.[36] Still some did not fall into the trap and, from the sixteenth century, became increasingly aware that their discussions are being obscured by the subterfuges of the merchants and the contradictory opinions of the doctors

---

[34] Ibid., pp. 45, 61.

[35] Joseph Shatzmiller, *Shylock Reconsidered: Jews, Moneylending, and Medieval Society*, Berkley, University of California Press, 1990, p. 6.

[36] See the voluminous works of Sigismondo Scaccia (ca. 1568–1618) of Raphael de Turri (ca. 1578–1666), and cardinals Juan de Lugo (1583–1660) and Giambattista de Luca (1613–1683).

of the church.[37] The Casuistic movement did fall into this trap, by refusing to see that the distinction between usurious and nonusurious contracts was only based on a sophisticated use of legal techniques, dressed in the language of friendship and gratitude, rather than that of justice and obligation.[38] Legislations were got around at every level of society and the rich peasants of Frioul knew how to switch from a contract for which the Republic had legislated to another that was not legally regulated to draw up their acknowledgement of debts, to say nothing of the fact that many were ignorant of the law.[39] But, on the other hand, if the subterfuge permitted lenders to escape, on the whole, from all earthly punishment, it did not save them from the fear of the hereafter, because numerous wills, which repay usurious loans at the last moment attest.[40]

Affirmation of the State and the Struggle to Maintain Social Hierarchies

The state, because it needs money and because the burden of debt weighs too heavily on the social structures, entered with determination into a game, hitherto mainly triangular, which took place between theologians, religious institutions, and civil society, even if the temporal power was, from early on, a partner.

The affirmation of the state took place in three stages. In the first stage, the church itself opened the way to its disengagement in advocating intention over fact. In a second, the state entered into judicial affairs at the expense of ecclesiastical power, and usury then became primarily a matter of temporal justice. Finally, the will to defend the social order and, in particular, the aristocracy against the destructive effects of usury and debt accentuated this intervention by the state in matters of credit.

[37] See, for example, the works of the Spanish Dominican, Domingo de Soto, quoted in de Roover, *L'évolution*, p. 72, or *Le Dialogue in which One Reasons on the Subject of the Changes and other Trade Contracts*, as well as *The Fairs of Chambery and Trent* published anonymously in Genoa in 1573 and quoted by Savelli "Modèles juridiques," pp. 403–20 (407–11).
[38] Clavero, *Antidora*, pp. 9, 49–56.
[39] Corazzol, *Fitti e livellpi a Grano*, pp. 35, 78.
[40] Benjamin. N. Nelson, "The Usurer and the Merchant Prince: Italian Businessmen and the Ecclesiastical Law of Restitution 1100–1550," *Supplement to the Journal of Economic History*, 7, 1947, pp. 104–22.

In fact, behind the debates intended to displace the crime of usury from fact to intention, the responsibility of control is at play. The logic was to disenfranchise church and the state in favour of the private conscience of the individual. Regarding the Protestants, the "Tubingen School" was at the root of this change. It was close to merchant circles. Gabriel Biel (1410/15–1495), Conrad Summenhart (1465/7–1502), and Johannes Eck (1486–1543, of whom Jacob Fugger was the patron), in the footsteps of Jean Gerson, argue that actions that seem wrong but that are not made with bad intent cannot be condemned just because they appear to be wrong. In Catholic doctrine, intention also plays an essential role since the compensatory gift is clearly allowed[41]: it is therefore necessary to decipher the generous intention bound up with the usurious intention. At the same, the doctrine of the Inquisition, which is more preoccupied with faith than morals, goes in the same direction.

If this debate was animated by Protestants, it must not hide the diversity of positions at the heart of Protestantism because Protestant theologians were divided according to the same lines as the Catholics: some rejected any form of loan; others questioned the rigidity of the prohibition except with regard to the needy. Thus, at the beginning of 1520, one of the faithful disciples of Luther, Jakob Strauss (1420–1534) launched a campaign against usury with his fifty-one theses founded in Deuteronomy. Luther rejected this strict adhesion to Jewish law without hiding his conservative views: he refused all forms of loan-bearing interest with the exception of those made for the survival of the church, priests, students, old people, widows, and orphans. Melanchthon (1497–1560), in a controversy with Strauss, held that the law of Christ should not necessarily be taken as the basis of secular society, giving to magistrates the right to govern in accord with civil law:

Lots of people, nowadays, become excited about contracts which are currently in use. It is appropriate to remember that it is not for private individuals or those who preach the gospels to judge contracts. It is necessary to bring every case before the magistrate; it is for him to determine which contracts are to be approved, as it is for the doctor to prescribe the appropriate medication for fever and pleurisy. For this reason, preachers cannot be allowed to give to themselves the authority to judge these contracts against the dictates of public laws.[42]

---

[41] Clavero, *Antidora*, pp. 59–63, and about *l'antidora*, which transforms liberality into obligation, pp. 85–89.

[42] Philippe Melanchton, "Commentarii aliquot politicos libros Aristotelis," *Opera omnia*, Corpus Reformatorum, XVI, quoted by Savelli, "Modèles juridiques," p. 420.

Calvin (1509–1564) is credited with having created a modern theory of interest. In fact, his ideas were largely circulated in the French-speaking world of the 1540s. They were in particular developed by Charles du Moulin (1500–1566) in his *Tractatus contractuum et usurarum reditumque pecunia constitutorum et monetarum* written in 1542 and published in 1547. It sets up a division between gift and loan depending on the circumstances and the situation of the borrower: it is necessary to provide free loans to the poor and to those who are temporarily in need but to lend with interest to the rich because they will make money with the loan.[43] Calvin expressed this same idea in 1545 in his famous letter to Claude de Sachins.[44]

The French,[45] Italian,[46] and English[47] debates of the end of the sixteenth century relied on these traditions in Catholic as well as Protestant circles. All agreed that usury should be denounced, but there was no agreement on what usury was or on what needed to be done to stifle it. Throughout the sixteenth century, three currents confronted each other: those who remained opposed to all forms of loan, those who rejected it only when the loan harms the laws of equity and charity, and those who wanted to be realistic and in keeping with civil practices. The definitions of usury always came up against the debates surrounding natural law. This diversity, which transcends the two confessions, is found in the books of arithmetic, as much in those written by Catholics as those by Protestants; the same nuances that range from neutrality to pejorative references are found equally among the two groups of writers.[48]

In the Netherlands, the merchant class obtained that Charles Quint authorize lending on interest only by traders, which was very liberal

[43] R. Savelli, "Diritto romano e teologia riformata: Du Moulin di fonrte al problemadell'interesse del denaro," *Materialli per una storia della cultura giuridica*, 23, no. 2, 1992, pp. 291–324. Jean-Louis Thireau, *Charles du Moulin (1500–1506)*. *Etude sur les sources, la méthode, les idées politiques et économiques d'un juriste de la Renaissance*, Geneva, Droz, 1980, in particular chap. 6.

[44] Benjamin N. Nelson, *The Idea of Usury from Tribal Brotherhood to Universal Otherhood*, Chicago, University of Chicago Press, 1969, pp. 73–5; and de Roover, *La pensée économique des scholastiques*, pp. 76–9.

[45] René Taveneaux, *Jansénisme et prêt à intérêt*, Paris, Vrin, 1977.

[46] Savelli, "Modèles juridiques," "Between Law and Morals: Interest in the Dispute on Exchanges during the XVI Century," *The Courts and the Development of Commercial Law* Vito Piergiovanni , ed., Berlin , 1987.

[47] Jones, *God and the Moneylenders*, pp. 43–5 et seq.

[48] Natalie Z. Davis, "Sixteenth-Century French Arithmetics on the Business Life, *Journal of the History of Ideas*, 21, 1960, pp. 18–48 (44).

for the times.[49] In Genoa, where no merchant guild existed since the end of the Middle Ages because everyone, from the feudal nobility to the poorest took part in trading activities,[50] the publication in 1582 of judicial decisions with respect to merchant courts shows that judges referred to tradition to avoid being drawn into a discussion on usury, that the ideas of du Moulin had permeated society and that if interest was allowed, it depended on the quality of the parties concerned. The *Decisiones* endorsed the social reality of the times by avoiding any discussion on principles that could expose it to doctrinal criticism, and these facts indicate that no money was lent without interest even to the poor.[51]

In England, nevertheless, between the end of the sixteenth century and the seventeenth century, the old tensions concerning time and work eased and the minority position, which accepted the loan and assimilated usury with high rates, became the majority view. Following the line of Martin Bucer (1491–1551), of Calvin, and of du Moulin, there are theologians who can broadly be called Puritan, who took the initiative, building on these initial ideas[52] and succeeding in disengaging the Protestant Church.

During the last third of the sixteenth century, the English Parliament put these debates onto its agenda. Its members had two convictions: first, divine law and human law must be in accord; secondly, men are saved more by faith than by good works and because God chooses who he is going to save, nobody can judge the secrets of the heart. In 1590, Miles Moses of Bury St Edmunds preached a series of sermons on usury that were published in 1595. *The Arraignment and Conviction of Usurie* makes usury a matter of personal conscience: "The sinne of usurie is to take or desire usurarious gaine: but usurie it selfe is the gaine which in its owne nature may be valued for money, and is demaunded principally for the dutie either of direct or coloured lending." It is the sin of usury that is condemned by God not the object of the usury. To commit the sin of usury, it is necessary to grant a loan, make a profit, seek gain, and not risk the principal.

---

[49] Schnapper, *Les Rentes au XVIe siècle*, p. 66.

[50] Giorgio Doria, "Comptoirs, foires de changes et place étrangères: les lieux d'apprentissage des nobles négociants de Gênes entre Moyen Age et âge baroque," *Négoce et culture*, F. Angiolini and D. Roche, eds., Paris, Editions de l'EHESS, 1995, pp. 321–48 (321).

[51] R. Savelli, "Between law and Morals", pp. 39–102 (87–102).

[52] Jones, *God and the Moneylenders*; see chap. 6, "Evolution of the Concept of Usury 1571–1624."

The distinction between the merchant's profit and the needs of the poor becomes increasingly clear. From 1591, for Gibbon, it is legitimate to make a profit with money, but not to the detriment of the poor. It is the same for Richard Rogers.[53] Finally, it was agreed that usury only existed vis-à-vis the poor and widows and that the right to loan with interest be given to orphans and religious ministers. Only consumer credit destined for the poor remains unacceptable.

These themes continue to give rise to quite a sizable number of sermons and debates, and from the 1590s, more and more people thought it necessary to leave the regulation of usury to magistrates. Thus, in England, from the end of the sixteenth century, it was accepted that the sin of usury was removed to the individual conscience and that the state, in its economic regulations, confined itself to acting on the secular economy.[54]

In the sixteenth and seventeenth centuries in France, French jurists, with the exception of Du Moulin, approved the rigor of the canonical prohibitions with regard to loans bearing interest. This is true of Bodin, Etienne Pasquier and d'Argentré in the sixteenth century and of Domat in the seventeenth century. After a long silence during the major part of the sixteenth century, usury was once again condemned in the pastoral theology of the church at the end of the century: between 1523 and 1594, the synodal statutes in the ecclesiastical province of Avignon are silent on usury; later, the bishops asked once again to be informed about the sins of usury. The Tridentine Reform is unquestionably at the origin of this.[55] Along the same lines, royal power, which had increased the derogations in the Middle Ages, passed legislation in 1579 firmly opposed to the loan bearing interest. Article 202 of the Ordonnance of Blois states that

Inhibitions and prohibition be on all people, whatever their status, sex or condition, to exercise usury or to loan deniers at profit or with interest ... and on pain, for the first offence, to honourable fine, banishment and sentenced to substantial fines of which one quarter will be accorded to the informers, and for the second offence, loss of property and incarceration.

This position was confirmed in 1629 and in 1673 when it was forbidden for shopkeepers to practice any form of compound interest. The legislation remained the civil transcription of ecclesiastical law.[56]

---

[53] Jones, *God and the Moneylenders*, pp. 48–50.
[54] Ibid., p. 163 et seq.
[55] Marc Venard, "Catholicisme et usure au XVIe siècle," *Revue d'histoire de l'Eglise de France*, 52, 1966, pp. 59–74 (68–70).
[56] Courdurié, *La Dette des collectivités*, pp. 62–3.

Charles du Moulin was the first to underline that the prohibitions, which were designed to protect debtors, had the opposite effect and only served to increase the cost of credit. He mocked, moreover, the trap into which the artfulness of contract writers was leading the doctors of the church: "I also leave their jargon and distinctions on real false and dry (réal, fict, et sec) exchange re-exchange and counter-exchange." Du Moulin who defends the loan bearing interest was, quite logically, persecuted for heresy and his writings were placed on the index.[57]

Shattering the cornerstones for behaviour, born at once of religious divisions and the affirmation of the State as another *locus* of power, leads to the creation of new ideological references and a redistribution of the roles and attributions at the heart of the institutions. Two authorities, religious and state, henceforth organized the practice as well as their symbolic and moral representations. Thus, in the seventeenth and eighteenth centuries, the royal tribunals acted with an increasingly free rein in matters that were previously religious. Cases of usury, however, continued to be brought before authorities of the church and the state throughout Europe: in France[58] as in England or in Italy.[59]

In parallel, the privileged became aware that usury is in the process of transforming society and utterly overturning old hierarchies. This realization began to dawn from the end of the sixteenth century in England and became widespread in the seventeenth century. Martin Bucer had already denounced merchants who practiced usury and monopolies, which endeavoured by gifts and toadyism to gain the favour of powerful people who were useful to them, which pushed nobles to spend, and ended up by taking possession of their lands, after having ruined

---

[57] de Roover, *l'Evolution*, p. 195; and "Scolastic Economics in Business," p. 319.

[58] In Lyon, registers of prisoners taken into custody for debt have been preserved from 1682 to 1694 and from 1702 to 1712. There were generally about a hundred prisoners with the number going up in some years such as 1688, 1690–93, 1705, and 1707. Similarly, bailiffs' records comprised "summons to appear for debt" before the lieutenant general of police. They show the extent of merchant-to-merchant, merchant-to-supplier and client-to-merchant indebtedness. Jean-Pierre Gutton, *La Société et les pauvres. L'exemple de la généralité de Lyon (1534–1789)*, Paris, Les Belles Lettres, 1971, p. 66.

[59] Vito Piergiovanni (dir.), *The Courts and the Development of Commercial Law*, Berlin, Duncker & Humbolt, 1987; Luciano Allegra, *La città verticale. Usurai, mercanti e tessitori nella Chieri del Cinquecento*, Milan, Franco Angeli, 1987, p. 26. In Piedmont, Episcopal and civic justice are in competition, as at Chieri, over questions of usury. In Rome in the seventeenth century, prison for debt was a reality experienced by many artisans, either as debtors, or as guarantors. See Renata Ago, *Economica Barocca. Mercato e istituzioni nella Roma del Seicento*, Rome, Donzelli, 1988, p. 18.

them, thereby provoking "the diminution of the Republic."[60] Ben Jonson echoed the common opinion that usurers were the ruin of gentlemen, a sentiment summed up in "Usurers live by the fall of heirs, as swine by the dropping of accorns."[61]

In the seventeenth century, the discourse on usury is the prelude to protective legislation in the service of maintaining social hierarchies. Everywhere in Europe, it came to the rescue of the aristocracy, whose foolish expenditure threatened its very existence. Usury was increasingly identified with the nouveaux riches. The increasingly widespread legislation is the corollary of two related movements: the domination of the state over the church (this is also shown in the formation of national churches) and the defence of the orders of society and, in particular, of the *Grands*. Although numerous studies have shown that the idea of the economic decline of the nobility had more to do with stereotypes,[62] the fear of the usurer and the possible consequences of indebtedness were no less great, a topic that recurred frequently in letters, travel diaries, and the literature of the times. This fear was strong enough to become a convincing argument in the battle against usury.

Depending on the country concerned, these movements have different chronologies. In England, the Parliament promulgated four statutes up to the end of the sixteenth century. The first general statute against usury dates from 1487. Until then, only the bishops concerned themselves with this fault against God. These statutes are along the lines of Thomas Aquinas's arguments condemning all loans bearing interest. Overall, the legislation relied on denunciation. In 1545, a new statute was passed because the old legislation was "soe obscure and dark in sentences wordes and termes, and upon the same soe many doubts ambiguityes and questions have risen and growen… that by reason thereof litle or noe punyshment hath ensued." The new formulation authorized a rate of interest up to 10 per cent. Beyond that, the creditor was liable for three times the value of the capital in fines. The legislation continued to count on informers to denounce the usurers. They received half of the fine and

---

[60] Quoted by M. Morineau, "Entre usurier et 'philistin': the 'bon marchand' and the 'négociant éclair,' *Cultures et formations négociantes*, D. Roche and F. Angiolini, eds., Paris, Editions de l'EHESS, 1995, pp. 421–38 (431).

[61] Ben Jonson, *Volpone; or the Fox*, [1606], Paris, Les Belles Lettres, 2012.

[62] Arlette Jouanna, *Le Devoir de révolte. La noblesse française et la gestation de l'Etat moderne (1559–1661)*, Paris, Fayard 1989, pp. 92–8. Charles Jago, "The Influence of Debt on the Relations between Crown and Aristocracy in Seventeenth-Century Castille," Economic History Review, 2nd series, 26, 1973, pp. 218–36 (227).

the Crown the other half. All reference to God had disappeared. It seems that these statutes did not keep interest below 10 per cent, and there were few prosecutions: in the Exchequer, only fifteen denunciations during the entire lifetime of the 1545 act are documented.[63]

By a new act of Edward VI in 1552, Parliament outlawed once again all forms of loan but softened the penalty: only the capital and the interest were forfeited and divided between the denouncer and the royal authorities. In 1571, the statutes of Elizabeth revived the 10 per cent limit and punished those who demanded higher rates of interest with the confiscation of three times the sums in question; those who contented themselves with less than 10 per cent were punished by the loss of only the capital. The new statutes contained a derogation for orphans and proposed the creation of a *mont-de-piété*, or "bill for poor mens' bank." But, above all, they added a section against brokers who are punished for arranging loans above 10 per cent and whose ubiquitous intermediation, as we saw in Chapter 4, increased greatly the cost of credit. The bodies competent to hear this type of plea were extended: more or less everyone down to the bailiffs. The ecclesiastical courts are not relieved of their competence but are left with cases of usury below 10 per cent. Of the four statutes, that of Henry of 1545 was the most liberal whereas those of Elizabeth of 1571 were much more conservative.[64]

The institutions that judged cases of usury were not only ecclesiastical; the royal courts were also charged with trials for usury. Europe dealt with these questions in a very uneven manner. England is the only country to have really brought usurers to justice in the modern period: the archives of the courts of King's Bench, Common Pleas, and Exchequer, the quarter sessions, the Court of Request, the ecclesiastical courts, and other jurisdictions contain hundreds of cases of usury. Most of these cases come from special commissions that were sent into the regions to inquire into usury. By contrast, the priest, everywhere the lender par excellence, figures only rarely in these cases for usury.[65]

---

[63] Jones, *God and the Moneylenders*, p. 50 et seq.

[64] Ibid., p. 92 et seq. 64. Written by men who think according to medieval traditions and those of canon law, the statutes are not a victory for Protestantism or a victory for ordinary men over theoricians as Tawney thinks. One cannot read them as victories for capitalism and for Protestantism over a medieval moral theology; on the contrary, they pursue the very same rationale. Moreover, they are aware that there is an underlying economic reality.

[65] In 1570–1571, one of these commissions went to Devon and Cornwall. It was surely sent because of the incessant complaints of the miners. Two hundred cases of usury were reported between 1566 and 1571 in these regions typical of the "truck system." They give

Generally, there are few cases in which the communities denounced usurers in their midst, but, in order to be effective, these courts depended on such denunciation. The role of the denouncer became a lucrative enterprise; however, the denouncer was a hated figure in Tudor society. But the system could not function without them. Between July 1571 and April 1575, two courtiers, Mackwilliams and Colshill, held a monopoly on seeking out crimes of usury as well as the right to arbitrate. Moreover, justice cannot be done without their assent. They take half of any fine imposed plus 10 per cent. These enormous powers were given to them because "it is reported that there is great remissness in the execution of the statutes aforesaid, partly caused by the corrupt dealings of those called promoters or informers." In 1575, their monopoly was abolished, but in the meantime, they made good use of their power by setting up a network of informers who reported to them. Their work was heavily criticized because they were reproached for thinking more about their own enrichment than about protecting the poor.[66] Moreover, it seems that the only cases involving prison were those in which the accused could not pay the fine to the informer: of the 13,649 cases investigated between 1559 and 1570, fewer than 1 per cent were concluded, and 84 per cent went no further than the initial hearing. Analysis of the Exchequer records shows that up to 1630 cases for usury were ridiculously few with the exception of the years 1560 through 1570 when the system of denouncers really worked.[67] After that time, there was a significant drop and trials for debt went down from 80 to 90 per cent of cases in 1640 to 32 per cent in 1750.[68] In the years 1760 through 1780, imprisonment for debt increased again before getting stabilized. Nonetheless, the fact remains that about half the prison population was

---

examples of interest from 10% to 100% and particularly hard conditions against those that do not pay on time. Cf. Jones, *God and the Moneylenders*, pp. 73–4 and 71–2.

[66] Ibid., p. 113. Quoting the example in 1602 of Thomas Bell of Helperby who is reproached for making the community pay for the state of absolute poverty in which he placed his debtors "By reason whereof he compelled Done to sell all he had, so now he is quite undone; And (yf his friendes mainteyne him not) he and his wife must be relieved at the charge of the parish"; ibid., p. 95.

[67] D. Lidington, "Mesne Process in Penal Actions at the Elisabethan Exchequer," *The Journal of Legal History*, 5, no. 3, 1984, pp. 33–8.

[68] C. W. Brooks, "Interpersonal Conflict and Social Tension: Civil Litigation in England, 1640–1730," *The First Modern Society*, A. L. Beier, D. Cannadine, and J. E. Rosenheim, eds., Cambridge, Cambridge University Press, 1989, pp. 388–90. W. A. Champion, "Litigation in the Boroughs: The Shrewsbury Curia Parva 1480–1730," *Legal History*, 15, no. 3, 1994, pp. 201–22 (216).

there for debts. Indeed, the logic of prison for debt incited creditors and debtors to accept it and even seek it.[69]

English legislative activity and, in particular, the Act of 1571, resulted in the setting of an official ceiling rate of 10 per cent. This should have helped to lower the rates of interest.[70] Although the earlier statutes of Henry VII, Edward VI, and Elizabeth make all loans punishable, there are no cases of rates below 10 per cent. After 1571, the towns and corporations used the act to borrow at 10 per cent and among the nobility, 10 per cent was the normal rate from 1600.[71]

The drafting of contracts designed to circumvent the law remained ever present: before 1545, they have to hide all interest charges; between 1545 and 1552, only those above 10 per cent; from 1552 to 1571, once again all interest; after 1571, again interest rates above 10 per cent.[72] The cases also show several tactics used to draw profit from the regulations. Thus, certain debtors, having borrowed, would hire an informer who would bring a suit against the lender. Having done this, they agreed with him a small sum, and then the case would be dropped, and they lend the money without any worry.

Then the interest rates fell very rapidly in Holland and England: loans from the bank of Amsterdam to the East India Company went from denier 16 in 1609 to denier 20 in 1620 before reaching in stages denier 40 (2.5 per cent) in 1723 and recovering to 3 per cent in 1746. In Great Britain, the maximum legal rate in 1624 went down from 10 to 8 per cent, then 6 per cent before the Restoration, and finally 5 per cent in 1713.[73]

In France, where the civil law followed ecclesiastical precepts, the practice was more chaotic. First of all, there are multiple derogations. Then, the king promptly granted others, such as the authorization given to the city of Lyon to borrow 850,000 pounds at 6 per cent in 1712.

[69] Joanna Innes, "The King's Bench Prison in the Later Eighteenth Century: Law, Authority and Order in a London Debtors' Prison," *An Ungovernable People: The English and Their Law in the Seventeenth and Eighteenth Centuries*, John Brewer and John Styles, eds., New Brunswick, NJ, Rutgers University Press, 1980, pp. 251–98. Paul H. Haagen, "Eighteenth-Century English Society and the Debt Law," *Social Control and the State, Historical and Comparative Essays*, Stanley Cohen and Andrew Seull, eds., London, Basil Blackwell, 1983, pp. 222–47 (223, 225–9).
[70] Jones, *God and the Moneylenders*, p. 117.
[71] Lawrence Stone, *Family and Fortune: Studies in Aristocratic Finance in the Sixteenth and Seventeenth Centuries*, Oxford, Clarendon Press, 1973, p. 530.
[72] Jones, *God and the Moneylenders*, p. 121.
[73] Pierre Goubert, *Beauvais et le Beauvaisis de 1600 à 1730: Contribution à l'histoire sociale de la France du XVIIe siècle*, Paris, 1960, p. 538.

Moreover, it was necessary to distinguish civil law countries from those of common law. In the former, there was a struggle to reconcile Roman law and royal ordinances, and the practice of interest tolerated by custom and the condemnations made against excessive usuries. Nevertheless, differences can be noticed between the parliaments: at Aix, excessive interest was deducted from the principal; at Toulouse or Bordeaux, the debtor could not ask for restitution of interest paid; by contrast, at Grenoble and Pau, as in the lands of Bresse, Gex, and Valmorey, the charging of interest for a money loan was tolerated. In the lands of customary law, any charge of interest on a loan was condemned, and the *Parlements* of Paris, Rouen, and Rennes punished it with exemplary severity: for them, any stipulation of interest was null and void, and all interest paid must be returned. Depending on the gravity of the crime, the penalties accruing ranged from admonishment, or a light fine, to banishment or a while in the galleys and, in the case of the repeat offense, the loss of property or life.[74] This panoply of sanctions was, in reality, rarely used, but the diversity of jurisdictions, the harsh punishment, and the arbitrary power of judges opened the door to blackmail and created a climate of fear in merchant circles.[75] At the same time, the official rates fell. The "denier du Roi" continued to fall in the seventeenth century. At the end of the sixteenth century, it stood at denier 12 and 14; in July 1601, it was denier 16, in March 1643, denier 18; from December 1665 to March 1720, it was at denier 20; and as it was again from June 1725 onwards.[76]

In March 1720, it reached denier 50, the maximum denier. This decision, referred to as Guyot, was not registered in any parliament, and theoretically it remained without execution; however, in some regions, we find annuities at denier 50. In June 1724, it fell again to 30 and in June 1725, it went back to the level of the 1665 ordinance. These edicts were not applied to the entire kingdom; they were in Beauvais, Amiens, and Paris. Normandy did not follow: the denier 14 remained legal until 1668; it was replaced by the denier 18, which held good until the Regency. In any case, this fall did not hinder usurers in any manner who had numerous ways to circumvent the law with or without the complicity of a notary

---

[74] Courdurié, *La Dette des collectivités*, pp. 65, 66.
[75] Emma Rothschild, "An Alarming Commercial Crisis in Eighteenth-Century Angoulême: Sentiments in Economic History," *Economic History Review*, New Series, 51, no. 2, 1998, pp. 268–93.
[76] Joseph-Nicolas Guyot, *Répertoire universel et raisonné de jurisprudence civile, criminelle, canonique et bénéficiale*, Paris, Visse, 1784–1785, V° Intérêt.

(sham sales or with the option to repurchase, sums declared and not paid, "offers" and underleases, business with the king).[77]

In Spain, from the end of the sixteenth century, there was a change of political thinking regarding foreign tradespeople. Commerce always seemed indispensable but not at the cost of heresy. After the peace of 1604 with England and the 1612 truce with Holland, the royal council issued new provisions concerning commerce with foreigners that marked the triumph of commercial law over the theological dogmatism that had previously held sway: "For the laws of commerce that follow peace not to be fruitless," it is asked that, "as long as foreigners do not give rise to scandal, nothing is asked of them regarding faith and religion and that neither their boats nor property nor merchandise are confiscated for this reason."[78] It is a first breach with the theological thinking that still largely dominated society, for, if the Inquisition above all judged only peasants in the sixteenth century, in the seventeenth century, it is mainly interested in merchants and tradesmen of all levels.[79]

The Loss of Social Relevance of Religious Discourse

Thus, between the sixteenth and seventeenth centuries, the state took charge progressively of the legitimacy of discourse on usury as well as control of credit practices. In so doing, if the church continued to raise these questions, its positions were no longer socially effective, and its word related to the religious institution and ceased to contribute to societal debate. In the eighteenth century, the system of theological thinking is markedly detached from any economic dimension.[80] Another principle for understanding the world now dominated. Not that this distinction had not existed here or there before, but now it became visible, and the actors became aware of it. The church's truth in matters of usury appeared increasingly alien to what its faithful believed, to take the words of Michel de Certeau,[81] and more to that which it uses to defend itself. The doctrine on usury became a sign of recognition more than the affirmation of a truth that it intended to impose on society. Moreover, the mercantile culture imposed its own practices and its legitimations,

---

[77] Goubert, *Beauvais et le Beauvaisis*, pp. 538–40.
[78] Contreras, *El santo oficio de la Inquisición*, p. 539, and Clavero, *Antidora*, pp. 145–8.
[79] Contreras, *El santo oficio de la Inquisición*, p. 580 et seq.
[80] Karl Polanyi, *The Great Transformation*, New York, Rinehart, 1944.
[81] Certeau, *L'écriture de l'histoire*, p. 134.

and everywhere the distinction between interest and usury was asserted, usury being an illegitimate interest or contrary to the good of the poor. Some examples show this disengagement of the church, the transformation of the status of its discourses, and the monopoly on economic affairs that was assumed by the state and the merchants.

From the end of the sixteenth century, this evolution is evident in England. People find credit too expensive. The monarchy needed money and wanted to see some of the creditors' profits. Members of the Parliament debated usury in 1604, 1606, 1614, and 1620–1621, and in 1623–1624, they pass a new statute. Francis Bacon, in *Usury and the Use Thereof*, pleaded for credit: all those who reject usury, he writes, "must be sent to Utopia." Moreover, interest rates had been fixed at 6 per cent in the Low Countries causing a disadvantage to England and upsetting the balance of trade. The evolution nevertheless took more than a generation. In 1603–1604, a new statute aims to protect creditors better against bankruptcy by including loans in the balance sheet. Then, until 1624, in spite of difficult debates in which the religious position had disappeared, the law did not shift and interest rates did not come down. However, brokers were subject to more controls than before.

To loan with interest is henceforth considered a normal activity that the state must regulate in the interests of economic success. Even if usury remains a sin, it is a sin that concerns individual conscience. The House of Lords' amendment to the 1624 law affirmed this distinction: men remain bound by their conscience and religion as regards their behaviour, and the state is only responsible for their economic behaviour insofar as it has earthly implications. In the text and preamble of the act, reference to God disappeared, which shows the distinction drawn between the laws of God and human laws.[82] The minority view in 1571 has become the majority one in the Parliament by 1624: a law against usury changed into a law controlling interest rates for the good of the economy in general.

Church discourse against usury did not, however, cease completely. In 1571, the bishops published a book of disciplinary canons, which were aimed against usury, adultery, incest, and all such odious crimes. Some bishops were particularly active. Archbishop Grindal of York is a good example. He demanded in 1571 that the supreme penalty of excommunication be reserved for the most abject crimes such as heresy, usury, treason, and murder. Promoted to the See of Canterbury, he insisted that, during pastoral visits in his diocese, it be asked if there are usurers and

[82] Jones, *God and the Moneylenders*, p. 183 et seq.

how they are being prosecuted. Usury was constantly linked to heresy, schism, simony, perjury, adultery, and incest. But the effect remains dubious: in spite of the instructions, visitors only rarely found usurers.[83]

Miles Mosse denounced the laxity of the church:

> But certainly it may be the complainte of the Commons of England, that many officials are too loose and remisse in pursuing of this offence. No man is presented, no man is ascited, no man is convicted, no man is punished ever since I could remember, by the ecclesiastical lawe for the committing of usury. And yet the poore people every where complaine of a number of men, that by one meanes or other take above the rate of tenne, yea of twentie in the hundred: the punishment of which excesse, the statute hath flatly permitted unto the ecclesiasticall governours.[84]

There were nevertheless some places where ecclesiastical authority proved more zealous, as in the very puritan Archdeaconry of Nottingham, where one finds cases of usury throughout the Elizabethan period which are brought before the supreme ecclesiastical court, the Ecclesiastical High Commission, under Archbishop Sandys of York.[85] Even if the cases of usury form "a distinctly minor part of the business of an ordinary English ecclesiastical court,"[86] Mosse's reckoning is hardly exaggerated. Nevertheless, compared to the number of cases of usury found in the lay courts, the church would seem less lax.

Despite some zealous bishops, the activity of the ecclesiastical courts remained very moderate for two reasons. The first is that behind usury, there is always an accord between a lender and a borrower, and so an attentive moralist, or an injured community, needs to agree to denounce a usurer before the ecclesiastical courts. Moreover, these courts, unlike the lay courts, could not levy fines of three times the capital nor invalidate the contracts. As the preachers liked to say, people seem blind to most forms of usury and nearly the world and his wife give in to it. In fact, even civil proceedings practically disappeared in the seventeenth century. Because of reforms in the rules for informing, the Elizabethan statute has practically ceased to be applied by 1624. In the previous ten years, the

[83] Ibid., p. 110.
[84] Miles Mosse, *The Arraignment and Conviction of Usury*, London, 1595, quoted in ibid., p. 110.
[85] R. A. Merchant, *The Church under the Law. Justice, Administration and Discipline in the Diocese of York 1560–1640*, Cambridge, Cambridge University Press, 1969, p. 218.
[86] R. H. Tawney, *Religion and the Rise of Capitalism. A Historical Study*, Harmondsworth, Penguin Books, 1980, pp. 165–6; Helmholtz, "Usury," p. 369; I. P. Ellis, "The Archbishop and the Usurers," *Journal of Ecclesiastical History*, 21, no. 1, 1970, pp. 34–5.

Exchequer receives only a dozen denunciations against usury each year. With the passage of the new law, this feeble volume dropped further until it reached just three denunciations in 1625 and, during the first five years of the reign of Charles I, the Exchequer only received seven denunciations and, in some years, none at all.[87]

In France, the eighteenth century saw a move to authorize modest interest charges in business. Philosophers ridiculed with irony and contempt the Casuistes, and the doctrine of usury was at the heart of the attacks. Véron de Forbonnais in his immense article on *usure* in the *Encyclopédie* is a good example.[88] He defended a definition of usury that

Is precisely the legal and compensatory rate of interest of a sum loaned to a well-off man, with the view to reciprocal advantage. Usury thus modified and reduced among us over a century to 20 deniers, is what I call legal usury; I contend that it is not contrary to natural law and that the practice is not less useful than so many other negotiations used and considered legitimate.

His argumentation is founded on the contradictions of the Casuists, the incoherence of custom between different *Parlements*, and the exceptions that were already admitted for dowry money and for orphans as well as for the king's borrowing, especially in the form of lotteries and annuities, in the borrowing of the *compagnie des Indes*, in the borrowing of general farmers and in the ordinary practice of the bank and commerce. Each was based on saying that he would have used his money in these cases and that by lending it to others, he automatically entered into the authorized cases of *lucrum cessans* or *dannum emergens*. He develops at length the analysis of the Old and New Testaments to show that they are concerned first with the poor and to react against the excesses of former times when insolvent debtors were reduced to slavery and where the rates were really usurious. Finally, he assimilates money with other forms of goods that can be rented out[89]:

[87] Jones, *God and the Moneylenders*, pp. 114, 197–8.

[88] *Encyclopédie*, ou, Dictionnaire raisonné des sciences, des arts et des métiers par une société de gens de lettres; mis en ordre & publié par M. Diderot... & quant à la partie mathématique, par M. d'Alembert, Geneva; Paris; Neufchastel 1754–1772, vol. 17, p. 545.

[89] Turgot is very clear on this point: "It is necessary that money be considered as a real good for which the price depends on the contract/agreement and varies, as with all other tradable goods, on the basis of the relationship between the supply and the demand." ("Il est nécessaire que l'argent soit considéré comme une véritable marchandise dont le prix dépend de la convention et varie, comme celui de toutes les autres marchandises, à raison du rapport de l'offre à la demande"). *Mémoire sur les prêts d'argent*, [1770], In: Gustav Schelle, OEuvres de Turgot et documents le concernant, Paris, F. Alcan, 1913–1923, vol. 3, p. 169. The interest rates must be free and negotiated.

No man has the right to benefit from the possessions of another, if he has not first agreed on some sort of compensation: a well-off man has no more right to his neighbour's money than to his ox, his donkey, his wife or his servant, thus nothing is more just than demanding some sort of indemnity for conceding for a time the product of his energy or of his savings, to a well-off man who increases by such borrowing his comfort.

He stigmatizes the practice of hiding interest within the capital, which occurs as often under simple contracts as before notaries and the practice of going to court to obtain interest when the term has expired:

Be that as it may, every advantage that the debtor gains from this imprecise prohibition on usury, he pays for it under the grand title "legitimate interest." In order for this transition from "usury" to "legitimate interest" to occur, it is necessary to have recourse to the courts and, naturally, to pay the expenses of such an endeavour. Thus, in brief, usurers paid for their practice of usury to acquire the honest title of "legitimate interest." Such developments led certain cynics to note that the judicial system is unjust since it considers its role as none other than to multiply the worries and costs of business for citizens.

Véron quotes Montesquieu: "the lender indemnifies himself against the risks of the contract" to emphasize how much these prohibitions serve above all to make credit expensive. The *Encyclopédie* reminds us finally that some forms of usury that do not exceed the legal rate were accepted in four cases:

1. In the contract setting up a rent; 2. For interests which arise ex mora & officio judicis; 3. In acts which require an obligation, apart from a loan, such as transactions for civil interest or rent, incorporeal rights, or moveable goods in gross; 4. For deniers of wardship, which only arise against the tutor, as long as the deniers are in his possession.

Added here is maritime usury because of the risk of losing the sums lent in commercial contracts in high-risk adventures and compensatory or legal usury, the "interest on the dowry, due and not paid, those of legitimate or partial inheritance, a shared hold, or the remainder of a wardship." It underlines finally that in certain regions interest on money lent between merchants may be set, as in Brittany and Bresse and at Lyon.

The economists of the eighteenth century were thoroughly aware that the prohibitions and controversies were no longer socially effective. Besides, the condemnations of the church came to be based increasingly on the letter of the sacred text to the exclusion of any rational argumentation: what the church wanted was a profession of obedience.[90]

---

[90] René Tavenaux, *Jansénisme et prêt à intérêt*, Paris, 1977, pp. 84–5, provides an excellent summation of the cleavages within the church and the evolution of Jansenism.

The number of people imprisoned for debt was absurdly low: 125 in Paris in 1771 in the aftermath of the economic crisis, and 89 the very next year whereas they were 1,250 in 1770 in London.[91] Turgot (1727–1781) asserts that the discussion was "born in the centuries of ignorance" and that it has "become a speculation that has been abandoned to rigorous theologians and, in practice, all commercial and financial operations rely on loans bearing interest without alienation of capital."[92] Condillac adds that the state itself does not respect its own laws:

Our legislators, if such is possible, reason worse than the casuists: they condemn loans bearing interest and they tolerate them; they condemn them without knowing why and they tolerate them because they are forced to do so. Their laws, products of ignorance and prejudice, are useless if they are not obeyed; and, when they are obeyed, they only harm business.[93]

Turgot, in his *Mémoire sur les prêts d'argent*, develops the reasons why demands for interest on money loaned should be allowed and its rate left free. His argumentation rests on reasons of commercial utility, on the contradictions between law and custom and on a redefinition of contract, ownership, and the relations between natural law and the order of divine law. He starts with a story about crooks who use the laws against usury to swindle merchants who have lent them money within the ordinary course of their business, the town of Angoulême itself was ground to a halt when the trade of money ended. From this example, he shows that the inapplicable laws only serve to create crooks and smugglers, "that the shame and risk associated with loans bearing interest are added costs that the borrower always pays," and that much money remains in the coffers. In the interests and for the enrichment of all, he asks then that the law be brought in line with practice.

The force of contracts, ownership and the laws of nature are at the heart of the conceptual apparatus. It is necessary to recognize the absolute force of "agreements freely entered" and "the inviolable law, attached to ownership, to be the absolute master of the thing, not to be deprived of it except with one's consent," writes Turgot, who adds that money is only a commodity and insists that conventions regulate "the reciprocal advantage

[91] Thomas M. Luckett, "The Debate over Imprisonment for Debt in Eighteenth-Century France," *Des personnes aux institutions. Réseaux et culture du crédit du XVIe au XXe siècle en Europe*, Laurence Fontaine, Gilles Postel-Vinay, Jean-Laurent Rosenthal, and Paul Servais, eds., Louvain-la-Neuve, Bruylant-Academia, 1997, pp. 163–72 (164).

[92] Turgot, *Mémoire sur les prêts d'argent*, vol. 3, p. 187.

[93] Condillac, *Le Commerce et le gouvernement considérés relativement l'un à l'autre*, pp. 311–312, quoted by Courdurié, *La Dette des collectivités*, p. 67.

of the contracting parties, and not the intrinsic and metaphysical qualities of the subject-matter of the contract." A petition of principle, which regulates the social question and eliminates the relations of power, completes the apparatus. According to these conventions, according to Turgot, "the value is always equal vis-à-vis both parties: but this is not by a principle of justice, it is because things cannot be otherwise." If generosity and charity are desirable, he adds, they only arise from the choice of the creditor, for in no case must the tradesman be liable to be prosecuted for usury. To support the validity of these assertions, Turgot explains that short-term lenders, who are especially active in the small grocery trade, render a service to their clientele, in spite of the high rates of interest that they charge, for the loans allow the borrower to earn a living. He also justifies consumption loans to the poor at high rates of interest with two arguments. The first is that they "do not cause the same harm as the former usurers who gradually led poor citizens, to whom they had offered disastrous help, to misery and slavery"; that is to say that with slavery being abolished, even if the poor man is completely deprived, he remains free. The second is that the instrument of credit for the poor is the pledge and that "he who borrows on pledge borrows with a possession which he is perfectly entitled to give up. If he is not in a position to return the capital and interest, the worst that can happen to him is to lose the possession pledged, and he will not be more unhappy than he was."[94] Turgot concludes that

The only really solid security against the poor man is the pledge, and the poor man considers himself lucky to find help for the time being without any other danger than that of losing the pledged possession. Thus, the people have more gratitude than hate for the small time usurers who help them in their need, even if they sell their assistance at quite a high price.

He recalls that when he had to report on a criminal case of usury at *la Tournelle,* he had never been so solicited in favour of the "unfortunate accused" and "even by those who had suffered the usuries that formed the basis of the case."[95] In his denunciation of usurers, Louis Sébastien Mercier's thinking is quite similar, and he compared usurers who lent on a weekly basis with those who profited from the ignorance and the weakness of young aristocrats.[96] Necker and the artisans, who had founded the official *monts-de-piété,* thought differently, emphasizing the damage caused by the all-too-frequent pledge of work tools.

[94] Turgot, *Mémoire sur les prêts d'argent,* pp. 138–9.
[95] Ibid., p. 139.
[96] Louis Sébastien Mercier, "Usurers," *Tableau de Paris,* Jean-Claude Bonnet, ed., vol. 2, Paris, Mercure de France, 1994 [1781–1789], pp. 300–303.

If the bishops of France maintain a different discourse, linking contract and morals, they nevertheless abstain from raising the debate. In 1700, the assembly of the clergy of France adopted a text drawn up by Bossuet, which attacks those who hold that only the loan bearing interest at the expense of the poor is forbidden and define in very rigorous terms the "nascent damage" and the "profit cessant," rejecting interest justified by assumed risk. But the embarrassment of the episcopacy is shown during the missions and in their recommendation vis-à-vis predicators and confessors. One reports that the bishop of Montpellier in 1743 instructs them "to be careful in their sermons on usury not to outrage the audience of usurers, present in large numbers in this town,"[97] and two archbishops of Lyon adopt the same attitude, as do moreover numerous priests who avoid the subject in the pulpit and in the confessional.[98] Deprivation of liberty was no longer commonplace except for fraudulent bankruptcy, and creditors did not use it against the poor, for, not only did they not recover their money, they would, moreover, have to pay the costs of keeping the debtor in prison as well.

In Italy, attacks against the doctrine of the church were made under cover of orthodoxy. As everywhere else, Italy was divided between traditional religious ideas and the widely held idea that usury was not a moderate profit, which must be licit but an exaggerated rate of interest to be extracted from the poor. The marquis Scipion Maffei (1675–1755) published *Dell'Impiego del danaro* in 1744, which defends the traditional ideas and which, in the last chapters, sustains the modern ideas and in particular invokes the *lex principis* that is to say the laws and customs of the country in matters of interest. The book created a storm. The pope orders the congregation of the Index to examine the work, appoints a commission of cardinals and theologians and issued the encyclical *Vix Pervenit* of 1 November 1745, which reaffirmed for the last time the old dogmas against usury. It confines itself to restating the traditional position of the church. Nevertheless, by introducing a notion of contract different from that of the loan for sums lent to the rich, where the demands for interest are modest or for profitable use of the capital by the debtor, the encyclical opens the door to wider interpretations:

The nature of a given contract is absolutely different from another and, as a consequence, the resulting effects are also totally different. In effect, profit based on

---

[97] *Nouvelles ecclésiastiques*, 14 April 1743, quoted by Courdurié, *La Dette des collectivités*, p. 59.
[98] Courdurié, *La Dette des collectivités*, p. 59.

the legitimate use of money, and thereby authorized in the internal sphere (i.e. private conscience) and external juridiction (i.e. competant courts) differs clearly from illicit profit which, precisely for this reason, is criticized by private conscience and by the law which requires its restitution.[99]

Some months later, a second edition of Maffei's book came out without a real change in its contents, although this edition published the text of the encyclical and was dedicated to Benoit XIV, an old friend of the author. Usury was no longer interest taken beyond the capital but that which exceeds the rate set by the law or custom. From that point on, if books were still written against all forms of interest until the nineteenth century, the authors brought nothing new to the subject and find themselves, without exception, in ultraconservative circles.[100]

In Spain, to read the synodal proceedings between 1675 and 1735 of a Catalan city, Villafranca,[101] as well as the pastoral visits from 1683, 1736, and 1818[102] shows how much the church had disengaged from the will to apply its moral directives against usury. The synodal proceedings insist on presence, assiduity, corporal discipline (to remain seated and abstain from abuse) and recall the need to read pontifical texts; in short, they aim to discipline the participants, not to transmit to them a morality. As for visits, when they were interested in questions of debt, it was a question of those concerning the church directly. In the visit of 1683, it is simply recommended to keep accounts for those who administer the church and to respect the wills of the dead in the question of masses, among others. In the 1736 visit, the bishop worried about the return of parish money and demanded that debts be publicized, giving ten days to creditors to make themselves known and to bring written proof of their credits. On the other hand, the bishop gives ten days to parishioners, under pain of excommunication, to denounce those who owe rents and *cens* to the church: this measure only concerned religious monies. In 1818, there was no longer mention of economic matters. In 1788, the bishop of Barcelona questioned the Episcopal commission on the subject of the bull *Vix Pervenit*, underlining how much credit is practiced everywhere and requesting to write to Rome so that he could learn exactly the contours of usury. In its response, the commission advised him to avoid the subject

---

[99] Ibid., pp. 47–54. Noonan, *Scholastic Analysis*, pp. 373–5. de Roover, "Scolastic Economics in Business," pp. 320–1.

[100] de Roover, "Scolastic Economics in Business," p. 321.

[101] Episcopal Archives of Barcelona (Arxúi diocesana), Acta synodalia, vol. 2, 1675–1735.

[102] Episcopal Archives of Barcelona (Arxúi diocesana), pastoral visit to Villafranca, years 1683, 1736, 1818.

and not to refer to Rome.[103] In 1818, there was no further mention of economic matters during the pastoral visits.

Similarly, the new paradigms penetrate Spanish society and the five large guilds (*gremios*) of Madrid asked King Charles III, citing jurists and theologians favourable to a moderate return (2.5 to 3 per cent per annum) on money, to allow a return on their own deposits of money, which was granted to them by the royal cedula of 1764.[104] Finally, the church took action over the disengagement of priests on these questions and developments and, in 1830, gave instructions to confessors not to annoy penitents who lend at legal rates and to leave it to the civil laws to sanction such matters.[105]

Thus, between the sixteenth and eighteenth centuries, the terms of reference were overturned, passing from a religious-based ethic to another born of economics. The conceptual pairings of credit and usury, gift and credit, and work and charity, as well as those of nature and of contract, are redefined. At the same time, the state has progressively taken charge of the disciplinary institutions for the practice of credit while concerning itself with protecting the aristocracy threatened by excessive debt. During the course of these transformations, the discourse of the church ceased to qualify practices in terms of credit and usury. It changed function, and from an operational discourse – in the sense that it had a practical effectiveness in pushing the operational institutions – it became a symbolic discourse given for the benefit of those advancing it. To participate in these debates, which no longer have social relevance, thus became a sign of recognition: it indicated membership of the religious world. The discourse against usury had changed vocation.

The word itself also changed meaning and now concerned only persons and very precise situations. Turgot enumerates them:

The word usurer is hardly ever used in society except to refer to short term usurers because of the high rates of interest they demand; to some second-hand dealers who lend on pledge to the middle classes and to artisans in distress; finally, to men of base reputation who make a livelihood of providing, at exhorbitant rates of interests, the means necessary for children from disturbed families to continue their libertine lifestyles and wild expenses.

[103] Episcopal Archives of Barcelona Barcelone (Arxúi diocesana).
[104] Carlos Petit, "Derecho mercantil: entre corporaciones y codigos," *Hispania. Entre derechos propios y derechos nacionales, Atti 'dell'incontro di studio Firenze-Lucca 25,26, 27 maggio 1989*, vol. 1, Bartolomé Clavero, Paolo Grossi, and Francesco Tomas y Valiente, eds., Milano, Giuffrè Editore, pp. 315–481 (360–7).
[105] de Roover, "Scolastic Economics in Business," p. 321.

It is precisely these categories that Mercier discusses in his chapter on usurers. But in spite of the evolution of minds, the legislation remains impermeable to credit. This denial of a reality, which totally impregnated society, prevented it from endowing itself with systems of regulation, be they economic (there was no lender in the last resort) or judicial – even if deprivation of liberty was no longer practiced except in fraudulent bankruptcy. It is evident that Turgot is right when he points out that the shame and risk associated with loans with interest are simply added costs to be met by the borrower.[106]

In October 1789, the National Assembly adopted a decree recognizing the loan bearing interest at a rate fixed by the law, and after the Revolution, the contract is completely secularized and the duty of solidarity left to the liberty of each person: "Each citizen is free to contract as he sees fit: the obligations that he agrees are to be executed in accordance with the terms and values stipulated" decrees a law of 5 Thermidor, Year IV in establishing the liberty to fix rates.[107]

Few historians have studied the influence of these ideological prohibitions on the economy[108]; it would seem as if the subterfuge lenders

---

[106] Turgot, *Mémoire sur les prêts d'argent*, vol. 3, p. 138.

[107] Quoted by Courdurié, *La Dette des collectivités*, pp. 75–6; and de Roover, "Scolastic Economics in Business," pp. 319–20.

[108] Hitherto, the debates on usury have been part of two types of problematic: that of economists who seek to measure the influence of the prohibitions on the development of capitalism and that of Max Weber who related economic behaviour to religious conviction; Max Weber, *L'ethique protestante et l'esprit du capitalisme; Les sectes protestantes et l'esprit du capitalisme*, Paris, Plon, 1990. John Noonan is the leading proponent of the theory that the prohibitions of the church would have prevented the investment of capital in the consumption loans market and would have thereby stimulated the practice of shared risk investments and, in so doing, increased the capital available for business, encouraging economic growth; Noonan, *Scholastic Analysis*, p. 195. Raymond de Roover does not share Noonan's, or indeed Weber's, beliefs but instead considers that capitalism developed independently of the church but that the latter always had a negative influence in inflating costs of credit and in increasing losses on exchange. These costs by affecting, all too often, the merchant's profits would have harmed economic growth by increasing not only the costs but also the risks of business. In particular, the church's prohibitions changed the history of banking by requiring merchants to use exchange to mask all their financial operations and by inflating the costs of credit because it was necessary to have recourse to foreign operators for all transactions; de Roover, *La Pensée économique des Scolastiques*, doctrines et méthode, Montreal, Vrin, 1971; de Roover, "The Scolastique, Usury and Foreign Exchange," *Business History Review*, 41, no. 3, 1967, pp. 257–71. These are ongoing debates, kept alive by medievalists and jurists, in Spain, Italy and France. See Actes du colloque de Narbonne (mars 1998), édité par *Alain Boureau et Sylvain Piron*, Paris, Vrin (Études de philosophie médiévale, 79), 1999. Giacomo Todeschini, *I mercanti e il Tempio. La società cristiana e il circulo virtuoso della ricchezza fra Medioevo ed Età Moderna*, Bologna, Il Mulino,

employed was enough to obliterate their effect, as if there were no point in discussing the subject, because prohibitions never succeeded in putting an end to practice of credit. The example of the pawnshops shows that it was nothing of the kind and that we would do well to fully integrate the role of ideologies and cultures seen as shared ways of viewing the world in studies on economic behaviour, in particular the two predominant types of behaviour in preindustrial Europe, namely, aristocratic behaviour and merchant behaviour.

2002; Giacomo Todeschini, *Richezza Francescana della povertà volontaria alla società di mercato*, Bologna, Il Mulino, 2004.

8

Political Economies and Cultures of Exchange

The first, of gold, who this inscription bears,
"Who chooseth me shall gain what many men desire" ...
The second, silver, which this promise carries,
"Who chooseth me shall get as much as he deserves"...
This third, dull lead, with warning all as blunt,
"Who chooseth me must give and hazard all he hath"...
  – William Shakespeare, *The Merchant of Venice,* Act II, Scene 7, 4–10

One part [of the army] shall fall upon Grangousier and his forces. By it shall he
be easily at the very first shock routed, and then shall you get money by heaps,
for the clown hath store of ready coin. Clown we call him, because a noble and
generous prince hath never a penny, and that to hoard up treasure is but a clown-
ish trick.
  – François Rabelais, *Gargantua*, chap. 33

Our analysis of credit and trust until now has shown that preindustrial
Europe followed two systems of exchange, which drew from different
economic cultures and, more generally, two divergent political economies. On one hand, we have the gift economy still very much in use and,
on the other, an assertive and continuously expanding capitalist economy.
Although each entailed a completely different set of practices, the two
were in constant interaction with each other.

Now, this duality was a subject theatre delighted in dealing with
between the sixteenth and seventeenth centuries. At times, a gentleman and a bourgeois wishing to acquire "polish" were pitted against
each other, as in the Bourgeois Gentilhomme; at others, the two cultures
entered into a head-on conflict, as in the *Merchant of Venice*; and at yet

others, aristocrats with a bourgeois-like behaviour were contrasted with other aristocrats who cherished the noble way of life, as in *Timon of Athens*. In fact, all three cases draw from real-life situations. In *Timon of Athens*, we see Timon's prodigality in the name of friendship clash with the calculative nature of his peers, revealing the antagonism between the two economic cultures, although in reality, neither existed in its pure state. The conflict intensifies in the *Merchant of Venice* with the depiction of another facet of aristocratic culture, namely, risk. When read along with other texts, in particular the memoires of Saint-Simon, a great aristocrat if there ever was one, these plays confirm the importance of the values of friendship and risk in the aristocratic culture. We then need to examine how the two economies corrupted each other, who were the intermediaries between the two worlds (intendants, servants, etc.) and look at the notions of credit, gift, market, and corruption in different contexts to understand the extent to which the existence of two rival economic and political cultures made their borders porous.

Historians are not in the habit of using theatre as a source, loath as they are to venture out of the archives. Yet, theatre is a product of its time. To keep its audiences engaged, it must speak to them about their problems and emotions with references they understand. It is in this sense that works that connect with their audience tell us about them, their interrogations in the face of a changing society, and the tensions and contradictions confronting them. This "community of interpretation"[1] between an author and his or her audience is what makes literary works an invaluable aid in understanding the questions agitating society in a manner no other source can: plays refract contemporary issues.[2]

Friendship and Economy

Timon of Athens was first printed in 1623 in the First Folio and was grouped together somewhat incongruously with *Romeo and Juliet* and *Julius Caesar*. A curious play written probably between 1605 and 1608, critics consider it incomplete, although it reaches its conclusion with the death of Timon. There is no evidence of it having ever been performed during Shakespeare's lifetime. To explain the play's incomplete nature,

---

[1] Stephen Greenblatt, *Shakespearian Negotiations. The Circulation of Social Energy in Renaissance England*, Oxford, Oxford University Press, 2000 [1988].

[2] Roger Chartier, "George Dandin, ou le social en representation," *Annales. Histoire, Sciences Sociales*, 49, no. 2, 1994, pp. 277–309.

literary criticism points to a number of indices: inconsistency of details, freewriting varying between prose and verse, and the existence of two main protagonists Timon and Alcibiades. Timon is the clear hero of the first half, but subsequently, Alcibiades steals Timon's thunder. The manner in which the other characters and walk-on parts are treated further strengthens the impression of incompleteness. A multitude of anonymous groups populate the entire play.[3] However, the systematic depersonalization of the characters leads it to acquire a theoretical dimension and this stance – or this moment in the work of the playwright – reflects the author's thinking about social groups.

Critics have always been uncomfortable with this play at the junction of two other plays of Shakespeare: *King Lear*, which deals with the suffering of a man hurt by the attitude of those close to him – as Timon is – and *Coriolanus*, which depicts the aggressiveness of a soldier in the face of public ingratitude as experienced by Alicibiades. "It is as if these two tragedies deal separately with what in Timon has been put together albeit somewhat imperfectly merged. Perhaps the sense of incompleteness comes from the feeling the playwright may have had about this impasse."[4]

Evidently, the play has been the subject of much commentary and several interpretations. A historical reading sees in it a critique of early capitalism at the turn of the seventeenth century. The play, moreover, forms part of an entire trend in English literature of the time in which greed and brazen and ruinous pomp along with all the attendant naivety and duplicity are recurring themes. In it, Shakespeare appears to observe, with a touch of nostalgia perhaps, the decline of the great aristocratic houses and feudal values; Timon, it would thus seem, is the incarnation of true nobility in the face of the onslaught by merchants and usurers under James I.[5] Some have pointed out more directly to the similarity in the behaviour of James I and Timon, going to the extent of concluding that it would have been impossible to stage the play before the king, because he would have found intolerable the mirror it held out to him.

---

[3] For criticism of this play, see Victor Bourgy's introduction to his translation in William Shakespeare and Thomas Middleton, *Timon d'Athènes*, Paris, Robert Laffont, 1995, pp. 229–243. See also Francelia Butler, *The Strange Critical fortunes of Shakespeare's Timon of Athens*, Ames, The Iowa State University Press, 1960.

[4] Victor Bourgy, Introduction, p. 243.

[5] H. J. Oliver, Introduction to *Timon of Athens*, London, Methuen (the Arden Shakespeare), 1959, pp. xliv–xlv takes into account this tradition that makes *Timon* a model symbol of the aristocracy.

A recent reading attempts to link feminism and psychoanalysis to provide a critique of masculine subjectivity and couple it together with "new historicism" interested in studying cultural practices and literary texts and their links with political structures and the social world.[6] My reading fits into this current, which sees in the play an exploration of the cultural forms of patronage in the Elizabethan and Jacobean eras and a confrontation between the culture of the gift and that of credit, their ambivalence, and their relationship with power.

Maintaining the play to be incomplete, most commentators lavish their attention on Timon and ignore Alcibiades. I have a different perspective: I believe we should look at the play as it is and see it as a work whose architecture is complete and whose surprising form is intentional. Viewed as such, it becomes a wonderful fable about the impossibility of living the aristocratic culture in a changed world. It may be seen as corresponding to the nostalgia of a noble audience for a bygone era, which undoubtedly never existed, but the evocation of which knits together its identity in a period when the ascending values were resolutely different.[7] Timon and Alcibiades are the two faces of the same culture, two facets of the same character and the same social group. Their divergent fortunes express the two possible reactions of a noble unwilling to adjust the rules of his life to the changing values of the social organization: one withdraws and flees a world he no longer understands, and the other takes to arms to destroy the political organization that marginalizes him. They represent two modes of expressing the values of the nobility: gift, charity, and patronage, on one hand; war, on the other. Moreover, the solidarity between the two men is complete and the only one in the play who stands the test of time along with the solidarity that binds Timon's servants to their master.

Through its geometry and play of opposition, the play's construction strengthens this single and dual image of the two main protagonists. One holds centre stage in the first half, the other in the second. We are watching the same man in two opposite situations (the lord in all his glory in his palace, then the ruined misanthrope in his cave), and two men who react with the same violence and inability to compromise with a society that excludes them, but each with a different weapon: Timon uses words,

[6] Coppelia Kahn, "'Magic of Bounty': Timon of Athens, Jacobean Patronage and Maternal Power," *Shakespeare Quarterly*, 38, no. 1, 1987, pp. 34–57.
[7] Norbert Elias put forward this disposition in his analysis of the liking for the poets of the Pléiade in the court society, Norbert Elias, *La Société de Cour* [1969], traduit de l'allemand par Pierre Kamnitzer, Paris, Calmann-Lévy, 1974.

and then the gold he finds to destroy Athens; Alcibiades chooses to take up arms. Both men turn against Athens; therein lies the strength of the city and the two men. The entire play works on this play of conformity and opposition: Timon is thrice rejected by three friends, and Alcibiades, betrayed by three senators. The characters come back and the scenes are repeated, but each time Timon perceives things and reacts differently: twice, the Painter and the Poet come and offer their works; the first time, Timon is fooled, and the second time, it is they who are fooled. Two banquets mark the play, one at which fine meats are served and the other where the guests are given water and stones. After an unreserved generosity that expects nothing in return comes the conditional generosity that buys only to destroy. The characters are equally schematized: we know nothing about Timon and hardly anything more about Alcibiades. They remain at the stage of character sketches and as such can be interpreted as two ideal types of the aristocracy. They move in an equally depersonalized world, made up of artists, artisans, lords, senators, inhabitants, servants, bandits, and so on and so forth. This partiality for anonymity gives the play a theoretical character: all the characters speak and act as representatives of the social group to which they belong. This aspect is all the more accentuated as Timon likes to explain the morality and reasons for his actions.

The social dynamics depicted show the radical difference between the two cultures that clash: the aristocratic culture of Timon and Alcibiades and the capitalist culture of all the others except Flavius, Timon's steward and servant who, like the other servants, participates in the culture of his master, although he moves in another world on account of his duties. Although Timon's failure to come to terms with a changing world announces unequivocally the end of a certain aristocratic culture, the details of the play bring to light the contradictory logics that govern the relationship with money, and it is this aspect that makes the play so interesting as it allows us to enter into the relationship with the economy of various social groups.

Friendship, for Timon, is a fundamental value, and friendship is at the heart of the aristocratic culture. It is in the name of friendship that he gives, to help and honour his friends. However, he gives excessively: these gifts are also an assertion of power. The two are linked: the number of "friends" is a measure of "credit." Here, there is subtle tension; on one hand, friendship creates a general solidarity among equals, a solidarity one cannot refuse, but on the other hand, Timon's excessiveness affirms his superiority, his power, and his strength, and Shakespeare often uses the adjective royal to describe his attitudes: we are thus not far from the mana of the anthropologists. In keeping with this logic, when Timon becomes aware of his ruination, he believes he can count on his friends; "unwisely, but not ignobly, have I given," he tells Flavius.[8] This line reveals the extent to which nobility was first and foremost a question of virtue. Arlette Jouanna likes to recall that *nobilitas est virtus* and this adage must be taken seriously. One cannot emphasise enough its obsessive character, she writes, for "real nobility" is neither power, nor ownership, nor the force of arms, but an inner quality, a human excellence that deserved to have pride of place.[9] Indeed, Alcibiades was the only one to offer him the little money he possessed; the others had long abandoned the values of Timon.

In the French context, Molière marks well the association between nobility and virtue. Don Louis explains this to his son Don Juan:

How do you think I can look on this multitude of unworthy actions, whose evil appearance can hardly be palliated before the world; this continuous succession of disgraceful quarrels, which compel us time and again to weary the kindness of our King, and which have exhausted in his esteem the merit of my services and the patience of my friends? Ah! how low you have fallen! Do you not blush to be so little worthy of your birth! Have you any right, tell me, to the least pride in it? And what have you done in the world to be a gentleman? Do you think that it is enough to bear the name and arms of one, and that it brings us glory to be sprung of noble blood, when we live infamously? No, no, birth is nothing where virtue is not.... Know that a man of noble birth who leads an evil life is a monster in nature; virtue is the prime title of nobility.[10]

True friendship does not stop at helping out occasionally, and rejects the direct repayment of help given. Thus, not only does Timon get Ventidius

---

[8] II, 2, 164.
[9] Arlette Jouanna, *Le Devoir de révolte. La noblesse française et la gestation de l'Etat moderne (1559–1661)*, Paris, Fayard 1989, p. 40.
[10] Molière, *Don Juan* (English version, Adolphe Cohn and Curds Hidden Page, eds., New York, G. P. Putnam's Sons, 1908), Act IV, Scene 6: "De quel œil, à votre avis, pensez-vous que je puisse voir cet amas d'actions indignes, dont on a peine, aux yeux du monde, d'adoucir le mauvais visage; cette suite continuelle de méchantes affaires, qui nous réduisent à toute heure à lasser les bontés du souverain, et qui ont épuisé auprès de lui le mérite de mes services, et le crédit de mes amis? Ah, quelle bassesse est la vôtre! Ne rougissez-vous point de mériter si peu votre naissance? Etes-vous en droit, dites-moi, d'en tirer quelque vanité, et qu'avez-vous fait dans le monde pour être gentilhomme? Croyez-vous qu'il suffise d'en porter le nom et les armes, et que ce nous soit une gloire d'être sorti d'un sang noble, lorsque nous vivons en infâmes? Non, non, la naissance n'est rien où la vertu n'est pas.... Apprenez enfin, qu'un gentilhomme qui vit mal est un monstre dans la nature; que la vertu est le premier titre de noblesse."

out of prison for debt, but undertakes to continue helping him: "Tis not enough to help the feeble up,/ But to support him after …".[11]

To the gift freely given is added the rejection of any visible hierarchy in behaviour, for if paraded, it would turn friendship into clientele. Accordingly, when the lords stand waiting respectfully as a sign of deference and social rank, Timon gives a lesson in political behaviour among aristocrats, inviting them to sit down without any ceremony, reservation or pettiness, for true friendship, he says, receives and gives with warmth. In rejecting the hierarchical organization of nobility, Timon is rejecting at the same time the transition of a friend into a client. Yet, his excessive generosity and his refusal to be reimbursed by Ventidius lend themselves to ambivalence: by this gesture, he excludes reciprocity and places himself above the others, behaving more like a king than a peer.

O, by no means, / Honest Ventidius. You mistake my love. / I gave freely ever, and there is none / Can truly say he gives if he receives. / If you betters play at that game, we must not dare / To imitate them. Faults that are rich are fair.[12]

Therein lies his fault, and Apemantus loses no time in telling him so when he refuses the food Timon offers him:

I scorn thy meat. 'Twould choke me, for I should ne'er flatter thee. O you gods, what a number of men eats Timon, and he sees 'em not! It grieves me to see so many dip their meat in one man's blood; and all the madness is, he cheers them up, too.[13]

In fact, after refusing Ventidius's offer to repay him, Timon adds: "Pray sit. More welcome are ye to my fortunes / than my fortunes to me." [14]

This ambivalence – or should one call it a transgression – can perhaps also be seen as a denunciation of the habits of James I who, in comparison to Elizabeth whom he succeeded, spent considerably to create and maintain his clientele. When she died, Elisabeth left behind about 40,000 pounds in debt and barely five years later, five years of peace, in 1608 James had already run up debts worth 600,000 pounds or six times the amount Elizabeth had accumulated after fifteen years of war. At the end of his reign, he owed 1 million pounds. Historians lay the blame for this indebtedness on the curialization of power and, along with it, the

[11] I, 1, 109.
[12] I, 2, 8–12.
[13] I, 2, 37–40.
[14] I, 2, 18–19.

generosity and royal munificence, with some even mentioning the king's compulsive need to give.[15]

But unlike Timon, James allowed himself to be persuaded by his ministers to take measures to maintain his income. The fact remains that although he was able to curtail his lifestyle and see to it that the cash kept coming in, he could not diminish his generosity because this was an intrinsic part of his role: to do so would be to lose honour. Thus, he could accept that his meat dishes be reduced from thirty to twenty-four, but he could not forego offering Lady Frances Howard jewels worth 10,000 pounds at the time of her marriage with his favourite Carr although his coffers had been emptied by the lavish marriage he had held for Princess Elizabeth.[16]

Friendship was a part of the political language. The campaign of the Duke of Newcastle in Sussex for his election to Parliament in 1761 illustrates how this notion was adapted to the needs of politics and parliamentary democracy. The duke conducted his campaign in the language of friendship, and his friends came from all sections of society: aristocrats rubbed shoulders with gentlemen, merchants, artisans, and even peasants. These friends sought to have him elected by all means, and he procured for them work, positions, credit, hospitality, and patronage from all kinds of institutions.[17]

The other difference with Timon was that the crown was not subjected to legal sanctions: creditors could not take the king to court and depended entirely on his whim. Thus a system of compensation, and a tax and financial structure similar to that of the French monarchy, came to be put in place, however, with one major difference, especially in a merchant country: the setting up of a far more effective customs administration, namely excise.[18]

Despite these safeguards, Timon's tragedy is very much in consonance with the royal practices and, just like his steward Flavius seeks to warn him

---

[15] Richard H. Tawney, *Business and Politics and Administration in 1603–1640*, Oxford, Clarendon Press, 1960; Lawrence Stone, *The Crisis of the Aristocracy 1558–1641*, Oxford, 1965; and *Family and Fortune: Studies in Aristocratic Finance in the 16th and 17th Centuries*, Oxford Clarendon Press, 1973. These features have been highlighted by Kahn, "Magic of Bounty," p. 42.

[16] Kahn, "Magic of Bounty," pp. 43–4, who uses his correspondence.

[17] Naomi Tadmor, *Family and Friends in Eighteenth-Century England Household, Kinship, and Patronage*, Cambridge, Cambridge University Press, 2001, pp. 218–19.

[18] Françoise Bayard, *Le monde des financiers au XVIIe siècle*, Paris, Flammarion, 1988; Daniel Dessert, *Argent, pouvoir et société au Grand Siècle*, Paris, Fayard, 1984; John Brewer, *The Sinews of Power, War Money and The English State*, London, Unwin Hyman, 1989.

about the dangers of his boundless munificence, the archbishop of York repeated the fears of the king's subjects in the face of his generosity when he gently pointed out to him that "the subjects of His Majesty understand and fear that his excellent and heroic nature be excessively disposed to giving, which in a short time will exhaust the treasury of the kingdom and bring much trouble."[19] Some critics opine that this similarity, also seen in the love for hunting and horses, would not have seemed respectful on stage and that this was probably the reason why the play was never performed during Shakespeare's lifetime and why it remained incomplete.[20]

Let us dwell for a moment on the dynamics of friendship. The bonds of friendship were forged in the sociability of families and neighbours. When a gentleman did a favour to another, the latter became the "obligor" of the former and thanked him with protestations of friendship, which were in fact an acknowledgment of debt, but one for which no time limit was set nor the manner in which it was to be repaid spelled out. Nobles wrote to each other and their correspondence acted both as a means to keep up their friendship and an acknowledgment of debt in which friends declared themselves to be their "friend," "obligor," and "servant."[21] Exchanges of letters, invitations, and gifts were the normal manifestations of friendship. However, solidarity did not preclude freedom and the obligation to repay the debt of friendship did not bar the obligor from enjoying certain independence. Indeed, at times it was in vain that a noble asked a friend to come and join him on the battlefield; other examples show that "friends" could change their mind and desert a battle they no longer approved of. Whatever be the case, the language was always that of an entreaty and not an order. In her treatise on the nobility in the form of advice to her son, Luisa Maria de Padilla, the countess of Aranda lays great stress on the importance of friends in social success but asks him not lose the ability to assert his authority in a relationship: she advises him to have highly placed friends but insists that such friendship does not go hand in hand with submission and that it behooves one to maintain the authority of a grandee:

Take care to win the friendship of Cardinals and Prelates, or those who occupy high posts in the Councils of the King as in the Militia, in order to support and

---

[19] Cited in Menna Prestwich, *Cranfield: Politics and Profits under the Early Stuarts: The Career of Lionel Cranfield, Earl of Middlesex*, Oxford, Clarendon Press, 1966, p. 14.

[20] Kahn, "Magic of Bounty," pp. 55–6.

[21] See examples in *Early Modern Institutions in their Social Context. An International Comparison of Local Justice, Politics and Administration*, Stefan Brakensiek, ed., Cologne and Vienna, Boehlau, 2005.

protect your servants and vassals by this means, and by others that may be befitting for you, but you must never do so by lowering your rank, but by preserving the authority and dignity of a grandee.[22]

These acknowledgements of the debts of friendship were distinct from the ties of fidelity and clientele. Through the bonds of friendship a system of mutual aid was built that could be pressed into service to face the vicissitudes of life. A stage was crossed when the goods were no longer distributed as "favours" but as pure and simple gifts, implying the pre-eminence of the giver. To keep open house and feed gentlemen every day, as also grant them regular pensions were ways to build a clientele. It was by imperceptible degrees that the relatively independent status of a friend changed into that of a client.[23] The Baron de la Moussaye used this transition to win his rank and reputation during his years in Brittany. He insisted that he was a great builder and a large consumer of furniture and jewellery, that he kept an open house, and that he "moreover lent money to those who needed it."[24]

Timon becomes the champion of friendship, understood as an insurance against the blows of fate, rooted in the complete gift of the self: he concludes by pointing to the guarantees that having many friends offers: "and what better or properer can we call our own than the riches of our friends? O, what a precious confort 'tis to have so many like brothers commanding one another's fortunes! O, joy's e'en made away ere't can be born: mine eyes cannot hold out water, methinks ...".[25]

Every gift made to him is returned with presents even more valuable: "Let the presents / Be worthily entertained."[26] When in Act 2 his need for money makes him turn to his friends, he is proud of his conduct as a perfect gentleman, certain that it will earn him gratitude.

The culture Shakespeare depicts is not merely literary: it is a moral reference for the European aristocracy. Saint-Simon describes with emotion the end of a treasurer who spared neither his time nor his money:

Poor de Harouys died at this time in the Bastille, where he had been for the last ten or twelve years; he had been for a long time the treasurer of the states of Brittany. He was the best man in the world and the most obliging; he only knew how to lend money, and never press to be repaid: with such a conduct,

[22] Luisa Maria de Padilla, *Nobleza virtuosa*, Zaragoza, 1637, pp. 59–60.
[23] Jouanna, *Le Devoir de révolte*, pp. 66–89.
[24] Quoted by Natalie Z. Davis, *Essai sur le don dans la France du XVIe siècle*, Paris, Seuil, 2003, p. 59.
[25] I, 2, 85–94.
[26] II, 2, 174–5.

he complied so readily that when he had to count the pennies, he could never get himself out of trouble. So great was the trust of the province and everyone in him that one had left him alone for several years without counting; that was his ruination. Many people lost heavily, Brittany had a great deal to do with it, and he remained utterly ruined. That, I think, is the sole example of an accountant of public monies with whom his masters and all the people lost without the slightest aspersion ever being cast on his integrity. The losers even pitied him, everyone was distressed about his misfortune: this was what made the King give him only life imprisonment; he endured it without complaint and served his term in great piety, visited by a great number of friends and helped by many.[27]

The vocabulary of love was the cement that bound these relationships of friendship and clientele, relationships that, moreover, were highly emotional. Arlette Jouanna gives several examples, and Sharon Kettering describes the rhetorical excesses used to express the feverish emotions that characterized the speech of the "malcontent."[28]

Timon acts in accordance with the emotional economy of his time, in other words, violently. Once ruined and rejected by his peers, he offers them a last banquet in which the fine meats are replaced by stones and water, and instead of championing the aristocratic values, as during the first banquet, he champions the very opposite of those same values. This was tantamount to a cosmic upheaval. Addressing the gods, he asks them to always keep something in reserve, for fear that their divinity be scorned, for if the gods had to borrow from men, men would abandon the gods.[29] In his last tirade, as he tears off his clothes and leaves Athens, he pushes the logic of what he is feeling to the extreme, and because he has been a witness to the overturning of morality and values, he calls for their destruction as well as that of all social ties: may children rebel, virgins prostitute themselves, servants steal, the bankrupt cut the throats of their creditors, he says, and his wishes rise in crescendo until he wants that all social relations, including that of friendship, be nothing more than poison.[30] He ends his diatribe by asking the gods to bring down Athens and to swell his rage against all humans for they have broken the link of divine kindness.

His new frame of mind materializes when in his cave he finds gold. He thanks the heavens for giving it to him, for "much of this will make /

---

[27] Saint-Simon, *Mémoires (1691–1701)*, t. 1, Paris, Gallimard, 1983, p. 664.
[28] See the examples given by Jouanna, *Le Devoir de révolte*, p. 102, n34 and pp. 103–11.
[29] III, 7, 60–2.
[30] IV, 2, 29–30.

Black white, foul fair, wrong right, / base noble, old young, coward
valiant."[31]

At this point, he unveils the divine bond that links God to men through
the aristocratic society and its values, as the noble values are rooted in
a social and moral architecture that comes directly from God to men.
He then gives away his gold to thieves so that they can continue stealing;
they are the only honest people as they openly profess their trade, whereas
all the rest steal while posing to be honest. Besides, in Elizabethan society,
sermons never failed to remind that wealth and fortune were the gifts of
God and not the fruit of man's labour.[32]

A chronicle by Pierre de l'Estoile about Marguerite of France, duchess of Savoy, sheds light on this link between God and humans through
the attitude of kings and the nobility. She preferred to give rather than
lend money to French gentry in need of money crossing her lands: "My
friends, ... you should not thank me, His [God's] will was to use me to
help you ... I am the daughter of kings who were so great and liberal that
they taught me not to lend, but to give liberally to whomsoever beseeches
me when in need."[33]

This filiation echoes Cicero's treatise on friendship *Laelius de Amicitia*,
which praises friendship without any expectation of return, without usury
in the vocabulary of the time, and above all Seneca's *De Beneficiis*, translated from the English in 1578, which enjoins the nobility to refuse the
transformation of gift into merchandise (III.xiv) and which recognizes
that the one who does good to others freely resembles the gods; but the
one who seeks something in return resembles usurers (III.xv).[34] The filiation is also present in the meanings of the word gift given in the dictionaries of the time: "Is equal to grace what is graciously given to man by
the hand of God, and in particular the gifts of the Holy Spirit. And it is in
the manner they are received that they must be given, you have received
freely, give freely (gratis accepistis, gratis date)."[35]

The language of the characters in the play expresses these cultural
oppositions. All, from the old Athenian to the senators and lords, only

[31] IV, 3, 29–30.
[32] Laura Stevenson O' Connel, "Antientrepreneurial Attitudes in Elisabethan Sermons and
    Popular Literature," *Journal of British Studies*, 15, 1976, pp. 1–20.
[33] Pierre de L'Estoile, *Journal pour le règne de Henri III (1574–1589)*, L. R. Lefèvre, ed.,
    Paris, Gallimard, 1943, p. 48, quoted by Davis, *Essai sur le don*, p. 32.
[34] Kahn, "Magic of Bounty," pp. 48–9.
[35] Le *Tesoro de la Lengua Castellana o Española* quoted by Bartolomé Clavero, *La Grâce
    du don, Anthropologie catholique de l'économie moderne*, Paris, Albin Michel, 1996
    [1991], p. 75.

use the language of money trading; Timon and Alcibiades alone do not do so. Thus, when Timon undertakes to endow his servant so that he can marry the girl he is courting, the agreement with the father is sealed by Timon giving his word of honour; however, the dialogue between the two evokes two economies: the Athenian uses the vocabulary of pawning and Timon that of moral commitment. The old Athenian says, "Pawn me to this your honour, she is his."[36] And Timon replies, "My hand to thee; mine honour on my promise."[37]

In the same scene of the same act while on their way to Timon's banquet, two lords discuss between themselves his generosity and the latter explains to the former that he returns six fold any favour and gives a far higher return on each present than what money could earn. The lords count, speak of interest and receipts and Timon for them is merely an excellent financial investment: "2 Lord.– ... Plutus the god of gold / Is but his steward; no meed but he repays / Sevenfold above itself; no gift to him / But breeds the giver a return exceeding / All use of quittance."[38]

But if friendship is the key word for Timon, for the others it is credit. Indebtedness, normally experienced as a loss, is for Timon a matter of pride, as it will give his peers the opportunity to demonstrate their friendship. Evidently, they will turn a deaf ear to his pleas for help and justify their conduct putting the blame on Timon's financial behaviour.

Customs also reveal these two moral economies: Timon gives his word and seals his promise with a handshake, thereby pledging himself; the others make bills, do the accounts or make crosses to conclude a deal, using first and foremost material procedures. Timon has a casket with gold and jewels, the others paper money. Timon is indifferent to time: he gives; the others turn time to good account: they lend, "have the date in count," the senator tells his servant when he sends him to Timon's to collect the repayment of the bills that have fallen due.[39] When Timon's collapse is clear, the misunderstanding is complete and in the same way as he had committed himself in all his economic transactions, he has only himself to give to pay back his debts, and he offers his heart and his blood in two replies which integrate the economy of the human body with the economy of mathematics: "Cut my heart in sums ... Tell out my blood."[40]

[36] I, 1, 152.
[37] I, 1, 153.
[38] I, 2, 275–9.
[39] II, 1, 34.
[40] III, 4, 86, 88.

He is stating the impossible conciliation of the two. But he adopts and hijacks the vocabulary of the others including the senators who, interceding with Timon in his cave so that he stop Alcibiades's revenge, use the vocabulary of arithmetic to describe their love: "sums of love," "the figures of their love."[41]

The use of the vocabulary of both gift and credit reveals the ambivalence of this generosity that is nourished by the very money of those for whom it is intended: the presents Timon offers the aristocrats have been bought with the money he has borrowed from them. His error lies in refusing to see that the culture of the gift is deeply embedded in that of credit. Behind the tragedy of the great Athenian lord, Shakespeare depicts the race for credit and the spiralling indebtedness of the aristocratic families in the court of James I.

The character of Flavius is essential in making the link among Timon, his master, and the capitalist economy: he is the steward who manages his fortune and who has to reconcile the two economies. He records the entries, keeps the accounts and books and, in doing so, shows that the real world is not that of the noble. Each and every act of Timon is translated by him into the two economic realities of the world: "O my good lord, / At many times I brought in my accounts, / Laid them before you; you would throw them off / and say you summed them in my honesty."[42]

He obeys, knowing full well that the culture of his master is no longer relevant and, when Timon asks him to bring his casket, he thinks rightly that "when all's spent, he'd be crossed then, an he could"; later, once the last presents have been offered, he observes: "His promises fly so beyond his state / That what he speaks is all in debt, he owes / For every word. He is so kind that he now / Pays interest for't. His land's put to their books."[43]

Flavius has to reconcile the ethos of disinterested friendship and the customary reciprocity among nobles with the merchant ethos based on the respect of contracts and payment of penalties in case of breach of commitment.

The character of Apemantus appears to the outsider, refusing to play the game. Further, he constantly pits the two economies against each other to show that neither redeems the other and that both are flawed, for man is essentially bad and individuals concerned only about themselves.

[41] V, 2, 37, 39.
[42] II, 2, 122–5.
[43] I, 2, 187–9.

In Act I Scene 1, during his first dialogue with Timon, when the latter invites him to dine with him, he answers, "No, I eat no lords,"[44] and later, he wishes on the merchant that his god, trade, be his ruin: "Traffic's thy god, and thy god confound thee!"[45] In his benedicite, he is equally dismissive of the two economies, for one must trust no one save oneself. Egoism reigns supreme:

Immortal gods, I crave no pelf. / I pray for no man but myself. / Grant I may never prove so fond / To trust man on his oath or bond, / Or a harlot for her weeping, / Or a dog that seems a-sleeping, / Or a keeper with my freedom, / Or my friends if I should need'em. / Amen. So fall to't. / Rich men sin, and I eat root.[46]

When he meets Timon again disgraced in his cave, he blames him for his inability to live with moderation, to place himself at the centre of humanity and compromise with it, for he knows only to live life in extremes and thus go from excessive refinement to rags. He says that beyond moral values, one has always to reckon with the selfishness of men.

Risk and the Economy

Friendship as the constituent value of the relationship among nobles is henceforth well recognized. But the cosmogony in which it was inscribed, in particular the link of men to God, has received less attention and the fundamental role of risk in this relationship insufficiently emphasized. Its importance stems from the conception the aristocrats have of the relationship with time and God. Time belongs to God and the only way man may experience it is in a relation of risk and chance and not in a relation of prescience and calculation. We have seen in the preceding chapter that in the debate on the lawfulness of credit, profit soon became legitimate, if, and only if, capital was at risk.

Taking risks was thus an essential aristocratic existential mode. It can be seen everywhere: in love as in the relationship with money. Although the question of risk is not ignored in Timon, Shakespeare places it at the heart of the *Merchant of Venice*. Because it brings out in all its facets the fundamental role of risk in the aristocratic culture, the play is an excellent entry point to understand this category. We may say that although the values that Timon defends are those of friendship, risk is the value

[44] I, 1, 206.
[45] I, 1, 237.
[46] I, 2, 58–67.

of the *Merchant of Venice*.[47] Risk is present at every level of the play: in economic ventures as in affairs of the heart, in the opposition between Shylock and Antonio as in the story of the three caskets of gold, silver, and lead that will open Portia's heart to the one who chooses well. The first casket, of gold, bears this inscription "Who chooseth me shall gain what many men desire"; the second, of silver, says "Who chooseth me shall get as much as he deserves"; and the third, in lead, declares "Who chooseth me must give and hazard all he hath"[48]; and that is the winning casket.

In the *Merchant of Venice*, the character of the Jew is complex; the dialogue reveals both his stigmatization and his humanity as well as his avarice, cynicism, and meanness. But this play is as much about usury as it about the Jew, for it is around the play on time and money that Shylock's and Antonio's hatred for each other crystallizes. Indeed, the Jews had been banned from specified places since the reign of Edward I, and there were few Jews in Elizabethan England; on the other hand, usury was a hotly debated social problem and a reality that weighed on everyone, on Shakespeare's audience as on his theatre, which, moreover, was financed by borrowings the interest of which carried a very heavy cost.[49]

The relationship with time and the building of trust were, as in Timon, at the heart of the opposition between the merchant world of Shylock and the aristocratic world of Antonio, Bassanio, and Portia. The play begins with Bassanio, the first to make the link between friendship and money: "To you, Antonio, / I owe the most in money and in love, / And from your love I have a warranty / to unburthen all my plots and purposes / How to get clear of all the debts I owe"[50] Antonio then urges him to unveil his plans, assuring him that "My purse, my person, my extremest means, / lie all unlocked to your occasion."[51]

Both respect the commitments of friendship: to help him conquer the woman he loves, Antonio does not hesitate to put his life in the hands of a usurer and one who hates him as well, for friendship is more important

---

[47] Pursuing this line of thought, see Gisèle Venet, "Valeurs et subversion: the merchant of Venice," *Etudes anglaises Grande-Bretagne-Etats-Unis*, 38, no. 1, 1985, pp. 1–12.

[48] II, 7, 5–7–9.

[49] William Shakespeare, *The Merchant of Venice*, J. R. Brown, ed., Arden edition, London, Methuen, 1955, Introduction. Stephen Greenblatt, *Shakespearian Negotiation*. For Portia and the place of women in exchange, see Karen Newman, "Portia's Ring: Unruly Women and Structures of Exchange in *The Merchant of Venice*," *Shakespeare Quaterly*, 38, no. 1, 1987, pp. 19–33.

[50] I, 1, 130–4.

[51] I, 1, 138–9.

to him than all else. The last enactment of the strength of friendship is left for Bassanio who, on learning that Antonio is in danger, leaves his wife the very day of their wedding and offers his life to save him.

More than the difference in faith, Shakespeare makes usury the driving force of Shylock's hatred for Antonio: "I hate him for he is a Christian: / But more for that in low simplicity / He lends out money gratis, and brings down / The rate of usance here with us in Venice."[52] He adds that Antonio hates his people, "my bargains, and my well-won thrift, / Which he calls interest …".[53]

Not only does Antonio act in accordance with the noble economy, but he also becomes its champion; he combats, stigmatizes, and despises the capitalist economy Shylock espouses. The dialogue between Antonio and Shylock on the subject of usury takes up the burning questions of the time. Antonio accepts to borrow for the sake of friendship: "albeit I neither lend nor borrow / By taking nor by giving of excess, / Yet to supply the ripe wants of my friend / I'll break a custom."[54]

Shylock answers with the story of the lambs that Jacob succeeded in multiplying and concludes that Jacob was blessed for that, for "This was a way to thrive, and he was blest: / And thrift is blessing if men steal it not."[55] Antonio then repeats the position of the church, saying that Jacob ran a risk and that gold and silver were not ewes and rams. Finally, Antonio becomes heated for he cannot bear to hear Shylock quote the Scriptures, "An evil soul, producing holy witness, / Is like a villain with a smiling cheek."[56] He stigmatizes the intention, the evil intention, condemned from now on by Protestants and Catholics alike.

The battle between the two men has begun and it is merciless. On the Rialto, Antonio is in the habit of publicly insulting Shylock for the money he earns and the interest he charges. Till then, Shylock had borne patiently being treated like a dog: "Fair sir, you spet on me on Wednesday last – / You spurned me such a day– another time / You called me dog: and for these courtesies / I'll lend you thus much moneys?[57]

Antonio assures him he is still capable of so treating him, of repelling him and spitting on him. He asks him to lend him money not as to a friend, but as to an enemy: "If thou wilt lend this money, lend it not / As

---

[52] I, 3, 37–40.
[53] I, 3, 45–8.
[54] I, 3, 56–9.
[55] I, 3, 85.
[56] I, 3, 94–5.
[57] I, 3, 121–4.

ti thy friends – for when did friendship take / A breed for barren metal of his friend? – / But lend it rather to thine enemy, / Who if he break, thou mayst with better face / Exact the penalty."[58]

These lines express perfectly all the violence that marked the debates of the time on the question of lending with interest. Today, charging interest on money loaned is legitimate and fixed in accordance with codified parameters. In Elizabethan England, it was a burning issue and those hostile to the idea of money growing with time considered the act of lending with or without interest as a social act intended either for a friend or for an enemy. The controversy was as bitter as Antonio's violence against Shylock, both verbal and physical, was public. Like all other Venetian aristocrats, Antonio too was a merchant, but a noble merchant, for the yield that he got from his money was through sea trade, which meant taking risks, the only mode that could legitimize the return on capital invested.[59] No sooner does Antonio suffer his first losses than Shylock reminds us again that the hatred between the two is born out of their conflict about how one should make one's wealth grow: "he was wont to call me usurer, let him look to his bond! he was wont to lend money for a Christian curtsy, let him look to his bond!"[60] He adds that Antonio had covered him with shame, laughed at his losses, mocked his gains, despised his race, hampered his business, dampened his friends and excited his enemies because he was a Jew.[61] When Antonio is at the mercy of Shylock, he knows he can expect no pity: "He seeks my life – his reason well I know; / I oft delivered from his forfeitures / Many that have at times made moan to me. / Therefore he hates me."[62]

As in Timon, the friendship that sustains the aristocratic economy is based on the gift of the self and each time he finds himself cornered, the noble offers his body in the literal sense of the word. Like Timon who asked his creditors to take his heart and blood as payment, Shylock demands a pound of Antonio's flesh as security for his loan. Both push to its limit the logic of the aristocratic economy that pledges the self: it is an economy of the body and social bonds, as we have already seen in the management of poverty in Chapter 1. The association between blood and aristocracy, man and wealth is a recurring one. In *Timon* in Act I, when Apemantus enters and Timon offers to dine with him, he replies, "No, I

[58] I, 3, 127–32.
[59] See Chapter 7.
[60] III, 1, 39–42.
[61] III, 1, 44–8.
[62] III, 3, 21–4.

eat not lords!"[63] and when Bassanio declares himself to Portia, he tells her, "all the wealth I had / Ran in my veins – I was a gentleman – "[64]

The blood of the aristocrat is his most precious good.

Risk and love are thus the principal categories of the gift economy. Even although the borders are porous, gifts are not strictly comparable to merchandise, for they are exchanged in a risk economy, in which time is indeterminate, and not in the economy of the moment, in which time is measured. It is within these borders that the limit between gift and bribe is located. Anthropologists have discussed the awareness that the actors have about the implicit exchanges that take place behind a gift and the obligation to return a gift offered.[65] Indeed, although there is only a fine line between gift and corruption, the line is nonetheless very real. Even if the gift is self-interested, it must not appear as such and it is precisely here that time and risk come into play: in societies of chance, to take time is to take the risk that the person may no longer be there to receive the counter-gift or to give what was implicit and expected in the first gift. Mauss recognizes that when a gift is given with a view to immediate gain, it is looked on with contempt.[66] In the aristocratic economy, exchange, mediated by individuals, cannot be reduced, as in a capitalist economy, to the clear and direct purchase of an object or service. On the contrary, in an aristocratic transaction, the motives as well as what is expected in return must never appear: they must remain indeterminate, for any clarification, by reducing the element of risk, would reduce, by the same token, the love and trust that are played and replayed out in each specific exchange. It would be to place objects before people, money before love, and this would overturn the order of the world, as Timon felt when his appeals for the reciprocity of friendship went unheeded, when material exchange came before emotional exchange and interpersonal relationships.

Chance, at the heart of love, the economy, and politics, lies also at the heart of noble entertainment. Everywhere in Europe, gambling was an aristocratic hobby as much in the court as in the cities and provinces. The habit developed in the seventeenth century and, in England, more particularly so after 1660. For a century and a half, it was to

[63] I, 1, 206.
[64] III, 2, 253–4.
[65] Alan Smart, "Gifts, Bribes, and Guanxi: A Reconsideration of Bourdieu's Social Capital," *Cultural Anthropology*, 1993, 8, no. 3, pp. 388–408 (394–7).
[66] Marcel Mauss, *Essai surle Don Forme et raison de l'échange dans les sociétés archaïques*, Paris, Presses Universitaires de France, 1991 [1923–24], pp. 145–279.

be for many a veritable obsession, a mania.[67] Lotteries were a part of everyone's lives: the royalty used them to fill its coffers, merchants increased their number in the city to sell their wares, and the Comte de Forge defended them.[68]

Some saw in the growth of gambling the influence of the fascination for problems of risk and the development of probabilities. Gaming was also encouraged by the increase in the number of opportunities for speculative gain during the wars against Louis XIV, especially those that came from gambling with public debt. The institution of lotteries had supposedly encouraged these tendencies.[69] Admittedly, these scientific developments may have encouraged gambling, but it seems to me that it was already there, at the heart of the aristocratic culture, and that its growth could, on the other hand, testify to the desire to distinguish and affirm the old values in the face of social groups whose rise was based on the values of calculation and prudence. This was to some extent what happened again in the eighteenth century with the infatuation for the old, extolled first by aristocrats to distinguish themselves from the bourgeois who had just come to power and then by the latter to legitimize their power by monopolizing these signs of distinction.[70]

The court was a place where gaming was daily affair and ubiquitous.[71] This tells us that hierarchies in aristocratic dignity, like Russian roulette, the other aristocratic paroxysmal habit based on chance, were determined by the capacity of the noble to be on first-name terms with Dame Fortune. Gambling was an integral part of ordinary life; in 1712, Saint-Simon narrates that even as the dauphin and the dauphine lay in their coffins waiting to be buried, the king went to Marly to resume gambling: "the King gave order for the recommencement of usual play at Mme de Maintenon's as early as the following Friday; and that M. and Mme la duchesse du Berry presided in the salon at the public lansquenet and brelan; and the different gaming tables for all the Court."[72]

[67] John Habakkuk, *Marriage, Debt and the Estates System. English Landownership, 1650–1950*, Oxford, Oxford University Press, 1994, pp. 294–5.
[68] Conte de Forges, *Des véritables intérêts de la Patrie*, Rotterdam, 1764, pp. 146–7.
[69] Habakkuk, *Marriage, Debt and the Estates System*, pp. 294–5.
[70] Grant McCracken, *Culture and Consumption*, Bloomington, Indiana University Press, 1988, p. ix.
[71] Olivier Grussi, *La vie quotidienne des joueurs sous l'ancien Régime à Paris et à la cour*, Paris, Hachette, 1985, chap. 4.
[72] Saint-Simon, *Mémoires (1691–1701)*, vol. 2, p. 480.

Gambling was not the preserve of the court and Parisians[73]; the aristocracy gambled as much in the provinces where the marquizes organized gambling sessions.[74]

Gambling was to consume money and as such, gaming debts were the only debts the aristocrats had to honour quickly. These were personal debts, debts of honour even though they were not recognized legally. For the families, paying back these debts was an absolute obligation as attested to by numerous examples in the case of England.[75] As for Mercier, at the end of eighteenth century, he was scandalized by aristocrats who did not pay their suppliers whereas they repaid their gaming debts: "In the evening, he stakes five hundred gold louis in gambling; and if he loses five hundred more, he pays them back the next day. A creditor of cards always prevails over a creditor of bread or meat."[76]

When debts became too heavy, the king or the family would help out the one who had had incurred excessive losses. Thus, in 1700 the king came to the rescue of Mme la Duchesse, who did not have the means to repay her gaming debts:

Madame la Duchesse, whose debts the King had repaid not so long ago, who showed herself to be very haughty to merchants in all manner of things, had not dared to speak of her gaming debts, which ran into large amounts. The debts kept swelling; she found herself utterly incapable of repaying them, thereby finding herself in the most awkward situation possible. What she feared the most was that Monsieur le Prince, and above all Monsieur le Duc, should come to know of it. Driven to extremes, she made up her mind to write to her former governess and expose to her plainly in a letter, in complete faith, which attracted her all powerful protection. She was not mistaken: Mme de Maintenon took pity on her situation, obtained that the King repay her debts, did not reprimand her in the least, and kept her secret.[77]

On the other hand, Saint-Simon was irritated by the misadventures of the duc de Mortemart, not because he began to play "hombre tête à tête with M. d'Isenghien" and peeved at losing, persisted stubbornly ending up with debts worth nearly 100,000 francs, but because the "payment gave rise to much talk," for it was late in coming and above all because

The ducs de Chevreuse and de Beauvillier attached themselves too literally to the dilapidation of the affairs of the duc de Mortemart, and to the reason of

[73] Francis Freunlich, *Le Monde du jeu à Paris 1715–1800*, Paris, Albin Michel, 1995.
[74] For examples for Toulouse, see A. Feugère, "Le capitoul David et les jeux défendus," *Annales du Midi*, XLIV, 1932–1933, pp. 305–11.
[75] Habakkuk, *Marriage, Debt and the Estates System*, p. 311.
[76] Mercier, *Tableau de Paris*, vol. 1, pp. 921–2, "Fournisseurs."
[77] Saint-Simon, *Mémoires*, vol. 1, p. 704.

conscience of preferring the debts of merchants and workers who were suffering, and of people who had lent their goods, over the debt that came from gambling and a heavy loss: they took much blame and had to listen to much from people … I could not help myself from warning MM. De Chevreuse and de Beauvillier about the commotion and the effect of such conduct and I had the greatest difficulty in making them understand how honour required the prompt payment of gaming debts, and how people were inexorable about it.[78]

This happened in 1710 just after the terrible economic crisis. The fact that the big players came to suffer shame and that nobles could prefer paying workers and merchants rather than clear their gaming debts was a sign of the changing attitudes even though Saint-Simon remained fastidious about the code of honour.

The wisest and most frequent course of action for an indebted gambler was to leave the court temporarily. Saint-Simon gives the example of Mme D'Elboeuf, who had managed to introduce herself in the court by gambling and who, in 1704, was taken away from there by her mother to prevent her debts from accumulating:

She [Mme D'Elboeuf] entered to such an extent [in the court], and even more so in playing for high stakes, dragging Mme la duchesse de Bourgogne with her in many debts that, either by order as it was believed, or by her mother's sagacity, she was with her daughter in her lands in Saintonge for eight months, and only came back to find M. de Mantoue in Paris [he will marry her].[79]

Interlacing of Two Economies

Between the two economies were a host of intermediaries. These issues, raised in the case of socialist economies,[80] were hardly ever discussed with respect to feudal economies. Yet, entrepreneurs and merchants had to develop their capitalist enterprises in a society that was not entirely so, and symmetrically, for a variety of reasons, many aristocrats, who were forbidden from trading, needed continuously to enter the market.

The antagonism of cultures, institutions controlled by the nobles and the necessary coexistence of men, with or without status, gave rise to a host of intermediaries. In all the previous chapters, we have met with some of these men and women: brokers, lawyers, and *revendeuses à la*

---

[78] Saint-Simon, *Mémoires*, vol. 3, pp. 985–6.
[79] Ibid. vol. 2, pp. 500–1.
[80] G. Grossman, "The 'Shadow Economy' of the USSR," *Problems of Communism*, 26, no. 5, 1977, pp. 25–40.

toilette, who allowed the passage from one world to the other and who knew how to use to their advantage this dual economy.

The intendant was the indispensable instrument of the nobles in their relations with the capitalist economy. Some worked in the interests of their master, others not. Flavius, Timon's steward, is the ideal intermediary in the service of his master. In his dialogue with Titus's servant, he denounces the nobles who deceived Timon, fully aware of what they were doing: "Why then preferred you not your sums and bills / When your false masters ate of my lord's meat? / Then you could smile and fawn upon his debts, And take down th'int'rest into their glutt'nous maws."[81]

But the reputation of the servants was not as commendatory: they were generally suspected of taking advantage of their situation. Saint-Simon recounts, for instance, how the valets of M. de La Rochefoucauld gained the upper hand over their master to the point where one had to "show all manner of consideration and accommodation if one desired to be a frequent visitor to the house." Among the valets, he mentions in particular Bachelier "who was one of the best and most honest of men I have ever seen in these classes, and the most worthy of his fortune." But he was the solitary exception, and the "spendthrift duke, incapable of looking after the house or any business, [was] at the mercy of valets who, as true valets, constantly took advantage of this, and all grew rich at his expense, and some off his credit."[82]

The capacity of some people to switch between the two economies lasted until the end of the ancien régime: Louis Sébastien Mercier and the Bastille archives provide us numerous examples of this. However, the monarchy and the families of the grandees had imposed safeguards on their own magnificence and surrounded themselves with institutions of financial control to check their generous impulses. Robert Descimon analysed the mechanism that Nevers, in imitation of the royalty, had put in place:

The characteristic feature in common between the management of Nevers and the royal administration (itself a seigniorial domination in the process of being modernized) is without doubt the permanent recourse to institutions of financial control the purpose of which was to limit the generosity of the prince. In the 16th century, the oath taken by the ordinary Barons of Nevers contained the following: and verify nothing that may be to my detriment unless I expressly order you to do so myself and warning me of it. Thus, swear and promise, and furthermore, as long as I am obliged and owe to another, whatever gift I may make, only allot

[81] III, 4, 50–3.
[82] Saint-Simon, *Mémoires*, vol. 4, pp. 725–9.

half of it and the other half to be acquitted, of which sound and loyal accounts shall be given to the lords, tax collectors and accounts officers. Article 46 of the "regulation of finances" of 21 May 1580 defined clearly the modalities of payment of sums given "as a pure gift to some respect worthy person or secret servant or then for some secret journey" (the equivalent of "cash" in the royal finances), but articles 53 and 54 stipulated that, as long as they had a large number of debts and annuities, the duke and the duchess would abstain from making gifts of more than fifty écus and prohibited secretaries, tax collectors, treasurers and the accounts people to enter and pay such amounts. This concern was shared by the king: since the 15th century, there were numerous edicts, for example the edict of Angers in 1498, stipulating that the donations of the domain would be worth only half their value and prohibited the Court of Accounts in Paris to register them for their nominal amount.[83]

The nobles also succeeded in entering the merchant arena either by using frontmen or by appropriating institutions, as we will see in the next chapter, with auction sales. Chroniclers of the time, from Saint-Simon to Louis-Sébastien Mercier, found this subterfuge amusing as also the large-scale influx of aristocrats into the trading world. They called it *business*. Writing about the wife of the Prince of Harcourt, Saint-Simon recounts in 1703, that "[s]he did business of all kinds, and would run as much for a hundred francs as for a hundred thousand. The comptrollers general could not get rid of her easily, and, as long as she could, she would cheat business people to make even more money."[84]

The "pecuniary pardons," to use the words of Saint-Simon, from which Mlle de Mailly benefitted in 1709, help us penetrate this art a little further:

Mlle de Mailly, the daughter of the Dame d'Atours, also received a pension of six thousand livres and twenty-five thousand écus for the town hall, in reward for a piece of advice her mother gave Desmarets, from which the king also drew some benefit. This is what is called doing business, and Desmarets was not a man, as forbidding as he was, not to listen to ladies in such matters, especially the ones who were so closely attached to Mme de Maintenon.[85]

The existence of two rival economic and political cultures makes it exceedingly difficult to separate credit, gift, market and corruption. In her essay on the gift in sixteenth-century France, Natalie Zemon Davis

---

[83] Robert Descimon, "Les ducs de Nevers au temps de Blaise de Vigenère ou la puissance de faire des hommes puissant," Blaise de Vigenère, poète et mythographe au temps de Henri III, *Cahiers V. L. Saulnier* n° 11, Paris, Presses de l'Ecole normale supérieure, 1994, pp. 13–37 (16–17).

[84] Saint-Simon, *Mémoires*, vol. 2, p. 272.

[85] Ibid., vol. 3, p. 334.

never ceases to encounter their porous borders.[86] They remained so at the beginning of the eighteenth century in Florence when Francesco Gondi, a Florentine patrician, noted in his diary not only the number of audiences he was granted by Grand Duke Cosimo III but also the gifts he received as grateful payment for his interventions with the sovereign.[87] In addition to the conceptual difficulties is the fact that in the sphere of exchanges, money was not supreme: it circulated as much in the form of goods as currency in all monetary exchanges, be they wages, purchases and sales, or even borrowed money that could be given partially in the form of goods.

Language liked to mix registers: the aristocratic political economy was founded on the language of the gift[88]: one neither lent nor sold; one gave, but these gifts had the knack of finding their way back to the market via brokers or jewellers, and Francesco Gondi never failed to note the market value of these presents.[89] Symmetrically, loans are contaminated by the culture of giving. Just as there is a whole grammar to be observed to fit into the tenses of reciprocity, repayment of loans also has its language showing that credit, even of the most commercial nature, is contaminated by the culture of giving: clearing one's debts, as Charles du Moulin recalled quoting an old proverb, is not always a happy ending because friends may turn into enemies if the debt link[90] is broken off. Such a refusal to close the accounts pervaded society all the way down to peddlers.

In the political arena, to maintain the thin line between gift and bribe, a ritualization of the gift took place with the purpose of detaching the gift from the immediacy of need. Rather than offering gifts to people in authority each time their help was required, which would immediately be perceived as an insult, in order to respect the spirit of the gift, presents were given outside the context of a crisis and followed time lines linked to family, festive, or administrative events. Accordingly, a good occasion could be the appointment of officers, at the time of every visit, every year, and so on; this continual flow of presents, not corresponding

---

[86] Davis, *Essai sur le don.*

[87] Jean-Claude Waquet, *De la corruption. Morale et pouvoir à Florence aux XVIIe et XVIIIe siècles*, Paris, Fayard, 1984, pp. 61–4.

[88] See Kettering for the seventeenth century, Sharon Kettering, *Patronage in Sixteenth and Seventeenth Century France*, Aldershot, UK, and Burlington, VT, Ashgate, 2002.

[89] See Chapter 4 and the examples in Waquet, *De la corruption*, in particular pp. 135, 63–4.

[90] Quoted by Davis, *Essai sur le don*, p. 99. See chapter 4 on gifts and sales.

to economic needs, made privileged assistance possible. In the sixteenth century, French law allowed all new officers to be honoured with presents even if the giver hoped to receive special favours in return.[91]

The scrutiny, for example, of the deliberations of the Alpine community assemblies shows that the act of offering presents to officers was a major concern of the elected village representatives. As we have seen, the occasions for gifting were ritualized and increased: welcome gifts and gifts offered during regular visits to pay "one's respects" cost dearly; all the more so because at every echelon, the individual took precedence over the post, which was tantamount to emphasizing the great freedom of those who held office and those in charge of the affairs of the state – and the powers of each one, although theoretically clearly spelled out, were in fact far more blurred. Thus, each time the holder of an office or a post changed, the advantages gained could be called into question. Therefore, communities had to be in position to influence all men who had a tiny bit of power on the road to royal will. This explains the great care taken to build and maintain a network of relations that could act like a pressure group, or a council. One had to have access to parliament, the election offices, and if possible have the ear of the intendant and the bishop. To enter these spaces, communities relied on personal relations, kept up with gifts and marks of submission, and, in Grenoble, paid one or several individuals likely to advise, represent, and defend them in court cases and legal proceeding.[92] These practices cost the community dearly: almost every month, the assembly would depute someone in Grenoble. Gifts, travel expenses, vacations, and wages all added up. Such influential men were not averse to being paid very handsomely for their good offices. The path followed was not very different from the gift offered to the king by his subjects, taxes collected for public good and the royal debt because the reason of state imposed it. But studying this fundamental aspect of state building is not the intention of this book; indeed, it would require another book to do so.

In public service, gifts to officials have a different meaning depending on the political regime; in a democratic one, gifts to public officials are seen as bribery; in aristocratic societies, they reflect links of subordination. In sixteenth-century France, both regimes coexisted until 1560

[91] Davis, *Essai sur le don*, pp. 135–6.
[92] Laurence Fontaine, *Pouvoir, identités et migrations dans les hautes vallées des Alpes occidentales (XVIIe–XVIIIe siècles)*, Grenoble, Presses Universitaires de Grenoble, 2003, chap. 8.

when a royal edict banned gifts to court officials. The following year, all gifts were forbidden by law, including perishable goods except for game from forests belonging to aristocrats, and, in 1579, all presents of whatever nature were banned.[93] This example shows the tensions within aristocratic societies when the monarchy asserts itself and what was at stake for the latter in monopolizing the symbolism of giving and the power it conveys.

But the desire to control officials and ensure better justice for the people did not withstand the traditional practices of giving, seen as a sign of respect and the foundation of aristocratic society. Making them perceived as instruments of corruption remained difficult to impose. However, another language gradually took form, and sufficiently enough to become law and be employed in their writings by Rabelais and Molière.

Indeed, behind the gift economy or the capitalist economy political stakes were involved: maintaining the aristocratic society with the personalization of the gift or the possible creation of a democratic society with the impersonality of the market. Montaigne perceived this and was clearly opposed to the links created by gifts:

For me nothing costs dearer than what is vouchsafed to me and for which my will remains mortgaged under the title of gratitude: I prefer to receive services which are up for sale. For the latter I give mere money: for the others, I give myself. Such knots as binds me by the laws of honour seem tighter to me and heavier than the knots of civil constraint. A lawyer ties me in his knots more loosely than I do myself.[94]

Like in the case of gambling, and later in the case of pomp, morality crept in as the process of becoming more bourgeois began; an echo of this can be heard in *Timon* with the lords having to learn how to count and miscount time. In this sense, the play acts as an identity reference, demonstrating nostalgia for a bygone era rather than a description of the present. Numerous contemporary texts echo this intrusion of the merchant

---

[93] Davis, *Essai sur le don*, pp. 136–7 and chap. 6. On Florence of the modern period, see Waquet, *De la corruption*, pp. 130, 141, 157, 230.

[94] "Je ne trouve rien si cher que ce qui m'est donné et ce pourquoi ma volonté demeure hypothéquée par tiltre de gratitude, et reçois plus volontiers les offices qui sont à vendre. Je croy bien: pour ceux-cy je ne donne que de l'argent; pour les autres je me donne moy-mesme. Le nœud qui me tient par la loy d'honnesteté me semble bien plus pressant et plus poisant que n'est celuy de la contrainte civile. On me garote plus doucement par un notaire que par moy." Montaigne, "Essais," *Œuvres complètes*, Paris, Gallimard, III, 9, 1962, pp. 943–5.

ethos in the aristocratic economy. Many letters from aristocrats warned their children, as Lord Burghley (1520–1598) writing to his son:

Beware when standing surety for your best friends; whoever repays the debts of another seeks his own ruin … Never borrow money from a neighbour or a friend, but only from a stranger, because once he's been repaid, you will never hear from him again, otherwise you will extinguish your credit, lose your freedom and yet pay him as much as others. But if you do borrow money, take great care with your word, because he who makes a point of honouring due dates is the lord of another's purse.[95]

A few years later, Sir Walter Raleigh (ca. 1552–1618), warns his son and posterity:

Amongst all other things of the world, take care of thy estate, which thou shall ever preserve, if thou observe three things; first, that thou know what thou hast; what everything is worth that thou hast; and to see that thou art no wasted by thy servants and officers. The second is, that thou never spend any thing before thou have it; for borrowing is the canker and death of every man's estate. The third is, that thou suffer not thyself to be wounded for other men's faults, and scourge for other men's offences; which is, the surety for another; for thereby millions of men have been beggared and destroyed, paying the reckoning of other men's riot, and the charge of other men's folly and prodigality; if thou smart, smart for thine own sins, and above all things, be not made an ass to carry the burdens of other men. If any friend desire thee to be his surety, give him a part of what thou hast to spare; if he press thee farther he is not thy friend at all, for friendship rather chooseth harm to itself, than offereth it. If thou be bound for a stranger, thou art a fool; if for a merchant thou puttest thy estate to learn to swim; if for a church-man, he hath no inheritance; if for a lawyer, he will find an evasion by a syllable or word, to abuse thee; if for a poor man thou must pay it thyself; if for a rich man he needs not: therefore from suretyship, as from a manslayer or enchanter, bless thyself …[96]

Only the pastors continued to make the contrast, such as the pastor Henry Wilkinson who, in a pamphlet of 1625 titled "The Debt Book," contrasted "the civil debt of money or goods" with "the sacred debt of love." In it, the pastor declared that "the bond of love is eternal among Christians" and that not asking the insolvent to pay back their debts and lending to one's neighbours in need must endure. But at the same time, he explained that being indebted was no longer a bond of dependence but a position of insecurity and that a family could allow itself to

[95] Quoted by Nelson Benjamin, *The Idea of Usury*, Chicago, University of Chicago Press, 1969, appendix, p. 147.
[96] "Instructions to His Son and to Posterity," *Works of Sir Walter Raleigh*, vol. 2, p. 351–2, cited by Benjamin, *The Idea of Usury*, pp. 147–8.

become indebted in order to fulfil its duties of hospitality only if it did not have the means to do so.[97] In France as well, merchant values penetrated the aristocracy progressively, and in 1712, Saint-Simon wrote, "The Duke de Richelieu, who had had the Duke de Fronsac, his son, put in the Bastille some time ago, paid his debts and got him out of prison, believing him to be properly punished."[98]

As in *Timon*, the language of trade progressively invaded all spheres of thought and activity; even the imaginary of spiritual literature was not spared. Michel de Certeau notes that the symbols and comparisons of this literature gradually dropped the natural elements, which had such resonance in the sixteenth century, then those of civil and technical life which appeared in the last quarter of the seventeenth century, to speak thereafter purely of trade and goods.[99]

[97] Craig Muldrew, *The Economy of Obligation: The Culture of Credit and Social Relations in Early Modern England*, Basingstoke, Macmillan, 1998, p. 241.

[98] Saint-Simon, *Mémoires*, vol. 4, p. 500.

[99] Michel de Certeau, *L'écriture de l'histoire*, Paris, Gallimard, 1975, p. 188.

9

Political Economy and Exchange Practices

DORANTE: I have a number of people who would gladly lend it to me; but since you are my best friend, I believed I might do you wrong if I asked someone else for it.

MONSIEUR JOURDAIN: It's too great an honour, sir, that you do me. I'll go get it for you.

MADAME JOURDAIN: *(Aside)* What! You're going to give it to him again?

MONSIEUR JOURDAIN: What can I do? Do you want me to refuse a man of this station, who spoke about me this morning in the King's bedchamber?

Gold give us, God forgive us,
And from all woes relieve us;
That we the treasure
May reap of pleasure,
And shun whate'er is grievous,
Gold give us, God forgive us.
End of the inscription set upon the great gate of Theleme
– Francois Rabelais, *Gargantua*, chap. 54

How did the two cultures – aristocratic and merchant- translate in practice? How did the various social groups go about the business of buying and selling? How did such transactions, from which no one could escape, play out in social relationships? In order to see if buying in its diverse forms reflected the various types of political economies and social strata, bargaining, which was the dominant mode of the market in the modern era, constitutes a good entry point as it enables us to see how various social groups used it and how credit and state action changed its nature and practice. Did the status of the nobility get translated in this market relationship? Furthermore, what does the keen interest that developed for collections in the seventeenth century tell us? The study of the circulation of art and collector's objects is another way to show how social status was reflected in trade and how aristocrats used the passion for curios to enter the market openly.

Uncertainty and the Economy of the Bazaar

The markets of modern Europe have often been described, and rightly so, as the economy of the bazaar because bargaining was the standard practice for exchange. Bargaining was the result of the fact that uncertainty weighed upon every aspect of the transaction: uncertainty about the quality of the products, nonstandardization of weights and measures, uncertainty about the value of currencies owing to the diversity of those in circulation and the practices of aging them and of cutting down, which raised doubts about their weight in precious metals. As uncertainty reigned at every level, the dominant form of the economy was the economy of the bazaar, characterized by price fixing after bargaining. In fact, it was a world of approximation where everything rested on the examination of what one had decided to negotiate over, by guesswork, drawing on a complex array of factors: knowledge of market price levels, the reputation of the seller, and, in particular, personal competences.

At the markets, bargaining was the usual mode of exchange: on each occasion, it implied a bilateral relationship between the seller and the buyer that was unique for each purchase. At each transaction, it took the form of an evaluation of the just price according to its general scarcity, and taking into account the quality and the specifications of each item. In the context of the technologies of the time, characterized by the absence of standardization, by very little information and very ineffective methods of control, bargaining fitted into a system that aimed to contain it within the strictest of limits. The objective was to make cheating as difficult as possible and to tightly restrict it.

For that, the organization of the places of sale, whether in the market or the town, was based on the criterion of specialization, so that one could rapidly go from one stall to another in order to compare products. The grouping together of products of the same type enabled access to the first prerequisite for bargaining: knowledge of the day's price range.[1]

---

[1] "The dispersal of prices is evident – and in fact a measure of the ignorance of the market." Quotation from Rothschild, as cited by C. Geertz, *Le Souk de Sefrou: sur l'économie du bazar*, Paris, Bouchène, 2003, pp. 123–264.

For the purpose of rapidly making this first evaluation, the arrangement of stores according to specialization was crucial: the investigation was thus conducted quickly. Equally important, this positioning also ensured that the whole profession could exercise an initial form of control over the conduct of individual members: all the information circulated very quickly, each could gauge the quality of the others' products: such a spatial grouping of rival interests was in itself a structure for exercising moral control, which allowed for a standardization of prices. In the same way, the very great fragmentation of market specializations served to demonstrate that each merchant was someone who knew what he was selling since he was very specialized. It was a mark of competence and, as such, a structure equally appropriate for reducing uncertainty: one could suppose that the merchant knew the quality of what he or she was selling.

A second layer in this structural context of community surveillance and specialization relates to the reputation of the merchant. A good reputation served to greatly reduce the margins of uncertainty regarding the way he or she was likely to use his knowledge about standards, measures, and currencies. Reputation was one of the most precious attributes that the merchant had to defend and maintain.

These two particular aspects of how the places of sale were organized laid the ground for the transaction undertaken between a seller and a buyer. This transaction took time. It required time for the buyer to assess the quality and the quantity of what he coveted and to relate them to the average market price. He needed to convince himself that the seller had not altered the quality or modified the quantity of the product. The words exchanged served to convey this information and, at the same time, to allow the buyer to examine the product and to check its qualities. Each transaction was an opportunity to use the practical knowledge that each possessed and had developed by virtue of going to the market regularly. It was also an opportunity to develop a personal relationship with the merchant, in the hope that he would want you as a valued client. This time had a price. The time spent on a transaction and on the socialization that went with it depended on the good and the players involved in the transaction. This time spent, in itinerant sales, in selling, and in building the trading relationship by means of regular visits that sustained trust, punctuating the visit with very modest purchases, or collecting a few sous on preagreed credit became a luxury when the industry allowed standardization. Fixed prices and the anonymity that followed from them, and that foreshadowed the existence of large stores, disqualified the peddler and undermined his profitability. In order to adapt to new products that enabled new trading relations, the peddler would have to overturn his own and revalue his time. The trade would thus cease to be profitable.

As Geertz has shown, the pursuit of information was really at the heart of the economy of the bazaar: "The search for information – laborious, uncertain, complex and irregular – is the central experience of the life of the bazaar, an enveloping reality."[2] But this information was sought not just before the transaction or in the verbal exchange, since this economy also rested upon the practical knowledge acquired progressively by each individual: the good purchaser was not just a well-informed man, he was a man who possessed a great technical culture in terms of the goods he was researching. The insistence on information in the analysis of Geertz, and in those people who have adopted his analyses regarding the economy of the bazaar,[3] is indeed central, but the quest for information was coupled with an individual technical culture, which does not appear in these analyses, so the information was acquired not just by means of informants: it arose from competences that were learnt in practice and absorbed by individuals in the course of experience. The study of after death inventories show that notaries were well versed in such a culture: all of them knew how to read multiple qualities and nuances of colours.[4]

Although bargaining actors tried to assess the parameters of quality and measurement, and, in the absence of such data, being fixed in advance, a good buyer was one who had mastered the art of determining the value of a good. Each one tried to master this market culture and negotiate his or her knowledge in the market encounter to fix the price. These fundamental uncertainties were reflected again on other notions and stakes of economic relations such as, in the first place, trickery. In a nonstandardized economy, the margin of negotiation was much wider

[2] Geertz, *Le Souk de Sefrou* p. 60.
[3] Valentin Groebner, "Towards an Economic History of Customary Practice: Bread, Money, and the Economy of the Bazaar. Observations on Consumption and Cheating in the Late Medieval Foodstuffs Market," *German History*, 12, no. 2, 1994, pp. 119–36.
[4] See, for instance, for France, Nicole Pellegrin, "Ruralité et modernité du textile en Haut-Poitou au XVIIIe siècle. La leçon des inventaires après décès," *112ᵉ Congrès national des Sociétés savantes*, 1987, pp. 381–4; and for Spain, Belén Moreno Claveria, "Familias y bienes en los siglos XVII y XVIII. Una sociedad en transformación a partir de los inventarios post-mortem," PHD thesis, European University Institute, October 2002.

and, at the same time, notions of trickery were more fluid and vague, as were the definitions of quality and of specification.

In order to function, such an economy was also dependent on informer-intermediaries who had a key role to play. Once again, it was women and brokers in large numbers who acted as informers. They would circulate information, sometimes good sometimes bad, for the opacity of the economy and lack of information increased instances of small and large scale fraud. The Bastille archives reveal several individuals who benefitted from this lack of information to usurp identities and status in order to win the trust of their dupes.

Credit

One element – credit – the complex role of which has never really been emphasized, although it is present in almost all transactions, distorts the apparent freedom that the profusion of merchants and circuits would seem to indicate and reduces the importance of the quest for information, because clients were bound to suppliers who offered them credit. We have seen in the preceding chapters the ambiguity associated with credit because it is both an economic instrument and a relational modality. To this extent, it is a good example of the contamination of both these economies, for closing an account was tantamount to the breaking of a relationship, and this practice was prevalent at all levels of trade, in the large establishments as well as among modest peddlers and shopkeepers. Here, the culture of the gift seeps into market culture. The peddler buys and sells on credit, and the few account books of peddlers available to us show that accounts were never closed and that credit and repayment were inextricably linked to each other. To gain the right to enter a house, small merchants never asked to be paid in cash. In this way, they developed personal relationships and were assured of their clientele whom they could visit every time they came by and receive some payment for prior purchases. When the peddler and the buyer decided to go over their accounts together, even if the peddler wrote the account had been settled in his register, he would add in the margin an outstanding amount; it could be very modest, but it was always there. The fact that these small debts were constantly carried over tells us how important it was never to fully clear an account. Such symbolic debts testify to the fact that this happened not for economic but cultural reasons. The market relationship was part of the sociability of trust and an always open account. Closing an account implied the end of a commercial and human relationship. The outstanding sums were also a guarantee for the small trader of maintaining his clientele in the next season.[5]

The analysis of the account books of shopkeepers all reveal the same phenomenon, whether they were those of Florence at the end of the Renaissance,[6] or of the small Lisbon shopkeepers at the end of the eighteenth century,[7] or the Catalan shops of the seventeenth and eighteenth centuries.[8] This process may also be found among the craftspeople, who practiced the same system of credit in relation to their clientele. In general, not insisting on payment in cash was a social obligation that, because it was a vehicle for honour and trust, was built on the personal relationship. The same debt mechanism was also found in paying employees and servants their wages; it was no different from the way goods were paid for.[9] The goods economy was thus embedded in a relational economy, and this relational economy, embodied by credit, disturbed the interplay of the bazaar and the apparent freedom that prevailed.[10]

The authorities have sought throughout the early modern age to reduce the margins of uncertainty in relation to the market through institutions that they have created and through normative production, they have enabled the development of new practices of exchange.[11] They have tried to impose quality through the institutionalization of the trade and they set out to reduce uncertainty regarding weights and measures, which could vary considerably within the same locality. The consuls for each

---

[5] Laurence Fontaine, *Le Voyage et la mémoire, colporteurs de l'Oisans au XIXe siècle*, Lyon, Presses Universitaires de Lyon, 1984, pp. 113–40. Pierre Martin-Charpenel, "Les colporteurs de l'Ubaye en basse Provence," *Annales de Haute Provence*, no. 291, 1981, pp. 3–57. Bernard Amouretti, "La tournée d'un colporteur dans les monts du Beaujolais sous le Second Empire, 1864–1868," *Cahiers d'Histoire*, 32, no. 3–4, 1987, pp. 350–2.

[6] Paul F. Gehl, "Credit sales Strategies in the Late Cinquecento Book Trade," *Libri, Tipografi, Biblioteche Ricerche storiche dedicate a Luigi Balsamo*, Florence, Leo S. Olschki, ed., 1997, pp. 193–206.

[7] Maria Manuela Rochas, "Crédito privato num contexto urbano. Lisboa, 1770–1830," PhD thesis, European University Institute, Florence, 1996.

[8] Lidia Torra Fernández, "Las botigues de teles de Barcelona: aportación al estudio de la offerta de tejidos y del crédito al consumo (1650–1800)," *Revista de Historia Económica*, 21, no. extraordinario, 2003, pp. 89–105 (98–102). It could follow the credit of the same families over several generations.

[9] See the examples for Lisbon in Rochas, "Crédito private."

[10] The same relationship to credit was already present in the Roman republic, as illustrated in Cicero's correspondence. See Marina Ioannatou, "Le code de l'honneur des paiements. Créanciers et débiteurs à la fin de la République romaine," *Annales HSS*, no. 6, November–December 2001, pp. 1201–21.

[11] Max Weber, *Economie et Société, tome I, les catégories de la sociologie*, Paris, Plon, 1995 [1922].

place were required to ensure the conformity of measuring instruments and that market regulations were respected. In seventeenth-century Lyon, they aimed to regulate exchange by prohibiting the purchase of defective weights and measures and by making the use of municipal weights obligatory; for the most sensitive professions such as millers, the rules were even stricter and forbade millers to keep weights, balances, or metal hooks at their dwellings; they were even required to "stand three or four steps away from the said weights" during the weighing. But at the beginning of the eighteenth century, the policing judges were aware that several dealers in "old furniture" also sold weights, balances, metal hooks, and scales that were often very defective. The authorities also sought to standardize the quality of products by increasing regulations and market controls.[12] When the two essential components to establish the price, quality, and measurement were assured, then bargaining was no longer necessary.

Sometimes a vicious circle occurred, the elements of which need to be understood, which led to general distrust such that each one expected the other to behave in an excessive manner to such an extent that each purchase began to resemble a psychological duel around a price range unrelated to the real value of items. During the eighteenth century in Paris, Louis Sebastian Mercier denounced this systematic game of overvaluation and undervaluation by seller and buyer on which the practice of bargaining was based:

Every petty merchant overprices his wares by about double: it's a scandalous thing! How does it happen? The buyer makes a bad offer. The smallest trifle is subject to a long discussion. If the merchant would offer his goods at half their value, he would nevertheless receive an even lower offer, since small traders have a reputation for overpricing beyond measure. How, in this debate, is a fair price reached? He who bargains is always afraid of being taken at his word; he plays for time, and often he escapes without having made the slightest offer.

Shouldn't merchants be obliged to abide by an inviolable law whereby they place a fixed price upon their wares? Once the tariff is set, trust would accordingly be re-established.[13]

If you pass by a small shop, you will hear the words *upon my conscience, upon my honour* between buyer and seller; you will ear them for the selling of a cane or of a cord of a watch; the gestures reply to the words, and they break their

---

[12] Anne Montenach, "Une économie de l'infime. Espaces et pratiques du commerce alimentaire à Lyon au XVIIe siècle," PhD thesis, European University Institute, October 2003, chap. 8.

[13] Louis Sébastien Mercier, "Surfaire" (Overpricing), *Tableau de Paris*, Jean-Claude Bonnet, ed., Paris, Mercure de France, vol. 1, 1994, pp. 1169–70.

word for a few coins. This is the negotiation of an infinite number of wretched quibblers who usurp the name of trader and even merchant.

The shop boys are called *runners* (*courtauts*) because the proprietor suddenly sends them after a buyer who, having offered a price, has gone away. The shop-keeper waits to see if he'll return; and when he doesn't turn straight on his heels he says to the boy: *Run (Cours-tôt) after him quickly.*

Such aberrations notwithstanding, the economy of the bazaar remained the best commercial organization to ensure that supply and demand coincided in a market economy characterized by numerous uncertainties. For instance, once again, in the nineteenth century, no label indicated the characteristics of the clothes, and buyers had to assess for themselves the quality and state of the clothes for which they were bargaining.[14]

Gift and Moral Economy

Bargaining implies a similarity of status: an implied equality between buyers and vendors in the interaction underlies the deal. However, the other feature of the economy, besides its uncertainty, was that society was very hierarchical, governed by inequality between its different levels. As in most countries, a nobleman could not trade; neither could he allow himself to bargain, so he would send his stewards or servants. Nonetheless, in spite of this use of substitutes, the status of aristocrat had to remain above board and his high moral code be seen in all areas of life, including in economic relationships. As we have seen, the gift economy that embodies both being and chance is the most appropriate mode to display nobiliary values. Even in those countries where the application of the rule forbidding nobility to trade was strictest, for example, as in Spain, the aristocrats, through their employees and "stand-ins" managed to see their wealth grow.[15] During the seventeenth and eighteenth centuries, the nobility succeeded in entering the market relationship openly by appropriating and diverting one of the most widespread forms of exchange in modern Europe – auctioning.

[14] Manuel Charpy, "The Scope and Structure of Nineteenth-Century Second-Hand Trade in the Parisian Clothes Market," *Alternative Exchanges: Second-Hand Circulations from the Sixteenth Century to the Present*, Laurence Fontaine, ed., Oxford, Berghahn, 2008, chap. 7.

[15] I. A. A. Thompson, "The Nobility in Spain, 1600–1800," *The European Nobilities in the Seventeenth and Eighteenth Centuries*, H. M. Scott, ed., London, Longman, 1995, pp. 174–236 (229–32).

But it was in the forms and rituals that surrounded the act that the nature of the gift in comparison to other forms of exchange was revealed. Even if people were aware of the fact that the gift was still a form of exchange, the economy governing the circulation on these "gifts" had to do not only with the value of the offered goods but also with the ranking of the people involved in the exchange. There was no strict balance between the value of the gifts offered and service received. One did not count either when offering or when receiving; depending on the status of each party, the exchange of gifts was also different. The social hierarchy which was at play in these exchanges, which were as much cultural as economic, could be interpreted and legitimized by the way in which the "gift" is presented. The obligation to give in return was not the same for everyone; it was the result of negotiation each time depending on the social ranking of each party and on the events which were the reason for the gift, some of these being more predictable than others. Because objects retained something of the people who possessed them, the same object gained therefore more or less value depending on who gave it. Money, which is intrinsically anonymous, was therefore not a natural tool of the aristocratic economy and this fact explained – apart from other considerations like the lack of cash – the great propensity of the nobles to pay with objects for services that could easily have been paid for with money.

Therefore, the line between the circulation of objects and the different forms of exchange in the marketplace is problematic because objects circulated as freely as paper money. The border between gift and market was far from watertight, with the two categories constantly overlapping each other in modern Europe. Secondhand objects were used as an alternative currency to feed multiple markets. Everywhere, monetary practices, which led people to hoard their money rather than to let it circulate, as well as the lack of cash, had allowed an economy based on the circulation of goods to develop.[16] In urban exchanges, bartering was still largely prevalent not only among traders, as we saw in Chapter 4, but also among peasants because there were many who paid peddlers with their harvest or the produce of their home based industry. Such practices led small merchants to make some members of their family specialize in trades that would enable them to make good use of payments made to them in kind, especially in cereals and in wine. Thus, in the Rhine

---

[16] See *Charpy, Alternative exchanges.*

plateau, Jews were active in the trade of cereals and wine,[17] and from the eighteenth century onwards, some merchant families from Auvergne who travelled through Castile specialized as milliners and bakers.[18]

Authoritarian Pricing

Among unequals, the price was fixed. The authority of the aristocrats, and especially that of the grandees, which was grounded on inequality of social status and on the asymmetry of relationships was translated in the market place to a culture of "his lordships pleasure and good will." This behaviour could be traced back to times when lords were masters of the wealth and of the men on their estates. Therefore, a merchant could not determine what the value of his or her goods should be, nor could he decide the terms of a contract between two parties because a contract implies equality of status, which meant that the nobleman would limit his liberty and authority by doing business with a merchant. This acknowledgment of the nobleman's ability to fix prices is well demonstrated in the play *Timon of Athens* when, in Scene 1 of Act 1, the jeweller who wants to sell a jewel to Timon declares that it is the task of the lord to determine its price, and he adds that the value of an object is in proportion to the status of the person who possesses it: "My Lord, 'tis rated/ As those which sell would give; but you well know / Things of like value differing in the owners / Are prized by their masters. Believe't, dear lord, / You mend the jewel by the wearing it."[19]

The jeweller was not wrong because in the following scene, Timon asked another lord to ennoble, by accepting it, the jewel he would like to offer him: "O my friends, I have one word to say to you. / Look you, my good lord, / I must entreat you honour me so much / As to advance this jewel. Accept and wear it, / Kind my Lord."[20]

When Shylock describes his hatred for Antonio, he says he hates Antonio because he is Christian, scorns Jews, lends his money free of

---

[17] Hans-Jorg Gilomen, "L'endettement paysan et la question du crédit dans les pays d'Empire au Moyen Age," *Endettement Paysan et Crédit Rural dans l'Europe médiévale et moderne*, Actes des XVIIes Journées Internationales d'Histoire de l'Abbaye de Flaran, September 1995, M. Berthe, ed., Toulouse, Presses Universitaires du Mirail, 1998, pp. 99–138.

[18] Rose Duroux, *Les Auvergnats de Castille. Renaissance et mort d'une migration au XIXe siècle*, Publications of the Faculty of Letters of the Université Blaise Pascal, Clermont-Ferrand, Publications de la faculté des lettres de l'université Blaise-Pascal, 1992.

[19] Shakespeare, *Timon of Athens*, I, 1, 172–6.

[20] Ibid., I, 2, 156–60.

interest, and heaps ridicule on him publicly for his bargains and the interest he charges on loans.

The nobleman assigns a value to things and grants accordingly a gratification. Tipping today has come down to us from such aristocratic practices: a tip really is neither a gift, nor a wage, nor an act of charity and is always a source of discomfort for the giver and the receiver as it continues to convey the idea of distance and social inequality; it is a mark of the whim of the one offers it.[21] Along with such gratifications, the aristocrat sets him- or herself apart by imposing delays of payments and by determining prices of goods and work. By the end of the eighteenth century, a system had been more or less worked out. Merchants and artisans included in their selling price interest due for late payments, and the stewards of the aristocratic houses, as treasurers for their royal masters, arbitrarily deducted about 10 per cent of the requested amount. This attitude was so common than when an accountant (steward) did not apply this reduction, he had to justify his decision.[22]

Purchases by nobles were also made upon credit. But credit did not take the same form for them. The noble settled as and when he wished, except for gambling debts. Mercier reflects this:

Only at Paris does one see these intrepid *suppliers*, who advance bread, meat, wine, furniture, groceries, medicinal compounds, to a marquis, a count, or a duke. It is the privilege of nobility. One would not lend in the same way to a bourgeois, one would press him; but one waits patiently, because he is a man with a title.

Such-and-such a noble house owes the butcher for six years' provisions, the grocer five, the baker four; even the servants accept credit in lieu of wages, whereas every commoner's household settles its debts at the end of each year.

When the suppliers, tired of waiting, finally ask for their payment, the steward comes as the Duke is rising, and says to him, My Lord, your butler complains that the butcher no longer wants to supply meat, as it is three years since he received a sou; your coach driver says that you have only one carriage in a fit state for use, and that the wheelwright no longer wants to have the honour of your custom, if you do not give him a payment of ten thousand francs; the wine merchant refuses to fill your cellar, the tailor to give you clothes ... The scoundrels! exclaims the master, let's go elsewhere. *I withdraw my protection from them.*

He finds other suppliers, even though the first have not been paid.[23]

---

[21] Viviana A. Zelizer, *The Social Meaning of Money*, Princeton, NJ, Princeton University Press, 1997, pp. 94–9. To remove the marker of social inequality, today, tipping is more often than not fixed as a percentage of the amount to be paid.

[22] Jean-Dominique Augarde, "Noël Gérard (1685–1736) et le Magasin Général à l'Hôtel Jabach," *Luxury Trades and Consumerism in Ancien Régime Paris. Studies in the History of the Skilled Workforce*, Robert Fox and Antony Turner, eds., Aldershot, Ashgate, 1998, pp. 169–88 (177).

[23] Mercier, "Fournisseurs" (Suppliers), *Tableau de Paris*, vol. 1, p. 921–2.

In fact, time was again central to the differences in behaviour between the classes. A very long time always elapsed before the memorandum describing the supplies, and work done was produced because the supplier or the artisan only presented his or her bill once he or she had finished or delivered almost everything that had been ordered. It was normal for four to five years to pass between the initial contact and the completion of the work. To wait was essential, it was part of deference due to people of rank, as a wine merchant explained to the duke of Fritz-James in the 1780s. Once the memorandum was written, there would be another period of waiting because the aristocrat would draw out the time before accepting it: his administrators would then cut the prices by 10 to 20 per cent. Once the memorandum was eventually signed, payment would then also be delayed because a nobleman was used to paying his debts a little at a time, so full payment would take several years. Weary and under pressure themselves by the passage of time, the suppliers would then start legal proceedings. In order to use time once more to his or her advantage, the aristocrat would finally appeal to the king who could stop the legal proceedings for one or more years by issuing a *committimus* or an arrest in state council.[24] Eventually, the respect shown to the social hierarchies and to the culture of nobility by the merchants in business relationships came against them in the eighteenth century; on one hand, they were reproached for supporting the vices of the aristocracy by allowing them to become so indebted and, on the other hand, for not asking enough security in the financing of the goods they had provided.

In every walk of life where money was involved, to preserve his honour, a nobleman could not stoop to bargaining be it for important as well as for minor things: Samuel Pepys recounts that everyone save aristocrats and the honourable would bargain over the price of their meal in the tavern,[25] and Mme de Cadillac, in a letter to Mme de Riquet, recalled it. Speaking of the temptation of certain aristocrats who, to move up the social ladder, tried to marry their daughters into more noble families and who, to attract better lineage, imprudently proposed large dowries for their daughters at a first meeting, she explains that those families, once the betrothal had taken place, would very much like to reduce the amount they had imprudently offered for

---

[24] Natacha Coquery, *L'Hôtel aristocratique. Le marché du luxe à Paris au XVIIIe siècle*, Paris, Publications de la Sorbonne, pp. 162–74.

[25] Samuel Pepys, *The Diary*, vol. 4, new and complete transcription, London, Bell, 1970–83, p. 131.

the dowries but, as she wrote, "once a first proposal is offered, it is not honourable to bargain."[26]

For culturally prized objects, auctioning was a means used by aristocrats to enter the market without revealing their identity. To grasp its specificity, it has to be viewed in the circulations of cultural objects in their entirety. The diverse forms of exchange relate to the values embodied in the contract's terms and conditions and illustrate the dynamics at work and the degree to which the various economies overlapped each other.

Circulation of Collectors' Items as Indicators of the Relationship with the Economy

Art is the love for beauty, and this attribute became a political issue in ancient Europe. As in the so-called primitive economies in which in any exchange the attributes of the giver were transmitted along with the object given, so too in the circulation of works of art, the quality and the beauty of the work were reflected on the owner. This alchemy conveyed the qualities of the work to the owner who had, it seems, placed art at the heart of the enactment of power. In aristocratic societies and even more so in the society of the court of ancient Europe, this consumption of art was indeed about pomp and show and the desire to dazzle, implying spending patterns that allowed neither imitation nor appropriation by other social groups. Social distance had to be evident both in appearance and in behaviour. Thus, only some people could own certain things, wear certain materials, and be obliged to constantly reactivate their status in a visible manner: wear distinctive clothing and exhibit for all to behold at ceremonies the objects they had acquired, an assertion of their brilliant and undeniable superiority. For in this elaborate show, power, in the way it was projected and projected itself, was always involved in the embellishment of things and the excesses of wealth acquired and exhibited.[27] But these presentations and ostentatious displays were always dialogues, and those who beheld them, without ever being able to own them, were an indispensible element of such power play. Accordingly, court societies had huge budgets for expenditure on festivities and art. An analysis of

---

[26] A. D. of la haute Garonne, 4-J, Mme De Cadillac to Mme de Riquet, 31 August 1746, quoted by Robert Forster, *The Nobility of Toulouse in the Eighteenth Century: A Social and Economic Study*, New York, Octagon Books, 1971, p. 131.

[27] Philippe Perrot, *Le Luxe. Une richesse entre faste et confort XVIIIe–XIXe siècle*, Paris, Seuil, 1995, p. 19.

the price of certain objects and the behaviour of princes to acquire them, I am referring here, for example, to the competition between Julius II and François I, or the manner in which Italian city-states used the arts in their political rivalries, reveals a cultural continuity in these practices that linked the competition in spending to the dignity of those who indulged in it. The various components of these self-presentations follow a genealogy that goes back to ancient Rome.[28] In the middle of the sixteenth century, the expenditure of the court of Ferrare on the maintenance and construction of buildings alone amounted to nearly 10 per cent of the budget,[29] to say nothing about the expenditure of monarchs such as Philippe II or Louis XIV.[30]

In turn, the aristocratic elite were caught in a spiral of unending consumption, for expenditure was in accordance with rank; one's being was measured by one's appearance, because appearance made visible the systems of social ranking. Residence, dress, way of life, and consumption were all markers of rank.[31] Finally, the will to curb consumption through sumptuary laws, just like the refusal to consume and the destruction of objects, was an integral part of this power play and political language in that the laws attested to the emergence of new regimes of meaning and values and the will to stabilize or reorganize politics. They also made visible other relationships with images that were not just aesthetic or artistic but that veered between adoration and destruction.[32]

The world of collector items, the first of which was formed in the European Courts, and which developed, during the seventeenth century, alongside the *salons*, gave rise to another economy of taste and an evolving notion of how one presented oneself. This emphasized moral

---

[28] Krzystof Pomian, *Collectionneurs, amateurs et curieux. Paris, Venise XVIe–XVIIIe siècle*, Paris, Gallimard, 1996, pp. 24–6.

[29] Guido Guerzoni, "*The Italian Renaissance Courts' Demand for the Arts: The Case of d'Este of Ferrara (1471–1560)*," *Art Markets in Europe, 1400–1800*, M. North and D. Omrod, ed., Aldershot, Ashgate, 1998, pp. 61–80.

[30] Norbert Elias, *La Société de Cour*, Paris, Calmann-Lévy,1969, chap. 2. John H. Elliott, "Royal Patronage and Collecting in Seventeenth-Century Spain," *Economia e arte secc. XIII-XVIII*, Atti della "Trentatreesima Settimana di Studi," Simonetta Cavaciocchi, ed., Florence, Le Monnier, 2002, pp. 551–65; Susanne Kubersky-Piredda, Spesa della materia und spesa dell'arte. Die preise von Altarfeln in der Florentiner Renaissance, dans *Economia e arte secc. XIII-XVIII*, pp. 339–54.

[31] Philippe Perrot, *Le Luxe*; Daniel Roche, *La culture des apparences: Une histoire du vêtement, XVIIe-XVIIIe siècle*, Paris, Fayard, 1989.

[32] *Border Fetichisms: Material Objects in Unstable Spaces*, P. Spyer, ed., London, Routledge, 1998; Olivier Christin, *Une révolution symbolique: l'iconoclasme huguenot et la reconstruction catholique*, Paris, Editions de Minuit, 1991.

qualities and showed a familiarity with the new worlds of excellence, those developed by travels and science, of which knowledge was essential. First, a library and then curios and scientific instruments became the necessary attributes of a man of taste.[33] As a result of these changes the traditional lack of culture of the aristocracy was replaced by an "ostentatious consumption" of time and wealth devoted to cultural objects. The time when the "social graces" obliged men to "show off their ignorance as a matter of honour," their consecrated right because of their social status[34] was over and the fad for curios begun. As a result of this new interest in collecting, nobility entered the business world and made the old practices of selling at auction its own.

In fact, from the Middle Ages to the modern era, works of art entered into four different forms of economies, which were variations of a fundamental opposition between the aristocratic economy and the market economy. Entering into the various circulations of these collector items represents faithfully, in the manner in which they mask or transform relations with the market, the diversity of relationships with the economy. One may thus isolate an aristocratic economy, with its extension in the court economy, and a market economy and observe hybrid forms such as the economy of institutions – with the church at the forefront – and a collectors' economy; the economy of institutions formed, at times, part of the aristocratic economy, even the court economy, and at others the market economy, giving it a specific colour. As for the collectors' economy, which grew in the modern era, it drew from aristocratic values but fit perfectly into the market economy, changing its frameworks. Each of these economies had its own modality of dealing with the economy, visible in the acquisition, circulation, and production of works.

Evidently, more often than not, the various economies coexisted in time and space, and although they could have different historical frameworks, they also overlapped. Finally, they were interactive through a complex series of exchanges and evolutions, which also fell within the province of technological transformations. However, by bringing out the peculiarity of each one and paying attention to it, we can refine their

[33] Pomian, *Collectionneurs*, p. 52; John Brewer, *The Pleasures of the Imagination: English Culture in the Eighteenth Century*, London, Harper Collins, 1997.
[34] Maurice Magendie, *La politesse mondaine et les théories de l'honnêteté en France au XVIIᵉ, de 1600 à 1660*, 1925, Geneva, Slatkine, 1970 [1925], p. 52; J.-P. Denz, *L'honnête homme et la critique du goût. Esthétique et société au XVIIe siècle*, Lexington, French Forum Publishers, 1981; J. Revel, *Les usages de la civilité*, in *Dictionnaire des sciences historiques*, A. Burguiere, ed., Paris, Presses universitaires de France, 1996, pp. 194–208.

logic, understand the complexity of market forms, and get a close view of the changing economic dynamics in which works of art were caught up. To illustrate these different economies, I deal with the various modes of circulation of works of art.

Princely circulations partook of four different modes: gift, commission, plundering, and patrimonialization. The gift was the princely circulation par excellence. It was at the heart of the aristocratic culture, of princes towards their courtesans and courtesans towards princes, as also of the religious world. Here is an example: in 1717, the regent visited the gallery of Raymond de la Sagette, chief clerk in the Parliament of Paris, and asked to buy three or four major canvases for his gallery in the Palais-Royal. "Sir," replied M. de la Sagette, "I do not sell my paintings; I offer them to Your Royal Highness": a generosity that proved to be ruinous, because the paintings of the Bolognese and Flemish schools were worth more than 50,000 écus. Nevertheless, the regent, who was duty bound to return the present, gave in return to the clerk a superb snuffbox enriched with diamonds and accorded him the title of state councillor in the name of the king.[35] Molière made use of this new culture of the connoisseur and of the aristocratic values of the gift and of friendship to convert M. Jourdain's father into an aristocrat:

Covielle. He, a shopkeeper! It is pure slander, he never was. All he did was this: he used to be very obliging, very polite, and since he was a connoisseur in cloth, he used to go about choosing it everywhere, and had it brought to his house, and gave it to his friends, for money.[36]

Indeed, the gift was the only mode of circulation never to be contested, allowing, for example, Louis XIV to acquire Veronese's *The Feast in the House of Simon*, presented to him by the Most Serene Republic of Venice in 1664; an acquisition that was never challenged whereas when he bought, in 1685, from the Savelli princes two famous antique sculptures, Pope Innocent IX immediately promulgated the most draconian regulations to control the export of works of art.[37]

Patrimonialization was another aristocratic mode that aimed at protecting princes and prelates from the logic of the market economy.

---

[35] Edmond Bonnaffé, *Dictionnaire des amateurs français au XVIIe siècle*, Paris 1884, quoted by Nathalie Heinich, *Du peintre à l'artiste. Artisans et académiciens à l'âge classique*, Paris, Éditions de Minuit, 1999, p. 57.

[36] Molière, *The Middle Class Gentleman (Le Bourgeois gentilhomme)*, Curtis Hidden Page, trans., New York and London, G.P. Putnam and Sons, 1908, IV, 5.

[37] Francis Haskell, *Conservation et dispersion du patrimoine artistique italien*, in *L'amateur d'art*, Paris, Librairie générale française, 1997, pp. 102–3.

This was the weapon to keep goods that, had market logic prevailed, would have been lost. Francis Haskell has made an excellent study of its use by the papacy. In the time of Michelangelo, Julius II and François I gave battle, spending huge sums of money, to secure the fame of a few great artists. The sums staked, quite unheard of, were not indicative moreover of an art market capable of maintaining such high prices, but of the battle being waged by the two greatest lords on the planet. Here, we are closer to potlatch than the market. But in the eighteenth century, when Rome could no longer stand up to the monarchs, to try and stop this haemorrhage of its works of art, the city offered not money, but decrees of patrimonialization.[38] It acted in the same way as the aristocracy had acted earlier, patrimonialising its lands to shield them from the claims of creditors. The Rhenish nobility did likewise with works of art, categorizing them increasingly as "male" property that could not go out of the lineage.[39] Besides, another specific trait of the aristocratic economy came to be associated with the ethic of the gift, namely the habit of not repaying one's debts. This feature was so deeply rooted in the customs that some firms refused to deal with the courts, and in 1680, the Dutch firm Forchout adopted this approach with respect to the court of Austria.[40]

Commissioning, an upstream stage of the production process whereas purchasing was downstream, became necessary when the work required an investment in time or material that exceeded the capacity of the painter (such as large history paintings), when linked to a specific exhibition space (frescoes and large decorative compositions) or to the person for whom it was intended (portrait). This mode imposed the tastes of the person who commissioned the work on the subject, as well as the dimensions, the place, the time limit, and restricted the circulation of works, kept in a secluded place, outside the market. It was said that the commission system – prestigious but restrictive – acted as a brake on the autonomy of production, the painter's independence, the mobility of the works and the growth of the market.[41]

Of course, princes and kings would mix the various circulations and knew how to use them all. François I, for example, commissioned paintings,

---

[38] Clément XII (1730–1740) then Clément XIV (1769–1774) and Pius VI (1775–1799) understood that the solution lay in the setting up of public museums. Ibid., pp. 90–146 (111).

[39] Christophe Duhamelle, *L'héritage collectif. La noblesse d'Eglise rhénane, 17e–18e siècles*, Paris, Editions de l'Ecole des Hautes Etudes en Sciences Sociales, 1998.

[40] Jean-Michel Montias, *Le Marché de l'art aux Pays-Bas (XVᵉ-XVIIᵉ siècles)*, Paris, Flammarion, 1996, p. 162.

[41] Heinich, *Du peintre à l'artiste*, p. 73.

had paintings offered to him, and acquired some as well through the intermediary of merchants.[42] However, on closer examination, it emerges that each of these choices obeyed a different logic: relational logic and – perhaps one may add – the logic of distinction and shame. There were hierarchies within these circulations, and the shameful circulations were handled by intermediaries of little distinction and were very often kept secret. Accordingly, the purchase of the collection of the dukes of Mantua by Charles I of England took place at the end of complex and secret negotiations conducted in the main by a Dutch merchant Daniel Nys. The duke of Mantua was keen that these be held in absolute secrecy, that their magnitude be hidden and that his collection travel sufficiently far so that no rival could boast of having bought it.[43] The merchant intermediary was also favoured when a personal relationship was not possible for works of artists outside the court or those who had died.

Auctioning was one of the traditional market modes appropriated by the aristocratic economy. It was the most common method of dealing in early modern times because it allowed one to fix the price, given the uncertainty surrounding the value of the goods and services, and to have those prices validated by the community that had gathered for the event, which, in fact, took the form of a real ceremony. Everything could be auctioned: food as well as political position, the construction of a house as well as publics buildings. Secondhand goods ended up in auctions for one of three different reasons: when an inheritance was being settled, when a business had failed, or when objects were being got rid of which had been pawned but not recovered.[44] Auctions guaranteed the transparency of the markets born out of politics: thanks to the publicity attached to the event, everybody could take part in it. It is indeed the selling style most appropriate to the individualistic and egalitarian utopia of the market place.

Nevertheless, numerous examples showed that, in order to monopolize the markets, the refusal to advertise the event was common practice. In politics, given the material profits political life generated, elected representatives devised strategies to maintain secrecy in order to distort the principle of auctioning. Because all contracts for which there was a likely market were awarded after a public auction, it could be in one's interest to ensure that, on the appointed day, not too many people showed up.

---

[42] Haskell, *Conservation et dispersion*, p. 93.

[43] Ibid., pp. 96, 98.

[44] Antoine Schnapper, "Probate Inventories, Public Sales and the Parisian Art Market in the Seventeenth Century," *Art Markets in Europe 1400–1900*, pp. 131–41.

Complaints against such practices were common. Thus, at Mizoen, a village in the Upper Dauphine, on 1 January 1678, the consul decided to hold an assembly to lease two tax rolls (one for the debts of the community towards the poor, the other to pay for repairs carried out in the church). Only four inhabitants were present. Two of them were ready to collect taxes for a fee of one sol per livre in revenue (5 per cent). But the affair came to be known, and five days later, a new assembly was convened for the same purpose, but this time, twenty-nine people were present. The result was completely different since the community decided that instead of preparing a roll for the poor with the expense that it entailed, it would be enough to "cross" the share of "the most needy" (to act as if they had paid their share) and to auction the roll of the church. And the auction, which was obviously digressive, began at a lower rate (4 per cent). We can thus point out several matters when the consul was accused of deliberately not having convened all the inhabitants or of having given as an excuse the urgency of the situation to award a contract or a paid position to a member of his clan without convening everyone publicly.[45]

As for the world of trade, Louis Sébastien Mercier denounced in general terms the way in which the shopkeepers dominated the secondhand sales, doing everything in their power to prevent access to private individuals. According to Mercier, *Les petites affiches*, one of the first French newspapers to announce the auctions which took place after a death, "are only of service to upholsterers, jewellers, merchants in the fashion business, and the young men who trade in horses, pictures and diamonds,"[46] whereas by making the information about these sales easily accessible the paper should have been helping individuals to break into this type of business.

But, in the world of men of taste, auctions became the stage on which the aristocratic element of society could show itself off as a connoisseur of collectible items:

they allowed agonistic behaviours to be freely expressed during a face to face in which people could express their taste simultaneously and their ability to give up some of their wealth in order to possess and also to demonstrate their financial strength. The sale of collectibles at public auctions thus became a privileged activity where social ranking was visible and where the usefulness of an object was lost as that object took on a new meaning. It is no wonder therefore that the major

---

[45] Laurence Fontaine, *Pouvoir, identités et migrations dans les hautes vallées des Alpes occidentales (XVIIe–XVIIIe siècles)*, Grenoble, Presses Universitaires de Grenoble, 2003, chap. 8.

[46] Mercier, "Journal de Paris," *Tableau de Paris*, vol. 2, p. 312.

auctions where well known collectibles changed hands, as happened in Paris in the 18th century, became society events which were discussed in the newspapers and letters of the time. No wonder if the major sales in which renowned collections were dispersed, as they were held in Paris in 18th century, became society events, commented in the press and the correspondences of the time.[47]

Of course, the art merchants fought against those markets which were in competition with them and the arguments put forward by both parties help us to understand why, backed up by certain painters, this form of buying and selling had become popular among aristocrats. In July 1642, some Dutch painters fought against the banning of public auctions that the merchants, with the support of their guilds, were demanding. The painters explained that banning public auctions would do great damage to them because it would prevent the formation of a knowledgeable public that these events – public auctions – helped to create. "Public auctions," they wrote, "give birth to lots of connoisseurs who, stimulated by the affluence and by the sight of all those objects of beauty, buy a piece of art, which they would not otherwise have thought much about." When these connoisseurs are allowed to resell the artwork which they have previously bought they become involved in the art world and end up buying "beautiful pieces by great masters" thanks to money which they put aside for that very purpose.[48] At the same time, in these auction rooms, the public could learn about artwork by buying and selling the works of young artists and by studying the printed catalogues that educated and disseminated good taste.

Thus, public auctions wiped out the marketplace by acting like an arena where learned people and social society could show off. By hiding the business aspect of the event behind the notion of a place for social and cultural meetings, public auctions became a place where it was important to be seen and to be involved; this alchemy made this method of circulation of goods so attractive to the aristocratic classes and why the shopkeepers never stopped asking that it be regulated.[49]

Finally, an economy of repute came up, redefining merchant circulations. Traditionally, paintings were sold by the producer to the consumer. The painter exhibited in his store or in the traditional painting sales outlets. In Paris, master-painters and merchant-painters were found at the Saint Germain fair, the Notre Dame Bridge, the Gesvre quay, and Place

---

[47] Pomian, *Collectionneurs*, pp. 53–4.
[48] Cited by Montias, *Le marché de l'art aux Pays-Bas*, pp. 145–6.
[49] See the examples in ibid., pp. 142–5.

Dauphine. In Holland, the guilds and the brotherhoods organized exhibitions and occupied the various markets (*pandt*) reserved for the sale of paintings.[50]

With the arrival of artists as a category and their inclusion in the academies, these circulations were redefined; academies forbade direct sales considered ignoble and developed various systems to exhibit works of art. By detaching exhibitions from all immediate financial transactions, the system succeeded in distancing the market aspect of the trade and direct purchase from the producer gave way to indirect purchase through an intermediary.

Initially the sale of paintings was conducted by haberdashers and many merchants added paintings to their banking or merchandise trade; then came the specialized art merchants, half way between connoisseurs and merchants, such as le Gersaint. Without going into the different systems behind the process, we would like to emphasize that the economy of repute, which came into place in the modern period at different moments in time, tried to reappropriate the market link, locating it not in an anonymous place of exchange but in the workshop where connoisseurs went and directly sought works of art. Studies about the layout of the workshops tell us a great deal as they describe the various settings of painters who would usually hide, behind the collection, the market exchange they tried to recover.

Once more, such a typology should not conceal the fact that many painters succeeded in turning various economies to advantage, as underscored by numerous historians,[51] who point out that very often there is a dual system of production: for the market, on one hand, and for a group of individual clients or sponsors, on the other. Besides, painters did not always work directly on commission ... It soon became a regular practice among painters to keep in their workshop a small number of canvases, often incomplete, that they would show as samples of their work to clients who came by. If a painting caught the fancy of a client, it would be completed once the price had been settled.[52]

[50] Ibid., pp. 138–41; Michael North, *Art and Commerce in the Dutch Golden Age*, New Haven, CT, Yale University Press, 1997, chaps. 5 and 6.
[51] Svletana Alpers, *L'Atelier de Rembrandt. La liberté, la peinture et l'argent*, Paris, Gallimard, 1991, pp. 239–40; John Michael Montias, *Vermeer and His Milieu; a Web of Social History*, Princeton, NJ, Princeton University Press, 1989; North, *Art and Commerce in the Dutch Golden Age*, 1977, chap. 5.
[52] Haskell, *Conservation et dispersion*, p. 15.

The example of the circulations of works of art allows us to grasp the extent to which the market as a category – in the sense we understand it today – was not the only mode. Once again, it emerges clearly that there was no single economy governing all the circulations of works of art, but several, if by economy we mean the different modes of relationships to economics. The complexity of the modes of circulation, as well as several other phenomena – foremost among which was the issue of copies, which it would be interesting to study how copies were perceived in the different economies (lauded in the court economy and by criminal in the capitalist economy) – show us the existence of various "worlds of art," each one maintaining specific relations with economics. The underlying values tell us about the political, economic, and social stakes involved in the diverse modes of exchange.

In this context, Simmel's analyses of money, which frees personal ties, are particularly relevant as monetary exchange effectively equalizes the objects exchanged regardless of personal ties[53] and the power that nonmonetary exchanges bring into play. Although the anonymous markets of the neoclassical model do not exist in economic life,[54] nonetheless, a social fiction that structures the new political economy exists: the fiction that impersonal market relations based on equality make possible the existence of a democratic society.

[53] Georg Simmel, *Philosophie de l'argent*, Paris, Presses universitaires de France, 1988.
[54] Marc Granovetter, *Le marché autrement*, Paris, Desclée de Brouwer, 2000, p. 96. Cf. discussion of Pascal Chantelat, "La Nouvelle Sociologie Economique et le lien marchand: des relations personnelles à l'impersonnalité des relations," *Revue française de sociologie*, 43, no. 3, 2002, pp. 521–56 (537).

IO

Building Trust

The King gave a pension of twenty thousand livres to marshal d'Humières'
wife, who, without it would have been reduced to very little, and this was
the first instance of such a large pension to a woman ... She was a pre-
cieuse, who at times bothered the Marshal and all his fine company, and
who, with an account book which she always kept before her, believed she
could do everything and did nothing but bring ruin upon herself.
— Saint-Simon, *Mémoires*, vol. 1, pp. 187–8

In a society completely integrated into countless credit relations, without practically any regulatory system to check its excesses, and in a
largely unpredictable economic climate, the question of building trust
assumes special significance. As a matter of fact, trust is an indispensable component of social relationships. It allows us to act in a world
of uncertainty and complexity by overcoming the information deficit. On the basis of Georg Simmel's seminal work,[1] the notion was
adapted in various ways by sociologists. Niklas Luhmann stresses its
capacity to reduce social complexity: in the face of "the mixture of
knowledge and ignorance" that each one has of the world, he writes,
trust "allows us to anticipate the future and behave as if the future was

---

[1] Georg Simmel, *The Sociology of Georg Simmel*, Glencoe, The Free Press, 1950 [1908],
pp. 318–20 (318). "Confidence, evidently, is one of the most important synthetic forces
within society. As a hypothesis regarding future behaviour, a hypothesis certain enough
to serve as a basis for practical conduct, confidence is intermediate between knowledge
and ignorance about a man. The person who knows completely need no trust; while the
person who knows nothing can, on no rational grounds, afford even confidence. Epochs,
fields of interest, and individual differ, characteristically, by the measures of knowledge
and ignorance which must mix in order that the single, practical decision based on confidence arise."

certain."[2] Using the functions it fulfils as his starting point, James Coleman emphasises its role in risk-taking behaviour and building social capital.[3] However, like Luhmann, he does not retain Simmel's emphasis on the sociopsychological factor, almost an article of faith underlying trust[4]; on the other hand, Antony Giddens chooses to keep it, stressing that the strength of trust lies precisely in its ability to make us suspend our perception of the unknown and the unknowable, based as it is on the belief that the other will not betray us and not act, even if he or she can do so, contrary to our interests.[5]

Nevertheless, the question of trust did not arise in the same manner for all social groups. The obligation to lend to one's family and near ones, like the political domination of the aristocrats, changed the terms radically: it was not so much about choosing one's debtors as it is about finding the right pretext so as not to meet one's obligations. Thus, the only group for whom the question was vital were the merchants, obliged as they were to strike a compromise between their family and social obligations and the demands of the market. This being the case, they are the focus of the present chapter.

In the context of the under institutionalization of the economy of the ancien régime, the ideal for every merchant was to work within an inter-knowledge network, which alone could supply the necessary information about partners and provide the best guarantee against risk and uncertainty. How did such networks generate trust? What kind of deciphering of the other was at work in the building of trust? Did this remain at the level of self-presentation? How much did reputation count for in the ways of gauging partners? Like all other exchanges, trade relations were also an exchange of values, and if so, what was their nature? What were the values on which good reputation was based? Finally, did the greater autonomy of the economy at the end of the eighteenth century influence the manner in which the other was judged?

[2] Niklas Luhmann, *Trust and Power: Two Works by Niklas Luhmann*, translation of the German original *Vertrauen* [1968] and *Macht* [1975], Chichester, John Wiley, 1979, pp. 10, 26. For an analysis of the entire work that draws from Georg Simmel, see Guido Möllering, "The Nature of Trust: From Georg Simmel to a Theory of Expectation, Interpretation and Suspension," *Sociology*, 35, no. 2, 2001, pp. 403–20.
[3] James S. Coleman, *Foundations of Social Theory*, Cambridge, MA, Harvard University Press, 1990.
[4] Möllering, "The Nature of Trust," p. 409.
[5] Antony Giddens, *Modernity and Self-Identity*, Cambridge, MA, Polity Press, 1991, p. 244. See also Allan Silver, "Trust as Moral Ideals: A Historical Approach," *Archives européennes de Sociologie*, 30, no. 2, 1989, pp. 69–87.

Trust and Networks

The best protected networks were what are today called "community networks" or "ethnic networks," because they were based, at times, on the common belonging to the same cluster of villages and, at other times, on a minority religion, as with the Jews or, in some places, the Protestants. These networks, whether Scottish, Alpine, Jewish, or Savoyard, activated the entire gamut of social relations in the village, starting from the merchants at the top of the market chain, some of whom were among the richest inhabitants of the cities in which they had settled, and, at the bottom, men who had barely anything to offer as guarantee for the merchandise entrusted to them.

A series of mechanisms helped reduce the obligations and tensions that arose from the economic and cultural heterogeneity of these networks and the multiple belongings of each one.[6] Sharing the same kinship developed a commonality of interest, the main guarantee that business relations would be conducted in the interest of all. A family "banking" system was the basis for kin groups to invest increasingly in public space by opening shops and factories. Each partner invested most of his or her family's property in the company. Such family firms were extremely flexible and could be expanded or reduced to match the needs of trade or of the enterprise and the death, enrichment, or impoverishment of some member. Normally, the association lasted between one and six winters: each one brought capital, and the profits were divided on a pro rata basis of the initial outlay. In case the company weakened by the death of one of its members, the contracts preserved show that measures were taken to tie up the capital invested until the end of the contract of association; the widow of the deceased merchant received fixed-term payments.

Endogamy was thus an essential part of the regulatory system to the extent that it aimed to protect the "banking" system and the attachment of each one to the merchant network. The exceptions to this rule can be attributed to the adjustments migrants had to make to enter the markets of the regions where they settled. The ban on marrying outside the group was also applied by trading companies, because this made it possible to

---

[6] Laurence Fontaine, *History of Pedlars in Europe*, Cambridge, Polity Press/Duke University Press, 1996, chap. 1; Marina Romani, "La tela del ragno: famiglie e banchi ebraici nell'Italia Centro – settentrionale (secc. XIV-XV)," *Cheiron*, no. 45–46, 2007, pp. 89–111. Corine Maitte, Les verriers d'Altare, Habilitation à Diriger des Recherches, university of Lille 3, December 2006.

move men quickly according to the needs of the company and gave ample opportunity to keep an eye on them through the family that remained in the village.

Between established entrepreneurs and migrant workers a bond of trust was forged because they belonged to the same village and were bound by the same social hierarchies: workers, peddlers, masons, and glassblowers were indebted to those who employed them and they left behind in the village their family and property over which the latter had a hold in case of any default. Uncertainty was thus reduced because of the power flowing through credit and employment chains.[7] Accordingly, analysis of merchant and migrant peddler networks shows that they were prisoners of multiple financial dependences and integrated into a system of social relations that helped them and watched over them. These organizations were founded on obligatory solidarities, surveillance mechanisms, and distrust. Association and guarantees were the two main obligatory forms of solidarity. But such solidarity was ambivalent and charged with tension because it implied that men were jointly responsible for both losses and profits. By linking together the property of one to the other, it caused the fall of one to weigh on the others, introducing yet another imbalance in the networks of relations.

For the moneylender, the extremely hierarchical organization of village migration and its rooting in the village elite, which played the role of both labour contractor and favoured intermediary between city trading and street trading, provided the maximum security. Although surety in standing obliged one to show solidarity, it also led to informing: if a peddler tried to escape his or her creditors, his or her guarantors, whose existence was threatened, would conspire with the merchants to find the peddler and compel him or her to pay. Such merchant solidarity secreted the elimination of black sheep and forced peddlers to assume collectively the responsibility for the failure of some. This morality imposed on the group was backed up by the strategies of the village elite, who kept a sharp lookout for any change in property or reversal of fortune. For this purpose, the elite relied on their own family, village notables and other peddlers who informed them about the state of each one's property and the changes in the composition of families likely to have an impact on the peddlers' solvency.

This example brings out the extreme rigidity of "local" merchant inter-knowledge networks as also the numerous constraints which compelled,

---

[7] On the subject, see the analyses of Luhmann, *Trust and Power*.

organized, regulated, and monitored trust. However, this should not lead us to overlook the dynamics that perturbed them, the imbalances they secreted, and the leeway they allowed. For in spite of all the surveillance systems, the networks were not free from the uncertainty characteristic of all merchant relationships with respect to human nature and the way behaviour changes when circumstances change.

In the case of such kinship and local networks, even if the risk was slight, it existed and shifted to the periphery of the network. For those in the inner periphery, the uncertainty was greater with respect to men who attempted to build an independent position for themselves. The outer periphery was located in the larger merchant relationships in which peddler networks had to be necessarily integrated. People had to know how to inspire trust to penetrate markets and give the impression that the risk involved in dealing with them was minimal. In this game, the image one projected of oneself was of the essence. The greater the risk, the more merchants moved out of inter-knowledge and the greater the importance attached to the outward signs of appearance and looks. In these situations, networks faced the problem all merchants face: that of safeguarding their reputation and giving the impression that they were trustworthy.

Trust and Exchange of Values

Building trust when partners do not have access to all the information that the family or the clientelist (in the political sense) networks can provide is an exercise that consists first and foremost in deciphering behaviour. Granting or not granting credit thus refers not so much to a rational calculation of the risk involved but to a means to revive a set of social, moral and political relations between creditor and debtor. Trust can then be observed at two levels: a certain way of presenting oneself physically and a certain moral construction of personality.

Trust and Appearance
Appearance was the first language. It was through their clothes that men sent out their first messages, and everyone was attentive to the effect of appearance; Samuel Pepys talked of buying a coat for 4 pounds because it was "worth wearing with credit."[8] A fortiori for the migrant merchant,

---

[8] Diary, IV, p. 332 cited by Craig Muldrew, *The Economy of Obligation, Culture of Credit and Social Relations in Early Modern England*, London, Macmillan, 1998, p. 25, 81.

concern for one's appearance was one of the means he favoured to attract trust: appearance was his initial "capital," a reflection of his assets, and an indication of the credit he could be given. Traders lent based on looks, and they themselves acknowledged it. Raymond Bellet, a bankrupt peddler, simulated the appearance of success to try his luck again: he returned to his village in a chariot, acted as if he were rich, and borrowed secretly to pay back the creditors in the village who complimented him and teased him about his newfound affluence. The following autumn, he travelled back in the same carriage to do business again, stopping in Lyon at his usual suppliers, who confessed later on to having been taken in by his grand style and agreeing to supply him with more merchandise than reasonable.[9] It was with his appearance that Noël Gille, a "book seller travelling through fairs" made a favourable impression on Paul Malherbe, an intermediary of the Typographical Company of Neuchâtel. His "heavily loaded" and "well-stocked" chariot as well as the assistant accompanying him inspired confidence in Malherbe: "he appears orderly. Provided the banned books which he sells in great quantity don't get him into a scrape, I don't believe he will cause losses. Besides he is married to Montargis" and so, for about 10 louis, he supplied him works worth 300 to 400 livres.[10]

Partnership contracts took into account the need for show and made provisions for silk stockings, shoes, and hose for each member to give him the appearance of a wealthy city trader.[11] Accordingly, the attention paid to dress was one of the specific features of merchant self-presentation. For migrants who had to work harder to inspire trust, the attention to dress was heightened all the more. The richest had expensive clothes. André Masson took with him to Paris two costumes so that he could be dressed all in red with his white tulle hose, or then more soberly in a grey brown costume enhanced with two white stripes.[12] In this manner, Masson showed that there were different dress codes for the various merchant communities and that one had to know how to make use of them

[9] A. D. Isère, 4U 321, trial of Auguste Bellet, 1862.

[10] Robert Darnton, "Un colporteur sous l'Ancien Régime," *Censures, de la Bible aux larmes d'Eros*, Paris, Centre Georges Pompidou, 1987, pp. 130–9 (134).

[11] The partnership of Simon and Claude Diaque with Vincent Albert was formed for six years with the right of termination at the end of three years. Provision was made for the partners to be taken care of for a month and be given silk stockings, shoes, and hose as well as the right to spend two months a year in the village. A. D. Hautes Alpes, 4E 4839, 6 August, 1686.

[12] A.N.F., MC, and /LXXXVI/213, 7 December 1610.

at the right time. Antoine Guy from Savoy only wore white, gray, or black silk stockings: he had 25 pairs.[13]

Employment and apprenticeship contracts always included, in addition to the wages in cash, a gift of some clothes. Jacques Roux, a merchant of Coltines, engaged the brothers Pierre and Guillaume Teyssal from Ussel as peddler's assistants for three successive seasons against one pair of shoes, a handkerchief, a collar and a bonnet, and 35 and 32 livres, respectively, per season.[14] After five years of apprenticeship, Mr Laurent Eytre Esquire, merchant from Hières, residing in Piémont, undertook to offer "a costume" to Jean Baille,[15] and at the bottom of the peddler hierarchy, Pierre Berthieu promised to give Antoine Arnaud, after eight months of apprenticeship on the road with him, 11 livres, "a hat and a pair of shoes."[16] Increasingly, other items of clothing were included to make a distinction: apprentice peddlers were given a costume to distinguish their gait from the stiff, almost starched walk of the peasant clothed in heavy drugget. Such attention to clothing was common to all temporary migrants. Martin Nadaul narrates how the migrant was appraised on his return. If he wished to borrow the money, he needed to set off for another season; he had to show by his appearance that he had worked well.[17]

The clothes offered, or brought back, with collars, handkerchiefs, and fine shirts being favoured, reproduced the merchant hierarchy in the hierarchy of appearance, setting apart at the same time the migrant merchant from the other villagers. The status of a man and his credit had to be read in the whiteness displayed. This was not an expression of greater attention to personal hygiene; rather, the desire for white linen was revelatory of a culture of appearance. In every encounter, one had to convey trust, and this even more so because between the migrants and the sedentary population this trust was not backed by the bonds forged through the belonging to the same inter-knowledge social group. Besides, being the elite of their village of origin, migrant merchants were duty bound to display their rank. The war of appearances was thus one of the modes of village competition. This competition was not gratuitous; it was also

[13] Catherine and Gilbert Maistre, *L'émigration marchande savoyarde aux XVIIe-XVIIIe siècles. L'exemple de Nancy-sur-Cluses*, Annecy, Académie Salésienne, 1986, p. 167.
[14] Abel Poitrineau, "Petits marchands colporteurs de la haute Planèze d'Auvergne à la fin de l'Ancien Régime," *Annales du Midi*, 88, 1976, pp. 423–36 (426).
[15] A. D. Hautes Alpes, 1E 4839, contract of apprenticeship between Pierre Baille late Jean, for his son Jean and Mr Laurent Eytre Esquire from Hières, 10 July 1684.
[16] A. D. Hautes Alpes, 1E 3839, 2 October 1685.
[17] Martin Nadaud, *Mémoires de Léonard ancien garçon maçon*, edition prepared and commented by Maurice Agulhon, Paris, Hachette, 1977, pp. 118–9.

one of the elements that determined a man's status and, consequently, his "credit." In the struggle for primacy in the village, extravagant expenditure was a favoured weapon. Magnificence was part of this culture of appearance, as seen in the altar decorations, paintings, and statues that the migrant offered on his return to the village church.

Trust and Reputation

But the act of lending and borrowing was not merely an exchange of money; it was also a cultural exchange. Along with power, which commands trust, and appearance, which indicates belonging to the same community or dazzling wealth, the merchant had to be able to put forward a certain number of personality traits in keeping with the image of a man "worthy of trust."[18]

How were reputations built? What were the signs? Reputation in the sense of repute, or *fama,* was one of the most precious attributes of any man desirous of obtaining credit. Since the Middle Ages, in every trial, judges enquired about the reputation of the accused. In the trial of Bondavid in 1317, witnesses defined *fama.* One opined it was the good or bad people said about a person; almost all the others defined *fama* in terms of its opposite, *infamis.* It was revealed through two types of conduct: bad habits (drinking, gambling, foul language), bad sexual behaviour, and going back on one's word.[19] It was thus not just about honouring one's commitments but also about showing in one's behaviour the internalization of moral values. These characteristics endured throughout the modern era. During the transition from the eighteenth to the nineteenth century, the printed circulars sent out regularly by trading houses to introduce themselves to their correspondents always contained ample information about the members of the company and their partners: deaths, marriages, family ties, professional record, and so on. Such information, which would have been considered confidential in the past, was disseminated freely because it helped build trust.[20]

[18] See John Brewer and Laurence Fontaine, "Homo creditus et construction de la confiance au XVIIIe siècle," *La Construction sociale de la confiance,* Philippe Bernoux and Jean-Michel Servet, eds., Association d'Economie financière-Caisse des dépôts et consignation, Paris, Montchrétien, 1997, pp. 161–76.

[19] Joseph Shatzmiller, *Shylock Reconsidered: Jews, Moneylending, and Medieval Society,* Berkeley, University of California Press, 1990, p. 41.

[20] Arnaud Bartolomei, "La publication de l'information commerciale à Marseille et Cadix (1780–1820): la fin des réseaux marchands?," *Rives nord-méditerranéennes,* no. 27, 2007, pp. 85–105 (93).

Rumour and word of mouth were at the heart of *fama*. As Defoe explains at length, a simple insult soon became a rumour that spread through the entire community, driving creditors to question the solvency of the debtor's family. Words could be "tossed about, shuttle-cock-like, from one table to another, in the coffee-house" and "every idle tongue can blast a young shopkeeper."[21] It was hardly surprising then that merchants were very attentive to what was being said, and insults were a very serious offense, especially when they called into question the reputation of men and women. An analysis of the trials for violence in a Castilian village reveals a large number of them to be on account of damage to reputation. In each case, the purport of the words exchanged in front of witnesses in the street, the inn, or the shop was that the man or woman in question did not keep his or her word or that he or she was unworthy of receiving credit. If there was no witness, the aggrieved party did not hesitate to whip out his weapon to take revenge,[22] because trust was always *fama* or what was said in public. A trader from Béarn Paul Barbanegre put it well when he was implicated by one of his colleagues from Tarbes in 1788. In a report, he wrote that the imputations against him

> were spread in the Province where [he] had a large business, where he was held in high esteem; it not for Mr Benquez Esquire [his accuser, a merchant from Tarbes] to make him lose it; it was therefore extremely necessary that he obtain genuine and widely known redress to restore the tarnished honour of a Trader whose state and existence depend on public opinion.[23]

Finally, the language of insult gave expression to the symbolic importance of reputation and attire. The worst possible insult in the migrant villages was the word *bankrupt*: the person who used it was made to pay, on average, 100 livres, in other words, between a fourth and a fifth of an average inheritance.

Sexual insults which sullied the reputation of a merchant and which concerned as much the behaviour of his wife as his own were devastating for his reputation. This tells us not just that the Europe of the time was

---

[21] Defoe, tradesman, pp. 132–5, quoted by Muldrew, *Economy of Obligation*, chap. VI.

[22] Scott Taylor, "Credit, Debt, and Honour in Castille, 1600–1650," *Journal of Early Modern History*, 7, no. 1–2, 2003, pp. 8–27.

[23] A. D. des Pyrénées-Atlantiques, IJ 449, "Mémoire pour le sieur Barbenegre, négociant et maire de la ville de Pontac en Béarn, contre le sieur Guillaume Benquez, négociant à tarbes et contre M. Le Procureur général en la Cour des Monnaie," Paris, chez N. H. Nyon, imprimeur du Parlement, 1788, p. 27, quoted by Patrice Poujade, Une société marchande. Le commerce et ses acteurs dans les Pyrénées modernes, Habilitation à Diriger des Recherches, Toulouse, 2006, p. 505.

steeped in Christian morality but also that this morality offered a financial guarantee, a fact noted by the correspondent of the Typographical Company of Neutchâtel when he lent unwisely to Gilles Noël: "Besides he is married to Montargis," he wrote, before supplying him works worth a considerable amount.[24] Because one was obliged to lend to one's friends, it was preferable that they led a settled, unblemished life. In the face of an uncertain economy and its crises, a debtor's being fearful of God and being faithful to one's spouse were two of the few elements creditors could cling to in the hope of recovering their money. It was one of the foundations of reputation and trust. Thomas Turner was careful that his "friends" be honest, believe in God, know to read and write, and be sober.[25] Such moral control extended to all aspects of private life, and a good potential debtor was one who was neither a gambler nor unfaithful and who knew how to mind his ten. The articles of association of guilds insisted on the morality of their members; for instance, those of the Università dei Servitori, the representative body of the Bolognese shoemakers' journeymen, transcribed in 1565, stipulated in chapter 16 that the company would not accept "blasphemers, gamblers and concubines."[26]

In an unpredictable world, morality and established patterns of conduct more than the nascent sophistry of calculation and forecasting were the basis for trust. This sentiment was a wager on the conduct of others, a wager sustained, as Simmel emphasises, by morality and by a quasi-religious faith.

Economic Discipline and Reputation

Reputation, based on the repute of the family and the morality it displayed in the conduct of its private life, was often associated with a corresponding training in economic discipline. However, an examination of the manner in which "good reputation" was defined in the eighteenth century reveals two contradictory poles. Merchant manuals defined a "good" trader, listing out the personal qualities by which he could be identified. The notion of discipline in work, with its consequences for time saving, was put forward forcefully. Less studied, but

---

[24] Darnton, "Un colporteur sous l'Ancien Régime," p. 134.

[25] Naomi Tadmor, *Family and Friends in Eighteenth-Century England Household, Kinship, and Patronage*, Cambridge, Cambridge University Press, 2001, p. 214.

[26] Mario Fanti, "Istituzioni di mutuo soccorso in Bologna fra Cinquecento e Settecento: la Compagnia dei lavoranti calzolari," *Povertà e innovazioni istituzionali in Italia del Medioevo ad oggi*, Vera Zamagni, ed., Bologne, Il Mulino, 2000, pp. 225–45 (230).

very present in the eighteenth century, was what one may call "the discipline of credit." It was first learned in social institutions (the most of important of which, in England, were voluntary associations and savings clubs). In France, Freemasonry was the club through which merchants met in large numbers. In the port cities such as Bordeaux and Marseille, it had been established as early as in the 1730s, and in both cases, there was a strong English influence that could be seen in the affiliation with British lodges, and in some cases even with other foreign lodges.[27]

As debt unfolds in two dimensions, time and space, it creates different times and spaces. The capacity to successfully manipulate these is at the heart of the success of a creditor, or debtor, as an economic agent. It was therefore not surprising that a didactic literature flourished, striving to develop measurement techniques, calculation, and rational prediction. Although such counsel advocated the use of specific techniques, such as account books or shared systems of measurement, it was never really followed, for merchant techniques remained very rudimentary: despite the massive dissemination of business correspondence manuals, the eighteenth-century French trader was hardly more informed than his sixteenth-century counterpart, even if it was easier for him to be looked on as a man of quality.[28] Interest in these new techniques was thus more the expression of an ideology that displayed to all the particularity of the person who devoted himself to their study. He became someone mindful of time management. The eighteenth century also witnessed the spread of instruments for measuring time. But owning a watch did not indicate merely the possibility of measuring time,[29] but also the fact of belonging to a world that reckoned with time.

Likewise, the affiliation with the Freemasonry and clubs with links abroad was also with the composition of libraries that kept commerce books and bilingual model letters, such as the bilingual Italian and French *Secrétaire des Négociants* by the Reycends brothers (1752 and 1763), *Secrétaire de Banque* (1768) in French and Spanish, or the *Lettres*

[27] John Brewer, "Credit, Clubs and Independence," *The Birth of Consumer Society*, N. McKendrick, J. Brewer, and J. H. Plumb, eds., London, Europa Press, 1982, pp. 217–21; Guy Chaussinand-Nogaret, *Gens de finance au XVIIIe siècle*, Paris, Bordas, 1972; Daniel Roche, *La France des Lumières*, Paris, Fayard, 1993, p. 156.
[28] Pierre Jeannin, "Distinction des compétences et niveau des qualifications," *Négoce et culture*, F. Angiolini and D. Roche, eds., Paris, Editions de l'EHESS, 1995, pp. 363–98.
[29] David S. Landes, *L'Heure qu'il est: les horloges, la mesure du temps et la formation du monde moderne* (French translation), Paris, Gallimard, 1987.

marchandes in French and Dutch,[30] was first and foremost a manner of stating familiarity with space.

A kind of precursor to the *Homo economicus* began to take shape in this novel literature. The continual insistence on forms of forecasting and calculation, institutionally rooted in the practices and rules of clubs, tells us of the familiarity with time, but was at odds with the commonly shared idea, acknowledged in didactic literature as well, that even the most well-informed, shrewd, and responsible merchant found himself generally disarmed when faced with a scarcity of money of which he could control neither the source nor the evolution. Of what use then was the knowledge of calculation when it brought no relief in a crisis of credit, which could prove ruinous?

Here, a second antinomic aspect of building reputation comes into play, adding to economic rationality a sense of compassion and moral values. Other elements thus get included in the portrait of a man worthy of credit. Indeed, in addition to qualities we put in the category of economic rationality, a good trader must project a certain type of personality. *The Tradesman's Director*, published in 1756, expresses this well:

Credit, that Jewel in Trade, that Flower that is so soon blighted, cannot be too tenderly nursed, or too earnest Endeavours used to establish and cultivate; and as the precious Possession so much depends upon the Good will of others, the Conduct of a Shopkeeper in his Neighbourhood and to his Fellow Tradesmen, should be such as, by practice of the former Instructions, and shewing an universal good Will and Friendship, to attract their Respect and conciliate their Affections; for his good Name, in Numbers of Instances, will greatly depend upon their Justice and Courtesy.[31]

If the end was to win trust, the means lay in the somewhat contradictory terms of "justice" and "courtesy." Justice called on the law, referring in particular to the laws on indebtedness, whereas courtesy evoked

[30] Roger Chartier, "Des 'secrétaires' pour le people," *La Correspondance les usages de la lettre au XIXe siècle*, Roger Chartier, ed., Paris, Fayard, 1991, pp. 159–207 (189). For the English examples, see *The Art of Letter Writing by a Gentleman of Fortune*, London, T. Osborne, 1762; *The Complete Letter-Writer: or New and Polite English Secretary*, A. S. Crowther & H. Woodgate, 1756. Jochen Hook and Pierre Jeannin, *Ars Mercatoria. Handbücher und Traktate für den Gebauch des Kaufmanns/ Manuels et traités à l'usage des marchands 1470–1820*. The first volume of this analytical bibliography has been published, Band 1: 1470–1600, Paderborn, Ferdinand Schöningh, 1989.

[31] *The Tradesman's Director, or the London and Country Shopkeeper's Companion*, London, W. Owen, 1756, pp. 9–10.

politeness, malleability, and discretion. In another passage, the same work spells out what this implies:

> From this Subject, we are naturally led to inculcate Compassion in the fortunate Tradesman towards his unfortunate Debtor; as he must have very extraordinary good Fortune if does not meet with many such in the Course of his Dealing: and surely no Men have more Reason to exercise this Virtue, seeing they are certainly in a constant hazardous Situation, and though perfectly circumspect and parsimonious themselves, as their Effects are in so many different Hands, may chance to be hurried in an Instant to the most distressful Ebb, by the failure of a Customer or Correspondent; or if he secure by his overgrown Riches from such a Turn, yet he ought, by paying this Debt of Charity, to acknowledge the Mercy that has set him from above and protected him from Danger. No favour indeed is due to the Fraudulent Bankrupt, but where the honest sinking Tradesman offers his All, that he has saved from the Wreck of his Fortunes, it must be a diabolical Temper that will refuse the first Motion to a Composition, and to give that Liberty that is absolutely necessary for the Support of himself and perhaps an innocent suffering Family: This is not only his Duty as a Man and a Christian, but might be proved to be the best and soundest Policy, and a Kindness done to himself.[32]

William Stout, in his autobiography, boasted of never having prosecuted any of his debtors because "to lose all was of more satisfaction to me than getting all to the great cost of my debtor, and to the preservation of my reputation."[33]

In *Le Parfait négociant*, Savary, too, insists on the quality of gentility with which debtors are to be treated: "One must not be overly concerned about debtors, for they cannot pay for the very reason of the cessation of their business, it is a time when they must be treated gently so as not to reduce them to bankruptcy."[34]

Likewise, Charles Davenant, an advocate of political arithmetic, links explicitly market and compassion towards one's neighbour: "Trust and confidence in each other, are as necessary to link and hold a people together, as obedience, love, friendship, or the intercourse of speech. And when experience has taught each man how weak he is, depending only upon himself, he will be willing to help others."[35]

---

[32] *The Tradesman's Director*, pp. 12–13.

[33] *The Autobiography of William Stout*, J. D. Marshall, ed., third series, 14, Manchester, Chetham Society, 1967, p. 120.

[34] Jacques Savary, *Le Parfait négociant*, Paris, 1665, second part, book 1, chap. 4.

[35] Charles Davenant, *Discourses on the Public Revenues*, in the Sir Charles Whitworth's edition, *The Political and Commercial Works of that Celebrated Writer Charles Davenant*, 1771, p. 151–2, quoted by Craig Muldrew, "Interpreting the Market: The Ethics of Credit and Community Relations in Early Modern England," *Social History*, 18, no. 2, 1993,

In France, the *Journal de commerce et d'agriculture* holds a similar discourse, which veers between the same poles: "We present him at the same time justice, integrity, good faith, fidelity and the punctual fulfilment of his obligations, selflessness, love for humanity, in a word, all the virtues, as the first basis of credit."[36]

These trade manuals viewed credit relations not so much as a rational economic choice of a partner but more as the knowledge of the partner's attitude and solidarity in times of a credit crisis. The purpose of all these recommendations was to instil a sense of generosity and Christian compassion, which would protect those who practiced it from the worst reverses of an unpredictable credit market. The ideal was to be like this friend of an eighteenth-century publisher "[who] was so generous to those indebted to him that only a villain could wish him ill."[37]

Although at first glance, the rhetoric seems designed to regulate the domain of credit – the advancement of the techniques of economic rationality, in fact, the purpose was to establish the merchant's "credit" to decrease the likelihood of his property being seized by his creditors. Given that the decision to act lay in the hands of the latter, the power to convince them of not acting, or first acting against others, was essential. Consequently, this play sent out contradictory messages. On one hand, the rhetoric of calculation and forecasting formed part of the merchant's identity, the knowledge of which could help strengthen credit and suggest that such and such person was a good risk in the matter of lending money; on the other, the ethos of generosity was what ensured that the elasticity of the system worked in favour of those who advocated it. Presenting oneself as a methodical and foresighted person was, at the end of the day, a means to ward off the violence of market forces. The business ideal of honour – and thus of trust – was constructed first and foremost to avert the dual threat of individual insolvency and collective bankruptcy: it acted both as a guarantee against risk and a mutual aid society. This explains the curious bankruptcy mechanisms that targeted first the newly established merchants, the ones the least integrated into the social fabric of the trading city, even if they were not the most indebted, and which protected others, defying all economic rationality.

---

pp. 163–83. The article puts into perspective the category of "self-interest" or "self-love" in the work of Adam Smith with the behaviour of the time.

[36] June 1762, p. 39–40, quoted by Thomas M. Luckett, "Crises financières dans la France du XVIIIᵉ siècle," *RHMC*, 43, no. 2, pp. 266–92.

[37] C. H. Timperlay, *Encyclopaedia of Literary and Typographical Anecdote*, London, H.G. Bohm, 1842, p. 630.

Accordingly, the study of bankruptcies teaches us a great deal about the cultural mechanisms of trust, as it brings out that they were not set off mechanically by an economic crisis, nor were they its direct indicator; on the contrary, they conveyed all the subtlety of the crises of trust. We learn that enterprises did not run the same risks in the face of legal bankruptcy and that the structures of the trading society were in the ultimate analysis determinant in choosing the bankrupt. Furthermore, the most affected were the recently established businessman, not very well-off, and who had just suffered a turn for the worse, and many houses well integrated in the city's social fabric were, on the other hand, spared even though their financial situation was as bad, if not critical. Thus, in their response to economic hazards, the trading society did not put all traders on an equal footing, because the ones the most well established in the merchant society were by and large never declared bankrupt.[38]

Hence, the merchant world was remarkably unregulated, whether by institutions (such as banks) or the law. Of course, a whole series of laws dealt with bankruptcy, especially in England where, at the end of the eighteenth century, the chances of finding oneself in the debtors' prison were much higher than for any other offense.[39] In France, since the sixteenth century, cases of default of payment were settled before a commercial court comprised of merchants. In 1720, sixty-five towns in France had such a court.[40] An analysis of the records of these courts shows however that few cessations of payment ended in a formal declaration of bankruptcy and that in comparison to England, imprisonment for debt was relatively rare in France; for all that, it remained the last recourse and a real possibility that haunted every bankrupt person.[41] Debt trials

[38] Jean-Clément Martin, "Le commerçant, la faillite et l'historien," *Annales ESC*, no. 6, 1980, pp. 1251–68.
[39] Johanna Innes, "The King's Bench Prison in the Later Eighteenth Century: Law, Authority and Order in a Debtors' Prison," *An Ungovernable People. The English and Their Law in the Seventeenth and Eighteenth Centuries*, John Brewer and John Styles, eds., London, Hutchinson, 1980, pp. 250–98.
[40] Jean-Louis Laffon, *Les Députés du commerce et l'ordonnance de mars 1673: les juridictions consulaires, principes et compétences*, Paris, Editions Cujas, 1979.
[41] Serge Chassagne, "Faillis en Anjou au XVIIIe siècle: contribution à l'histoire économique d'une province," *Annales ESC*, no. 2, 1970, pp. 477–97; Pierre de Saint Jacob, "Histoire économique et sociale dans les archives de la juridiction consulaire de Dijon, 1715–1789," *Bulletin de la Société d'histoire moderne*, no. 4, 1957, pp. 2–10. Maurice Garden, "Aires du commerce Lyonnais au XVIIIe siècle," *Aires et structures du commerce français au XVIIIe siècle*, Pierre Léon, ed., Lyon, Publication of the centre d'histoire économique et sociale de la région lyonnaise, no. 5, 1975, pp. 265–99.

were numerous everywhere; however, given the widespread use of credit, they were finally of little importance.⁴² But, by focusing the attention of each one on the risk of an infamous exclusion should he lose the trust and support of the other traders, such trials acted like a moral and social deterrent.

Paradoxically, as a consequence, appearing to be a homo economicus was the way to avoid being treated like one. The business honesty of a merchant was thus built around a split personality – someone whose interest required that he be at the same time coldly calculative and warmly compassionate. In the context of obligatory credit, widespread indebtedness and the unpredictability of financial crises that characterized preindustrial Europe, in which the economy was enmeshed in social relationships, the question of the bond of trust arose differently than in the contemporary era. Trust was not found where we expect to find it today. It was not so much a question of verifying, before entering into a relationship of credit, the degree of disengagement of a future debtor vis-à-vis his social obligations as of securing, given the violence of credit crises, the benevolent support of those with whom one shared a business relationship. In this sense, trust was closely linked to reputation.

However, each individual belonged at the same time to several communities with the expectations of some being inimical to others. One of the strengths of migrant networks was precisely the ability to control these multiple and contradictory interests of individuals. Two examples will serve to show the complexity of such cultural encounters that the economic rationality of the act of lending could obscure and that such economic exchanges could link together different registers and bring into play contradictory belongings.

How did economic rationality become reconciled with the behaviour expected among relatives? When a lender who, fulfilling the obligations of kinship, had lent money within the family (and we have seen how frequently this was the case) and discovered that his or her relative was a bad payer, he or she had contradictory feelings: on one hand, the lender did not want to lose money, and on the other, he or she had to face enormous family pressure to dissuade him or her from taking the relative to court. If, in spite of everything, the lender chose to do so, there was every likelihood of his or her being ostracized by the family. He or she would have won his or her credit in court, but would have lost it among the

---

⁴² In Yébenes, a town of 2,000 to 3,500 inhabitants to the south of Toledo, 550 of the 1,030 criminal trials were for indebtedness. Taylor, "Credit, Debt, and Honour," p. 10.

family.[43] This is what happened in 1711 when a London soap manufacturer furnished the government with a detailed account of the soap business, enabling the introduction of a new tax on soap. This initiative led to his ruination: he was rejected by the other merchants, who took their revenge by refusing him any credit, and he was soon led to bankruptcy.

These two examples underscore the fact that we cannot study in isolation the notions of communities of individuals and communities of credit made up of individuals, united and distinct not just by the fact of borrowing and lending but also by the shared conceptions of what such transactions mean. Moreover, each community was not inward looking and maintained relations with other groups whose moral references were not necessarily compatible. In this context, understanding how bonds of trust were built is not an easy task, because it requires the reconstruction, within the credit markets, of the various credit communities and a study of the ways in which the multiple belongings of the individual and the group made their commitments compatible or conflictual.

William Stout's attitude faced with his relations' commercial debts illustrates this combination of social and moral obligations that affected even English merchants who could have been expected to manage to keep economic and private spheres apart. It also shows that, in order to uphold his reputation, a merchant must not restrict his generosity to his peers but extend it to the poorest. One of his former apprentices, John Thoughton, was jailed for debt, and a commission of bankruptcy was issued against him by a merchant from Liverpool to whom he owed 100 pounds. To avoid the expense of the commission, Stout took the trouble and time to sell Thoughton's shop goods at auction, because, he stated, "as he had been my apprintice, and the begining of his creddit by my recomendition, I thought my selfe obliged to use my endevours to make the most for the creditors." Later on, his nephew, to whom he had sold his business, borrowed more than 900 pounds in one year, and Stout took it on himself to repay more than fifty creditors because many "were my particular friends, and he my near relation, and I had recommended him." In fact, he claimed in his diary to have been "tender of oppressing poor people with law charges ... for the preservation of my reputation," because, he added, "losing everything was more satisfactory

[43] Margaret Hunt, "English Urban Families in Trade, 1660–1800: The Social Relations of Early Modern Capitalism," unpublished PhD thesis, New York University, New York, 1986, chap. 2.

for me and my reputation than recovering everything at great expense for my debtor."[44]

Friendship and Information

Thus, at every level of society, "credit" was according to the number of "friends" one could gather around one.[45] Since the curialization of aristocracies, credit was the extent to which the noble had the king's ear, for it was at the court that largesse was dispensed. "Friendship" was understood as a moral relationship, one of aid and reciprocity. It cut across kinship as much as relationships chosen, principally among equals; however, politics could add an unequal dimension to it, composed as it was of all kinds of economic and emotional exchanges. One lent money to one another other when the need arose, introduced one's "friends" to influential people, entertained one another, and these relationships were stated in the language of affection. Some personal diaries allow us to take a closer look at the way friendship networks were formed. The diary of Thomas Turner, from eighteenth-century England, mentions relatives and nonrelatives, and provides an insight into the political sphere; on the other hand, Turner systematically excludes his neighbours and partners whom he met every day from his circle of "friends." Yet, he often spoke of the disappointment he felt at the selfishness and coldness of his friends, the expectations he had of them, and the help, consideration, and warmth he hoped to receive from them.[46]

The lessons of bankruptcies were shared by the actors of the time: they knew it was the lack of friends that led to the fall of new entrants. Thus, when a Swiss merchant went bankrupt in Lyon in the eighteenth century, his brother reproached him bitterly for being incapable of widening his circle of "friends": "had you made yourself known in Lyon, as I had always recommended to you, we would not have lacked for money."[47] The Dutch merchants shared the same concerns and mentality:

A merchant was dependent on others and it was often difficult to know who was trustworthy. One had to rely on reputation ... People made a clear distinction

[44] Stout, *Autobiography*, pp. 148–9, 208–9, 225, and 120, quoted by Muldrew, *The Economy of Obligation*, p. 257.
[45] Arlette Jouanna, *Le Devoir de révolte. La noblesse française et la gestation de l'Etat moderne (1559–1661)*, Paris, Fayard 1989, p. 65.
[46] Tadmor, *Family and Friends*, pp. 212–15.
[47] A. D. Rhône, série B, papiers Cuentz, liasse XV, Paris, 28 October 1721, cited by Pierre Léon, Jacqueline Fayollet, and Maurice Garden, "Recherche conjoncturelle et milieux économiques: hommes d'affaires suisses et mouvement économique lyonnais sous la Régence," Publications of the Faculty of Economics and Social Sciences, of the University of Geneva, 20, 1969, pp. 101–19 (113).

between "us" and "them," between "friends" and "foreigners." The one who did not belong to the circle of friends was a stranger about whom one could never be completely sure.[48]

It was always a problem of information. Before the advent, in the nineteenth century, of businesses specializing in information on other businesses, each business developed an information network through correspondence. This consumed a great deal of time and energy, and required a large staff.[49] The information was so unreliable and difficult to obtain that many opted finally for a very small number of regular business partners, although they did not give up the habit of using every exchange of letters to inform themselves about the state of affairs and reputation of men and women. Thus, Melchior Philibert, a prominent trader from Lyon in the first half of the eighteenth century, kept up a vast network of correspondents even though he did business with only a few of them: one or two large companies per area. There was a list of about ten names that always referred to the largest companies in each city. It was with them that he did at least 90 per cent of his business. It was from them that he sought information about the many traders who wished to do business with him. To his correspondent from Carcassonne, Philibert wrote one day, "I am delighted to see what you have marked to me about him, for as you know, it is not gracious to run risks by pleasing one's friends."[50]

Jean-Baptiste Bruny in Marseille was one such friend, and the two companies developed a loyal friendship. The exchange of business letters was thus coupled with an interest in private and family affairs. In return, these rare friends received preferential economic treatment: "There will always be money in the till for friends such as you, for whom I have genuine consideration, and complete trust," wrote Melchior to Raymond

---

[48] L. Kooijimans, "Risk and Reputation in the Mentality of Merchants in the Early Modern Period," *Entrepreneurs and Entrepreneurship in Early Modern Times*, C. Lesger and N. Noordegraaf, eds., The Hague, Stiching Hollandse Historische Reeks, 1995, pp. 27, 32, cited by Peter Mathias, "Risk, Credit and Kinship in Early Modern Enterprise," an essay in honour of Jacob Price. See also his analyses on the obligations of friendship in the context of enterprises, pp. 402 and seqq. I thank Peter Mathias who gave me this manuscript.

[49] A fine example in Robert Chamboredon, "Toutes antennes déployées: les enseignements de la correspondance des frères Fornier entre Nîmes et Cadix (1748–1786)," *Rives nord-méditerranéennes*, no. 27, 2007, pp. 65–84.

[50] Quoted by Maurice Garden, "Le grand négoce lyonnais au début du XVIIIe siècle. La maison Melchior Philibert: de l'apogée à la disparition," *Colloque franco-suisse d'histoire économique et sociale*, Genève, Librairie Georg et Cie, 1969, pp. 83–99.

Bruny on 21 June 1721. During the same year, when one of Bruny's nephews asked Philibert that he be given the same reduced provisioning rate as his uncle, he was explained the exceptional nature of this favour granted to Bruny "on account of our old association, and not wishing to look closely into their affairs, but they are the only friends with whom I have such dealings."[51] In this, his brother followed Savary's advice that wholesalers should avoid looking for funds on the marketplace and prefer instead the security of "special friends,"[52] and these ties of friendship and business between large trading houses were commonplace in Europe.[53] Seventeenth-century Rome shows that even the more modest artisans turned towards the security of networks and looked for credit and guarantors among relatives and friends.[54]

Changing Values at the End of the Eighteenth Century

In the seventeenth and eighteenth centuries, trust therefore did not lie where one would expect it today. It reflected both, as Furetière's dictionary emphasized, the deeply social nature of credit in the modern era, the "power," the "authority," the "wealth one acquired through the reputation one had gained," and its fragile nature, for this reputation, founded on the values of generosity and benevolence, was required more to attenuate the violence of the economy than help rationalize one's own economic commitments.

At the end of the eighteenth century, credit was increasingly held responsible for the economic and moral crises. One did speak of bankruptcies and the scarcity of money, but credit in itself was stigmatized and accused of corroding morality by inciting people to buy, especially luxury goods, whereas they did not have the means to do so. Now, the legal and institutional machinery to fight against indebtedness and repeated bankruptcy was no longer adequate; what had to be changed was people's relation with debt. Laws against fraudulent bankruptcies were promulgated at the end of the eighteenth century, and the very notion of fraud changed: its scope was extended in discussions and regulations beyond the concealment of property alone to the condemnation of the usual behaviour and practices of each one. The term fraud now covered actions

---

[51] Garden, "Le grand négoce lyonnais au début du XVIIIe siècle," pp. 83–99 (86–7).
[52] Savary, *Le Parfait négociant*, pp. 6–7.
[53] Jean-Yves Grenier, *L'économie d'Ancien Régime. Un monde de l'échange et de l'incertitude*, Paris, Albin Michel, 1996, pp. 129–30.
[54] Renata Ago, *Economia Barocca. Mercato e istituzioni nella Roma del Seicento*, Roma, Donzelli, 1998, pp. 23–7.

such as accepting a loan when its repayment was not certain, living an extravagant life on borrowed money, or failing to anticipate foreseeable difficulties or then not trying hard enough to avert going into default. Words such as reasonable, extravagant, avoidable, and enough used in these new definitions of fraud are extremely subjective. They reveal a desire to act on cultures and behaviour.[55]

At the same time, between the sixteenth and the eighteenth centuries, an entire range of practices changed the relationship with credit and was translated in the semantic shifts of words such as fortune, corruption, interest, and credit in the publication of information, given that access to information was a key element in any transaction, in the competition among creditors, in the emergence of specialized intermediaries in finance and in the greater institutionalization of guarantees.[56] These changes, inseparable from the political transformation of society, were one of the essential elements in the formation of money markets that detached themselves increasingly from the play of interpersonal relations alone. They marked the advent of contemporary trust as an ownership set of things and not beings.

The manner in which trust was built also shows the merit of taking into account the complexity of social categories: historians like to define the merchant as a social type, inscribed in the continuum of all those involved in buying and selling, from the small hawker to the large trader; now, this role in credit shows the merchant to be perceived as a dual being, of whom contradictory behaviour was expected and who had to come to a compromise with the other facets of his social context and reconcile, with all their incompatibilities, his various belongings and the demands of his profession. Certainly the professionalization of trade was to lead to the progressive separation of the spheres of activity, but the borders were always porous. We need to pursue studies that link credit with civil society and economic activity through the reconstruction of credit commitments to see where, when and for whom the obligatory aspect of credit relations was set aside, in favour of more freely chosen behaviour, and to find out by what mechanisms and changes the question of trust could be raised in terms of economic rationality and not just of mutual protection. These studies should then allow us to grasp how that part of Antonio and Shylock that exists in every creditor changed.

---

[55] Paul H. Haagen, "Eighteenth-Century English Society and the Debt Law," *Social Control and the State, Historical and Comparative Essays*, Stanley Cohen and Andrew Seull, eds., London, Basil Blackwell, 1983, pp. 222–47 (230–1).

[56] Renata Ago, *Economia Barocca*, chap. 6.

Finally, what were the repercussions of obligatory trust and wide-spread credit on the general functioning of the economy and the ways individuals related to it?

From Micro to Macro: Economic Imbalances and Individual Behaviour

An Unpredictable and Speculative Economy

The mechanisms of obligatory trust and widespread credit had serious repercussions on the general functioning of the economy. First, we are talking of an economy in which credit was easily available: it was simple to borrow. Moreover, private debt increased by the same mechanisms as public debt, for it was simpler to borrow than raise taxes. However, the eulogizing of the royal gift, ubiquitous in the sixteenth century, became muted in the seventeenth century and turned into criticism in the eighteenth century.[57] Until the end of the eighteenth century, credit was not stigmatized, even when a result of extravagance, and in addition, excessive debt was fuelled by the aristocrats' lack of interest in their debts, the aristocratic culture being very comfortable with the notion of indebtedness. If few nobles were concerned at the swelling of their debts and if few felt the need to reduce them, the same spirit guided them when it came to lending, which they continued to do even after being alerted about the borrowers' insolvency; traders followed, willingly or unwillingly, the same culture, because they rarely turned down the requests of their aristocratic clients. The protection of noble property may have possibly encouraged the indebtedness of aristocrats in the long run.[58] Hence, not only was borrowing relatively easy in the society of the ancien régime, but the legal remedies available were also quite ineffective, because numerous lands and properties escaped debt guarantees, and prison was not a deterrent, especially in England, where the subject had been well studied.[59] As a result, society as a whole was caught in the debt logic, and

[57] Robert Descimon, "La vénalité des offices comme dette publique sous l'Ancien Régime français. Le bien commun au pays des intérêts privés," *La dette publique dans l'histoire*, Jean Andreau, Gérard Béaur, and Jean-Yves Grenier, eds., Paris, Comité pour l'histoire économique et financière de la France, 2006, pp. 177–242 (182); Alain Guery, "Le roi dépensier. Le don, la contrainte, et l'origine du système financier de la monarchie française d'Ancien Régime," *Annales ESC*, 39, no. 6, 1984, pp. 1241–69.
[58] John Habakkuk, *Marriage, Debt and the Estates System. English Landownership, 1650–1950*, Oxford, Oxford University Press, 1994, pp. 302–4, p. 338; and see our analyses in this book, Chapter 3.
[59] Haagen, "Eighteenth-Century English Society and the Debt Law," pp. 222–47.

the wealth of the elite was primarily paper wealth, the foundations of which were economically extremely volatile and sensitive to any downturn. It was truly a case of "the ruinous expedient of permanent capitalisation" of which Adam Smith spoke.[60]

In addition to credit not being stigmatized was the culture of the obligation to lend, which we have seen at work in all social groups. This was also responsible for the individual's lack of rational control over credit: one was duty bound to lend to the family even if one knew that it was not in position to honour its commitments just as the landed elite could not refuse credit or late payment of rent to their farmers. Finally, information about the state of indebtedness of each one was very difficult to obtain and hardly circulated. Thus, the obligation to lend tended to maintain general over-indebtedness: every social group was potentially in a state of bankruptcy. Unregulated currency was created, because the notes exchanged and in circulation, like paper money, were for the most part not secured against any real goods. Admittedly, periods of expansion allowed the reduction of indebtedness: every family and every social group was not continually in a state of excessive debt. But, bringing to light this potentiality intrinsic to the credit mechanisms, and the difficulty for social agents to act rationally in the management of their credit was a structural feature of the ancien régime, which acted on credit related culture and behaviour.

All credit systems worked as long as no one really needed to recover his debts. But no sooner did some people demand to be paid at a time when credit had increased than financial panic broke out. The panic was all the greater, given that there was no bank to regulate the issuance of credit and play the role of lender as a last resort. This is the likely explanation for the volatility of the credit systems and the unpredictability of the financial crises.[61] The impossibility of anticipating crises and the conscious helplessness of the economic agents, when faced with their occurrence, geographical spread, and duration, made them difficult to control.

The geographical spread of the scarcity of money compounded the ordinary merchant's helplessness as he was sucked into the crisis. The crisis of 1760, for example, spread over a very wide area in France:

Bankruptcies, writes a merchant from Lorient, are not yet close to ending, as in this letter we are informed of the bankruptcy of Mr. Georges Fitzgerald in

---

[60] Cited by Habakkuk, *Marriage, Debt and the Estates System*, p. 337.
[61] Hyman P. Minsky, "The Financial Instability Hypothesis: Capitalism Behavior and the Economy," *Financial Crises: Theory, History and Policy*, C. P. Kindelberger and J. -P. Laffargue, eds., Cambridge, Cambridge University Press, 1982, pp. 13–47.

London, which is said to be considerable and dreadful, and there have also been one or two in Lyon and (in) the previous ordinary (letter), we also learnt of the troubles of Mr In. Testar and C. (from Amsterdam).

In Paris, the number of imprisonments for debt went up rapidly the following year.[62]

These characteristics of the economy fuelled speculation. The speculator was, like most economic agents of the time, someone who did not have a likely source of income sufficient to pay his short-term debts. This person was thus compelled either to sell his assets or to borrow even further to meet his obligations, a Hobson's choice which made the speculator vulnerable to the conditions of the asset market and constituted his main threat. Admittedly, such people were unwilling speculators: they had not planned to live with this type of financial behaviour, but if one takes into consideration the fact that their debtors were incapable of respecting the repayment period and above all the large number of bad payers, we realize that the speculative mentality was inherent to the functioning of the economy of the ancien régime.

In this incessant demand for credit, a mere trifle could create panic, leaving the social actors with no choice but to continue finding more risky finance to meet their due dates. The system held good only as long as conditions continued to be favourable. A study of the credit networks of peddlers brought out clearly their vulnerability to the vagaries of the economy; they borrowed for six months from city traders and sold on credit during the season such that after the first months, they were only repaid in the following season. A client just had to become insolvent for these peddlers to be unable to pay for their own purchases and compelled them to borrow from family and friends to pay their suppliers. In this way, they would make the debt go back to the village and would transform it into a long-term debt. In the middle of the nineteenth century, mountain villages were indebted for thrice the value of their goods, and their inability to overcome such structural indebtedness left them hollow: permanent emigration replaced temporary emigration.[63] This short-term debt structure, characteristic of speculative finance, was not specific to migrant merchants: the more the debt structure was on a short-term basis, the greater were the obligations in relation to the receipts of income, and the more the debts in circulation were chronically higher than assets.

---

[62] Luckett, "Crises financières dans la France du XVIIIe siècle," pp. 266–92.
[63] Laurence Fontaine, "Le reti del credito. la montagna, la città, la pianura: i mercanti dell' Oisans tra XVII e XIX secolo," *Quaderni Storici*, 2, no. 68, 1988, pp. 573–93.

This is why Minsky, in his analysis of financial instability in the first phase of capitalism, pointed out that volatile systems of credit were always subject to violent short-term fluctuations.[64]

The same phenomenon was at work in periods when money was scarce, there being a vast difference in the evolution of long-term and short-term credit. Long-term credit, essentially annuities, remained stable at 5 per cent during the eighteenth century, whereas short-term interest rates constantly fluctuated, depending on the market forces, and as soon as the interest rate reached 6 per cent, money became scarce. Besides, although there was no clear linkage between money scarcity and grain price movement, the partial bankruptcy of royal debt and the arbitrary measures taken by the minister of finance were clearly a trigger. This was the analysis of Véron de Fourbonnais, who observed, even then, that "the greater the lack of trust in the state, the scarcer money becomes."

To manage crises, the solution was always to extend the repayment period and transform short term debts into long term ones. Indeed, we have shown that structural over-indebtedness of society went hand in hand with the extension of repayment periods. In 1767–68, the inspector of the Caen Fair wrote that this was the general trend in the world of trade and that "[i]n spite of all that we have said (concerning the scarcity of money), there have been very few prosecutions and no imprisonment for debt. Merchants prefer to come to an agreement and extend the repayment period with the result that most prefer to receive new long term obligations."

The rate of interest was no longer significant in periods of money scarcity, since people could no longer find cash, whatever the rate of interest.[65]

Even at the turn of the eighteenth century, Pierre de Boisguilbert said that in a country filled with goods such as France, the abundance or lack of currency had no role to play in the scarcity of money:

Such that when one protests against the scarcity of money and blames the scarcity or transport of cash for the difficulty in finding it, one is completely mistaken, because one does not reflect that there being two things which make any kind of material dear, the first its scarcity, and the second, the unexpected increase of those in need of it, money suffers the fate of scarcity on account of the second cause, and one has blindly chosen to attribute it to the first.[66]

[64] Minsky, "The Financial Instability Hypothesis."
[65] Luckett, "Crises financières dans la France du XVIIIe siècle"; Martin, "Le commerçant, la faillite et l'historien," pp. 1251–68.
[66] Pierre le Pesant de Boisguilbert, Mémoire sur l'assiette de la taille et de la capitation, présenté au roi en mai 1705, in Marcel Marion, Les *Impôts directs sous l'ancien régime principalement au XVIIIᵉ siècle*, Paris, 1910, pp. 269–273.

The problem was that credit notes had no forced currency. Thus, in such phases of expansion, no one bothered to see if the credit notes were backed by cash, but the moment any difficulty arose, everyone wanted to be repaid at the same time and in cash. When money was scarce, those with a little cash clung to it; this was their only security against prison for debt in case they were required to pay back their own debts. In other words, money did not go out: it remained where it was, hidden carefully to cope with any mishap that might befall them on account of their debts. The example of Samuel Pepys has already taught us that. Philibert, a prominent merchant from Lyon, adopted this habit followed by all merchants whenever a crisis seemed imminent. All would unanimously agree to not ask for the repayment of credit. In 1772, when money was scarce, Philibert expressed his concern to his friend and correspondent from Marseille Raymond Bruny about the fact that his correspondents from Carcassonne were "demanding" of payment of exchange bills of exchange, whereas they should have waited for the crisis to blow over, for Philibert could not tolerate being put in a situation of having to borrow to guarantee a bill of exchange.[67] In times of crisis, it was his habit and advice to always "hold the reins in one's hands" and to not "force friends" or expose one's paper or credit."[68]

Effect on Individual Behaviour
These specific features of the economy produced a *homo economicus* who tended to hoard money, liked to shroud his or her affairs in secrecy, and showed a preference for illiquidity.

To cope with the crises of credit and not risk losing one's money due to the hazards of the obligation to lend, the most effective ploy was the one Pepys adopted, which was simply to withdraw his money from circulation and hoard it. Many eighteenth-century economists, following Locke, stigmatized this refusal to make wealth circulate. Boisguilbert thus wrote to the comptroller general on 1 July 1704:

There is dead money and live money. The first is that which, being immobile and hidden, is of no more use to the State than if it were stone; and the other, live, is that which is always on the move and never at rest.

Accounts of his contemporaries emphasized the extent of hoarding.

---

[67] Garden, "Le grand négoce lyonnais au début du XVIIIe siècle," p. 87.
[68] Ibid., p. 88.

I have been talking for a week to all the shrewdest traders either for their business, or for exchange: they all agree that (their) distrust does not stem from a lack of money, and that there is much more than needed in a place like this, wrote the intendant of Bordeaux on 23 March 1715.[69]

An inquiry conducted by the office of the comptroller general in Marseille in 1783 estimated that the total cash supply was about 3 million livres tournois, but that only 1.8 million was in circulation. The intendant stated that the remainder was kept in reserve, depending on the circumstances.[70] The dead money was a precautionary saving, insurance in the face of the uncertainty and unpredictability of crises.

Furthermore, at every level, the actors did their best to maintain secrecy over the extent of their indebtedness and the number of their creditors. We have seen that this was the mentality of all migrant merchants,[71] not just characteristic of individuals but of institutions as well. When in the eighteenth century the Hôtel-Dieu de Marseille experienced financial difficulties, the directors informed the intendant, but they also demanded that he maintain secrecy in the name of the services he rendered:

The limited resources that maintain our hospital and which all put together are not sufficient to meet half the annual expenditure … it is nevertheless essential that the public does not know of it; knowledge of our situation would make us loose trust for sunk investments; we would then have to put the poor on the streets and capital up for auction.[72]

Secrecy was maintained by avoiding at all costs the publicising of businesses, and the manner in which they were registered was part of this desire to shroud one's economic activities in secrecy. Although we have seen the migrant merchants were systematic in their use of private agreements and their refusal to have their businesses registered, institutions in difficulty such as the Hôpital de Marseille did not hesitate to look for creditors who paid for the rectors, and the latter accepted unregistered credit in the presence of a notary in order that the city did not come to know about and thus discover the bankruptcy of the institution.

Finally, we come to the preference for illiquidity. The concept was first introduced in studies on developing countries after observing that people in these countries preferred investing their gains in valuable items

---

[69] Quoted by Grenier, *L'Économie d'Ancien Régime*, p. 203.

[70] Ibid., pp. 203–4.

[71] Fontaine, *History of Pedlars*.

[72] Lettre à l'intendant, 26 Septembre 1752, quoted by Courdurié Marcel, *La Dette des collectivités publiques de Marseille au xviii* siècle. Du débat sur le prêt à intérêt au financement par l'emprunt*, Marseille, Institut historique de Provence, 1974, p. 212.

rather than keeping cash and thus be obliged to save. This mechanism helped them to keep a check on their expenditure, since they would have to reconvert into money the money they had kept aside in the form of goods. This phenomenon was observed in all strata of society: in the inventories after death of aristocrats, the proportion of items in precious metal increased as families became richer. Accordingly, in Brittany during the sixteenth and the seventeenth centuries, gold-plated pewter became increasingly commonplace and reserved for the poorest families. With pewter going out of favour, especially since the seventeenth century, all the more-well-off social categories preferred to buy silverware in large quantities. It was present in all large inventories of which it formed a sizeable share, varying from a third to half of the total value and this, taking into account only the weight of the metal.[73] The memoires of Saint-Simon abound in stories of silverware being converted into money or vice versa, depending on the circumstances. The presence of a large number of itinerant jewellers at country fairs is another indication that farmers and villagers kept their savings in the form of jewels and precious metals. In the city, we have seen the success of luxury goods and the ease with which the same could be end up in the hands of brokers or pawnshops. If this preference for illiquidity shown by society as a whole was an insurance against the uncertainty of the future, it was also a means to evade the obligation to lend.

When all is said and done, the unpredictable nature of the economy, with its intrinsic speculative tendencies, characterized states, which were both the creators of and dependent on these social and cultural dynamics. They were caught in a double bind: the economic obligation to compete for credit all the more fiercely as they were engaged in war and the political obligation to ensure their credibility in their relations with their principal money lenders, especially merchants and citizens in general. While looking at the domino effect that state policies had on credit relations as a whole in society, we must not forget that behind this there was, quite obviously, a political problem: that of the conflict between arbitrary and imposed behaviour, and the widespread need in society for socially shared and predictable codes and conducts. Accordingly, what vanished when money was scarce was not so much money as credit in the old sense of the term: public trust in the credit system. In 1758, a merchant put it succinctly: "With trust and good

---

[73] Jean Meyer, *La Noblesse bretonne au XVIIIe siècle*, Paris, Flammarion, 1972, pp. 340–1.

commercial papers, a large part of business is conducted without any great need for money."

In the face of the general crisis of trust secreted by the state and the aristocratic society, different countries responded in divergent ways: some overturned the system; others refined it.[74]

[74] We may be permitted an excursus in relation to this work, for the collateral effect of the inquiry on which it is based reveals similarities, striking to say the least, between the financial panic during the ancien régime and the subprime crisis that triggered a chain reaction, paralyzing all banking systems since the summer of 2008. What was it about? Real estate loans were given to low-income clients at variable interest rates with the possibility of a steep hike. As the interest rates went up and real estate prices fell from the summer of 2008, many borrowers were unable to repay their loans and their homes were foreclosed by the banks. In early modern Europe, the obligation, so to speak, to lend to one's near ones and to the political elite led to an uncontrolled accumulation of debts. Credit was very easily accessible, just as it was recently, in the course of the last few years that witnessed low rates and an increase in the number of lending institutions. But in the ancien régime, information about debts was scarce such that suspicions of portfolios being crippled by bad debts were rife. The plethora of dubious papers thus created financial bubbles that could burst at any moment. The crisis began with the bankruptcy of a large business house that, like a powder trail, spread across the whole of Europe, following the trade chains. The financial panic was due not to a lack of liquidity but of trust and information: business houses, which also acted as banks in a financial system not regulated, unlike our time, by any lender in the last resort refused to lend: they preferred to keep their liquidity until the crisis was absorbed with the sole purpose of being able to satisfy the demands of their own creditors should they be hit by the financial panic. These crises make one think irresistibly of the current world economic crisis where credit is distributed easily and where the outsourcing of dubious debts, a product of the American mortgage loan markets, aroused the suspicion of banks about the securities in their portfolios. Soon after, panic broke out when Northern Rock, a small English business bank, went bankrupt, paralysed by insolvent debts; the British government had to privatize and bail it out to prevent a spate of bankruptcies across the board, in the international network of financial institutions. Very soon, the U.S. Federal Reserve lowered its discount rate and injected liquidity into the market to sustain economic activity and the large banks followed suite (the European Central Bank, the Swiss National Bank, the Bank of Canada and the Bank of England). Simultaneously, banks recapitalized themselves and governments put their hands into their pockets to clean up the balance sheets of the banking institutions in a bid to boost sagging confidence. In exchange, they began asking for greater transparency, a sign of the realization for the need to regulate financial capitalism, which, at the end of the day, made taxpayers pay for its highly speculative and risky behaviour. The ancien régime was left with no choice but to let the crisis blow over. But it seems that once again something is changing in the world financial order: the contemporary banking system controlled by central banks was filled out by the arrival of operators whose role as financial investors escaped the control of central banks and who played on the leverage effect of more risky but more remunerative investments. This diversification of finance, where all kinds of operators made investments and indulged in financial speculation, is reminiscent of the unregulated world of the old financial Europe and creates the same interdependence of systems and institutions. It portends the return of the major uncontrollable crises that periodically shook the economy of the ancien régime: today it is the subprime crisis; tomorrow it will be something else, and already there is talk of giving credit to shaky enterprises to protect investors from their bankruptcy, unless stricter rules of transparency and capitalization are imposed.

Conclusion

From the Ancien Régime to the Twenty-First Century: A Journey Back and Forth

If some polls are to be believed, more than 50 per cent of the French fear that some day they will find themselves homeless. In that, they are no different from the inhabitants of ancient Europe, where 80 per cent of the people lived with the threat of losing their homes. In fact, the absence of a minimum wage in an uncertain world made poverty a risk for most people. Poverty and the strategies employed by the vast majority of the population for survival thus seem a good starting point for gauging the efficiency of the values of solidarity.

Nowadays, poverty is viewed as a state determined by economic thresholds, and the state, as the custodian of national solidarity, is duty bound to help the poor. The poor are the victims of the vicissitudes of life; they are the casualties of economic circuits. In preindustrial Europe, poverty was regarded in a more complex light. It was also held to be a state by the social elites, one ordained by God. The duty of solidarity fell first and foremost on the family and the social networks around the poor. However, such networks were not activated of their own accord and required the active engagement of those who needed them. Although impoverishment depended on phenomena over which individuals had no control, the lack of insurance against the blows of fate or circumstances condemned these very individuals – we would do well to recall that more than three-fourths of the population was likely to fall into a state of poverty – to be active. The fundamental issues we are dealing with are therefore those of risk and uncertainty, the efficiency of social networks and the ways in which the status and social roles of individuals influenced their capacity to act. The capacity of the poor to shake off their condition and to organize the future in such a way as to prevent falling back into poverty hinge on considerations such as these.

Neither the paucity of ready money nor the reduction of daily life to mere biological survival can be the sole determinants of poverty. Poverty, whatever it may seem, is never one-dimensional: it can be absolute or relative. A socially constructed phenomenon, poverty is the way individuals perceive themselves and is measured in relation to the rest of the population. A social group that does not grow rich in an environment where others improve their position or income is a form of poverty; not being able to maintain the lifestyle imposed by one's status or the group to which one belongs is another form of poverty. Such poverty, subjective but no less real, was recognized during the ancien régime. Today it has acquired worldwide dimensions with the globalization of the media and the circulation of men and goods. In fact, global inequality between rich and poor countries, of which the people of the developing world are fully aware, is the great purveyor of migrants from the countries of the South to the affluent countries. This perception of poverty also highlights the different needs people have, depending on the society or social group to which they belong. In his analysis of contemporary poverty, Amartya Sen emphasizes this point: participating in collective life – which, along with keeping oneself alive, is one of the foundations of human life – assumes in the rich countries the possession of goods such as a telephone, a television set or, in the United States especially, a car, goods which are not indispensable for collective life in the poorest countries.[1]

Social Networks

The alter-globalist ideology, in the sense of a coherent and inclusive worldview, and, more broadly speaking, the advocates of the Other economy, view networks as central to the reorganization of society. These would permit the patching up of social ties and help build trust, and consequently a more humane economy: "Networks are built through gifts and trust is maintained through the renewal of gifts,"[2] a scheme whereby the "embedding" of the economy and morality takes place through social networks. Now, social networks were the bedrock of society in

---

[1] Amartya Sen, *Development as Freedom*, Oxford, Oxford University Press, 1999, chap. IV.
[2] Alain Caillé, "Don," *Dictionnaire de l'autre économie*, Jean-Louis Laville and Antonio David Cattani, eds., Paris, Folio, 2006, pp. 176–9.

early modern Europe. An analysis of their functioning gives us an initial insight into the ethics and solidarity of an "embedded" economic society. We would do well to recall that the notion of "embedding" was first put forward by Karl Polanyi in his work *The Great Transformation*, a demonstration that the self-regulated market is neither natural nor universal: historically, the distinguishing feature of the West is presumed to be the raising of economic activity to an institution independent from the others.[3] Although local, national and even international markets connected by exchange to other markets have always existed, structurally everyone remained a constitutive part of society (they were embedded in the wider set of social relations), whereas the market society is thought to embrace society as a whole, reducing all material and immaterial activity to market activity.

The first thing anyone who cannot make ends meet will do is to ask for credit and an extension of the repayment period.[4] In ancient Europe, and in the absence of banking institutions, people turned to credit circles: family, friends, employers, the political elite, and finally foreigners whose business was finance. Each network had its own requirements, an analysis of practices showing that the farther one moved away from one's kith and kin, the more stringent were the conditions for granting loans or an extension of the repayment period. To social proximity were added cultural factors, which coloured these relations in varying ways. The nobiliary ethos, for example, was more alive to the duty of friendship and assistance than the bourgeois ethic. Furthermore, and even in ancient society, not everyone had access to family or friends networks; these were never given but had to be built: it requires time and money to maintain social ties. We can thus not speak of a network society in general without dwelling on its concrete forms and the reciprocal commitments it implies.

Moreover, some migrant groups were, and still are, organized around "local" networks. Then, like now, such organizations built enterprises whose success was lauded everywhere. However, their functioning was based not just on alliance and mutual help that favoured integration but also on the labour force of fellow countrymen. Indeed, the primary reason for their success was the power the elite had over labour via the debts migrants contracted from them, for the elite was essentially a labour contractor. An analysis, for example, of how migrant networks built trust

---

[3] Karl Polanyi, *The Great Transformation: The Political and Economic Origins of Our Time*, New York, Rinehart, 1944.
[4] See Chapters 1 and 2.

in their midst[5] shows the patient gathering of information, supervision, and constraints that held them together. The gift therefore came into play not so much among the members of a network but more between the networks and the outside world, which viewed them with distrust. Gifts and money loans helped them enter the markets of the countries where they wished to settle. Today, scholars tend to overlook these relations of dependence that link migrants to each other, an oversight resulting from the belief that the contemporary market economy is totally disembedded. Now, what is it that circulates in these networks? Money lent and assistance, no doubt, but equally domination and exploitation – which, from the time of Michel Foucault, has been habitually referred to as power.

Although networks no longer organize society as a whole, they remain nonetheless an essential element of social reproduction, in particular of the elite, who alone have the time and money needed to maintain family and friendly sociability. Indebtedness to family continues to remain a salient feature of the poorest in France.[6]

In preindustrial Europe, there were multiple debt logics. Debt was a means to seize land, control other markets such as labour and food markets, and above all to assert power over people.[7] It was "a bond of life and a knot of death."[8] In the non-European world and some outer parts of the Western world, it is still a way to control other markets and a social bond to secure the labour force of those who have not managed to free themselves from their own and their family's debts. For a graphic illustration of this, I recommend the magnificent film by the Chinese director Jia Zhangke, *Still Life*. The film tells two stories that unravel around the Three Gorges. The one, which interests us here, narrates the tribulations of a miner from the north. The wife he had bought left him, fleeing to her province of origin and taking her daughter with her. Seventeen years later, the miner sets out to look for them. In the end, he finds his ex-wife on a barge where she works and lives to pay off her brother's debts. If she is to go back with the man who was her husband, something she too wants, she must first be bought back through the settlement of her brother's debts. On the other hand, debt can be the guarantee of being fed by one's creditors in exchange for one's labour. In India, workers freed, thanks to

[5] See Chapter 10.
[6] Report of Geneviève de Gaulle-Anthonioz to the economic and social council in 1995, quoted by Jean-Michel Servet, *Banquiers aux pieds nus. La microfinance*, CITY Paris, Odile Jacob, 2006, p. 160.
[7] See Chapter 3.
[8] Charles Malamoud, *La dette*, Paris, Editions de l'EHESS, 1980.

the law, from the bondage of debt are quick to contract a fresh loan from their former master, or another, so that they have a secure job once again, however badly paid[9]; Rabelais made light of this mechanism, but even in modern Europe, the poor sought to make use of it.[10]

Microcredit and Market

In addition to using social and debt networks, the inhabitants of preindustrial Europe, like those of the developing countries, tried to minimize the risk of falling into poverty by practising "polyactivity." Increasing sources of income involves a dual strategy of legal and illegal activities and the possibility, or not, that such activities develop entrepreneurial capacities. Polyactivity strategies assume a certain opacity, which obstructs the historian's view whenever the poor work more than do the others in the shadow of what is called the "informal" economy. Now, the part-time casual work of men, women, and children, although extremely widespread, is never recorded in the official statistics and evades the regulations of the contemporary world.

An analysis of survival strategies in modern Europe reveals that access to the market is a particularly significant factor, for it alone creates strategies for advancement.[11] But everyone does not have access to the market. Along with the necessary proximity to demand, access to capital and the capacity to take initiative, restrained at times by cultural and political taboos, are required. Thus, families who live near a city can find more economic opportunities than can those living in the hinterland. Similarly, constituting an initial capital, however modest, either through borrowing or pooling of resources, requires access to a wage labour generated surplus, social networks or a foothold in the market. In ancient Europe, many families pooled dowries and inheritances to start a business, thereby enabling entire villages to experience entrepreneurship. One could argue that everyone stood to gain because families could continue to live in their villages, but it also gave rise to great social inequalities among villagers. Conditions have changed in Western Europe, and so

---

[9] Isabelle Guérin, "Servitude et protection: quelques réflexions à partir du secteur des briqueteries en Inde du Sud," French Institute of *Pondicherry* working document, Pondicherry, 2005.

[10] See Chapter 2.

[11] *Household Strategies for Survival, 1600–2000: Fission, Faction and Cooperation,* Laurence Fontaine and Jürgen Schlumbohm, eds., Cambridge, Cambridge University Press, 2000.

too the relationship with money and family credit. Such family business forms, the ambivalence of which has been highlighted, can now be found only in non-European countries: China, India, and Latin America offer us good examples. But entrepreneurship remains out of bounds for the very poor, as credit is prohibitive and the securities asked for disproportionate in relation to the sums loaned.

A major difference between yesterday and today is that in modern Europe, everyone was a merchant of some kind. Many poor people survived by putting their meagre home- made goods on the market, and through small resales, because resale chains of every conceivable item including food, could be found across the city. However, to enter the market, all required access to capital, the tiny amount of money needed to set up a small business. This need for capital, coupled with the absence of social networks, was at the heart of the city's financial economy. It gave rise to a whole host of usurers and intermediaries, more or less honest, who created funding chains in which many poor people did not scruple to live off the needs of other poor people, selling their services very dearly.[12] The ubiquity of usury remains one of the features of contemporary financial life and the cities of the developing world are driven by the same abundance of informal finance, which allows a whole host of small traders to make a living. When looking for capital, the rich have access to banks and family credit, and the poorer people to the informal usury circuits. From this point of view, nothing has changed: in the Europe of yesterday as in the world of today, the poorest are those who have neither family to help them nor access to the banking circuits, thus none of the small credit that would allow them to tide over a bad patch or give shape to their economic plans, however modest. The only finance they can hope for is informal finance, which soon becomes usurious.

It is with this in mind that contemporary microcredit has developed, the institutionalization of which provides an alternative comparable to the establishment of pawn shops in the Middle Ages and motivated by the same desire to fight against usury by providing the poor access to cheap credit markets. Muhammad Yunus, a professor of economics in India, noticed that the hawkers he met on his way to the university bor-rowed from usurers the money they required for their small businesses. These moneylenders charged them a steep rate of interest for the capital they borrowed on a daily basis. This gave him the idea of setting up a

---

[12] See Chapter 4.

bank which would supply credit at a reasonable rate. The idea began to take seed in the 1970s, and in 1976, Yunus founded the Grameen Bank.[13] Since then, there has been an increasing interest inmicrocredit, so much so that 2005 was declared the "Year of Microcredit." The same mechanisms existed in preindustrial Europe[14] with many activities being dependent on tiny loans given on a daily basis at usurious rates: thus, in Paris, to purchase the foodstuff needed for their small trade, women at the Halle borrowed from usurers who, like the Grameen Bank today, asked for a joint and several guarantee. Given the magnitude of such usurious practices, a dual debate was initiated in Europe since the Middle Ages: first, to win recognition for the service rendered by credit and, second, to set up institutions to provide cheap and readily accessible credit to the poor.

The pawnshops did a relatively good job in fulfilling their role; however, they were faced with a dilemma that not been resolved to date and which all small credit institutions continue to face: Are they to give charity or credit? Is it assistance or banking? These questions influenced the functioning of economic aid establishments, obliging them to hedge between the two poles of gift and profit.[15] Many pawnshops went into crisis due to a lack of capital, because the church rejected profit-earning financing and it became difficult to keep up operations purely based on gifts. The borders between gift and profit are still very fluid and the subject of much discussion.

Consequently, pawnshops turned into municipal credit. They developed their banking activities in the twentieth century, however, without completely stopping lending against securities. Three types of social groups still use them: rich individuals wanting to pawn a painting or precious object to meet an unexpected financial commitment, those excluded from the banking system who can thus borrow, and new clients, migrant populations with a tradition of informal finance. The last category has a preponderance of women – Indian, Asian, and African – and gypsies, the traditional clients of institutions lending against security. The migrants of North Africa also make regular use of them. All of these clients know how to turn the functioning of such institutions to their advantage. Thus, they use them as much as a vault for the safekeeping of their precious objects during their periodical visits to their home country as for quickly

[13] "Grameen Foundation," Grameen Bank, http://www.grameenfoundation.org/
[14] See Chapter 7.
[15] See Chapter 6.

raising capital to reinvest. These appropriations are identical to those practiced by the people of ancient Europe.[16]

The debate on microfinance, ideological in nature and wavering between charity and profit, is taking place in terms similar to those of the debate on the setting up of pawnshops[17]: the primary mission of such institutions is to support those excluded from the banking system, yet for them to continue working, they have to find ways of being profitable. Next is the difficult question of from where the resources are to come, their remuneration, and how the profits are to be used. The answer to each of these questions has repercussions on the functioning of such establishments and the services they can provide. The thorny issue of the use of profits eventually sounded the death knell of pawnshops. What is one to do with the profits? Are they to be reinvested to improve the instrument, or should they be used to help other poor people? Modern Europe chose in the end to utilize the profits for financing other charitable works, for example, starting with hospitals, rather than modernizing the pawnshops. In this way, morality and social hierarchies remained intact, but in the longer term, the lack of modernization raised operational costs to such an extent that in the nineteenth century, some private lenders became less expensive.[18]

In addition to the functioning of the pawnshops was the question of their efficiency: it is not enough to get capital to start a business, even if the initial idea is good. You need know-how, the can-do spirit, and, possibly, support networks. These three factors transcend the framework of economic action alone, for they have to do with education, individual rights, social roles, and social capital. The past few years have seen banks for the poor, especially the Grameen Bank, run training programmes to provide new entrepreneurs the know-how for their economic activity and offer them hand holding in place of the social capital they lack. But the can-do spirit still remains a major problem. At this stage, only an analysis in terms of "capacities"[19] will allow us to calculate the price individuals pay on account of their political, economic, and legal marginalization as also their physical handicaps. The existence of cultural and political

---

[16] Discussion with the managers of regional banks during the campaign "un objet un prêt," October 2005.

[17] Servet, *Banquiers aux pieds nus*.

[18] See Chapter 6.

[19] Amartya Sen, *Commodities and Capabilities*, New Dehli, Vedams eBooks, 1999; Amartya Sen, *On Ethics and Economics*, Wiley-Blackwell, 1991; Amartya Sen, *A New Economic Model: Development as Freedom*, Oxford, Oxford University Press, 1999.

taboos has much to do in determining the range of possibilities such that all family members are not equally capable of developing all types of activities.

In many countries, the legal status and the roles imposed on women restrict them to a limited number of activities. For them to develop small enterprises, for example, they need to have sufficient control, or power, over their property and in the family decision-making process. Not only access to education but also to property and legal responsibility, as well as explicit and implicit contracts that regulate redistribution within the family, are so many factors which, in varying degrees according to the era and civilization, delimit the little space, the fringes where women and children can take initiative and use their limited power to negotiate and bargain within the family. Because these capacities are denied to them, the bulk of the world's poor are women.

The example of women shows very clearly how legal regulations restrict their capacity to act.[20] In ancient Europe, women's rights changed depending on the stage in their life cycle: women who were of age, single or widowed, as well as female traders (the category did exist) had far more rights than did married women whose person and property were under their husband's authority. The fact of women's rights being linked to the life-cycle stage they were in had, in my view, the following consequence: women knew that some day they would have a greater say in managing their property, which, in my view – and contrary to other civilizations, such as India and China, where women remain dependent on men, irrespective of their age or family situation – made them think about their lives more independently. Similarly, all the little spaces of freedom allocated to women in countries where guardianship is strong are fermenting change in the entire feminine condition.

The inequality of status and rights, of which individuals and groups including migrants are the victims, pushes them into the informal economy and towards forms of the solidarity economy. Women were behind the setting up of tontines as they function in Africa and Asia; women are also the main beneficiaries of microcredit programmes and constituted 70 to 80 per cent of the members of barter clubs during the Argentinean experiment.[21] However, apart from legal rules, other factors also circumscribe potential individual strategies; the control over resources exercised by certain families or specific groups as a result of social values can also

---

[20] See Chapter 5.
[21] Heloisa Primavera, "Monnaie sociale (2)," *Dictionnaire de l'autre économie*, p. 475.

reduce the number of opportunities, as witnessed in African cultures of solidarity, which require the needs of the kin to be satisfied before those of individual enterprises.[22]

The history of women and the battle to win their rights in Europe compels us to conclude that in the long run – although much still remains to be done – social transformations, such as the recognition of the status of women, the proclaimed legal equality of men and women, and access to education are what changed their capacity to come out of poverty more than any successful economic experiment conducted here and there. This tells us clearly that microcredit is not a miracle cure; however, the fact remains that in countries where such rights do not exist, assistance to women and migrants in setting up microenterprises is a means of giving them greater autonomy as well as the wherewithal to live from day to day rather than handing out humiliating charity intended more to promote political clienteles than to train citizens. Furthermore, success stories always have a positive effect in the battle of representation, indispensable for creating awareness and the will to act on the part of such marginalized populations. Microcredit is by no means a universal panacea, but it does have the virtue of bringing entrepreneurial creativity to certain segments excluded from the banking system, as well as a lever to create greater awareness. Alerted to the social stakes, which go beyond mirco-credit programs and limit their scope, increasingly organizations are including training in addition to their banking activities. In this way, they are promoting other roles and social models, which, in the long run, can generate the need for change to fight against injustice.

The market has always been an important resource for survival strategies. The inhabitants of ancient Europe had easy access to the market both as buyers and as sellers. The extent of informal activities was, moreover, a reflection of this permanent familiarity with the market. However, entering the market is no longer as simple, and people in the West go there mainly as consumers. The growth of capitalism and the rise of a wage earning class have made less necessary and more difficult such contact, which remains at the centre of the survival strategies in non-European countries. The study of poverty in modern Europe between the seventeenth and nineteenth centuries highlights the role of the market in

---

[22] Alain Marie, "Du sujet communautaire au sujet individuel. Une lecture anthropologique de la réalité africaine contemporaine," *L'Afrique des individus. Itinéraires citadins dans la société contemporaine (Abidjan, Bamako, Dakar, Nyamey)*, Alain Marie, ed., Paris, Karthala, 1997, pp. 53–110.

the strategies for survival as well as the progressive exclusion of the poor from most markets to which they traditionally had access. The hygiene standards for the trade of secondhand goods and foodstuffs, and the continuous requirement for more capital this entails along with urban reorganization, tax initiatives and constant competition from the established merchants have progressively chased away the weakest from the market, starting with women and migrants.

Today, we are witnessing the reappropriation of the market by individuals and, once again, the resistance of the well-established traders in a bid to try to prevent or curtail their entry. Three phenomena are becoming more and more visible: an increase in the number of garage sales all over the territory, especially in the large suburbs, where the poorest come to shop and where each and every one is becoming with increasing frequency a trader for a day – a trend strongly opposed by the professionals to whom it provides competition; the success of eBay and other auction and sale sites on the Internet, allowing a greater number of individuals to appropriate these new markets and supplement their income through reselling or buying and reselling on the Internet; finally, the development of microcredit, which enables people to acquire the capital needed to set up a micro or a small trading enterprise and which would have been of great use in helping, for example, women in the eighteenth century adapt to the new market and product standards. The new circuits coming up offer new spaces where the poorest can shop.[23]

The various survival strategies and their possible implementation bring out forcefully the centrality of the concept of poverty and its acceptations in any analysis of the moral economy. More than ever before, for a proper understanding of things, let us stop looking at poverty as a state that has to be remedied and the poor as patients who have to be taken care of. Let us accept poverty for what it is: a dynamic phenomenon that is both a risk whose modalities of uncertainty we need to understand and a set of strategies employed by the poor to deal with it in the space delimited for them by the physical and cultural, institutional, and economic blockages that, in turn, inhibit their capacity to act. From this perspective, not only

[23] They also reveal a need, that of being able to access the market without intermediaries, a need echoed in *Le Monde* in its last issue of 2007. At the request of its readers and based on the administrative difficulties encountered by one of them, Jamal, unemployed for a long time, who wanted to set up in a village in Côte-d'Or a street trading enterprise for pizzas and kebab sandwiches, *Le Monde* informed its readers, with bibliographical references in support, about the procedures to be followed, the pitfalls, and the various legislations for occupying public space.

does the contemporary definition of poverty as a threshold expressed in monetary terms ignore the subjectivity of social suffering, but it also glosses over the risks ordinary people face every day and the fact that all individuals are not equally equipped to deal with them.

Rehabilitating the Market in Favour of the Poor

The general perception and the reigning ideologies hold that the market can have no positive role. It is argued that the old national and aristocratic culture has instilled until today value hierarchies that look down on trade. Onto this substratum, Leninist ideology grafted in turn a loathing for the market and concrete economic activity. Keeping in view our cultural environment, or what Braudel called "long-term prisons,"[24] it is all the more important that historians, economists, sociologists, and ordinary citizens must not let down their guard and stop using their critical faculties. The analysis of survival strategies in modern Europe and the contemporary world lead us doubly to take a close look at the role of the market and enhance it – not the market as it functions currently with the sole ambition of being king – but a market from which all could benefit. It is an institution like any other and can be regulated, because it already is in several respects. Globalization, the loss of full employment and insecurity are again compelling us to try to democratize access to the market for the least well equipped at a time when life is becoming less secure.

It appears that the historical and economic rehabilitation of the market as an instrument for the struggle against poverty is diametrically opposed to all blueprints of an Other economy, which its promoters claim is based on the gift and solidarity. The alter-globalist discourse for public consumption is that modernity's "disembedding" of the economy is driven by the will of the State to free the economy from the rules that governed it in the earlier periods.[25] It is as if a golden age, an age when the economy reflected the values and morality of society from which it was inseparable, were followed by an amoral economy.

The theoretical basis of this position was drawn, as we have recalled at the outset, from the works of Karl Polanyi.[26] In 1932, Polanyi

[24] Fernand Braudel, *Écrits sur l'histoire*, Paris, Flammarion, 1969.
[25] AUTHOR Jean-Louis Laville et Antonio David Cattani, "L'autre économie. Enjeux pratiques et conceptuels," *Dictionnaire de l'autre économie*, pp. 12–13.
[26] Polanyi, *The Great Transformation*. A collection of essays with a preface and a postface bringing out their relevance even today has just been published: *Essais de Karl Polanyi*, Paris, Seuil, 2008.

explained the autonomization of spheres in *Economy and Democracy* as follows:

> There is a gulf between economics and politics. This, to put it baldly, is the prognosis of the time. Economics and politics, these two forms of social life, have been autonomized and are constantly at war with each other ... The left is rooted in democracy, and the right in the economy. It is precisely in this way that the dysfunctioning between economics and politics unfurls in a catastrophic polarity. From the domain of political democracy emanate forces which affect the economy, disturb and hamper it; the economy hits back by a general assault against democracy, presumed to embody irresponsible and unrealistic anti-economism.[27]

This text is a good example of the generality in which Polanyi's thinking is located: the complexity of political struggle and social groups is reduced to the polarity between economics and politics in which there can be no place for the actors who emerged during the last century: women, the colonized, and those excluded from paid employment. For lack of contextualization of Polanyi's thinking, we are unable to understand the fracture lines, the differentiations and the exclusions it carries within it, the most constant and the most important being women.[28] At the time, it is true, women did not have any rights, wage earners and large industry dominated, and the big question of the depletion of the world's natural resources did not figure on the agenda. Polanyi, in the footsteps of Marx, defined as "a temporal" the relations between humans and nature, unlike the relations between humans that, he said, were historical.[29]

The only way in which Polanyi's thinking can be approached is by historicizing it. He died in 1964, and his universe spans the previous century, the 1929 crisis, fascism, Leninism and Stalinism in Russia, the Second World War, and the Cold War. It is in this universe that he theorizes about the separation of economics from politics, sees the destruction of democracy in favour of fascism and defines a state socialism in control of the ownership of the means of production, the fixing of economic and industrial objectives, and the redistribution of profits in order that each one can receive a "fair wage" and buy at a "fair price":[30]

> There is patently another solution, which consists in preserving democracy and abolishing capitalism. This is the socialist solution. Indeed, in the same way as

---

[27] Polanyi, "Economie et démocratie," *Essais de Karl Polanyi*, 1932, pp. 353–7 (353).

[28] Gareth Stedman Jones, *Languages of Class: Studies in English Working Class History, 1832–1982*, Cambridge, Cambridge University Press, 1983.

[29] Polanyi, "Communauté et société. La critique chrétienne de notre ordre social [1937]," *Essais*, p. 457–64 (461).

[30] Polanyi, "la comptabilité socialiste," *Essais*, pp. 283–315 (302–5).

capitalism needs the fascist political system as a complement, democracy needs a socialist economy which would be its extension. Socialism is democratic or it is not; it is only functional because it is democratic.[31]

To buttress his conviction, Polanyi provides a cursory overview of the past when societies – archaic and preindustrial European – were supposedly based on solidarity, and the economy of the gift and redistribution. Then he makes two changes: he separates economics from politics, and redefines democracy as the place where consumer organizations and producer groups take decisions, necessarily good and reflective of the general will, for when men are brought together they can only work for public good and eschew their private interests.[32] While waiting for this general will to emerge spontaneously, it is necessary to educate the people:

Politics, parties, and Parliaments have become suspect. Democracy has been discredited. Large masses to the left as to the right have opposed it.

Hence the conclusion: nothing can save democracy today, other than a new mass culture founded on a political and economic education. This alone can keep it from suicide.[33]

While awaiting the new person, who, through education, will always declare him- or herself in favour of the General Will, it is incumbent on the state to plan the economy:

in a truly democratic society, the problem of industry would resolve itself through the planned intervention of the producers and the consumers themselves. Such conscious and responsible action is, indeed, one of the embodiments of freedom in a complex society. But, as the contents of this article suggest, such an endeavour cannot be successful unless it is disciplined by a total view of man and society very different from that which we inherited from the market-economy.[34]

---

[31] Polanyi, "Le fascisme et la terminologie marxiste," *Essais*, 1934, pp. 425–9 (427).

[32] Polanyi takes up this idea in a manuscript of 1943 on the propositions of Jean-Jacques Rousseau. He writes that "Rousseau calls the will to survive 'the general will,' and he is right to do so; he calls the particular wills of individuals 'the will of all.'" If voters are well-well informed about the problem, we will observe that they all want almost the same thing and will thus proclaim the general will, be it war or peace. "We can thus conclude that in a free society, as long as individuals express their particular wills and are well-informed, the will of all will be perceptibly close to the general will"; p. 532 in "Jean-Jacques Rousseau: une société libre est-elle possible?" *Essais*, 1953, pp. 529–37, and "Nouvelles considérations sur notre théorie et notre pratique," pp. 327–35 (333–4).

[33] Polanyi, "Economie et démocratie," pp. 354–5.

[34] Polanyi, "La mentalité de marché est obsolète!," *Essais*, 1947, pp. 505–19 (519).

The vision that the market economy imposes universally is one of a reality from which no one can escape:

> The market functions as an invisible line which isolates each individual, as a producer or consumer, in his everyday activity. Everyone produces for the market and buys from the market. Individuals cannot move out of the market, however much they may want to be of use to their fellowmen. Every attempt to offer their assistance is immediately frustrated by the market mechanism.[35]

When we relate Karl Polanyi's analysis to what we know about the economy of early modern Europe, it is obvious that it fails to take into account the plurality of exchange logics within the same society, and the permanent coexistence of the gift and patrimonialization with the market; it also ignore women's labour, invisible on the market. Even so, alter-globalism has today chosen to endow it with all manner of qualities. Although admitting that Polanyi's hypotheses have been weakened by the scientific refutation of his vision of primitive economies, alter-globalism retains his construction of the *homo economicus*, a product of history and "the great transformation," as well as of the "disembedding" of the economy from "traditional social relations." The advocates of the Other economy thus hope to undo what history has done, namely, rediscover, along with the market, "the logic of reciprocity – that is to say of the gift/counter gift – or of patrimonial or state redistribution"[36] – and take away from the market labour, land, and capital.

> Polanyism thus characterised appears as sort of Marxism with a human face, as the only substantial general theorisation in the social sciences capable of founding and nurturing radical socio-democratic thought. To those disappointed with Marxism, like those disappointed with economic liberalism, Polanyi offers the hope of building a humane society, decent and master of itself, without giving in to the illusions of the omnipotence of politics or the market.[37]

Roughly four articles form a charter: (1) democracy is not a product of the market; (2) the State must play an active role in the creation of the market; (3) the self-regulated market creates the psychic conditions for the aspiration to totalitarianism, and thus the destruction of democracy; and (4) the transformation of institutions requires changing each individual.[38]

[35] Polanyi, "Communauté et société," pp. 457–64 (459).
[36] Alain Caillé and Jean-Louis Laville, "Postface. Actualité de Karl Polanyi," *Essais*, pp. 565–86 (567).
[37] Ibid., p. 568.
[38] Ibid., p. 569.

The first article, therefore, is that democracy is not a product of the market. The analysis of exchange in preindustrial Europe shows that the market, because it was based on the equality of those who entered it, was fundamentally more capable of ushering in democracy than the gift economy.[39] Moreover, the aristocratic economy could not accept equality of status; consequently, all exchanges had to bear the mark of nobiliary superiority. Thus, beneath the fine word *gift*, what we find is plundering and forced labour, submission and arbitrariness. Consequently, even in the sixteenth century, Montaigne preferred the market to the gift, for in the market, he wrote, "I give only money" whereas with the gift "I give myself." This only goes to reiterate the fact that all exchange of goods is also an exchange of values and that these values are so many vectors of power and the arrangement of societies.

Breaking the link between economics and politics allows us to analyse anew such historical configurations and rearrange their elements. Dissociating democracy from the market makes it easier to criticize the latter; separating aristocratic power from the gift economy can give rise to an economy of solidarity. Following Polanyi, alter-globalists have thus brought about a dual disembedding in the history of preindustrial Europe: by undoing the link between politics and the market, they are to some extent reinserting democracy in a political regime of a socialist nature that did not bring democracy, and, by breaking, but this time without stating so explicitly, the link between the gift economy and the aristocratic regime, they are inserting the gift economy in a regime that would show solidarity and that they call democratic. All these attempts at historical surgery are devoid of any kind of legitimacy, as proved by the analyses of the political economy of the ancien régime.

Furthermore, Polanyi's new man, as well as that of the alter-globalists, likes unanimity, not open debate; and for men to see the world in the same way, they must be remodelled:

Clearly, it has to do with developing ways of experiencing in behaviour a vision of the world, and this appeal to reality experienced is not without evoking the grammar of the social struggles of Alex Honneth; with the concern that economic organisation embodies it, and here one thinks of Edward P. Thompson's moral economy. It is important to generate ways of acting, but also "discursive regimes," that is to say ways of thinking which conceptualise experiences by combining theoretical and empirical research.[40]

---

[39] See Chapter 9.
[40] Caillé and Laville, "Postface," p. 581.

The belief in a possible transformation of society draws continually from Edward P. Thompson's moral economy. It is an integral part of all contemporary pleas for an Other economy and serves as their archaeology.[41] After disembedding, they now call for a democratic reembedding of the economy in which reference to solidarity would be primordial.[42] Such reembedding is possible in the future, as it was in the past, with the moral economy of the popular classes being rediscovered and reinstated by E. P. Thompson.[43] Utopia was reality in times past.

The advent of capitalism, with its rationality and individualism, is presumed to have sounded the death knell of the moral economy. Can one still believe, with E. P. Thompson, that the moral economy, abandoning relations between social groups, remained alive only amidst the people, who, as its sole custodian, put it into practice during their revolts? The desire of Marxist movements to legitimize the domination of the proletariat, or more precisely, the sole party supposed to embody it, led such movements to endow the people called upon to govern with a moral essence that transcended them. Communist historians then buckled down to the task of finding the foundations of this moral economy. E. P. Thomson did precisely this in his famous article in *Past and Present* in which he rooted working-class revolts in peasant riots,[44] in accordance with, when all is said and done, a rather simple schema. He first asserts that during the food riots, the peasantry acted in keeping with a morality that imposed the imprescriptible duty of fulfilling the needs of the poor. Next, he locates the foundations of this morality shared by all peasant communities in a corpus of old and ancient customs and laws, which were codified in England between 1580 and 1630 and which became obsolete during the Civil War. These customs, he said, were never absent from popular consciousness. To explain their permanence, E. P. Thompson brings into play memory, a memory that is "extraordinarily long, especially in an oral society," enabling consciousness to travel across time and space. Accordingly, after the rural exodus, the community culture came to the city and reemerged among the workers of the textile cities in West England. Once attuned to

[41] J. T. Godbout, *Le don, la dette et l'identité*, Paris, la découverte, 2000; Revue du MAUSS, Qu'est-ce que l'utilitarisme?, no. 6, 2nd semester, 1995.
[42] Jean-Louis Laville, "Economie plurielle," *Dictionnaire de l'autre économie*, p. 254.
[43] E. P. Thompson, "The Moral Economy of the English Crowd in the Eighteenth Century," *Past and Present*, 50, 1971, pp. 76–136.
[44] Ibid., For a deconstruction of this approach, see Sakari Saaritsa, "Beneath Moral Economy: Informal Assistance in Early 20th century Finland," PHD thesis, European University Institute, Florence, 2008.

the class world, it would establish the right of the poor to take, in case of extreme necessity, what they lacked. Food riots and stealing raw materials from the workshop and factory are the two poles of the resurgence of a moral economy. This economy supposedly legitimized the opposition to the market and the questioning of the right to property of the rich, which itself was a historical construction. At the end of this historical reconstitution, akin to a historical reconstruction, customs that had become obsolete were said to have founded the right to temporarily deny the right to property and given the people a collective consciousness.[45]

"Disembedding" and the Plurality of Economies

All analysis of the Other economy is based on the certitude that historically, society moved from one system of production to another, in an unquestionable and visible manner. Now, the first lesson from our study of the Ancien Régime is precisely that the modes of production and political economies did not succeed each other in a linear fashion, but rather various forms coexisted and were in constant competition. Competition is at the heart of the contemporary world as well, for even today, various kinds of economies – capitalist, socialist, caste based, to name only the major ones – clash, merge, and coexist with each other. Rejecting the linearity of production for concomitance and overlapping of political economies amounts to recalling that before the eighteenth century, there had never been unity between society, economics, and religion, and thus, the empowerment of the economy during the century of Enlightenment does not mean there was a separation between economics and morality.[46] The economies and moralities in the Europe of the ancien régime and preindustrial Europe were always in competition with each other. Such ideological conflicts left their mark on Christianity as well, the debate on usury being a case in point.[47] Now, not only did the battle around credit involve symbolic, political, and material stakes, but the fracture lines, which today oppose diverse political economies and cross all religions, are also still and will always be about power and identity.[48] The ban

---

[45] James C. Scott, *The Moral Economy of the Peasant. Rebellion and Subsistence in South Asia*, New Haven, CT, Yale University Press, 1976; Peter Linebaugh, *The London Hanged: Crime and Society in Eighteenth-Century London*, Penguin Books, 1993.

[46] Noëlle M. P. Lechat, "Economie morale," *Dictionnaire de l'autre économie*, pp. 220–8, in which the opposite is advocated.

[47] See Chapter 7.

[48] See Chapters 8 and 9.

on lending on interest, which continues to be discussed in the Muslim countries, is one such example.

In ancient Europe, there was a clash of two economies, the aristocratic and the market economies, one deriving its strength from an aristocratic political regime and the other awaiting the birth of democracy which was to be more or less widespread.[49] Admittedly, it is difficult to compare sixteenth-century merchant capitalism with modern-day financial capitalism, not to speak of the fact that each country adapts, to a greater or lesser degree, capitalism to its own culture, but the soil in which both flourished is the same. In modern Europe, this great clash took place because of the attempt by the aristocratic economy to confine the market and the capitalist economy to a few well-defined pockets, something the Chinese political leadership is attempting to do today.

Studying the plurality of the various economies in the contemporary world, and even within each country, helps us rid ourselves of old-fashioned ideas, and the singular and synthetic solutions they offer. There has never really been a "disembedding" of the economy, for the economies were plural and embedded, each one in political and moral value systems. But we have seen shifts in the balance of power – and a contamination – between the different values systems and the political and social regimes that uphold them. For the historian, capitalism is plural; it is to be studied chronologically but also geographically, given the wide diversity of ways in which political regimes adapt the individualistic values of the market economy.

The transition to capitalism of some truly socialist societies gave rise to studies on the manner in which both economies coexisted. The problematic merits a systematic investigation in other countries to understand how local political economies are connected with the market economy and the various forms of capitalism. China offers us a remarkable laboratory where the question is, Can there be economic pluralism without political pluralism? More generally, the analyses of the moral economy of modern and preindustrial Europe would stand to gain from a systematic study of the linkages between the economy, national culture, and politics. These linkages are not obvious; indeed, each day we are discovering just how indiscernible and subtle they are: we now know that when the West attempts to impose democracy, it is corruption that first spreads to all levels, just as it did in early modern Europe with the overlap of market and aristocratic economies. These facts are a challenge for the aid policies

[49] See Chapters 8 and 9.

of states and major international organizations that, all too often, fail for want of taking interest in the values and workings of the societies they claim to help and relieve.[50]

The analyses of the relationship with debt and credit in the preindustrial society of the ancien régime bring out the full relevance of the attention given to the values that structured other societies.[51] Thus, contrary to the simple economic image we have of them today, the transactions illustrate the diversity of stakes, expectations, and cultures of the various social groups. The same complexity is at work today in the mutual misunderstanding between borrowers and employees of microfinance organizations: the latter insist loans be repaid on time and, on first default, immediately invoke joint and several guarantee, so to speak, whereas in such societies, individuals are accustomed to never reclaiming a debt within the stipulated period and to playing for time.[52] Similarly, for a long time the border between gift and corruption remained hazy in modern Europe, as it the case even today with respect to the development policies advocated by the Western world: the nondemocratic societies for which these policies are intended have to contend with other power structures in which the general interest can be understood only in terms of region, religion, and the family structure of origin.

Such cultural differences apply at every level of activity, and everyone understands them implicitly, as shown by the behaviour of the poorest. In a market economy, they favour forms of self-presentation that suggest they successfully belong to the market world. Families and individuals invest in clothing, jewellery, or luxury items that proclaim success but that can also be sold or pawned if the need arises. Conversely, in status-related economies that advocate charity and assistance, the poor strive to take on the appearance of deserving poor to obtain help from various charitable institutions. Lack of access to the market or losing such access also has an impact on individual economic attitudes: from being citizens, they become political clients, as happened in socialist economies and as is happening today in Africa in those areas where marabouts control access to the protected markets they reserve for their protégés on whom in return they impose private and religious conducts. But this intuitive knowledge of the moral codes of the various political economies

---

[50] Joseph E. Stiglitz, *Globalization and its Discontents*, New York and London, W.W. Norton & Company, 2002.

[51] See Chapters 2 and 3.

[52] Servet, *Banquiers aux pieds nus*, pp. 151–2.

also develops in the poorest a culture of cunning that exploits imposed and experienced identities and social roles.

In the same way, the modes of trust building, which are at the heart of market exchange and which guarantee its proper functioning, will differ depending on the political economies. Today, trust has been institutionalized in Western societies: contracts specify commitments and courts ensure they are respected. But under the ancien régime, as in numerous other societies, trust is built within various cultures of honour – cultures that can be found in market organizations working outside the law as well as in many migrant entrepreneur networks, where monitoring and control mechanisms regulate trust.

Freeing Oneself from Morality and Solidarities

Although morality and religion permeate behaviour, techniques to escape their severity are always available. Everywhere and at all times, irrespective of which religion proclaims the ban on usury, individual lenders always manage to circumvent it. The legal ploys used by the casuists in modern Europe,[53] who devised contracts in which credit was passed off as a gift or a purchase, are also employed by Muslim traders, who camouflage lending on interest as sales followed by buybacks, as the Muslim Lebanese traders in Africa do, disguising lending on interest as fictitious sales: the merchandise used to prop up the transaction is sold at a higher price to include the hidden interest. No sooner has the good been bought than the client resells it in another shop, but at two-thirds the price, that is, excluding the interest. Such a system gives the lender a huge margin on short-term loans, just as was the case of the usurers of ancient Europe, still very active in some regions of the developed world such as in the south of Italy and in Japan and in many parts of the developing world. In all societies, individuals know how to twist the rules and morality and take advantage of every available loophole.

What do value systems become when a crisis creates havoc? Analyzing poverty and creditor circles[54] illustrates the difficulty in putting into practice value systems, even when they are shared, when situations worsen. Furthermore, the farther you move away from small inter-knowledge structures, the more difficult it is to impose those values. Before the French Revolution, aristocrats showed much more solidarity towards

[53] See Chapter 7.
[54] See Chapters 1 and 2.

poor farmers than towards the middle classes: they allowed debts to be prolonged, lowered interest rates in difficult times, and often cancelled them in their wills. All these behaviours are also found nowadays in contemporary status-based societies. But in times of crises, many aristocrats circumvented prohibitions, and in spite of advocating a culture of gift and charity, got rid of bad debts by selling them on the cheap to lawyers or prosecutors who knew how to make the most of them because they were not bound by a moral contract to the lords' farmers. In fact, the farmers, for whom the sale of debts often meant economic downfall, called them "penny-grabbers" (*grippe-sols*).

By virtue of being transferred from aristocrats to the middle classes, debts moved from one moral sphere to another; they left a network of interdependency and solidarity – owing to the paternalistic power of the aristocracy – for a world of relationships claiming anonymity and governed by observance of contracts. The practice of transferring debt collection to economic or financial agents not bound to debtors by a moral contract has survived through the centuries. Nowadays, in spite of the example they want to set, large corporations who like to talk of ethics also sell their bad debts to private banks responsible for collecting them. Yesteryear's penny-grabbers are now called "vulture funds": they enable banks, after winning court cases, to collect most of the income of particularly poor countries.

The historical enquiry on informal finance, which develops spontaneously to meet the capital requirements of the poor, and the institutions established to give it a moral framework,[55] makes us wary of postcapitalist scenarios seeking to extend to society as whole scattered circuits of the solidarity economy. Apart from the fact that informal finance is expensive, the utopia of linking together in networks an increasing number of consumers, enterprises, and sectors of the solidarity economy to the point of creating a post capitalist society[56] faces another impediment: that of finding ways to fight against fraud in networks the moment they exceed a limited number of participants. Argentina has already experimented with such forms during the 1996–2000 crisis years. At the time, some Argentineans attempted to restructure their economy and society by building an economy based on the direct exchange of goods and services. But as soon as the number of participants increased, especially when an equivalent for direct exchange was needed to streamline needs

---

[55] See Chapter 4.
[56] Laurent Fraisse, "Changement social," *Dictionnaire de l'autre économie*, p. 101.

and supply, the experiment came a cropper because the paper money issued in the form of bonds for the exceedingly large variety of goods and services available was devalued by counterfeiting, thereby demolishing the ethical principles on which it was built.[57]

Everyone, even the poorest in the social solidarity networks, tries to find a pretext to evade the duties solidarity imposes. The best expedient is illiquidity. It is difficult to turn away relatives and friends when they come to you for help, so the surest way of not being parted from your savings is to keep them in the form of objects rather than cash. Such behaviour shows us to what extent even money, considered an impersonal mode of circulating value, can be transformed by the cultures and practices of the social agents. Besides, in modern Europe, the interplay of various types of currencies was an important manifestation of usury. Accordingly, several kinds of currencies and liquidities were created depending on the different needs.[58] In this way, morality was preserved, but at a price, for it was with heavy depreciation that the goods were put on the market again, as we saw in the example of eighteenth-century Paris.[59]

In the end, the insistence on the presumed validity of Polanyi's hypothesis for drawing up the blueprint of an Other economic and social future is reminiscent of the interminable debate on credit, which carried on in the West for four centuries and which, even though it had no practical worth in the eighteenth century, continued in spite of all the controversies, the nature of its function having changed so vastly: it was no longer about taking a stand on commonly accepted practices but about asserting political identity.[60]

From this point of view, anti-utilitarianism would do well to attribute less generously to the gift- in the sense that Marcel Mauss understood it: "giving-receiving-returning" – virtues which it never possessed as such the gift has never ceased to exist, even in a financialized economy in whose functioning it coiled up without being necessarily at odds with the relations of economic interests and power.[61] Instead, anti-utilitarianism should, as Amartya Sen suggests, look for practical ways and means to

---

[57] *Alternative Exchanges: Second-Hand Circulations from the Sixteenth Century to the Present*, L. Fontaine, ed., Oxford, Longham, 2008.

[58] Viviana A. Zelizer, *The Social Meaning of Money*, Princeton, NJ, Princeton University Press, 1997.

[59] See Chapter 4.

[60] See Chapter 7

[61] *La société vue du don. Manuel de sociologie anti-utilitariste appliqué*, Philippe Chanial, ed., Paris, La Découverte, 2008.

make every man and woman participate in public debate through the right to vote, the circulation and sharing of information as a common good, the refusal to let it be commodified by monopolies, and the setting up of institutions which guarantee everyone free and equal access to the basic necessities, namely, security, education, health, and the impartiality of the state.[62] Instead of the restitution of an anti-utilitarian gift economy, a more ambitious goal for humankind would be to help each one live the life he or she wants.

---

[62] Sen, *Development as Freedom.*

Printed in the United States

Printed in the United States
by Baker & Taylor Publisher Services

Printed in the United States
by Baker & Taylor Publisher Services